THE NEW PhD

The New PhD

How to Build a Better Graduate Education

Leonard Cassuto and Robert Weisbuch

JOHNS HOPKINS UNIVERSITY PRESS
Baltimore

© 2021 Johns Hopkins University Press
All rights reserved. Published 2021
Printed in the United States of America on acid-free paper

9 8 7 6 5 4 3 2 1

Johns Hopkins University Press
2715 North Charles Street
Baltimore, Maryland 21218-4363
www.press.jhu.edu

Library of Congress Cataloging-in-Publication Data

Names: Cassuto, Leonard, 1960– author. | Weisbuch, Robert, 1946– author.
Title: The new PhD : how to build a better graduate education / Leonard Cassuto
    and Robert Weisbuch.
Description: Baltimore : Johns Hopkins University Press, 2021. |
    Includes bibliographical references and index.
Identifiers: LCCN 2020011604 | ISBN 9781421439761 (hardcover) |
    ISBN 9781421439778 (ebook)
Subjects: LCSH: Doctor of philosophy degree.
Classification: LCC LB2386 .C376 2021 | DDC 378.2/42—dc23
LC record available at https://lccn.loc.gov/2020011604

A catalog record for this book is available from the British Library.

*Special discounts are available for bulk purchases of this book. For more informa-
tion, please contact Special Sales at specialsales@press.jhu.edu.*

Johns Hopkins University Press uses environmentally friendly book materials,
including recycled text paper that is composed of at least 30 percent post-consumer
waste, whenever possible.

To our partners,
Debra Osofsky and Candy Cooper

CONTENTS

Introduction

Why We Need a New PhD and How We Can Create One

Imagine an entering cohort of eight doctoral students sitting around a table in a department seminar room or laboratory conference room. They've just arrived at graduate school, and they're eager to see what their new adventure will hold for them. All of them know that the academic job market is depressed, but most (perhaps all) are hoping for a college or university teaching job of some kind.

Now let's flash forward in time. According to current statistics, four of the eight—50 percent!—will not complete the degree.[1] Of the remaining four who do finish, two will not get academic positions and will seek jobs elsewhere. The remaining pair will get full-time teaching jobs, most likely at teaching-intensive institutions. Perhaps they'll get tenure-track assistant professorships, though the supply of those positions has been shrinking. And maybe one of those two will get a position at a research university like the one where those eight students assembled years earlier.*

---

*We are of course dealing with aggregate (and pre-COVID) statistics here. Certain disciplines, such as economics and computer science, produce different outcomes, but the contours of this thought experiment apply broadly across disciplines.

Now flash back to the seminar table again to regard those eager beginners and consider: all eight of the first-year students at the table will be trained according to the needs of that one of them who might snag a job at a research university. The curriculum of most graduate programs in the arts and sciences emphasizes research above all, and it's contoured to prepare students to compete for the rarest and most competitive jobs that sit atop the academic status pyramid.

During the seven or eight (or perhaps more) years that the typical graduate student spends getting a PhD, she may find herself confused by unstated expectations, pushed to becoming a clone of the research university faculty members who are training her. If she's a scientist, she typically will have a single adviser who will dictate her work and may, in the process, narrow her imagination. If she's a humanist or a social scientist, her adviser may go missing in action. Then, having been persuaded (explicitly or otherwise) during her years of study that the only jobs worth having are professorships at universities like the one she is now attending, she will enter the academic job market with little chance of getting the job she has been taught to wish for.

Or else, having endured enough frustrations along the way, she may be one of the 50 percent of all beginning doctoral students who do not graduate at all, and she may leave only after some years, for half of those departures come late—after years during which students could have been doing something more productive, enjoyable, and lucrative. Given such prospects, why would any talented potential applicant not agree with a pundit who wrote simply, "Just don't go"?[2]

As this thought experiment suggests, graduate school in the arts and sciences prepares students for jobs that don't exist. And while it prepares them, it teaches them to want those jobs above all others. Yet the number of doctoral applicants in most fields has increased steadily over the past half century. As the academic job market has contracted, the gap has increased between students' training and the jobs that they actually get. Some have felt victimized by an institutional Ponzi scheme. But not all: surveys of graduates show that most would do it again, even those who didn't enter the professoriate. So as we seek to improve doctoral education, we need not only to rethink its inhumane logic but also to extend its strengths: the opportunities to delve deeply into a cherished field of study and make discoveries, to work closely with expert faculty, and to bond with other students who share the same interest and dedication.

The status quo presents a picture of incoherence of process and goals. The PhD isn't working right now. It isn't serving students because it doesn't prepare them for the realities that they will face in their professional lives. That disjunction creates anger, bitterness, and unhappiness—and manifest disapprobation from outside the university too. Those outcomes don't serve the faculty or the university either. Not for nothing did Derek Bok describe graduate school as "woefully out of alignment with the career opportunities available to graduates."[3]

The price paid by our society is higher still. We waste human resources—and humans—when we channel them in only one direction. "People pursuing PhDs are deeply curious," writes Katina L. Rogers in her new study of the humanities doctorate. They are "exploratory, and passionate about their work. . . . Imagine what could happen if doctoral students were invited to apply a similar approach of inquiry, creativity, and exploration to their professional lives beyond the university's gates."[4] Actually, we don't have to imagine this, as there are thousands of striking but underpublicized examples out there already. Statistically speaking, they constitute a new normal.

We've written this book to help administrators, faculty, and students fix graduate school in the arts and sciences. We want to help programs align the work of administrators, faculty, and students in pursuit of common goals that are scholarly, professional, and—because we're talking about people's lives here—personal too. Revising the doctoral career path requires rethinking the requirements for the degree, and with this book we want to facilitate that thought process. In the following chapters, we will present many examples of best practice from graduate schools, departments, and programs around the country. They address the range of doctoral education, from the humanities to the sciences, from admissions through career outcomes. And we consider how to recuperate the master's degree. We also examine some less exemplary practices in a survey of failed reforms from the 1990s and 2000s. We gather these well-intentioned but ineffective efforts together for the first time, for their shortcomings are instructive and help clarify the way forward.

We offer many suggestions in the pages that follow but no cure-all. Specifics ought to be up to the faculty in their own disciplines. The potential renovation of the PhD has attracted no small amount of suspicion from defenders of the doctoral faith, but to reflect on our educational practice is no heresy: teachers revise their curricula all the time. That the prospect of changing the PhD could become a lightning rod for controversy ought to tell us something about the educational culture we live in. Academia is socially and culturally conservative, and that's mostly to the good: it's not supposed to yield to fads. But graduate school is conservative even by academic standards, and the structure of doctoral education has changed little in more than a century since it was introduced in the United States. We're long overdue for an assessment of our customs and expectations. Such an assessment is all the more crucial as academia confronts an economy battered by the COVID-19 pandemic. Yet the will to reassess has been strengthened as graduate faculty have learned to adapt radically new teaching methods in lieu of classroom instruction. We hope that this recent confidence in making swift and dramatic changes will further fuel the growing movement to rethink the PhD.

We're going to begin that assessment and outline some procedures by which programs can continue to examine their own practices with an eye toward keeping what works and changing what doesn't. But that approach needs historical consciousness, because we can best meet our problems if we know where they came from.

How Did We Get Here?

Complaints about the state of doctoral education are nothing new. They date back at least to William James, whose "The Ph.D. Octopus" (1903) eerily anticipates our current problems in certain respects. Speaking of the allure of the PhD, James wrote that "we dangle our three magic letters before the eyes of these predestined victims, and they swarm to us like moths to an electric flame."[5] More than a century later, Louis Menand (the author of a renowned study of James) similarly scorned the waste of talent: "It takes three years to become a lawyer. It takes four years to become a doctor. But it takes from six to nine years, and sometimes longer, to be eligible to teach poetry to college students for a living. . . . Lives are warped because of the length and uncertainty of the doctoral educational process."[6]

For all of the consistency of these complaints, efforts at remedy have been vexed by contradiction. We thought we knew what doctoral education in America meant at one time, and then we were less certain. Is its aim to produce the next generation of university scholar-teachers? At a deeper level, should the doctorate be, as its early American founders saw it, a degree intended to honor scholarly and scientific discovery? In the United States, that purpose has always existed in tandem with a mandate to educate undergraduate students, a tension that arises from the planting of the doctorate in an American higher educational field already filled with colleges of the teaching-centered English model. These two institutional types have coexisted over these many generations in the United States, but their purposes are not entirely symbiotic.

On the one hand, the culture of the college model is (and remains) explicitly student centered. On the other, research university culture is fundamentally faculty centered. Teaching shall be "secondary" at the new University of Chicago, wrote its incoming president, William Rainey Harper, in 1888. Such teaching would be performed by researchers because "it is only the man who has made investigations who can teach others how to investigate."[7] In other words, graduate school faculty make the best university teachers because they can impart techniques of discovery, but they nevertheless shouldn't teach very much because they have more important work to do.

Early public universities drew on both the teaching and research missions. The Morrill Act, which President Abraham Lincoln signed in 1862, called for the founding of land-grant institutions that would "promote the liberal and practical education of the industrial classes in the several pursuits and professions in life."[8] Founded in profusion in the decades surrounding the turn of the twentieth century, land-grant institutions became research universities that had to serve the public at the same time. The result has been a tension that might be called productive—sometimes of symbiosis, sometimes of disjunction.

"The fundamental problem," says Nicholas Lemann, is that the United States has "adopted two noncongruent ideals of higher education."[9] The coexistence of the teaching and research missions in American higher education has informed its history for about a century and a half, and we need to be conscious of it. Must such alternatives be at war, or can they coordinate?

Training in teaching gained an unsteady foothold in doctoral education once it was found that graduate students could serve as bargain-basement instructors. But historian Thomas Bender suggests that PhD training in later years may have moved backward, to become more traditionally oriented toward pure research than ever before: "By the 1990's [the PhD] could fairly be considered a research degree, pure and simple, perhaps even a hyper-research degree."[10] This movement was driven in large measure by the tightening academic job market, which raised the credentialing bar ever higher. And with the enormous growth of government-sponsored scientific research assigned to universities, research gained a new prestige well beyond the sciences. Yet there has always been a loyal opposition to the purely scholarly degree, arising from the American ideal of democratized education as a means to produce citizens.

But those concerns were barely considered during earlier times of postwar academic plenty. Higher education expanded rapidly in the postwar era, with growth peaking in the 1960s. Doctoral education in the arts and sciences grew rapidly from 1962 to 1970, with double-digit annual increases in graduate students and an overall tripling in size in less than a decade. (Over the ensuing 45-plus years, growth has been much slower, averaging between 1 and 2 percent per year, including some small decreases.)[11] Heady increases in college attendance during that same period led to a swelling of undergraduate enrollment in the humanities and social sciences and a growing and ambitious national agenda for the bench sciences tied to university research. As a result of these and other factors, the postwar doctorate became a highly desirable degree, promising great opportunity for its holders.

As early as the 1970s, though, this welcoming edifice began to teeter. The number of academic positions in the humanities suddenly and badly trailed the number of doctoral graduates, and unemployed and underemployed humanities PhDs became commonplace. The slowing of growth, coupled with cuts in federal and state funding of higher education—which have continued for decades since—contributed to the straitening of the academic job market. That funding uncertainty made cheap labor attractive, and those work conditions led to the rise of both adjunct and graduate student labor. As William G. Bowen and Neil Rudenstine documented in a 1992 study, the time to degree for doctoral students in the humanities had swelled beyond eight years, and the rate of attrition of entering students had surpassed 50 percent—shocking data that this publication first made widely known.[12] In the 1990s, many graduate students sought unionization, a movement for recognition that continues a generation later. (The rise of adjunct unions today is a delayed response to the same conditions.) Student union movements began to appear at the same historical moment when conversations about institutional reform of graduate programs were also starting to take place in earnest. One result of this confluence was infighting: the reform movement split between activism and pragmatics.[13]

Just as membership in a poorly paid, disrespected, and migratory adjunct work force has ensnared far too many doctoral graduates in the humanities, career-stalling postdocs have confronted many graduates in the sciences. Recommendations for improving the lot of postdocs share some issues with calls to improve the lot of adjuncts in the humanistic disciplines. Academic positions in the sciences have been in decline as well, as federal and state support of higher education continues to decrease. Time to degree remains terribly long, with more than eight years from the start of a program to graduation still the norm in the humanities. (The numbers are slightly lower in the social sciences and a bit less still in the sciences, but the sciences have the longest path of all when one includes the usual postdoc years.)

Meanwhile, the cyclical grant-making mechanism of the sciences has built a structure that relies on student populations to staff laboratories to do the work that gets the grants renewed. Grants provide faculty members with funds to hire students into their labs, and their work leads to more grants—and so on and on. Such research exigencies, then and now, have severely compromised the academic and intellectual development of doctoral students, even when many lab-oriented programs have beginning students rotate through several labs and meet with the professors in different subspecialties before joining one lab group.

More generally, throughout the arts and sciences, a disconnect developed—and remains in force—between the kind of training research universities have provided and the responsibilities of those PhDs who get hired as new professors in a wide variety of teaching-intensive colleges and universities. Worse still, the needs of those considering a career outside of academia were—and remain—largely ignored, yet this group constitutes, at minimum, a very large minority in the humanities and a majority of students in the sciences. Our opening example of the eight students highlights this disconnect: the doctoral curriculum bears scant relation to student outcomes.

The 1990s magnified these considerable challenges to higher education. The academic job market had been shrinking for a generation, since the 1970s. As the 1990s progressed, discontent with the doctorate quietly increased, following two decades of shortages in tenure-track positions. Adjunct replacements for full-time tenure-line positions became a lightning rod, but beneath it lay structural trouble in the national economic models for higher education. States cut budgets for public universities and colleges.[14] They raised tuition to cover the shortfalls, to levels greater than many students could afford. Private colleges likewise struggled, as costs outpaced revenues once the public no longer agreed to support annual tuition increases significantly greater than overall inflation. And beneath those economic changes, a rising demand for utility challenged the humanistic disciplines and made science education all the more beholden to funded research.

Higher education was widely viewed as a valuable public good during the postwar era. Beginning in the 1980s and since, it has increasingly been seen as a personal investment, a view that persists today. For these and other reasons, a near-doomsday sensibility took hold in doctoral education, at least among those who refused to wear blinders. By 2000, in the humanities and social sciences, the labor pool of people seeking full-time academic positions at least doubled the size of the supply pool of such positions. It was around this time that the long-held conviction that the employment shortfall was merely a temporary market correction began to give way. It had become a hope too desperate to comfort any but the most Panglossian of faculty members.

Nevertheless, this realization took hold only slowly. One reason for the lag was an unfounded optimism encouraged by William G. Bowen and Julie Ann Sosa's *Prospects for Faculty in the Arts & Sciences* (1989). Bowen, a distinguished economist serving as head of the wealthy and influential Andrew W. Mellon Foundation after two decades as the president of Princeton University, held great sway throughout academia. (Sosa was his graduate student researcher.) Bowen earned his reputation over and again. His 1998 *Shape of the River*, coauthored with Derek Bok, made the best case for diversity and affirmative action in academia, and he established major policies to enact his remedies.[15] Along with taking on international issues involving higher education, especially in South Africa, he helped to found JSTOR, the indispensable digital repository of articles from scholarly journals. "Had Bowen been a rock musician," Len wrote upon Bowen's death, "his greatest hits would have filled at least a double album."[16] But the highly influential *Prospects for Faculty in the Arts & Sciences* would not have been included on it.

Bowen and Sosa argued that a coming increase in the number of college-bound students would soon necessitate the hiring of many more new professors. They forecast a faculty shortage, especially in the humanities and social sciences, areas where they said graduate student enrollment levels were particularly insufficient to meet the coming influx. PhD graduates in the humanities had in fact declined, largely because of the poor academic job market, from 4,873 in 1973 to a low of 2,749 in 1988, a drop of 49 percent, just as Bowen and Sosa were concluding their research.[17] This finding bolstered Bowen's argument to the Mellon board for maintaining and increasing support for graduate students. The authors carefully hedged their projections, but the many news reports that summarized the study omitted the authors' qualifications and trumpeted joyful tidings. Faculty and students—who had struggled with an academic job shortage that began in the early 1970s—relied more on the news reports than the dense book itself, and they took heart. They renewed their patience.

The Bowen Report, as the book was quickly nicknamed, proved persuasive, but it also proved wrong. The market for professors changed rapidly in ways that Bowen, for all his perspicacity, did not anticipate. When the large cohort of professors of Bowen's own generation retired, they were mostly not replaced by new tenure-track hires. Nor did the anticipated increase in undergraduate enrollment—which Bowen and Sosa relied upon in their projections—lead to more tenure-track jobs. Instead, we have witnessed the adjunctification of academia: the rise of a new generation of contingent faculty working full and part time in non-tenure-track positions. We "just didn't anticipate" the move to adjuncts, Bowen later acknowledged in an interview with the *Chronicle of Higher Education*.[18] Faculty and administrators—and especially graduate students—didn't see it coming either. They continued to wait for an academic job market recovery that never came. College and university administrators, accustomed to abundance, also expected that it would one day return—so programs grew in anticipation of a return to previous funding levels.

That moment never arrived. The situation worsened, in fact, after the national economic downturn in 2008 (as it likely will again after COVID). The consequences were grievous in doctoral education in the arts and sciences: generations of PhDs were taught to expect professorships that never materialized when they graduated. This disjunction informs many problems that developed, such as increased time to the doctoral degree, and formed the basis for many of the ethical difficulties that plague doctoral education today.

The same disjunction helped push doctoral education toward incoherence. Perhaps the most-quoted sentence that powered reform efforts from 1990 forward appears in an influential Pew-sponsored 2001 report by Chris M. Golde and Timothy M. Dore, ominously titled "At Cross Purposes": "The training doctoral students receive is not what they want, nor does it prepare them for the jobs they take."[19] (Such frank pessimism still alternates with nostalgia. For example, Golde is also a coauthor of a Carnegie Foundation–sponsored volume in which the history of this nation's PhD is lauded as "by almost any measure . . . a tale of success—and a typically American one at that.")[20]

The number of academic positions in the United States actually did increase gradually until 2007, but the number of graduates in the humanities and social sciences increased far more rapidly. For example, there were

563 doctorates awarded in history in 1986,
663 in 1991,
861 in 1996, and
1,031 in 2001, a near doubling over 15 years.[21]

The Bowen-Sosa findings, along with faculty and administrative eagerness to believe them, helped stoke an enrollment boom that easily outpaced this small growth in professorial openings and led to a continuation, even an intensification, of the academic employment bust. During the succeeding 15 years, from 2001 to 2016, the number of doctoral graduates in history rose by only 21 percent compared to an overall increase of 29 percent in PhD students in all fields. In English, growth essentially ended, with just a 1 percent increase in the following 15 years.[22]

These figures sum up the story in more ways than one. The optimism of the Bowen Report contributed to unrealistic hopes and encouraged enrollments in PhD programs, while the eventual unmasking of the report's false premises, key among them the failure to anticipate adjunctification, led to still lower morale. An even more profound pessimism soon took hold in the humanities disciplines. And while discontent in the sciences was more muted, there was a growing conviction of a disconnect between training (which assumed graduates would opt for an academic career) and the actual intentions of a majority of the students, who did not plan to remain in the academy.

That pessimism led to a flurry of activity. Administrators and foundation officers moved to study doctoral education in the United States. They agreed on the need for data on its shortcomings, and they determined to try to solve the problems that it faced. An especially intense decade of reform around the turn of this century sought to turn this consensus into action. Major players with names like Carnegie and Mellon sought major reforms—with major lack of success. (We'll look closely at those efforts in chapter 1.)

The ensuing reform impetus wasn't all due to the dismal academic job market. While there were fewer good academic jobs, it now took longer and longer to earn a doctorate to apply for one. The extreme buyer's market pressured graduate students to publish their work while still in school. And the scarcity of academic jobs led students often to linger in graduate school, where they lived on a subsistence wage that was still perceived as better than nothing.

Added to the lengthening time to degree were other embarrassments. These included, in some fields, a scattered and narrow course selection that suited faculty members' research but hardly added up to a rational curriculum. (This patchwork is essentially a hangover from the days when departments offered so many courses that there really was something for everyone.) Following coursework, students now underwent perfunctory and often haphazard teacher training before they entered the classroom themselves. Another failing was the low numbers of students of color and (in some fields) women, that had academia trailing almost all other social sectors (such as the military and business) in improving racial and ethnic diversity.[23] The numbers did improve in succeeding decades—most in the health sciences and least in the humanities—but overall at an agonizingly slow pace.

And this partial failure in turn slowed attempts to reflect the diversity of a new American population in doctoral education. For educators who liked to see themselves as progressive, this result was galling.

Whatever the near and far causes of growing discontent, the shortcomings we have outlined across all fields of the arts and sciences had become obvious to educators. Mathematician Tony Chan wrote in a Carnegie-sponsored study in 2006 that "there is no shortage of ideas about *what* we need to change. We have to decide whether or not we *want* to change."[24]

What Should We Do Now?

We need a PhD that looks outside the walls of the university, not one that turns inward. There's nothing new about a public-facing PhD. Its roots lie in the American academic past, before the Cold War expansion of academia created a temporary demand for professors, along with a seemingly permanent sense that this demand would endure forever. Engagement of multiple and diverse publics is a much older aim of American education than the model of pure scholarly replication. Most private colleges and universities were founded by religious groups seeking to improve society through learning and the good works of their students who possessed that learning.

Such an emphasis on public use and usefulness is coiled into the DNA of American higher education, and it affected the early direction of universities as well as colleges.[25] American colleges were designed to serve the public, and when universities supplemented them, they incorporated this aim along with their emphasis on research. Public usefulness was a prime tenet in the founding of state universities beginning in the nineteenth century. While those universities founded by land grants were intended to emphasize "the useful arts" such as engineering and agriculture, it is worth noting that not a single one of the public universities, including the land grants, failed to offer a full array of the liberal arts disciplines. In this way they fulfilled the language of the Morrill Act, which calls for both "liberal and practical education." In this spirit, John Dewey wrote that a discipline "recovers itself . . . when it ceases to be a device for dealing with the problems of philosophers and becomes a method cultivated by philosophers for dealing with the problems of men" (and women, we would add).[26]

This expansive vision of higher education proved hugely influential in the decades around the turn of the twentieth century. Many institutions, both new and existing, followed the vision of the Morrill Act, not just the land grant institutions, which gave the law an influence that exceeded its strictly legal boundaries and shaped higher education's modern contours. The interdependence in American universities of the intellectual and practical remains in force today.[27]

A movement outward is now underway, and it should continue. It marks a restoration more than an innovation when, in his excellent short history of higher education, Douglas C. Bennett lists experiential and service learning among six "frontiers of innovation." And more recently Andrew Delbanco concludes his book *College* with a set of examples illustrating "a growing movement promoting education for citizenship."[28] In all, there is a burgeoning sense in higher education that academic learning should not merely critique social realities but should likewise constitute them. It's also useful to achieve public impact: a greater orientation toward applying knowledge to the public good actually helps when graduate programs advocate for themselves with deans, provosts, and university presidents.

We need to go back to the future then, and there's no time to lose. Jacques Berlinerblau has recently updated Dewey's suggestions. He urges "an engaged humanism" and cautions that "the humanities had better start serving people, people who are not professional humanists."[29] The tonal contrast between Dewey and Berlinerblau is instructive of what transpired in the years between the statements: Dewey offers guidance, while Berlinerblau sounds a warning.

When doctoral education fails to heed these calls, the result can be a terrible waste of human talent for both individual people and the community. Consider the case of Erin Bartram, a visiting assistant professor of history who had been seeking a tenure-track position since earning her PhD in 2015. In 2018, she decided to stop trying. She made her decision public in an essay, "The Sublimated Grief of the Left Behind," first posted on her blog and then, after it went viral, republished in the *Chronicle of Higher Education*.

"I got a Ph.D. in history because I wanted to be a historian," Bartram wrote. "Now I have to do something else." At first, she wrote, she suppressed the sadness she felt ("I didn't feel I had a right to grieve") and then she released it. Bartram's essay quickly gained a prominent place in a subfield of "quit lit" that might also be termed "pushed out lit." (Before that, the best-known work in that category had been Rebecca Schuman's anguished "Thesis Hatement," which was published almost five years before.)[30]

Bartram is clearly angry, but grief animates her above all. She questions the value of her scholarly work ("valuable to whom?") and considers her learning "utterly useless." She determines that the time she spent in academia "doesn't matter in the way that I hoped it would," and concludes, "I don't know what I'm going to do. I don't know what I'm good for."[31] When someone with a doctorate doesn't know what she is good for, that's more than an expression of personal despair. It also says something negative about graduate training and academic culture. We should expect holders of the highest academic degree not simply to know a great deal but to know what to do with it, both within the academy (teaching, for instance, is one enactment of knowledge) and beyond it.

We're not singling out Bartram here—quite the opposite. Graduate students and PhDs are highly resourceful people, but we don't see their resourcefulness often or broadly enough. Doctoral students learn to work with information in sophisticated ways and to communicate to different kinds of audiences. But too many can get stuck because they aren't aware that they possess those skills.

They also get stuck because graduate education has taught them that only a professorship truly justifies the long pursuit of a PhD.[32] The message that a tenure-track job is the only honorable career goal can be implicit, and it isn't always intentional. But the fact is, the doctoral curriculum is modeled on the work of a professor at a research university—a career goal that the vast majority of doctoral graduates won't (or will not wish to) achieve.

If students or their teachers would realize it, doctoral graduates are valuable in myriad ways. But we don't typically help our students perceive their own versatility—and with it their many potential means for success and happiness. In *So What Are You Going to Do with That? Finding Careers outside Academia*, first published in 2001, Susan Basalla and Maggie Debelius write, "We understand that being forced to leave a career you love because of a weak job market is heartbreaking." They also warn that "if you think that you can't possibly be happy outside academia, you probably won't be." Most PhDs don't become professors, but that's only a problem if we teach them to feel like failures when that happens. It's much more than ironic that, when PhDs leave the academy, most are happy with their choice.[33]

Good graduate training should unlock and direct students' creativity. Instead of narrowing their vision, we should broaden it, practically as well as intellectually. Writing in a forum entitled "What Should Be Done?" Brian Croxall says simply, "Every doctoral program should discuss and encourage other career opportunities. The culture of graduate school needs to change so that it becomes possible to recognize other options outside the tenure-track position."[34]

In short, we professors and administrators need to stop sponsoring the kind of despair that Erin Bartram so vividly expresses. It easily becomes a self-fulfilling prophecy. That doesn't mean encouraging graduate students to abandon scholarly pursuits—the PhD is a scholarly degree—but it does mean integrating other skills into the curriculum that students will need outside of the university as well as within it. It means enabling students to better understand the full range of career possibilities opened to them by their graduate training.

After more than 45 years of shortages of academic positions for PhDs in all fields, we have reached a tipping point. Speaking of the humanistic disciplines, Sidonie Smith writes emphatically that "the model of success narrowly focused on one outcome—completion of the long-form proto-monograph and then a tenure-track position at an R-1 institution*—has run its course. It is exhausted; it is exhausting; it is no longer tenable in terms of student interests and prospects."[35] Far more programs than ever before are initiating changes. Julia Kent, who directs communications at the Council of Graduate Schools, and Maureen Terese McCarthy, who led the office of research, observed that English departments often have been the most resistant to considering nonacademic outcomes for graduate students, but the two remarked in 2018 that, "Compared to ten or twenty or even five years ago, this is a new moment, and the resistance to a more public or applicable English degree, though still potent, is much reduced."[36]

In the bench sciences, more students enter their programs with nonprofessorial career expectations, but their programs again train them as if they all will become professorial researchers. In most bench sciences, fewer than half of graduate students anticipate an academic career, and fewer still end up in one. The number of professorial positions in these fields has been dwindling as well, and doctoral study in science similarly neglects preparation for diverse career options. "The real crisis in American science education," according to *Scientific American*, "is a distorted job market's inability to provide careers" for young scientists "worthy of their abilities." The editorial (which is unsigned) points to an anomaly: we hear about a shortage of US scientists and engineers at the same time that we also hear about an "oversupply" of doctoral graduates in the sciences.[37] In *Graduate STEM Education for the 21st Century*, a recent major report from the National Academy of Science, the authors write that the graduate student "mind-set" needs to be "readjusted to recognize that some of the better students will not pursue academic research but will enter careers in other sectors, such as business or government."[38] Differing data sets provide different estimates, but they agree that more than half of all STEM doctoral graduates will work outside the academy.

---

* R-1 (Research 1) is a category in the classification system developed by the Carnegie Commission on Higher Education in 1970 and updated many times since. R-1 universities demonstrate "very high research activity." Carnegie Classification of Institutions of Higher Education, "2018 Classification Update," News & Announcements, https://carnegieclassifications.iu.edu/.

Two Cultures, One Doctorate

We focus our historical view in this book on graduate education reform efforts since 1990. The preponderance of these concern the humanities and social sciences, and our emphases often will follow suit—
but not always. We've sought information about best practices in the
sciences, and we also looked at reports in which scientists assess their
own enterprises.[39] What immediately stands out is the degree to which
scientists and scholars in the so-called softer disciplines share major
concerns. There's a marked tendency to talk about changes in science
and nonscience fields separately, as though they were different species
that require entirely different care and feeding. Of course there are differences, starting with the different economic models that underwrite
graduate education in science and nonscience fields. The grant-
supported academic science laboratory educates and funds graduate
students in a specific way. But graduate school is still graduate school,
and many concerns of graduate educators and students overlap across
the disciplines. Doctoral programs take place on the same campuses,
not on different planets, for reasons intellectual as well as practical.
Truth seeking and discovery making are the properties of all disciplines,
though methods for learning and objects of discovery may differ
broadly. The ancient philosophers *were* scientists, and much Roman-
tic poetry exhibits scientific interest and understanding. The divorce
of what C. P. Snow famously (and infamously) termed "the two cultures" is a relatively recent phenomenon that dates back to the late
nineteenth century at the earliest.

We consider doctoral education as a whole, rather than limiting
ourselves to the humanities and humanistic social sciences, because
it's more practical. We have a great deal to learn from each other's
practices. For example, departments in the bench sciences often administer diagnostic exams to entering students to determine when a
student may need additional coursework. The requirements for undergraduate science majors tend to be more directive than those in the
humanistic fields, so such early assessment might appear more appropriate, but nonscience departments concerned with student knowledge

beyond individual specialization might have all the more reason to consider imitating that practice. While the loose organization of the dissertation in the humanities might benefit by more stringent advising and collective exchanges, the micromanaged, lab-oriented science dissertation might benefit by offering students some of the creative self-direction prevalent in the humanities.

But it is equally instructive to emphasize common challenges. We surveyed six recent science reports, and all six featured two topics: nonacademic career preparation and new academic partnerships between business and government (with three of the reports recommending increased opportunities for off-campus internships). These concerns are likewise central to reformers of doctoral education in nonscience fields.

All but one of the science reports focused on improving pedagogical training for doctoral students, a concern that's easy to find in humanistic fields but is no less important for scientists. (In the humanistic fields, concern centers on the low status of the courses that graduate students are given to teach, while in the sciences, the dissatisfaction is with the low standing of all teaching and its status as last resort for students not yet eligible or not chosen for grant-funded lab research.)

Four of the reports called for greater and novel efforts in recruiting students from underrepresented groups. In recent history the sciences (especially but not only the health sciences) have succeeded better at this than the humanities. Four also recommend greater transparency in reporting student career outcomes, better data collection, and more thorough program assessment. These concerns likewise arise in nonscience fields—and we'll be addressing them in this book.

Three of the science reports call for better training for students in communicating with different kinds of audiences, invoking what is essentially public scholarship. Two reports echoed our own concerns—elaborated in different places throughout this book—with better faculty advising of students and curricular innovation. Three of the reports recommmend more interdisciplinary study as well, and three urge rethinking the master's degree, yet another concern outside the sciences that we also address here. Informing many of these recommendations, as in nonscience fields, is a burgeoning realization that PhD outcomes are more diverse than has been assumed, and these reports model a new spirit of not just toleration but encouragement of such career range.

The sciences also stand apart in certain areas. Most important, five of the reports call for more training grants (that is, grants aimed at student training) as opposed to research grants (under which graduate students become paid enactors of a faculty member's research agenda). That's why three of the reports also call for measures to encourage student creativity. And three give welcome and overdue attention to the elephant in the graduate science lab: the proliferation of postdocs. This contingent army—the rough equivalent of adjunct instructors in the humanistic fields—is supported by soft money (that is, competitive grants whose future is always uncertain). They publish as much as they can, hoping for a break that might lead to running a lab of their own. Postdocs have become such a fixture that some data collectors wonder whether postdoctoral years should be figured into time-to-degree data, even though they follow the doctorate.

But perhaps the most profound difference has to do with the more exclusive emphasis on research in the bench sciences, where everything, including curriculum, points toward hands-on lab work. Perhaps that's why science reformers sometimes bemoan the lack of big-picture ethical and even methodological reflection provided for students. Inversely, humanities and social science reformers often call for a more hands-on application of learning to local and global social concerns.

The overlaps, as well as the differences, suggest how much academics stand to gain by learning more about the other of Snow's "two cultures." Humanities labs, which are being tried at colleges and universities around the country, present one obvious possibility of improvement by imitation. There are many others, some to be found through a comparison of scientific and humanistic dissertation traditions and advising cultures. We already see one impressive import from the sciences: myIDP (Independent Development Plan), the STEM-oriented online service begun by the AAAS (American Association for the Advancement of the Sciences), an interactive site that allows each student to match interests and abilities with career options, has now been complemented by a similar website for doctoral students in all disciplines, ImaginePhD, initiated by the Graduate Career Consortium of more than 400 career counselors. (Both are described in the next chapter.)

We want to single out the *21st Century* report from NAS for its exemplary consideration of how to turn recommendations into actions. We might infer that its force results from frustration. So many previous reports fell on deaf ears, or received nominal assent and practical neglect, even within the organization that sponsored the report. But whatever the cause, a refreshing emphasis on the can-do makes *Graduate STEM Education for the 21st Century* recommended reading for all audiences concerned with graduate education in any field. We acknowledge its influence on our work with pleasure, and we will borrow from it in our own concluding proposal for a national agenda for foundations, universities, programs, individual faculty, and students.

In short, career diversity extends across disciplines. But it's new, and we still have to figure out how to do it well. However, the work has begun, and with this book, we hope to contribute to a constructive and hopeful reenvisioning of doctoral education.

Simply put, we see no reason to expect that the number of professorial positions will increase. In fact, steeper decreases appear far more possible, especially in the wake of the economically destructive pandemic that is raging while this book is in press. Some of the problem is due to a loss of government support that may in turn be traced to a breakdown in trust between higher education and the society that supports it. We will discuss some of the ways that we might begin to repair that trust, beginning with an outward-facing public scholarship. And throughout, we discuss how we can live best with the reality that faces us right now.

A further diminishing of professorial positions is more likely than any other prospect at the moment. Berlinerblau predicts that what he calls the "Academic Misery Index" (i.e., "the percentage of doctorates in one field graduating in a given year who will never land a tenure-track job") "will rise from something like 65 to 75 percent for the

The Counterargument: Man the Barricades

The "perma-temping" of the faculty has led some commentators to put forward a Manichaean theory of academic job prospects in which university capitalists consciously and deliberately structure an exploitative system instead of creating permanent teaching jobs.[1] Michael Bérubé, Cary Nelson, and others are right to urge us not to lose sight of the fact that academic institutions employ doctoral students and graduates as cheap labor. Administrators are beset by sharp decreases in public funding and by large increases in the costs of benefits and other material and human aspects of running a college community. Adjunctification becomes their shelter from a financial storm—and the upshot for doctoral education is plain. As early as 1994, Bérubé and Nelson argued that the apprenticeship model of doctoral education was gone, for it presupposes that those apprentices will get the jobs for which they are being apprenticed.[2] But the fix, we believe, is not achieved by broadsides or even by supporting unions (as we do). We support transparency in general. History tells us that except for that one brief, abundant period of postwar expansion, PhDs have always sought work outside as well as inside the academy. With that in mind, we believe that the sustainable solution is to promulgate job prospects in every social sector for the gifted people that doctoral graduates are. Capitalism or no, a closed economy is a bad economy.

Part of the problem is simple demographics. Colleges and universities are competing for fewer traditional-age students—their largest segment—and the downturn will increase with the coming generation. This has already led to a growing dependence on foreign students wealthy enough to pay full tuition. Many small colleges and BA-centered universities are expected to merge or outright fail over the next few decades, and all but the wealthiest will require even steeper budget reductions than many have already suffered, as the financial model for private schools without billion-dollar endowments has become fraught.[3] Tuition increases have evidently exceeded public tolerance, resulting in a rhetoric of barely managed panic on the part of students and their parents. Financial aid continues to increase, with the result that net tuition is static while costs continue to grow.[4] At the same time, public universities, including research-centered flagships, continue to suffer cuts from their state legislatures.[5]

In unfurling this depressing roster, we do not wish to repeat the mistake of assuming that all is certain or that we should consider the further degradation of professorial positions as fated. Unforeseen events could change these projections; and certainly all academics should commit to restoring public enthusiasm for higher education in general and the liberal arts in particular, beginning at the undergraduate level—because if we don't succeed in attracting undergraduate majors in liberal arts fields, it will obviously become difficult to argue for support for graduate study in those fields.[6]

---

1. "It's the capitalism, stupid," as Marc Bousquet remarks. "California Is Burning," *Chronicle of Higher Education*, Brainstorm (blog), November 19, 2009, https://www.chronicle.com/blogs/brainstorm/california-is-burning/8915. He criticizes PhD career diversity as a cop-out, a distraction from necessary reforms of the academic workplace. Evil administrators and their foolish cost cutting are solely responsible for the academic job shortage, which can be fixed easily: "It should be clear to all responsible observers that movement of a few percentage points toward the tenuring of teaching-intensive faculty members would cause the 'oversupply' of people with doctorates to vanish. Instead, a vast, sucking 'undersupply' would occur." "Graduate Humanities Education: What Should Be Done?," *Chronicle of Higher Education*, April 4, 2010.

No, it wouldn't, and it is ironic that such a fierce critic of Bowen's faulty projections would promulgate such a fantasy. It *is* about capitalism in that there isn't anything like the money to perform this conversion: a junior faculty member receives about $100,000 in salary and benefits for teaching six courses a year, while adjuncts do the same at some institutions at $3,000 per course, for a total of less than $20,000. In this context, hiring adjuncts is a forced choice. Wallace Loh, the president of the Maryland system, in a 2010 *Chronicle of Higher Education* forum, described "the staggering budget reductions that most universities have suffered in this Great Recession," but the reductions began before then and have continued to the present.

2. Cary Nelson and Michael Bérubé, "Graduate Education Is Losing Its Moral Base," *Chronicle of Higher Education*, March 23, 1994, https://www.chronicle.com/article/Graduate-Education-Is-Losing/91381.

3. See, for instance, Clayton Christiansen and Henry Eyring, *The Innovative University: Changing the DNA of Higher Education from the Inside Out* (Baltimore: Johns Hopkins University Press, 2011); and Christiansen's more radical comment at the "Innovation+Disruption Symposium in Higher Education" in May 2017, that "50 percent of the 4,000 colleges and universities in the United States will be bankrupt in 10 to 15 years" (quoted in Abigail Hess, "Harvard Business School Professor: Half of American Colleges Will Be Bankrupt in 10 to 15 Years," *MakeIt*, November 15, 2017, https://www.cnbc.com/2017/11/15/hbs-professor-half-of-us-colleges-will-be-bankrupt-in-10-to-15-years.html). A *Forbes* article notes that it is the for-profits that mainly have failed since the publication of the book, and even the stern warning from Moody's, the credit rating system, predicts only that "a few" private colleges will cease and the number of closures and mergers will accelerate. Derek Newton, "No, Half of All Colleges Will Not Go

Bankrupt," *Forbes*, September 11, 2018, https://www.forbes.com/sites/dereknewton/2018/09/11/no-there-wont-be-massive-college-bankruptcies/#4114f172d75b. The "few" turns out to number about 75. Observers agree about the severe financial pressures on private, nonprofit colleges in particular. See for example, Rick Seltzer, "Days of Reckoning," *Inside Higher Ed*, November 13, 2017, https://www.insidehighered.com/news/2017/11/13/spate-recent-college-closures-has-some-seeing-long-predicted-consolidation-taking, on the closure of four colleges, the merger of another into a large university, and the forced selling of land by others. In the nonacademic press, see Michael Damiano, "Boston's Colleges Are Going Broke—and We May All Have to Pay," *Boston Magazine*, January 29, 2019, https://www.bostonmagazine.com/news/2019/01/29/college-problem/.

4. See for instance, Scott Carlson, "Rising Tuition Discounts and Flat Tuition Revenues Squeeze Colleges Even Harder," *Chronicle of Higher Education*, July 2, 2014, https://www.chronicle.com/article/Rising-Tuition-Discounts-and/147465; and Steven Johnson, "Private Colleges Set New Record on Tuition Discounting," *Chronicle of Higher Education*, May 10, 2019, https://www.chronicle.com/article/Private-Colleges-Set-New/246281. The latter article cites the annual Tuition Discounting Study published by the National Association of College and University Business Officers and describes "an upward trend that has persisted for more than a decade" to the point where the average discount for an incoming first-year student is "estimated at 52.2 percent" for 2018–19, topping the half-off mark for the first time. Further, "most increases in tuition and fee listed prices have largely been offset by even higher institutional discounts," leading the author to question "whether tuition-discounting practices are sustainable."

5. While Greg Toppo's "A Marginally Better Year for State Funding," *Inside Higher Education*, January 21, 2019, https://www.insidehighered.com/news/2019/01/21/state-support-higher-ed-rises-37-percent-improves-over-2017, cites a 3.7 percent increase overall in fiscal year 2018–19, following upon a 1.6 percent increase the previous year, Jon Marcus reports on PBS that, once you adjust for inflation, annual state support of higher education has decreased over the past decade by $9 billion, according to the Center on Budget and Policy Priorities. A decade ago, public school students and their families "paid for about a third of university operating costs. . . . Now they pay for nearly half," according to the State Higher Education Executive Officers Association. "Most Americans Don't Recognize State Funding for Higher Ed Fell by Billions," PBS.org, February 26, 2019, https://www.pbs.org/newshour/education/most-americans-dont-realize-state-funding-for-higher-ed-fell-by-billions.

6. One promising undergraduate initiative, the Cornerstone Integrated Liberal Arts Program (https://www.cla.purdue.edu/students/academics/certificates/cornerstone.html) debuted at Purdue in 2017 and already shows promise to increase undergraduate liberal arts enrollments. With the support of the Teagle Foundation, the university hopes to expand and showcase the program for possible adoption at other state universities. See Leonard Cassuto, "A Modern Great Books Solution to the Humanities' Enrollment Woes," *Chronicle of Higher Education*, November 10, 2019, https://www.chronicle.com/article/A-Modern-Great-Books-Solution/247481.

class of 2016 to maybe 85 to 90 percent in a few decades." Of tenure, he suggests that "in a worst-case scenario, it perishes in a quarter-century," while "the likeliest future for tenure in the liberal arts is that everything will stay the same—and somehow gradually get worse."[40] We can't disagree—unless we succeed in improving our own lot.

An emphasis on careers beyond the academy does not mean we're neglecting the scarcity of good academic positions. Like every other professor we know, we want an academic job market that offers full-time, tenure-track opportunities for young scholars and teachers. Adjunctification hurts the experience of teachers and students alike.

Yet opportunities inside and outside of academia actually support each other. A closed economy is a weak economy, and our doctoral graduates in many fields suffer from that fact. If more doctoral graduates consider the professoriate as one of many opportunities, ultimately the academic job market will need to respond by competing for those graduates, as many professional schools in law, medicine, and business now do. That is a goal, not a present reality—but if we start with a "both/and" perspective, we will serve our students better.

The Nine Challenges

We've structured this book around nine challenges that span the process of graduate education, from admissions through the dissertation and employment. We've framed the chapters according to those challenges: we limn the problems and propose solutions.

Reformers for the past quarter century have been seeking solutions to the same problems, and that fact is an important place to start. Many of these concerns connect, which bears out Michael Bérubé's observation that the problems facing graduate school are "a seamless garment of crisis." Once you start tugging on a thread, the whole thing unravels.[41] For example, admissions committees working with good intentions nonetheless employ processes that privilege the privileged and thereby depress racial, ethnic, and socioeconomic diversity, as Julie R. Posselt has shown in her important recent study.[42] Admissions committees also select against another kind of diversity when they de-value applicants who are not certain they desire a professorial career. This preference relates to the crisis in career outcomes, which is another problem we describe below.

Herewith, the nine challenges:

Program Elements

1. *The Opening Out of Graduate Education: Career Diversity and Public Focus.* Doctoral education in most disciplines is hermetic and fails to prepare graduates to address a variety of public audiences or to apply their learning throughout social sectors. Half or more of PhDs do not gain academic positions (including those, especially in the STEM disciplines, who do not wish to), and yet graduate programs are designed with the assumption in mind that academia is the sole or default career possibility for holders of the degree. Figures again differ, but when you take attrition into account, perhaps 1 in 10 beginning doctoral students will get a faculty position at a research university or selective small college. It may be for this reason, which stands out among others, that graduate programs often lack knowledge of the postdegree careers of their own graduates. Because rigorous self-assessment is rare, programs are frequently unaware of the career plans of their current cohorts.

2. *Admissions, Attrition, and Student Support.* Admissions criteria typically go unexamined and may prove naïve: for example, professors mostly scorn the GRE exam, even as they rely heavily upon it. The national attrition rate from doctoral programs is about 50 percent, and as we earlier pointed out, about half of these students often drop out too late, at the dissertation stage. Diversity of all kinds (intellectual as well as racial, ethnic, socioeconomic) is thwarted by this limited vision, as it is by many of the practices described in each of the other challenges we list. The current doctoral cohort not only fails to represent the population in its diversity, but the increases in minority PhDs over the past half century and more recently—

while real (and especially impressive in the health sciences)—also trail badly the gains made in almost all other social sectors. Because diversity is a multifaceted high-stakes issue, we will treat it throughout the book rather than isolate it artificially. To admit more students from underrepresented groups, or more women in male-dominated fields, while challenging, is just a beginning. To address questions of racial, ethnic, and gender justice requires rethinking all aspects of a program—and that rethinking may make any program more attractive to underrepresented students in the first place.

3. *Time to Degree*. The PhD in the arts and sciences takes far too long to complete. While methods of calculating time to degree differ, a figure of seven to nine years in a doctoral program is typical. The bench sciences reduce that figure by perhaps a year, but the presence of "the postdoc chute" delays the opportunity for scientists to seek a faculty position by more years. Financial support for students is related to both time to degree and attrition. Inadequate support at some institutions is an obvious problem, one that a more practically designed PhD might help to alleviate. That the unthoughtful application of aid and support sometimes can encourage drift is less obvious, and that is a main subject of our attention.

4. *Curriculum and Exams*. Course offerings, especially in the humanities, are often haphazard and may turn the curriculum into an incoherent scattering of faculty research interests that bears no relation to developing student abilities. Responsibly limiting the number of doctoral students—a good thing—exacerbates this problem when fewer courses are offered. Moreover, interdisciplinary opportunities may be limited or administratively hindered. Doctoral programs typically acknowledge the importance of multidisciplinary opportunities but then make them minor, ancillary add-ons to the disciplinary mission. Within disciplines, subfields may be emphasized at the expense of breadth, rendering graduates incapable of teaching widely scoped courses or collaborating

with colleagues. Finally, qualifying exams in some fields assume a model of coverage that the curriculum fails to deliver. The typical exam forms more of a time-consuming barricade before the dissertation than a bridge to it.

5. *Student Advising*. At the graduate level, the relationships between students and faculty are crucial, even determinant. Yet advising is fragmentary, insular, and focused too tightly on that dissertation to come. In the sciences, the grant structure that underwrites graduate education supports the faculty member's creativity while undermining the student's. In the humanities and humanistic social sciences, practices of advising are individual and therefore inconsistent, and so run a gamut from similarly dictatorial to disastrously laissez-faire. In each case, we may be grateful for so many sensible, student-dedicated advisers—but nothing structural guarantees this, as too many students know from experience. Skilled advising at the graduate level should not happen by chance. It is as close to a right as any we can name.

6. *Pedagogy*. Teaching needs attention—and rethinking. Teaching *by* graduate students is a well-documented economic calamity: their employment as underpaid and overworked undergraduate instructors is a failure of responsibility and social justice. But it's also a failure of instruction, a failure in the teaching *of* graduate students. Throughout their graduate years, students simply teach the courses that faculty do not wish to teach (often with little training), and by this necessity, little attention is given to a sequence of teaching opportunities that might develop their pedagogical abilities.

7. *The Dissertation*. Dissertation advising in the humanities and social sciences is inconsistent, eccentric, and haphazard. It encourages drift. By contrast, in the sciences, advisement is so tightly tied to faculty members' own grant-funded projects that it may discourage original investigation by graduate students. Across the disciplines, there is insufficient reflection on what a dissertation means, or ought to mean—or of its alternatives, such as a master's degree that means something.

Program Outcomes

8. *Insufficient Oversight.* Doctoral education is rarely afforded the administrative oversight that would attend to student interest and spread best practices. Graduate schools and their deans too often lack the resources and the authority to forward student interests and to encourage and spread best practices. Bok says that graduate school is the most poorly administered of all schools in the university.[43] Too often, no one takes responsibility—because no one (not even the typically disempowered dean) is in charge.

9. *Data and Assessment.* The widespread faculty antipathy toward anything that smacks of assessment is well established, but how else do you know whether change is actually happening or whether reforms are working? It's important not only to develop rational measures but also to measure the right things—as part of a partnership between administration and faculty, with input from students. In our second chapter, we suggest a method of planning, executing, and assessing that makes assessment relevant and not a statistical substitute for thought and creative refinement.

Each of these challenges has attracted attempts at solutions over the past generation or more, but at present the results are uneven, scattered, and piecemeal. With this book, we seek a more unified plan that can repair Bérubé's "seamless garment of crisis." "The most important and necessary thing to do" right now, says Maria LaMonaca Wisdom, "is to support our graduate students in becoming agents of their own academic and professional trajectories."[44]

How to Use This Book

We want you to think of the book you've begun as an instrument for change. We will explain why the PhD needs changing—but our emphasis is on how to do it. We've designed that "how" for multiple audiences: especially for university departments but also for university administrations and national organizations, individual faculty members, and yes, graduate students too.

The book opens with a "pre-fix." Chapter 1 surveys the reforms of the past generation, and then examines current efforts, many of which hold promise. "Then and Now" provides historical background, and an instructive context. Chapter 2, "Purpose, Then Path," designs a discussion-based process by which a department or program might reflect on its current practices with an eye to changing them. It's a user's guide to a group approach to the issues.

From the pre-fix, we move to the fix: the largest part of the book centers on program elements. Chapter 3 addresses career diversity. We make a case for it, outline the challenges we face in instituting it, and then present some examples of best practice from around the country. Chapter 10, on public scholarship, has the same architecture—and indeed, we see career diversity and public scholarship as intimately connected. It's hard to do one without verging on the other. We've positioned these two important practices at the beginning and end, to frame the discussion of program practices and elements, but we invite our readers to read these chapters consecutively if they wish.

Chapter 4 centers on admissions and attrition. Here we encourage our readers to question assumptions and the often-ossified practices that they lead to. In chapter 5, on student support and time to degree, we encourage programs to think beyond the economics of these issues—for there is more to student support than money. Like many of the practices we examine in this book, support connects to school and program culture, a fact that is easier to see when we consider the challenges of retaining students from disadvantaged groups.

We spotlight curriculum and exams in chapter 6, advising in chapter 7, and pedagogical training in chapter 8. Here and elsewhere, we describe how these practices might be given a student-centered approach. We do the same in chapter 9, on degrees: here we encourage the examination of the norms that underlie the dissertation. Chapter 10 follows the degree holder out of the gates of the university: the focus is on public scholarship—which is in tandem, as we've said, with the idea of career diversity.

We were tempted to write a chapter on diversifying the doctoral cohort in race, ethnicity, and gender—which would enrich the national intellect. Instead, we decided to treat this issue throughout. Given its importance and complexity—from recruitment through retention—we determined instead to treat the challenge of mirroring the nation's diversity in several of our chapters, including admissions, multitasking, advising, teacher training, and public scholarship.

Our conclusion looks back as well as forward. How can we create the best conditions for thoughtful change in graduate education in the arts and sciences? This question animates the book, and our answer is twofold. First, give the person in charge enough power to do things. Across the country, graduate deans have to fight for their place at the deans' table. Economically hamstrung, the graduate dean too often possesses little influence and little power to effect change. Change happens best when it's pushed by leaders from above *and* below. For that influence from above, we advocate for an empowered graduate dean.

Second, for change to happen, we have to be able to look at the process. We need to see what's working—and what isn't. One of the signal lessons of the reforms of the last generation is the need to stay engaged. The book ends with hypothetical case studies of departments that prioritize different elements. We imagine what change might look like, so that you might imagine what it might look like for you.

The New PhD is new because it puts students first and subordinates faculty interests. All good education does this, but it's particularly important for this most personal of degrees. To the students we say with Woody Guthrie, "This land is your land"—or "This life is your life." And to their teachers, we say, if you give the initiative to your students, your own professional life will improve along with theirs.

ONE

Then and Now

Two Recent Eras of Reform

Overview: Fixing Graduate School

The past generation featured an unprecedented boom in PhD program reform followed by an equally unprecedented outcome bust, as reform efforts dwindled or fizzled out. Which raises the obvious question: Why review the era of failed reform at all?

The most obvious reason is to learn from some very instructive failures. At a conference he held to discuss problems in doctoral education in the humanities, Mellon Foundation president Earl Lewis noted that he was hearing the same complaints that he and Bob had heard when they led one of the reform efforts 15 years earlier. In this chapter, we review with a critical eye the reforms of a recent earlier period (roughly 1990–2005). We will catalogue current reforms that, after a breathing period, were initiated from 2013 forward—and we'll note a major difference between the two periods. During the first period, widening a student's career opportunities beyond a future as a professor was one main topic among several. In the more recent reforms, career diversity has become the chief focus without exception. But a less obvious difference, and an encouraging one, is that today's generation of reformers has learned from the previous one, often by fixing what didn't work.

For example, some of the earlier initiatives left too much leeway for endless faculty discussion, and nothing really got done. At the opposite extreme, some other reformers preempted discussion and sought to command from above, with a result akin to a cartoon of a military officer shouting "Follow Me!" with no one behind. How can the faculty enthusiastically engage without turning shared governance into snared governance? That question, obvious now, did not engage earlier reformers sufficiently.

The Who's classic "Won't Get Fooled Again" can serve as a motto in reviewing the first era of modern doctoral reform. If we are to identify a sustainable path forward for graduate education, we have to track our failures along with our successes. When we consider them together, we may be able to see patterns. Certainly we can learn lessons. The melancholy history of graduate school reform has been a largely untold story before now. As institutional custodians, we haven't done a very good job of keeping track of our own work, which invites us to make the same mistakes over and over.

More positively, each of the failed initiatives had strengths that can be capitalized upon. These included good diagnoses (which helped to clarify what needed doing) and some useful early steps to remedy specific problems. The range of issues treated is impressive, from attempting to rein in time to degree to improving the scope and sophistication of training students as teachers and educators, to promoting career outcomes. Even if widespread changes did not take place, many individual institutions did innovate brilliantly to meet challenges that were extant then and even more pressing now. (We'll be reviewing some of those successes in greater detail in future chapters.) Further, these efforts yielded information that remains useful going forward. This is true especially in the case of the Mellon-supported effort, which was by far the most amply funded (to the impressive level of nearly $100 million).

Both the reforms and their results warrant a much closer look. The sweat and treasure of many committed and talented people went into these efforts, but even after such a substantial investment, we haven't looked closely enough at their aftermath. In fact, no one has ever examined these reform efforts all together. We have much to gain by doing so. This generation's reformers can sidestep some of last generation's difficulties.

Going forward is our business here. Paradoxically, that's why we turn first to a survey of what has *not* worked to improve the doctoral experience and its outcomes. A comprehensive overview of why the seeds of reform have fallen upon hard and unyielding ground may seem a gloomy way to begin, but before graduate schools and their programs can formulate plans for improving practices and outcomes, they will do well not to reinvent some square wheels.

Of course, a main and savage impetus for reform had to do with the shortage of professorial positions. But the reform impetus wasn't all about the job market. While there were fewer good academic jobs, it took longer and longer to earn a doctorate to apply for one. Meanwhile, programs continued more or less as they had. A sense of habit devoid of reason perpetuated program elements, with inadequate advising as an overarching constant drawing the problems together.

It's worth lingering on that last point. In the sciences, reports urged giving students greater freedom from their advisers' research grants to develop their abilities as teachers and their creativity as scientists. Yet the alternative of training grants (as opposed to research grants) was losing the ground the reformers said it needed to gain. As an example, the 2012 National Institutes of Health report observed that in 1979, about 7,500 biomedical students were supported by working on their professor's grant, while nearly as many had traineeships, and a like number had fellowships or support through teaching. But by 2009, 25,000 students were being supported by work on their professor's grant while the number of traineeships remained at 7,500. In all, research assistantships increased from about one-quarter of all student support to nearly half, and the NIH working group again urged the institute to provide more traineeships.[1] (Writing in 2006, chemist Angelica Stacy went further. She proposed that funds be provided directly to students, who would then be free to choose an adviser.)[2] The bottom line here is that the same organizations whose committees recommended more training grants and fewer research grants tended to increase the proportion of research grants. It's a vivid example of bureaucracy working at cross-purposes with itself.

During these times of increasing trouble and turmoil, almost every major foundation and association related to graduate study in the arts and sciences launched an initiative to improve graduate education. The most prominent of these included the Andrew W. Mellon Foundation, the Carnegie Fund for the Advancement of Teaching, the Woodrow Wilson National Fellowship Foundation, the Council of Graduate Schools, the National Science Foundation, the National Institutes of Health, and the National Academy of Sciences.

As this impressive group of policy heavyweights entered the arena, we should also note which groups did not: the national associations of the various disciplines. This disjunction may well be what doomed the larger groups' efforts, many of which were highly thoughtful and strategically savvy. But the absence of the disciplinary associations points to a faculty resistance that may have led to proposals that were big on verbiage and small in consequence. This effective refusal by the arts and sciences disciplines to participate despite accepting funding shocked the reformers at the time. "All told," the Mellon team sadly concluded, "redesigning doctoral education in the humanities has proved harder than imagined at the outset."[3]

By 2005, various reform initiatives were winding down. Foundation funding had departed the campuses of universities and moved largely to the K–12 sector, where it remains. The lack of obvious results in doctoral innovation discouraged those who funded it. Today, inertia, resistance, and stasis continue to oppose a now widely acknowledged need for essential change. But it is also true that a dramatically increasing number of universities, programs, and national organizations are taking up the challenges of these times. And this time around, major disciplinary organizations, like the American Historical Association and the Modern Language Association, are taking the lead.

The difference between the reforms of a generation ago and now results from more than the persistence and deepening of the academic job shortage. Educators are more open to rethinking the doctorate now. They take a wider view and are willing to examine their own programs and practices. We appear to have reached a new tipping point compared to even just a decade ago.

Before we describe the particular efforts of the previous era of reform, though, we pause to take up one more reason for the difficulties the efforts faced.

James Grossman, the executive director of the American Historical Association, has often pointed out that each stakeholding group in doctoral education—faculty, students, administrators—cites recalcitrance on the part of the other two as a reason nothing can be done. In other words, everyone believes that it's someone else who has to change. Just so, speaking of the group of essays commissioned by the Carnegie Foundation from leaders in various fields collected in *Envisioning the Future of Doctoral Education* (2006), Kenneth Prewitt observes that those proposed reforms "are bold" in concept but "timid, in fact mostly silent, about who will have to align institutional habits, budgets, rules, and incentives if the reforms are to move from pages . . . to practices."[4]

Grossman's and Prewitt's points dovetail, and both arise partly from the fact that graduate education is highly localized in individual departments, with little or weak oversight. Their observations illustrate an imperative: if proper and sufficient authority is not assigned and if faculty members are not sufficiently informed of the realities facing the graduate school workplace, the institution cannot change to meet its challenges. Various reform efforts—such as the Carnegie effort and Mellon's Graduate Education Initiative—relied heavily on departmental self-study, but the results were minimal. Mellon's effort to make graduate study more time efficient (which we will discuss further below) also relied on the graduate deans, and the Woodrow Wilson Responsive Ph.D. initiative followed suit, with similarly disappointing results. In brief, too many programs that signed up for one or another reform effort took the money and ran.

We wrote this book on the assumption that programs may need to reform themselves by themselves, but we want to emphasize again how much more dynamic and effective these efforts can be when they're exerted from above as well as from within. An administrator—an empowered graduate dean or her equivalent—with authority and resources can spearhead a more institutionally comprehensive effort. Graduate education deserves an administrative structure worthy of the highest degree that a university offers.

From the disappointments that we document in the following section, we derive a set of not-to-do's that could benefit both national organizations or grad school administrators and also any group of faculty attempting to improve their program. These cautions include not to talk about specifics without first establishing action goals, not to spend money on those goals without strong and continuing assessment, and not to expect change when responsibility is not assigned and consequences are not clearly stated and enacted. These desiderata would be far more easily achieved if universities gave their graduate deans greater authority and resources, and we will make a case for that change in our final chapter. But we cannot wait upon a basic change in the administrative norm to rethink the doctorate.

We will propose a process for individual programs to follow that invites openness, ensures faculty engagement, and nourishes reform. Much effort went into the initiatives we will describe. The best way to honor the labor of past years is to make it all work this time.

National Reform Efforts, 1990–2006

The central challenges for every reform effort begin with creating a collective will for rethinking and change. Reformers must decide who in the graduate structure—faculty themselves, a dean, a provost, students—can do this. They must determine how they are to go about it, to create a reasonable strategic consensus without endless debate, leadership with authority, and the means to achieve the agreed-upon goals. All of these moves must be accompanied by ongoing assessment. Each of the major reform efforts we examine addresses these challenges, and it is to those specific efforts that we now turn. It is worth repeating that, in doing so, we confront more failure than success, but we will discover valuable features that did succeed or might have flourished if they had been accompanied by a more effective strategy. We also can diagnose what didn't work and fix it.

This section ends at 2006, after which several years of hibernation occurred—partly because funding by philanthropies shifted focus to public K–12 education, but also because of the economic downturn of 2008 and, perhaps, because those most concerned with reform were exhausted. A revival followed, and the following section will summarize ongoing efforts that began several years later.

Graduate Education Initiative (GEI), the Andrew W. Mellon Foundation
TIMELINE: 1991–2000

The first reform effort of this period was also, at least financially, the most dramatic. In 1991, The Andrew W. Mellon Foundation's Graduate Education Initiative (GEI) funded grants to 54 humanities departments (including the humanistic social sciences of anthropology and political science) at the 10 research universities most often attended by Mellon graduate fellowship awardees. The grants were employed to provide students making good progress with one year of Mellon support at the dissertation stage. Data from programs at these and three other unfunded universities would be considered as a control group. These 13 universities together accounted for 18 percent of all PhDs in the humanities, a considerable number. The aim of the program was greater efficiency in graduate education, and the foundation selected two "key indicators" as measures of effectiveness: attrition rates and the average time to the PhD.[5]

> *Goals*: Reduce time to degree in chosen humanities departments to six years; reduce attrition rates, particularly in later years of a student's graduate career; encourage improved efficiency and better practices at the departmental level to reach these goals.
> *Participants*: Fifty-four departments at the 10 major universities attended by the greatest number of Mellon humanities fellow-

ship awardees and, by providing only statistics and student responses to a survey, nearly the same number of unfunded "control" programs at these 10 and an additional 3 well-resourced universities.

Strategy: Led by graduate deans at each university, departments would submit plans and subsequent reports for achieving the goals. Students making good progress would receive extra financial support to speed their way to degree completion. Mellon funds totaled nearly $85 million in all.

Results: Very small reductions in time to degree and attrition rates, though certain enthusiastic departments showed more robust results. Future reformers gained the benefit of an extraordinary data set.

Key Publication: Ronald Ehrenberg, Harriet Zuckerman, Jeffrey Groen, and Sharon Brucker, *Educating Scholars: Doctoral Education in the Humanities* (Princeton University Press, 2010).

Lessons Learned:

Need for:

- Assessments with consequences
- Faculty participation in planning
- A strengthened graduate deanship, collaboration with provost and dean of faculty, or both
- A greater range of participating institutional types

The GEI program's aim of reducing time to degree was motivated by Mellon president William Bowen's view that upcoming retirements and competition from professional schools for graduate students would create a faculty shortage. (We discussed that consequential miscalculation in the introduction to this book.)

The GEI came on top of a preexisting program, the Mellon Fellowships in Humanistic Studies, which created a competition for first-year fellowships for graduate students. The fellowship program had no explicit reforming purpose (unless you count the broadening of the definition of humanities by the inclusion of the humanistic social sciences such as cultural anthropology) but rather simply sought to ensure that the most promising undergraduates would pursue academic careers. The fellowship program began in 1983 by offering multiyear student support, then moved a decade later to providing only an initial year of support, and ended in 2005, when Mellon determined that the more prestigious doctoral programs were already providing such student support themselves. Interestingly, the foundation decided a few years later to provide one-year research and writing funds for sixty-five students annually who were making on-time progress to graduation. Offered in conjunction with the American Council of Learned Societies, the Mellon/ACLS Dissertation Completion Fellowships program, in other words, was more in line with the reform effort we are describing here, as it also provided dissertation funding.

William G. Bowen and Neil L. Rudenstine, the first and second in command at the Mellon Foundation, had determined that high attrition and lengthy time to degree arose partly because of inadequate student funding. But they also discovered that simply increasing student stipends did not help, as the recipients of the extra money finished at about the same rate and fared no better than the general doctoral population.[6] Thus, the Mellon GEI initiative determined to act through conditional funding to departments (with some supervisory attention from the deans of the graduate schools at each institution). To receive continuing funds, each department would have to reconsider the design of its doctoral programs. The funding would ultimately go to students, but only to those progressing in a timely manner.[7] At the same time, Mellon sought not to be too prescriptive. Programmatic changes had to "be consistent with . . . improving effectiveness, lowering attrition, shrinking [time to degree], redesigning programs, and funding graduate students in line with helping them move expeditiously toward completion."[8] That is, aside from graduating students faster to replenish the faculty, the initiative sought to reduce two kinds of waste: first, the waste of years of students' early professional lives, both for those who chose to withdraw after several years and those who graduated but took seven or eight years to do so; and second, the waste of institutional funds on those who would not finish and on those who required extra years of support to graduate—an increasing worry as politicians and the public had become more skeptical about higher education.

The GEI program was greeted with enthusiasm, in part because economist William Bowen was as close as academia ever came to having a godfather. After two highly successful decades as president of Princeton, he arrived at Mellon, already a leader in supporting the humanities, with an abundance of ideas on how to spend the foundation's abundant funds. And aside from his deserved reputation as an expert on the economics of higher education, Bowen's prediction of an upcoming shortage of faculty positions cheered faculty and students who had suffered already through nearly two decades of job shortages.

In all, Mellon spent nearly $85 million—more than double the $35 million expended over the life of the Mellon Fellowship program for individual students—over a decade to support the GEI: $58 million in aid, an additional $22.5 million for sustaining the new practices after the formal period ended, and another $4 million-plus for planning grants and funds for data collection. The project also included much data and analysis in a valuable attempt to determine links between practices and effects.

One obvious limitation of the project concerned the choice of universities, which were all among the nation's wealthiest and most prestigious. The lessons and data from Harvard or Yale have their value, but they don't necessarily apply fully, or much at all, elsewhere. However, there is a follow-the-leaders tendency in higher education that gives credence to Mellon's practice of rewarding the richest. Moreover, the fact that a prestigious foundation was calling attention to problems at the doctoral level focused new attention on the issues.

But the results were decidedly disappointing. Mellon's own voluminous report on the GEI is commendably frank. To begin with, many programs did not live up to their agreement to reform their own practices. "Improving effectiveness was," the authors say, "a less pressing matter" for them than continuing graduate education in its deeply rutted grooves.[9]

The reported gains proved modest indeed: over the 11 years surveyed, mean time to degree stood at 7.27 years before the initiative and 6.98 years afterward, a difference of about three and a half months. In comparison to the unfunded control programs, the difference was negligible, only a matter of weeks. Further, the mean time to attrition (that is, how soon a doctoral student chose to leave a program) declined in funded programs from 6.35 to 5.86 years, again only a bit better than in the control group.[10] The authors cite the poor academic job market as a possible cause for the program's poor results, but it seems clear that faculty recalcitrance was the prime reason.[11]

Despite the disappointing numbers, the GEI accomplished far more than might appear from a cursory and purely quantitative look. The Mellon researchers note that the necessary averaging of results masks some important differences, such as that 10 of the GEI-funded departments improved their eight-year completion rates by more than 20 percent.[12] As well, funded departments often reduced the size of entering cohorts, by two to three students on average, allowing for a greater concentration of monetary and faculty resources.

There were also many improvements in department culture, as a survey suggests, starting with clarification of program expectations. Departments reported improved curricular planning, and advising and mentoring, as well as more group workshops, greater summer and research support, and a reduction in the number of semesters doctoral students spent teaching. These innovations may not have had much effect on the two targeted indicators of attrition and time to degree, but they did improve the student experience.

Extrapolating further from Mellon's outcomes survey data, if we consider a sample of 40 entering students in these most prestigious programs, 22 would graduate (a 45 percent attrition rate), 12 to tenure-track positions, 6 of those at doctoral institutions (with 3 of those 6 appointed at a doctoral institution ranked in the top 50 by *US News & World Report*), and one more on the tenure track at a prestigious college. Graduates who did not go into academia did not tend to become adjuncts. Rather, they gravitated to professional jobs.[13]

The data are extraordinarily suggestive and skillfully presented, but there is no denying the lackluster results. "There was no active disagreement with the goals of the GEI," the authors observe. "The faculty simply lacked the enthusiasm for the necessary changes or the continuity of leadership that could make them happen. . . . In some departments, the very idea of changing the program came as a shock."[14] One admires the patience evinced by such comments, although one might also question, after expending $85 million on such marginal improvements, the lack of indignation on the foundation's behalf. Periodic reports to the foundation were required, and the authors commend how the foundation was being kept up to date on "how well the intervention is proceeding while it is in process." But in light of the results, it's clear that some departments were either exaggerating their activity or else getting a pass.[15]

In light of such conservatism, the Mellon team reluctantly concluded that it was harder to reform doctoral education than they originally thought.[16] This confession radiates with suppressed regret and disappointment. The foundation's effort makes plain that reforming doctoral study is no simple task.

Preparing Future Faculty (PFF), Association of American Colleges and Universities and the Council of Graduate Schools
TIMELINE: 1993 to the Present.

Sponsored in 1993 by the Association of American Colleges and Universities and by the Council of Graduate Schools, and funded first by the Pew Trusts and then by the Atlantic Philanthropies and National Science Foundation, Preparing Future Faculty (PFF) was designed to provide graduate students with experience at institutions other than the research universities where they receive their degrees: liberal arts colleges, community colleges, and comprehensive universities such as branches of state universities. The students were to observe and learn about faculty responsibilities in a variety of settings. "The key purpose of PFF," its leaders write, "is to promote expanded professional development for doctoral students." Not only do many doctoral students gain very little teaching experience in their home universities, but those who do often get assignments "that do not provide opportunities for grappling with the full array of serious intellectual and practical challenges of teaching, learning, and shaping an educational program."[17] In other words, while graduate students teach at their home institutions, their experience can be rarified, not resembling the sort of work that many do later at teaching-intensive colleges and universities. The most important recommendation of the PFF leaders is that "the doctoral experience should provide increasingly independent and varied teaching responsibilities."[18]

Goals: Expand professional development for graduate students to become effective teachers, active researchers, and good academic citizens. Emphasis on teaching and service.

Participants: Institutional numbers varied through the years, but at the program's height, it enrolled 44 departments at 25 lead research universities, with 130 partner departments at other kinds of higher education institutions, across 11 disciplines representing the sciences, humanities, and social sciences.

Strategy: Graduate departments send students to undergraduate institutions to shadow faculty.

Results: Over the first decade of the program, 4,000 graduate students participated but often were given little preparation by their home institutions and received minimal teaching experience. Mostly, they learned about the daily lives and the culture of faculty at different kinds of institutions.

Key Publications: PFF Occasional Papers; J. Gaff, A. Pruitt-Logan, L. Sims, and D. Denecke, *Preparing Future Faculty in the Humanities and Social Sciences: A Guide for Change* (Washington, DC: AACU and CGS, 2003); "Preparing Future Faculty," in *Paths to the Professoriate: Strategies for Enriching the Preparation of Future Faculty*, ed. Donald H. Wulff and Ann E. Austin (San Francisco: Jossey-Bass, 2004), 177–93.

Lessons Learned: Value of creating partnership with a range of BA colleges and the need for doctoral students to actually have teaching experience at these colleges to make the required investment of time worthwhile.

The PFF plan—to bring graduate students who were being educated in research universities into contact with people working at the kinds of professors' jobs that far outnumber those at research universities— was well founded. The home university was expected to provide some kind of instruction in teaching and learning or faculty life and careers, or to offer designed sequences of teaching assignments, or at least to deliver a workshop and "informal student activities." The partner institutions would "assign a faculty member to work with doctoral students, invite students to attend department or faculty meetings, include them in faculty development activities, and offer supervised teaching opportunities."[19]

It proved a considerable task for PFF to bring together different kinds of colleges and universities to collaborate in the professional preparation of graduate students. The program responded to the reality that most graduate students, trained at research universities, would find themselves unfamiliar with and unprepared for academic positions at teaching-intensive institutions with fewer resources. Given that both the graduate schools and the partner institutions were aware of the need that PFF was designed to meet, the lack of communication, even locally and regionally, among the various kinds of institutions of higher learning was (and remains) counterproductive and notably depressing— partly because it's not especially surprising.

The program remains extant at a low ebb, but it fell short of its purpose early on. Presented with a range of possible activities on both sides of the partnership, participants tended to provide the minimum (e.g., an occasional workshop or job shadowing program). In almost all cases, the graduate students never actually engaged in classroom teaching. Further, the service component at the partner institution generally meant simply internal committee work without public engagement. Thus, many PhD-granting institutions soon opted out of the program because the benefits did not seem to justify the amount of time required of their students.

If the effects of the Mellon GEI initiative had been constrained by the decision to involve only elite universities, the PFF initiative proved limited by the opposite. A high number of programs participated—first 17 lead universities, then 25 (with 130 partners), and a large number of disciplinary societies. This wide participation was a clear strength, but it resulted partly from modest requirements: little was required of home or partner institutions; indeed, the leaders of PFF stressed its low cost. But few of the most prestigious departments took part.

The PFF program is a superb conceptual design, and it persists in some graduate programs, usually in diluted form. But the initiative fell short in one of the key areas that also hampered the Mellon GEI, which the Mellon authors would later identify as a failure to "define the objective of the intervention clearly and repeatedly and to build in an enforcement mechanism.[20] Even so, a 2002 survey of PFF alumni who secured academic positions revealed a positive view of the program, with the preponderance believing that their PFF participation helped their job search, enabled them to hit the classroom running at their new jobs, and even allowed them to immediately become resources for their new faculty colleagues.[21]

Perhaps more important, the most ambitious institutional participants—interestingly, those with the strongest reputations—did provide a helpful model for future collaborations between doctoral-granting universities and a range of other kinds of institutions of higher education. At Indiana University, 20 students each year spent one or two semesters teaching two courses each term with guidance from a faculty member. At the University of Washington, nine students working intensively with mentors from their department or a partner received scholarships to design and teach a course or attempt an alternative instructional innovation. At Duke, the biology department offered a teaching certificate that included a course in teaching and learning issues, teaching with supervision, and faculty mentoring. We detail such efforts in chapter 3.

In retrospect, we might say that PFF demanded so little from its participants because its leaders were aware they were breaking new ground. By bringing extended focus to teaching and professionalization, the PFF program argued in effect that a PhD degree required something more than time in the seminar room, the library, or the lab.

It isn't condescending to say that perhaps the most important effect of PFF is that it existed—and exists—as an important reminder to more privileged students of a larger academic world beyond the institution that will award them their degrees. In chapter 8, on students as teachers, we will cite examples of other programs that, while not formal participants in PFF, nevertheless propagate its values.

Re-envisioning the Ph.D., the University of
Washington Graduate School
TIMELINE: 1999–2002 (following a four-year longitudinal study)

If the PFF program sought to widen the sense of teaching opportunities, the University of Washington went far beyond that in considering the PhD in terms of a whole range of outcomes that would include not only faculty positions across the spectrum of colleges and universities, but also K–12 schools, government agencies, nonprofits, and industry. The project, wrote its leaders, Jody Nyquist, Bettina Woodford, and Diane Rogers, "is built on the premise that doctoral education is not *owned* by any one educational level, type of institution, or social or academic constituency." Instead, "the analytical skills and problem-solving habits developed in Ph.D's are of great concern to a range of employers that hire Ph.D's both inside and outside of academia."[22]

> *Goals*: To prepare students for a full range of roles and careers in the various social sectors, including those beyond higher education.
>
> *Participants*: An extraordinary range of interviewees in academia, business, public education, nonprofits, and government agencies.
>
> *Strategy*: To engage all parties to articulate a new vision of the PhD by conducting research on students, interviewing all stakeholders, bringing together faculty and a full range of potential employers, and collecting innovative practices.
>
> *Results*: International website, extensive bibliography, compilation of 300 promising practices, and a national working

conference with leaders from all sectors, followed by an ongoing virtual discussion.

Key Publications: J. D. Nyquist, A. Austin, J. Sprague, and D. Wulff, "The Development of Graduate Students as Teaching Scholars: A Four-Year Longitudinal Study (2001; rpt. 2004, in Wulff and Austin, *Paths to the Professoriate*), 46–73; Jody Nyquist and Bettina Woodford, *The Ph.D.: What Concerns Do We Have?* (2000), https://depts.washington.edu/envision/resources /ConcernsBrief.pdf; Nyquist, "The Ph.D.: A Tapestry of Change for the 21st Century," *Change* 34, no. 6 (2002): 12–20.

Lessons Learned: The value of bringing together doctoral students and their teachers and employers for wide-ranging discussions, and institutional awareness that career possibilities beyond the professoriate abound.

Because it was based at a single institution, Re-envisioning the Ph.D. relied primarily on the publication of internal reports to document student attitudes and spread the word intramurally on innovative practices. It culminated in a major conference in 2000 and a website that continued to describe promising practices for several years.

The project leaders began with a decidedly Jeffersonian goal for the doctorate, "to meet the needs of society." They sought to provide "an environmental scan of the landscape of doctoral education" and to document concerns (e.g., an urban college dean's worry that his new professors tended not to understand or respect working-class students, often older part-time students with jobs, who comprised his college's student body) and innovations.[23]

To realize this varied agenda, the leaders of the initiative spoke with the widest range of stakeholders yet considered in relation to the degree: students and faculty, of course, but also leaders of all kinds of institutions of higher education, of K–12 schools, government, funding agencies, foundations and nonprofits, disciplinary associations, accrediting agencies, and even college trustees. Then it brought them into conversation.

This range provided the initiative, undertaken by a single university and beholden to no outside agency, with a certain rhetorical boldness of approach, evidenced in this statement of purpose: "To safe-guard its vitality, including its very raison d'être, the Ph.D must get to know change, and must embrace it."[24] The project report lists "three pervasive myths": that research universities are solely responsible for determining the PhD and that the graduates should emerge "in the tradition of their mentors," that traditional research is the only endeavor worth a student's time, and that graduate faculty know what is best for their students' career choices.[25] They proposed instead a vision that would adapt PFF's emphasis on the array of academic careers and then added a much greater emphasis on nonacademic careers. This amounted to no less than a mandate to change the graduate school culture at the university.

For the next few years, the University of Washington became a leader in doctoral innovation, and some of its programs to enlarge career perspectives have been sustained. We describe several in succeeding chapters. But a change in graduate school leadership tended to mute the effort and led the university to hand off national efforts to the Woodrow Wilson Foundation's Responsive Ph.D. initiative (described below)—but not before an unprecedented meeting in 2000 stirred national interest and led to Woodrow Wilson's alliance with the leaders of the University of Washington effort.[26]

At that 2000 national conference, the Re-envisioning leaders convened representatives from all sectors—producers and "consumers" of PhDs alike—to consider what contributions each sector could make to doctoral education. Further, they built an ambitious website "as a clearinghouse for transformative ideas and strategies," a bibliography of works concerning doctoral education, a description of 300 practices (some more promising than others), and links to 500 external partners. The conference itself was one of a kind. Participants from outside the academy criticized some practices in the current educational model but also engaged the issues informing those practices. They were critical but friendly, and the insiders consequently heard criticisms and proposals that were genuinely fresh and surprisingly strategic.

This kind of conversation, much more open, interesting, and focused than most of the conversations in a faculty lounge, has unfortunately not been repeated in the ensuing 20 years. But it remains a potential model for individual institutions, or even a renewed national initiative. And the Re-envisioning project itself encouraged others to create reforms, inspired perhaps by a statement from a graduate student quoted in a Re-envisioning report: "The academic environment is still very insular. And our society is not insular and people who are well-prepared should have a multitude of experiences and interactions with people in different sectors. And that's still not happening, it's still not there. And it's desperately needed."[27]

Following the conference, the Woodrow Wilson National Fellowship Foundation, whose leaders had participated, worked closely with the Washington group to act on what the Re-envisioning team had discovered. And while change at Seattle was real but limited, the effort would spread to more than 20 universities via Woodrow Wilson, and would encourage the Carnegie Foundation for the Advancement of Teaching to start an additional major effort. To many reformers, Jody Nyquist, the head of the Washington group, is the Thomas Edison of all doctoral reform efforts since—because she and her colleagues first acted on the insight that the doctorate matters not just in academia but throughout society.

The Humanities at Work, the Woodrow Wilson National Fellowship Foundation
TIMELINE: 1999–2006

Reacting to the academic job shortage in the humanities disciplines, the Woodrow Wilson National Fellowship Foundation led an early initiative to create awareness of nonprofessorial careers for doctoral graduates. It sought to extend the reach of these disciplines into the social realms by two means: summer stipends for doctoral students to work outside of academia, and a sponsorship of full-time jobs outside of academia in nonprofits and industry for graduates.

Goals: To encourage greater career opportunities within and beyond the professoriate for doctoral graduates in the humanities.

Participants: Sixteen graduate schools for academic postdocs, 200 doctoral students for summer grants, 30 students for career post-docs and 30 for academic postdocs, 30 corporations and nonprofits.

Strategy: Summer Practicum Grants, pilot programs for both nonacademic and academic postdocs to serve as a model for graduate schools to emulate through their career and alumni offices.

Results: A follow-up study in 2013 by the American Historical Association revealed a high degree of student satisfaction with experiences beyond the academy, especially among those who pursued academic careers.

Key Publications: Robert Weisbuch, "The Humanities and its Publics," American Council of Learned Societies Occasional Paper No. 61 (2006).

Lessons Learned: Awareness of the value of nonacademic internships even for those students in the humanities who pursue academic careers; of the variety of opportunities available to humanists in nonprofits, government agencies, media and other corporations, and of the strong interest of students in working for the public good; of the persuasive challenge required to enlist the support of human resources departments at for-profit corporations, and of the need to get the CEO or other high-level executives involved.

The Humanities at Work centered on two programs, one for current graduate students and one for graduating PhDs. Current doctoral students could apply for modest summer stipends, practicum grants of up to $2,000 to help support internships beyond the academy, with the caveat that the students needed to find those opportunities themselves. More than 100 awards were made during a four-year period, with dynamic and promising results. A cultural anthropology student at the University of Texas worked at a home for delinquent teenage girls who had been molested as children, for example, employing autobiographical writing, dance, storytelling, and drawings to improve the girls' self-images. An English student at Texas worked for NASA on the biographies of astronauts, and an art history student at Stanford found a trove of Latino art at Self-Help Graphics in San Francisco and mounted an exhibition.[28]

In 2014, as the American Historical Society began its Career Diversity for Historians initiative, its researchers located several history graduates who had won the summer awards years earlier. A surprising majority had in fact entered the professoriate, but all of them attributed a good part of their success to their summer experience outside of academia. They reported that the demands for planning, explaining, and bringing work to term to meet deadlines had honed skills in a way that their doctoral programs had not.

The parallel postdoctoral effort, aimed at new PhDs and keyed to the for-profit world in addition to the nonprofit world, established more than 30 substantive job openings at such institutions as A. T. Kearney, the *Wall Street Journal*, Verizon, and the National Park Service. The program, which continued for two years, provided a model that universities—drawing on networks curated by their alumni offices— could replicate, perhaps with less difficulty. The foundation also collaborated with several research universities to offer academic postdoctoral awards, as the foundation's directors considered it necessary to show that support for extra-academic careers did not constitute an abandonment of the professorial job track but rather an extension of it. The foundation provided $10,000 per year for two years for each postdoctoral award, while the participating universities provided double that sum and benefits.[29]

This program, and its enlarged follow-up, The Responsive Ph.D. (described below), was limited by Woodrow Wilson's lack of internal resources. Following World War II, many nonprofits termed themselves "foundations" even when they were dependent on outside funding. Woodrow Wilson, with an endowment that never exceeded $5 million, was not a philanthropy in itself. It either enacted programs financially sponsored by wealthy foundations or proposed scholarship programs of its own to these same foundations. Woodrow Wilson was funded from its beginnings by the Ford, Carnegie, and Mellon Foundations. At the time of The Humanities at Work program, the early 2000s, these philanthropies (and others) were not ready to buy into the idea of nonprofessorial careers for doctoral students, and so Wilson used its own very limited funds in matches with employers and universities while seeking outside funding that ultimately did not materialize. In this respect, The Humanities at Work was an idea ahead of its time.

Intellectual Entrepreneurship Program, the University of Texas.
TIMELINE: 1997–2003 (continues to the present as an undergraduate program)

This campus-specific effort, begun in 1997 by the indefatigable Richard Cherwitz, then the associate dean of the Graduate School at the University of Texas at Austin, went beyond the humanities disciplines to enlist all graduate students in the arts and sciences in an effort "to discover how they can use their expertise to make meaningful and lasting differences in their academic disciplines and communities—to be what the program calls 'citizen scholars.'"[30]

> *Goals*: Creating citizen-scholars to work on community challenges.
> *Participants*: The University of Texas at Austin's Graduate School and a range of community groups.
> *Results*: High student participation, but the program was ended by changes in graduate school administration. It continues at the undergraduate level.
> *Key Publications*: Richard Cherwitz and Charlotte Sullivan, "Intellectual Entrepreneurship: A Vision for Graduate Education," *Change* 34, no. 6 (November–December 2002): 23–27.
> *Lessons Learned*: How participation by graduate students (including those from disadvantaged backgrounds) could be enlisted in efforts with a social mission, evidence of the viability

of team learning in doctoral programs, importance of higher administrative understanding to implement changes in institutional culture.

The Individual Entrepreneurship program at the University of Texas at Austin offered several cross-disciplinary, credit-bearing elective courses along with internships in such areas as consulting, ethics, communication, and technology. The program leaders also worked with community organizations to create "synergy groups," provided advice on portfolios for students, and established a consulting service. Students were encouraged to "develop visions for their academic and professional work by imagining the realm of possibilities for themselves"— to take responsible ownership of their education, learn to think across disciplinary boundaries as well as across the boundary of academia itself, and gain experience in collaborative work.[31] As a result, a doctoral student in mechanical engineering worked with a historian to develop storytelling techniques to increase scientific literacy. A PhD student in theater working on its role in community development designed a business plan for a local arts incubator. A biology student, while pursuing specialized research, also developed means for explaining the more technical aspects of his field to a wide audience. And in the wake of the September 11 attacks, a doctoral student in government created an online network of political scientists to employ political theory to address real-world concerns.

In all, more than 3,000 students in 90 programs participated in the Individual Entrepreneurship program over seven years. It nevertheless became expendable after changes in the graduate deanship and was ultimately moved out of the graduate school to become an undergraduate-oriented program. It continues today in a robust and well publicized form. In our view, Individual Entrepreneurship provides a highly useful model for graduate education that deserves to be reincarnated at the graduate level and funded. It fits the needs of our times at least as well as it did when it was founded.

The Responsive Ph.D., the Woodrow Wilson
National Fellowship Foundation
TIMELINE: 2001–2006

Given its earlier Humanities at Work initiative, it was natural for Woodrow Wilson to participate in the University of Washington Re-envisioning project, and the foundation partly inherited the project following the Seattle conference in 2000. Its purview included the social sciences and bench sciences as well as the humanities. The foundation initially enlisted 14 universities to extend the initiative and soon added six more. It sought range in geography and resources, and a mix of public and private institutions.[32]

> *Goals*: Student diversity, interdisciplinary scholarship, pedagogical development, career options in all arts and science disciplines, community engagement.
>
> *Participants*: Twenty graduate schools, led by their deans.
>
> *Results*: Innovations in funding of programs, some strengthening of grad school deanships, local improvements (including the addition of a graduate student focus to some career development centers previously devoted exclusively to undergraduates), new relations with alumni for student internships, a few innovative recruitment and retention efforts for students from underrepresented groups, and graduate student conferences. In all, the program offered some notable initial efforts toward career diversity for PhDs.
>
> *Key Publications*: Robert Weisbuch, "Toward a Responsive Ph.D.," in Wulff and Austin, *Paths to the Professoriate*, 217–35; *The Responsive Ph.D.: Innovations in U.S. Doctoral Education*, pamphlet and CD (Princeton, NJ: Woodrow Wilson, 2005); *Diversity and the PhD: A Review of Efforts to Broaden Race and Ethnicity in U.S. Doctoral Education* (Princeton, NJ: Woodrow Wilson, 2005), pamphlet available on the website of the Woodrow Wilson National Fellowship Foundation.

Lessons Learned: The enthusiasm for innovation varied widely depending on institution, with the greatest will to change at those on the rise but not yet on the highest rungs of the prestige ladder. The program demonstrated the need to prioritize goals and efforts more rigorously, the need to provide graduate deans with greater scope and authority, and the reluctance or inability of leadership to tackle issues of race and ethnicity.

The Responsive Ph.D. initiative was organized through graduate deans. The foundation saw graduate schools in a struggle to survive and noted that at some universities "graduate deaning is a subfunction of the office of research" and that the position of graduate dean did not exist at some others. While acknowledging the "locally controlled, decentralized" character of graduate education, the foundation observed also that these decentralized structures constitute "our most balkanized and least regularly evaluated level of education."[33] The foundation thus sought to support graduate deanships in theory and practice by acting through them, just as the Mellon GEI initiative had, and by encouraging them to create, among other things, local versions of Washington's Re-envisioning dialogue between the producers and the consumers of doctoral degrees."[34]

The foundation insisted upon action, noting that too many reports had led to very modest concrete results. Employing grants from the Pew Trusts and Atlantic Philanthropies, it seeded actual projects on the participating campuses in four areas.

New Paradigms was the first of the four. It "evolved out of a rebellion among participants against the scholarship-as-enemy implication of some of the previous studies" and posed the question of what could encourage truly adventurous student scholarship.[35] A program at Duke allowed doctoral students to take additional courses toward a cognate master's degree in another field at no additional cost—which anticipated a current program at Brown University—and another program at Arizona State provided special fellowships for students attempting interdisciplinary studies.[36] The initiative also encouraged campuses to apply to the NSF Integrative Graduate Education, Research, and Teaching (IGERT) program, partly because of its interdisciplinary emphasis.

New Practices focused on making pedagogy "truly developmental" and on enlarging the notion of service to include community engagement and career opportunities outside academia. (We will have more to say about this effort in chapter 10.) Thus, both Howard and Duke offered certificates in teaching that encouraged greater work on teaching philosophies and strategies and even, at Howard, research into the learning process. The Intellectual Entrepreneurship program at Texas and the Preparing Future Professionals program at Arizona State were two efforts aimed at expanded service and more diverse career goals. Yale created a networking database to connect current students with alumni outside of academia, and the career offices at the University of Pennsylvania and Washington University in St. Louis for the first time provided nonacademic career advice and contacts for doctoral students. The University of Colorado Boulder's Center for Humanities & the Arts offered internships for graduate students to learn to translate their skills into nonacademic settings. Combining these two themes of teaching and expanded service, the University of California, Irvine, created the Humanities Out There (HOT) program to promote collaborations with K–12 public schools. Similarly, Wisconsin's K-through-Infinity initiative introduced STEM students to teaching in the schools.

New People aimed to recruit more students of color into doctoral programs. It resulted in a document, *Diversity and the Ph.D.*, which offered useable data and a set of recommendations to increase student recruitment. (Most provocative were the recommendations to increase the disciplines' social engagement, to reject the choice between race and need as bases for fellowship aid because each requires funding, and to create a "united nations" of funders so that efforts could be better coordinated.) In terms of actual campus initiatives, though, the results were disappointing. Michigan augmented its summer program of eight weeks of orientation for merit scholars, a practical introduction to graduate work, and Washington, Yale, and Wisconsin created peer mentoring and support groups. But there was a lack of truly new ideas.

Finally, New Partnerships picked up the theme of the original Washington Re-envisioning initiative to seek "an essential and continuous relationship between those who create and maintain the doctoral curriculum and requirements and all those who employ its graduates."[37] While the deans involved did respond in various ways to strengthening bonds with organizations beyond academia, the conversation, begun in the Washington program, never really germinated in the later Woodrow Wilson version.

Even with the initiative's emphasis on concrete actions and its highly specific renderings of them in the *Responsive* booklet and CD (still available from the Woodrow Wilson National Fellowship Foundation along with their *Diversity and the Ph.D.* report), it is unclear how many of its recommendations might have been enacted simply on the initiative of the participating graduate schools without any Wilson encouragement, for by design this initiative was targeted at a group of activist deans. Nonetheless, the deans clearly learned from each other and were able to adapt general concepts to their particular circumstances.

Some of these deans designed programs around money—for instance, Duke and Washington offered greater financial incentives for departments to innovate in student-centered ways—while several other deans worked to provide clear data on career outcomes to incoming students and to faculty. In this way, they responded to something that had shocked the leaders of the Mellon initiative: the degree to which individual programs and graduate schools lacked information on student experiences (time to degree, completion rates) and outcomes. But there was no opportunity to add to the original initiative or disseminate what had been achieved. Looking back, Bob, who led the Woodrow Wilson effort with Earl Lewis, believes that greater emphasis on dissemination through publishing would have been useful. The lack of both internal funds and philanthropic interest further reduced the impact of The Responsive Ph.D. Woodrow Wilson changed direction soon afterward, focusing on K–12 teacher training, and thus an uneven but impressive demonstration by these graduate deans of what could be accomplished never gained the publicity that might have made other institutions take notice.

Carnegie Initiative on the Doctorate, the Carnegie
Foundation for the Advancement of Teaching
TIMELINE: 2002–2006

This same general trend away from higher education philanthropy finally hobbled another major effort, but it left us with an extraordinary treasure trove of discussions of the PhD. The Carnegie Foundation for the Advancement of Teaching took a tack opposite to that of The Responsive Ph.D. in that it bypassed graduate schools to work instead with faculty members in individual departments. "Honoring the disciplines" was their mantra—or more precisely, "increasing power of the disciplines and the departments that house them."[38] However, the gifted leader of the Carnegie effort, George Walker, also emphasized that "appropriate modification of the incentive systems is more a top-down effort, carried out by leaders who look across the entire landscape and see how the elements fit together."[39] That this might be the description of an empowered graduate dean's office goes unmentioned.[40]

The Carnegie Initiative on the Doctorate (CID) enlisted more than 50 departments among six varied disciplines—chemistry, English, history, mathematics, neuroscience, and education—and first asked them to reflect on the goals of their programs and then to consider whether their existing "curricula, practices, and assessments" of student progress "are robustly contributing to those outcomes."[41]

Goals: Wise stewardship of the academic disciplines.

Strategy: To raise basic questions of purpose and effectiveness in individual departments through leadership teams, with the commissioning of a published collection of 16 essays as conversation starters.

Participants: Eighty-four departments and programs in 44 universities in six disciplines: chemistry, education, English, history, mathematics, and neuroscience.

Results: Modest. Some changes in program requirements and newly created experiences, but departments mainly hewed to customary interactions and practices. Two fine books did emerge (see below).

Lessons Learned: That faculty participation in discussion must lead to plans of action, and that such plans need consequential assessment.

Key Publications: George E. Walker, "The Carnegie Initiative on the Doctorate," in Wulff and Austin, *Paths to the Professoriate*, 236–49; Chris Golde and Walker, eds., *Envisioning the Future of Doctoral Education: Preparing Stewards of the Disciplines* (San Francisco: Jossey-Bass, 2006); Walker et al., *The Formation of Scholars: Rethinking Doctoral Education for the Twenty-First Century* (San Francisco: Jossey-Bass, 2008).

The idea of stewardship of the disciplines was the only assumption that the CID explicitly presented. Stewardship was a concept "encompassing a set of knowledge and skills, as well as a set of principles," and an academic steward was one "capable of *generating* and critically evaluating new knowledge; of *conserving* the most important ideas and findings," and of "understanding how knowledge is *transforming* the world in which we live, and engaging in the transformational work of communicating their knowledge responsibly to others."[42] But perhaps the message to the faculty—a flattering one—was, you're in charge and you must be an enlightened and ethical agent.

Carnegie set before its stewards three skillfully phrased sets of questions:

1. What is the purpose of the doctoral program? What does it mean to develop students as stewards? What are the desired outcomes of the program?
2. What is the rationale and educational purpose of each element of the doctoral program? Which elements of the program should be affirmed and retained? Which elements could usefully be changed or eliminated?
3. How do you know? What evidence aids in answering those questions? What evidence can be collected to determine whether changes serve the desired outcomes?[43]

One could argue that this emphasis on discussion invited faculty to do what academics do all too readily—namely, substitute endless debate for action. However, these questions encouraged the stewards to question the assumptions behind such tendencies. The authors of the Carnegie report emphasize that they pushed against the habit of "conflict avoidance" that leads graduate program administrators to perpetually renew the status quo simply to keep departmental peace.

Some departments, such as English at Columbia under David Damrosch's leadership, were usefully stirred into action: the department began with a student survey that "provided a wealth of statistical information and many thoughtful, creative ideas for change, many of which made their way into our final package of reforms."[44] The University of Nebraska's mathematics department used the Carnegie questions to develop a document "that actually reflects what we believe," a statement "that fits on two sides of a sheet of paper; a description of the three possible career paths; and a list of eight goals."[45] That document is also used for assessment at exit interviews. At the University of Kansas, the traditional comprehensive exam had come to seem a "data dump" that placed a drag on time to degree. It was cashiered in favor of a professional portfolio, which students begin to compile in their first term. That portfolio was designed to include a CV, research papers, any publications, a 15–20-page essay providing a rationale for the student's major fields, and related research issues, teaching materials, and a dissertation prospectus—all due one semester after course work is completed.

But these thoughtful practices proved exceptions. The outcomes after five years confirmed the view of the skeptics: collected on a website ironically titled *The Keep* but now unused for several years, they are few and not very innovative. George Walker argues persuasively for a program goal signified by the acronym PART (purposeful, assessable, reflective, and transparent), then concludes, "but none of this can happen without a profound change in *faculty attitudes and habits*,"[46] a change that did not take place under Carnegie's gentle hand.

The underwhelming results of the CID, notably lacking in any sense of urgency, characterize many of the initiatives that we've described here. If there has been broad agreement that something needs to be done, that consensus does not extend to what that "something" ought to be or whether it ought to be done anytime soon. Confronted with an imperative, most would-be reforms defaulted to the status quo.

That status quo is untenable on two levels. First, it's unsustainable. Graduate education is under siege on many fronts and has to change somehow to meet these threats. Second and as important, graduate education as traditionally conceived does not adequately serve its most important constituents: graduate students themselves. These uncomfortable facts leave us again face to face with the difficult challenge of who can achieve change and how, even with a strong consensus about what needs changing. But whatever the right levers are—and we believe some exist—the three basic sets of questions raised by Carnegie should prove extremely useful for any effort going forward.

Graduate Teaching Fellows in K–12 Education (GK–12), National Science Foundation
TIMELINE: 1999–2011

The program provided funds for graduate students (and advanced undergraduates) in STEM disciplines "to acquire additional skills that will broadly prepare them for professional and scientific careers in the 21st century. Through interactions with teachers and students in K–12 schools and with other graduate fellows and faculty . . . , graduate students can improve communication, teaching, collaboration, and team building skills while enriching STEM learning and instruction in K–12 schools."[47] Grants were provided to institutions, typically for three to five years, with renewal possibilities that could lead to up to eight years of funding.

This was a highly popular program that made more than 300 institutional awards involving thousands of students, but it was ended without warning in 2011. The American Institute of Physics applauded the program for "providing models for potential adopters" but argued that evaluations suggested only mixed success in improving students' research skills. More to the point, perhaps, "the program design limits the ability of participants to gain enough in-depth experience in K–12 teaching to impact student learning."[48] However, Abt Associates conducted a program evaluation in which over 90 percent of surveyed teachers reported a positive effect on their students' knowledge as well as increased interest in science and math. The assessors also pointed to the intangible effect of role models for the K–12 students. Over 84 percent of teachers said they were now more likely to use hands-on teaching, and two-thirds said they were more confident in using this kind of teaching.

Nineteen of the original 188 awarded programs carried on after the demise of the GK–12. The 1:10 ratio can be viewed pessimistically, or we might look to the brighter aspects: the 35 awardees that followed up with general outreach, online resources for K–12 teachers, and certificate programs for grad students.[49]

Among universities that did not continue the work, most blamed lack of funding and, more suggestively, the lack of any built-in sustainability plan. Further, those universities that received only one three-year grant were much less likely to continue on their own than those that were funded for longer. Several other programs were discontinued because a key faculty member or administrator departed, and here again we see the importance of grantees making a real commitment. As we see it, the main lesson here is that no initiative should ever be funded without a plan for sustaining the program after the grant ends.

Grantees also showed uneven commitment to the question of how much teaching and preparation for teaching would be required of students. As with PFF, this is understandable given the novelty of the program and its challenge in particular to PhD norms and expectations. But here again the lesson is that only a deep, whole-hearted commitment will be successful, not only in the sciences, mathematics, and engineering but in any discipline.

> *Goals*: To involve upper-level undergraduates and graduate students in the STEM disciplines in K–12 teaching careers and to improve K–12 education by partnering teachers with advanced-learning students.

Strategy: Partnerships between universities and schools created by placing advanced college and graduate students in partnership with K–12 teachers in their classrooms.

Participants: Among 188 universities, thousands of graduate student trainees, and thousands of K–12 teachers as well as tens of thousands of K–12 students.

Results: Uneven and contradictory evaluations ranging from "weak tea" to highly influential. Only 19 programs were continued by the participating universities after NSF funding ended, though another 35 maintained some relationship with the students and the schools.

Diversity Efforts

We describe under this heading various efforts at inclusion of under-represented groups in the doctoral student cohort. This compilation was researched and presented initially by Dr. Johnnella Butler, formerly provost of Spelman College and currently professor of women's studies there. We've updated her helpful compilation.

We begin with the observation that most of the diversity efforts we discuss focus on student recruitment and financial support. Important as these are, they represent no more than a segment of the graduate school experience. Only a few of these initiatives take up the important questions of culture—that is, the experience of students of color, and of women, while they are in doctoral programs. And none spotlights the questions raised by admissions practices or attrition (which we will consider in chapter 4). Throughout this book, we discuss what faculty, programs, and graduate schools (and also foundations and other philanthropies) can do to support students from underrepresented groups and help them succeed. Here we offer a brief summary of recent and current efforts to improve racial, ethnic, and gender diversity in the PhD cohort.

- *Ford Foundation Diversity Predoctoral, Dissertation, and Postdoctoral Fellowships* (1966–present): Ford currently funds

60 predoctoral fellows annually, providing $24,000 for each of the final three years of graduate study, 36 one-year dissertation fellowships worth $27,000 each, and 20 postdoctoral fellowships at $45,000 per year for three years at partner institutions. The awards, administered by the National Academies of Science, Engineering, and Medicine, go to students who contribute either personally or in their studies to diversity in the academy, in most disciplines of the arts and sciences. Awardees attend an annual conference and participate in a liaison network with past awardees and others.[50]

- *Gates Millennium Scholars* (1999–present). This is primarily a program for funding underrepresented minority students at the undergraduate level, administered by the United Negro College Fund. Gates also provides continuing support for students who pursue graduate study in computer science, education, engineering, library science, mathematics, the sciences, and public health. One thousand students are selected each year, for a total program cost of $1.6 billion. Three of eight students (37.5 percent) go on to enter graduate programs. Awards differ, to provide funds for unmet needs and to obviate pressures to work or incur debt.[51]

- *Southern Regional Education Board Doctoral Scholars Program* (1993–present; previously the Compact for Faculty Diversity). This program arises from a partnership of state and institutional funding for graduate students from underrepresented groups, with the state providing the first three years of funding and the institution the final two, as well as a tuition rebate for all five years. Additional funds are available for travel and research. Students in all arts and sciences fields are eligible, with special emphasis on (and at least half of total funding set aside for) the STEM disciplines.[52]

- *Alfred P. Sloan Foundation Minority Ph.D. Program* (1995–present): Sloan provides funds to nine universities for mentorship of students of color in various STEM disciplines.[53]

- *Mellon Mays Undergraduate Fellows (MMUF) and Social Science Research Council-Mellon Mays Graduate Initiatives*

(1988–present): This combined undergraduate and graduate program seeks to redress the shortage of college and university faculty from underrepresented minority groups. Mellon awards fellowships to high-achieving students in the arts and sciences (though now limited to the humanities and humanistic social sciences) who are seriously considering a career as teacher-scholars. Students are chosen after their sophomore years as they are declaring college majors. The undergraduate program began by making awards to students at eight colleges and universities and has since expanded to 48 schools and three consortia, including a consortium of historically black colleges and universities and three South African universities.

Those fellows who enroll in a doctoral program within 39 months of college graduation become eligible for Predoctoral Research Grants. Originally, Mellon also provided Dissertation and Travel and Research Grants, now replaced by a range of seminars and conferences on such topics as preparing for the professoriate and professional development, and a retreat on dissertation writing. As of 2019, more than 5,000 undergraduates had become fellows, with more than 800 already having earned the PhD and more than 700 currently enrolled in doctoral programs.[54]

One can question why only undergraduates who have been fellows are eligible for the graduate-school funding and programs. But this start-to-finish approach takes into consideration the reality that achieving a truly diverse doctoral cohort requires spotting talent and interest well before the graduate application process begins.

- *Ronald E. McNair Post-Baccalaureate Achievement Program* (1986–present): Administered by the US Department of Education, this long-established program provides grants on a competitive basis to universities (28 institutions, with more than 100 programs represented to date). Grants average around $200,000 for each institution and are earmarked for financial support and academic counseling for 20 to 30 disad-vantaged students. Two-thirds of awardees are first-generation students from low-income families, with the remainder from underrepresented groups only. The program is decentralized, with directors at individual campuses recruiting students and organizing their mentoring.[55]

- *National Science Foundation (NSF) ADVANCE—Organizational Change for Gender Equity in STEM Academic Professions* (2001–present): Aims to increase the representation of women in academic science and engineering careers for a more diverse workforce. Because it focuses on improving faculty equity, it's not specifically a PhD-oriented program, but we've included it here because it has a bearing on academic careers and is bound to be of interest to doctoral students and pro-grams. More than 177 universities and colleges and 13 profes-sional societies and nonprofit groups have shared in grants totaling more than $270 million "to address various aspects of STEM academic culture and institutional structure that may differentially affect women faculty and academic administra-tors." The grants target both "policy and practice" and "orga-nizational culture and climate." In recent years, the focus has broadened to include racial and ethnic minorities along with women, with a parallel emphasis on community colleges and minority-serving institutions. These awards do not go to individual students but to organizations working at either the undergraduate or graduate levels, with a maximum grant of $3 million.[56]

- *NSF Alliance for Graduate Education and the Professoriate* (AGEP, 1998–present): The AGEP coordinates institutional efforts rather than dealing directly with students. As of 2005, the AGEP works to link related programs, such as an NSF undergraduate research program and the Sloan Foundation's minority PhD program, to foster collaboration among institu-tions that encourage students in STEM disciplines.[57]

- *Council of Graduate Schools Award for Innovation in Promoting an Inclusive Graduate Community—now known as the ETS (Education Testing Service) Award and previously as Peterson's Award* (1994–present): This award recognizes promising efforts from admissions through completion in a graduate degree program, with emphasis on improving the success of a diverse student population.[58]
- *Others*: on an international basis, the Schlumberger Foundation Faculty for the Future Awards, for women in developing nations pursuing the doctorate anywhere in the world in the STEM disciplines, currently makes 155 new awards annually. Several programs are no longer supported, including the GE Foundation Faculty for the Future Program, which provided financial support for minority and women students in the sciences, engineering, and business. Two others may be of special interest as potential models. MOST (Minority Opportunities through School Transformation), administered by the American Sociology Association from 1994 to 2002, provided 11 departments with funds to address a more inclusive curriculum, better research training, enhanced mentoring, climate issues, and pipeline recruitment at both the undergraduate and graduate levels for students of color. As a result, more than half of sociology courses at the target departments included some consideration of diversity, sociology majors from minority groups almost doubled to 33 percent, and minority faculty rose from 22 to nearly 30 percent.[59] Finally, the NSF program on Integrative Graduate Education and Research Training (IGERT) combined an interest in increasing minority student participation in STEM and social science fields with new models of interdisciplinary education and training. In operation from 1997 to 2012, the program made a total of 215 awards to 100 institutions. IGERT also aided the sponsored programs in recruiting a diverse cohort of students.[60]

A New Era of Reform: 2011 to Tomorrow

The change in emphasis at the Woodrow Wilson foundation to K–12 teacher preparation in 2008 may be traced to a renewed sense of crisis in elementary and high school education, a naïve belief that colleges and universities were all wealthy and should use their own funds for any initiatives, and the limited results of the initiatives themselves. These three factors motivated foundations to search for higher-impact uses of their money. Some major donors, such as Atlantic Philanthropies and the Pew Trusts, simply got out of the higher education business. Other long-standing organizations such as the American Association of Higher Education and the Council for Basic Education went out of existence entirely. And of course, the recession of 2008 and slow recovery further discouraged reform efforts—even while rendering them all the more necessary, as academic job opportunities, already scarce, plummeted. The movement to reform graduate education paused. Educators dedicated to improving the PhD experience and outcomes will need to advocate skillfully to avoid another pause in the wake of the COVID-19 pandemic.

The general lack of change through this first series of reforms also revealed a basic challenge that we keep in sight throughout this book: it takes a great deal to get a little done in doctoral education. With competing worldwide causes such as poverty and inequity, disease and health, and many more, the reform of doctoral education might seem an extravagant luxury, especially given the well-publicized wealth of the most renowned universities. But as we have seen, such wealth and reputation can cement the status quo and discourage change.

The professorial job market failed to recover with the economy. Driven by this deepening need, a new series of reform initiatives emerged in recent years. The ongoing efforts to which we now turn have benefited from the pause, for they take into some account what did not succeed before. Perhaps of greatest importance, and a source of optimism, is that each of the programs we describe below are led by the same disciplinary organizations that chose not to get involved a generation ago.

Another change is more concerning: the three humanities-oriented efforts are funded by just one philanthropy, Mellon. Other major philanthropies that previously took interest in graduate education, like Ford and the Carnegie Corporation (separate from the Carnegie Fund for the Advancement of Teaching, which organized the initiative mentioned earlier in this chapter) continue to sit out.[61] Equally worrisome is a lack of new national initiatives to promote a more ethnically and racially diverse cohort of doctoral students. The case for the seminal influence of doctoral education on the well-being of society remains to be made anew.

But on the positive side, there's a growing faculty recognition in all fields of the need for fundamental rethinking of the PhD, and of graduate school in the arts and sciences generally. Resistance to change remains high, but it's dropping, especially as younger people—who understand the current difficulties from personal experience—enter the debate. More professors have had to confront the scarcity of professorial jobs. They may be the lucky survivors of a Darwinian struggle, or to put it differently, the academic equivalent of the 1 percent, but most are aware that they are the exception rather than the norm. It's true that a change in faculty attitude must ultimately be accompanied by a change outside the academy in the perception of PhD graduates as possessing flexible skills that are everywhere valuable, but that change must begin inside the academy and then migrate outward. The shift may be uneven, but it is underway. We believe it will continue to grow.

Public Fellows Program, the American Council of Learned Societies (ACLS)
TIMELINE: 2011–present

Funded by the Mellon Foundation and administered by the ACLS, the Public Fellows Program annually places up to 22 recent PhDs in the humanities and humanistic social sciences at select government and nonprofit organizations for a two-year fellowship term as an employee.

Goals: To expand the reach of doctoral education in the United States by demonstrating the wide applications of advanced study of the humanities.

Participants: ACLS, Mellon, various government agencies and offices, and nonprofit organizations.

Strategy: To place recent PhDs from the humanities and humanistic social sciences into two-year staff positions at partnering organizations.

Results: Highly successful, both in soliciting public institutions' participation and in the career outcomes of the postgraduate participants.

Key Publications: None, apart from the descriptions on the ACLS website.

Lessons Learned: That there now exists much greater faculty and student acceptance of career diversity, especially work at nonprofit organizations with strongly idealistic social purposes (compared to opportunities at for-profit organizations); that the skills of humanities doctoral graduates may be applied to a wide range of purposes, some of which are not obvious.

The ACLS Public Fellows Program is designed for those who make "an affirmative decision to commit their abilities and energy outside the classroom."[62] The ACLS does the outreach to create these opportunities and collate them. Prospective fellows apply for specific positions within the host organizations, and the Mellon Foundation subsidizes their salaries for the first two years to smooth their touchdown in the nonacademic sector.[63] Fellows work in such positions as communications manager (Tenement Museum of New York), communications program analyst (Audubon Society), legislative studies specialist (National Conference of Legislatures), program analyst (American Bar Association Rule of Law Initiative), senior program manager (Nexus at Carnegie Museum of Pittsburgh), senior manager of audience development (Public Radio International), strategic outreach manager (Central Park Conservancy), and policy research manager (American Civil Liberties Union).[64]

John Paul Christy, director of public programs for ACLS, reports that approximately 85 percent of fellows from the first cohorts are employed in their new career fields, while others have returned to tenure-track academic positions.[65]

One chief strength of the program is also a possible weakness. The nonprofit status of the participating employers neutralizes the anti-corporate sentiments of many professors and students and leads to enthusiastic participation. This result mirrors the much-earlier Humanities at Work summer fellowships sponsored by the Woodrow Wilson foundation, where the great majority of student applicants chose to find internships for themselves at nonprofits, while only a few worked at companies.

Humanists, unsurprisingly, tend to be progressive idealists. But is there really a great difference between, say, a position at the nonprofit Public Broadcasting System and another at the for-profit History Channel, which regularly employs PhDs? By excluding for-profits from membership in programs like this one, are we not making a decision for our doctoral graduates that they ought to make for themselves? First impressions matter, and this initial exclusion limits graduates' opportunities. It also neglects the influence of humanities-informed graduates on the business sector. We reflect further on these questions in chapter 10, on public scholarship.

Career Diversity for Historians, the American Historical Association (AHA)
TIMELINE: 2013–present

A multistage, multifaceted project, Career Diversity for Historians began with work by the American Historical Association (AHA) to identify the essential skills that historians ought to possess both inside and outside the academy. The organization then distributed substantial grants, funded by the Mellon Foundation, to history departments at four pilot institutions to implement some or all of these goals as they saw fit. Reports from these "early adopters," presented at conferences organized by the AHA, informed a second series of smaller grants to a new group of departments to reform their practices. The program is ongoing, with periodic reports disseminated at convenings such as the AHA's annual meeting.

Goals: To better prepare graduate students and early-career historians for a range of career options, within and beyond the academy.

Participants: The American Historical Association, the Mellon Foundation, many partner universities (starting with the four pilot participants: the University of Chicago, the University of New Mexico, UCLA, and Columbia University).

Strategy: Pilot programs launched at four history departments to prepare doctoral students to pursue a wide spectrum of career opportunities. A later series of smaller grants have been made to aid further specific reforms at a second set of departments.

Results: Ongoing.

Key Publications: Anthony T. Grafton and James Grossman, "No More Plan B: A Very Modest Proposal for Graduate Programs in History," *Perspectives on History*, October 1, 2011, https://www.historians.org/publications-and-directories/perspectives-on-history/october-2011/no-more-plan-b; see also the follow-up essay, "Plan B: The Debate Continues" by Grafton, Grossman, and Jesse Lemisch, *Perspectives on History*, December 1, 2011, https://www.historians.org/publications-and-directories/perspectives-on-history/december-2011/letter-to-the-editor-plan-b-the-debate-continues; AHA, "The Many Careers of History Ph.D.'s: A Study of Job Outcomes," 2013, https://www.historians.org/jobs-and-professional-development/career-resources/the-many-careers-of-history-phds; and the AHA website, "About Career Diversity" (ongoing), https://www.historians.org/jobs-and-professional-development/career-diversity-for-historians/about-career-diversity.

Lessons Learned: The page of the AHA website devoted to this program lists five findings and outcomes from the pilot phase: "Only one in six history PhDs pursue careers as faculty in R1 institutions," says Emily Swafford, the AHA's director of academic and professional affairs, "despite the fact that most graduate programs are designed with this career outcome in mind." Accordingly, academic and nonacademic job preparation overlap and need not be considered separate tracks; teaching is essential, including engaging with scholarly literature on history education; experiences and learning opportunities with an eye to academic and nonacademic careers should be integrated into the curriculum rather than be made supplemental; and a first step toward reconsidering a doctoral program should consist in articulating its purpose.

Led by its dynamic executive director, James Grossman, the AHA has been the most active disciplinary organization in devising and promoting alternative careers for PhDs. Its strategies and emphases translate to other humanities disciplines, and to the social and bench sciences as well. Indeed, while we plead innocent to collusion (though Bob did consult with AHA on the program's pilot phase), the AHA's efforts often overlap with the issues and strategies we offer throughout this book.

As preparatory for the pilot stage of the Career Diversity program, the AHA published a report titled "The Many Careers of History Ph.D.'s" in 2013. Of the PhDs surveyed, one-quarter were employed outside the university.[66] This careful statistical analysis is based on extensive efforts to locate all PhDs who received their degrees between 1998 and 2009. It revealed that about half (50.6 percent) were tenured or held tenure-track positions at four-year institutions (with another 2.4 percent at two-year colleges). Approximately 15 percent were teaching in nontenure track positions. About a quarter of the surveyed group work outside of academia.

Through focus groups and interviews with historians, the AHA identified five skills that graduate school in history ought to teach in order to turn a graduate student into a fully skilled historian: communication, collaboration, quantitative literacy, digital literacy, and intellectual self-confidence.[67] Through its continuing pilot programs, the AHA

A Model for Disciplines to Track PhD Outcomes

In 2018 the AHA released Where Historians Work, an interactive, online database that allows users to track what happened to 10 years of history PhDs.[1] An impressive amount of work went into this project. First of all, AHA researchers located nearly 95 percent of the 8,515 people who got a history PhD at an American university between 2004 and 2013. The designers chose that 10-year period because it bridges the Great Recession of 2008 and so offers a picture of PhD employment both before and after.

Then they sorted their data to allow for comparison across years, subfields, geography, and other categories—including, of course, outcomes. The result is a compilation of graphs, charts, maps, and other interactive visual tools that allow the user to manipulate data within categories.

Emily Swafford, director of academic and professional affairs at the AHA, and Dylan Ruediger, coordinator of its career diversity program, offered some preliminary observations in a 2018 article in *Perspectives*, the association's newsletter.[2] In some cases, the data confirm long-held suspicions: for example, ever since the 2008 recession, fewer historians have gotten tenure-track positions and more of them work in non-tenure-track, full-time teaching jobs than was the case prerecession. The database also showcases some unexpected findings: the employment patterns of women PhDs are virtually identical to those of males—meaning that there is no gender gap at the point of hire.

As to who's getting hired where, Where Historians Work offers a detailed pie chart. Some basic facts:

- About 51 percent of the decade of PhDs sampled are either tenured or tenure-track professors, with jobs at four-year colleges and universities accounting for nearly all of that total.
- About 16 percent teach full time in non-tenure-track positions
- So about two-thirds of the total PhDs surveyed teach full time at the college level.
- About 7 percent work for nonprofit groups, and another 7 percent in the private sector.
- Almost 4 percent work in government, and almost 6 percent in higher education staff or administration.

Other findings fairly beg for further study. "Graduates of many programs remain clustered in the cities or regions where they earned their degree," Swafford and Ruediger observe, "while other programs' graduates seem to scatter." Are some locations more likely to produce wider job searches than others? We'd like to know the answer to that one.

Where Historians Work enables assessment backed by actual data. Swafford also hopes "that prospective graduate students will use it as they contemplate whether to pursue a Ph.D." She speculates that "the diversity of outcomes may encourage a more diverse pool of applicants." It will also help all of us reflect on our practices running graduate programs, from admissions to curriculum to all forms of student support.

---

1. The database is located on the AHA website at https://www.historians.org /wherehistorianswork.

2. Emily Swafford and Dylan Ruediger, "Every Historian Counts," *Perspectives on History*, July 9, 2018, https://www.historians.org/publications-and-directories /perspectives-on-history/september-2018/every-historian-counts-a-new-aha -database-analyzes-careers-for-phds.

is tasking departments to develop ways to integrate such preparation into courses and curricula.[68]

Pilot initiatives were funded through a 2014 Mellon Foundation grant awarded to the AHA to demonstrate in practice how graduate programs in history can prepare students for a range of careers. The first three-year phase of the career diversity project funded pilot programs at four universities (Chicago, New Mexico, UCLA, and Columbia) that were chosen for geographical and institutional variety. Chicago and New Mexico chose to plan and host workshops and conferences to think through and publicize the initiative. Chicago developed events that focus on professionalization and skill building, and continues to place students in internships to emphasize public speaking and outreach. New Mexico implemented a monthly workshop series and employs faculty-student teams to maintain its fellowship placement program for career development. UCLA hired a graduate career officer who assists students in marketing themselves outside the academy, and the department has modified its curriculum to integrate professional development into course offerings, including classes on career preparation and on the various career trajectories available to historians. Columbia created awards, courses, a conference, and History in Action Research Assistantships in which students work with host organizations to develop and apply their skills outside the university.

Ten other doctoral history programs, also geographically varied but all at public universities, later received smaller grants to improve "programs and activities aimed at career preparation for graduate students." We summarize the overall results and insights of the participating programs in the "Lessons Learned" listing above. In effect, programs came to an understanding that their vision of the PhD needed to expand, to encompass teaching as something more than a sidecar, and to enable student engagement beyond the library and the archive. To do this requires mindful action of the sort that we describe in chapter 2.

A second phase of the Career Diversity Project, also funded by Mellon, began in late 2016. This next stage aims to spread the word and head toward a "new normal." The initiative now supports a cohort of Career Diversity Fellows, which the AHA describes as "essentially two-year assistantships in higher education administration working with faculty teams." This experiment is being conducted in up to 20 history departments. Departmental eligibility entails participation in a series of faculty institutes over a year's time that "will emphasize the convergence between maintaining rigorous research standards and preparing PhD students for work both beyond the professoriate and as teachers in higher education." Details are available on the AHA Career Diversity website.[69]

We particularly applaud the specific responsibilities listed for the fellows, for throughout our own work we emphasize that doctoral programs seeking better career outcomes for their students need to make more friends.[70] That is, they should connect to relevant offices throughout the university—because it really does take a village. Thus, among their prescribed duties, AHA Fellows will "create links to career and alumni offices, centers for teaching and learning and other appropriate units such as humanities centers" as well as create on-campus internships and assist faculty in course development, including a professionalization course that encompasses nonacademic opportunities along with academic ones.

We view the AHA's program as the current state of the art in terms of career diversity, and we admire its vision and practical savvy. While we encourage programs in other disciplines to learn from this initiative, we're also aware that other disciplines in the humanities, such as English and philosophy, lack the more obvious links to government work and other nonacademic endeavors that history traditionally enjoys. However, we don't see this difference as inevitable or insurmountable, and the career diversity efforts we enumerate in our subsequent chapters could establish new links between the academic and wider social sectors that can become traditions of their own in time.

Connected Academics: Preparing Doctoral Students
of Language and Literature for a Variety of Careers,
the Modern Language Association (MLA)
TIMELINE: 2015–present (though the original
funding period has ended)

The MLA, again with Mellon Foundation support, launched Connected Academics: Preparing Doctoral Students of Language and Literature for a Variety of Careers in 2015.[71] The program encompasses interrelated initiatives focused on careers for PhDs outside the professoriate.

Goals: To support initiatives that demonstrate the wide applications of humanities doctoral education to a wide range of careers.

Participants: MLA, Mellon, selected partner institutions (Arizona State University, Georgetown University, and the University of California Humanities Research Institute).

Strategy: Pilot programs at partner institutions, data compilation on career paths, graduate proseminars given by MLA, mentoring activities, workshops at national and regional meetings, and boot camps and model courses on career diversity.

Results: Ongoing.

Key Publications: *Report of the MLA Task Force on Doctoral Study in Modern Literature* (MLA, 2014), https://www.mla.org /Resources/Research/Surveys-Reports-and-Other-Documents /Staffing-Salaries-and-Other-Professional-Issues/Report-of-the -Task-Force-on-Doctoral-Study-in-Modern-Language-and -Literature-2014; "Connected Academics," https://connect.mla .hcommons.org/.

Lessons Learned: Connected Academics offers perhaps the best curricular model for expanding career horizons beyond the academy; it uncovered the continuing reluctance of many literature professors to reconsider the goals of the PhD and modeled strategies to overcome that reluctance.

MLA's Connected Academics program grew out of certain recommendations of the 2014 *Report of the MLA Task Force on Doctoral Study in Modern Literature*. Russell Berman commissioned the report and chaired the task force while serving as MLA president. Among the report's recommendations were a reduction in time to degree and a call for programs to change rather than shrink: rather than "a retreat designed to preserve a national paradigm," task force members call instead for "transforming the paradigm by broadening professional horizons in the interest of preserving accessibility to a humanities Ph.D." The report argues that "professional formation" should not be limited to becoming a professor. In an interview with *Inside Higher Ed*, Berman characterizes resistance to extra-academic career outcomes as "a prudish hesitation," adding, "we do our students a disservice when we limit their career horizons."[72] The report also recommends questioning traditional requirements of literary-historical period coverage and urges a range of experimental alternatives to the usual form of the dissertation. The Connected Academics initiative focused on those task force recommendations that urged a broadening of career horizons.

Like the AHA, the MLA sponsored pilot programs that emphasize alternative careers. These were housed at Arizona State University, Georgetown University, and the University of California Humanities Research Institute. At Arizona State, faculty and administrators focused on advising across the timeline of graduate study, with advisers reviewing applicants and committing to a formal mentoring relationship prior to student acceptance. Advisers correspond with advisees in advance of enrollment, assist them with course selection and background preparation, and facilitate the creation of the student's personal "doctoral advisement plan" that aims for a five-year course to the PhD. Georgetown, which does not offer a doctorate in English, developed a prototype for a Center for Public Humanities as part of its initiative to integrate humanistic expertise into the public sector. The UC Humanities Research Institute organized twice-annual graduate career workshops. The MLA has hosted annual institutes at these locations to assess their programs, test models, and develop further plans, and it has also run annual, year-long seminars in New York City for students, recent PhDs, and adjuncts to consider diverse careers.

These pilot efforts were less deeply founded than those of the American Historical Association. This is perhaps owing in part to greater faculty resistance to nonacademic outcomes in the MLA's many language and literature disciplines. But with the leadership of its new executive director, Paula Krebs, and the head of the Connected Academics initiative, Stacy Hartman, the MLA stepped up its outreach efforts to a far greater range of participants compared to the AHA. The MLA also collaborated with the AHA on data collection and joint presentations on career diversity and other subjects at the organizations' annual conventions.

Beyond the three participating pilot institutions, the MLA expanded mentoring and networking activities at its annual national convention and organized workshops for graduate program directors and placement officers. It now routinely hosts convention sessions on job-seeking skills for those seeking diverse careers. Further, with help from veteran graduate school reformer Chris Golde of Stanford, the MLA has established summer boot camps for instructing students on how to prepare for

The Changing MLA Convention

The annual convention of the Modern Language Association draws thousands of scholars each year, making it the biggest meeting of its kind in the humanities. For years the convention offered a smattering of sessions on academic career issues—with an emphasis on "smattering." Job seekers could attend a workshop on interview skills or a handful of sponsored sessions on careers. But the troubled faculty job market has changed things in recent years. Now there are so many sessions, panels, and workshops on professional issues that you could migrate from one to another and never notice you were at a language and literature conference.

For years, the MLA convention offered a small menu of sessions aimed at professional development. Now there is a boatload of them. The 2019 conference contained dozens of panels that weren't about literature and language but instead about the profession of studying them—and especially the troubles besetting that profession. Most of the panels were aimed at graduate students and recent PhDs. Virtually every time slot over the course of four days had at least one professional-development panel. There were sessions on how to build your online presence and on reimagining the dissertation (in different formats). Other panels tackled political issues, such as legislative strategies to support contingent faculty members. Some panels were aimed at more-established academics, such as one on making the transition from faculty member to administrator.

The 2019 convention also had more hands-on workshops than a meditation retreat. Predictably, there was a CV workshop and another on résumés. But there were also workshops on topics like the role of LinkedIn in hiring. Other panels—like the Connected Academics presentation by PhDs working outside of academia—were open meetings in which the audience could go from one presenter to another, who were positioned like booths at the book exhibit.

Paula Krebs, the MLA's executive director, said that the association's leaders "are always asking ourselves: What can the national association's convention offer that the gatherings of smaller sub disciplinary groups cannot?" With that in mind, they are now looking to create "more structures" that will enable earlier and more sustained mentorship of PhDs. "The convention changes as the profession changes," she said. And that's how it should be.

diverse careers (and once-disrespected academic alternatives such as community college teaching) and gain employment. The boot camps also served as a model for a course piloted at the University of Michigan, team-taught by Hartman and English Department chair David Porter.[73] These efforts were complemented by an active website and workshops for graduate directors at regional meetings as well as the national convention. Indeed, at recent national conventions, a heartening number of sessions included a rethinking of various aspects of graduate education, often with an emphasis on beyond-academic careers.

Finally, in conjunction with the AHA efforts to track doctoral outcomes in history, the MLA is collecting data on career paths of PhDs between 1998 and 2009. History has finished its database (discussed above), but the MLA version has taken longer because it has more graduates in more fields.

Next Generation Humanities Ph.D., Council of Graduate Schools (CGS)
TIMELINE: 2016–2019

The Next Generation Humanities Ph.D. is a program interrupted. Conceived by the Council of Graduate Schools (CGS) as a multifaceted response to the constricted academic job market for humanities PhDs, the Next Gen planners intended to use National Endowment for the Humanities (NEH) funding to move from planning grants to a wide array of implementation grants. Institutions that received these awards would form a community in which they would share their findings, learn from each other's experiences, and hone their reforms together.

> *Goals*: Various, with a central mission to broaden career pathways of humanities doctoral students. The initiative also encompassed everything from administrative structure and reviews to funding models to student recruitment to pedagogy to scholarly requirements.
>
> *Participants*: The CGS and 25 humanities teams at different universities. The teams were given planning grants and three (at

the University of Chicago, Duke University, and the University of Delaware) were awarded larger implementation grants.

Strategy: Individualized by school and highly varied. Implementation grant outcomes ranged from professional development boot camps (at the University of Chicago) to a widely scoped African American public humanities program (at the University of Delaware).

Results: Excellent publications but uneven outcomes. The project was hindered from building on initial ideas by the 2016 change in federal administration.

Publications: "Promising Practices in Humanities PhD Professional Development: Lessons Learned," https://cgsnet.org /promising-practices-humanities-phd-professional-development -lessons-learned-2016-2017-next; "Summary of Prior Work in Humanities PhD Professional Development," https://cgsnet .org/ckfinder/userfiles/files/NEH_NextGen_PriorWork.pdf; and "Rethinking Humanities PhD Resources" (a bibliography on such matters as careers, admissions policies, and teaching), https://cgsnet.org/rethinking-humanities-phd -resources. All originally organized by Maureen Terese McCarthy.

Lessons Learned: As stated in the report, the importance of choosing vocabulary and framing to support goals, developing strategies for stretching resources, engaging important voices, and removing administrative roadblocks. But perhaps an additional lesson is the need to exercise assessment and accountability more strongly.

It is difficult to assess this NEH-funded project because the granting agency changed course in midstream when the Trump administration came to power. Thus, it is something of an unfinished edifice. Some of the partner institutions were able to make salutary changes. For example, Binghamton University created an individual development plan for each humanities graduate student, while both Lehigh University and the University of Iowa created summer opportunities for graduate student development and support. Georgia State created a graduate certificate program in digital humanities. Other teams were less ambitious, creating podcasts or websites.

The Next Gen publications are helpful. They collate realistic and strategy-oriented advice, illustrate it with interesting examples, and present data. The bibliography, though not comprehensive, is usable and interestingly organized.

Though the Next Generation initiative was interrupted, it has led to a subsequent project from CGS that includes but also goes beyond the humanities disciplines. Ph.D. Career Pathways tracks PhD career outcomes at greater depth, longitude, and detail than any study before it.[74] Twenty-nine universities and 21 additional affiliates are surveying the career outcomes and goals of students while they are in graduate school (in their second and then fifth years) and afterward. Doctoral alumni will be surveyed 3, 8, and 15 years after graduation. The information gained will surely lead to better understanding and professional support for students and graduates. The Career Pathways project is funded by the Mellon Foundation and the National Science Foundation. Because it is not directly concerned with reform, we're not listing it separately, but we believe that the data it produces will inform future initiatives.

myIDP (Individual Development Plan), American
Association for the Advancement of Science
TIMELINE: 2003 (in an earlier form)–present

A free online tool, myIDP is designed to help STEM students match their abilities and interests to career possibilities.

> *Goals*: To reduce career anxiety for STEM students by allowing them to privately match their abilities and interests to career possibilities.
> *Participants*: American Association for the Advancement of Sciences (AAAS); University of California, San Francisco; University of Massachusetts Medical School; Federation of

American Societies for Experimental Biology; Burroughs Wellcome Fund.

Strategy: To adapt online the kinds of individualized development plans already employed by industry for graduate student and postdoctoral explorations of careers in the sciences.

Results: There is no published data on usage, but myIDP has become well known and influential.

Publications: The myIDP website has links to several articles, including Jennifer Hobin, Cynthia Fuhrmann, Bill Lundstaedt, and Phillip Clifton, "You Need a Game Plan," *Science*, September 7, 2012, https://www.sciencemag.org/careers/2012/09/you-need-game-plan.[75]

Lessons Learned: As the number of science PhDs who enter academia has decreased from 55 percent in 1973 to 44 percent in 2008 (presumably lower today) and the number of science PhDs holding tenured or tenure-track positions after five years from graduation has declined by a third since the early 1990s, the understanding of nonacademic career options has become more and more vital for students and teachers alike.[76] The myIDP tool arises from these lessons and also contributes to them.

We have placed myIDP out of chronological order for a reason: to call attention to the unacknowledged overlap of doctoral challenges across all disciplines of the arts and sciences. It began in 2003 exclusively for graduate students and postdocs in experimental biology, and even then it was borrowed from a traditional industry practice. Several years later, the AAAS became a partner in the project and adapted the website to be used by students throughout the physical and life sciences. And now, in recent years, the Graduate Career Consortium, a group of career counselors focused especially on careers for humanities and social science students, has developed its own version of the tool, ImaginePhD. While we could discover no data on how many students use these online resources, their wider adaptation suggests that they have some value.

ImaginePhD, Graduate Career Consortium
TIMELINE: Fall 2017–present

ImaginePhD is a sophisticated interactive online tool that helps graduate students figure out their interests, inclinations, and skills, with the
goal of helping them identify work that they might pursue. A kind of
practical personality test, it was designed by the Graduate Career Consortium as an aid to graduate student career counseling.

> *Goals*: The most concrete outcome yet of 30 years of discus-
> sion of broadening graduate student career paths, Imagi-
> nePhD aims to match graduate students and postdoc users in
> the humanities and social sciences with appropriate career
> options.
> *Participants*: Currently has more than 18,000 users from more
> than 90 countries.
> *Strategy*: A free, online career exploration and planning tool that
> can be customized by the user.
> *Results*: Still to be determined.
> *Publications*: None yet.
> *Lessons Learned*: None yet.

ImaginePhD is an exciting project. Inspired by the myIDP online
career tool for STEM fields, enthusiastic administrators enlisted disciplinary and career experts "to gather data to match skills and interests" of users to "sixteen job families"—that is, collections of related
careers and job titles. In their interactions with this online tool, users
are encouraged and aided to perform a self-assessment, to explore and
then narrow options, and finally to develop a career plan.[77] ImaginePhD was developed by an ad hoc group from the Graduate Career
Consortium, a network of career professional and graduate school
professional development staff members at different universities who
offer career advice for PhDs and postdocs. The group created the website and the interface, which allows students to discover their broad
career matches online. The challenge for ImaginePhD is publicity: How
many faculty and students yet know of its existence?

Research Traineeship Program (NRT), National Science Foundation

The NRT awards training grants to lab leaders and their teams to engage in interdisciplinary research. The program emphasizes student learning in the pursuit of interdisciplinary inquiry and goals.

Goals: To "increase the capacity of U.S. graduate programs to produce diverse cohorts of interdisciplinary STEM professionals with technical and transferable skills for a range of research and research-related careers within and outside academia"; and to "catalyze and advance cutting-edge interdisciplinary or convergent research in high priority areas; develop innovative approaches and knowledge that will promote transformative improvements in graduate education."[78]

Participants: Each year 14–15 awards are given to faculty leaders with teams of graduate students, each receiving a budget of up to $3 million for up to five years.

Strategy: Lab leaders compete for substantial training grants. There are highly defined guidelines for proposals and requirements for the host institution to extend the proposed program elements beyond the funded students to benefit non-funded trainees and non-trainees. Additionally, grantees are required to disseminate their outcomes and insights widely and engage in "robust formative assessment" (deemed "central to the traineeship"), which "routinely informs and improves practices."

Results: While no formal evaluation of the program exists, we judge the quality of past funded proposals to be impressive.

Publication: The only real NRT publication is the announcement and guidelines for the program on the NSF website; the announcement mentions that the program has been shaped and subsequently modified in part by several recent reports on graduate STEM education. These reports include *The Path Forward: The Future of Graduate Education*, by the Commission on the Future of Graduate Education in the United States, 2010; *Advancing Graduate Education in the Chemical Sciences*, by the American Chemical Society, 2012; *Biomedical Research Workforce Working Group Report*, by the National Institutes of Health, 2012; *Understanding PhD Career Pathways for Program Improvement*, by the Council of Graduate Schools, 2014; *Revisiting the STEM Workforce: A Companion to Science and Engineering Indicators of 2014*, by the National Science Board, 2015; *Professional Development: Shaping Effective Programs for STEM Graduate Students*, by the Council of Graduate Schools, 2017; and *Graduate STEM Education for the 21st Century*, by the National Academies of Sciences, Engineering, and Medicine, 2018.

Lessons Learned: It's too soon to say, but the authors of the program description cite "increasing recognition that addressing the grand challenges in science and engineering requires interdisciplinary and convergent approaches, as well as broader professional training that is atypical for most graduate programs."

We saved the best for last. This NSF program, funded in the tens of millions of dollars, takes up what we see as the major challenge facing doctoral education in the sciences. For decades now, every advisory report on science education has urged fewer research grants and more training grants. (Research grants subordinate graduate student training to their work on the principal investigator's project, while training grants give priority to the developmental education of the student.) Yet often the same granting agencies issuing these reports have ignored their own recommendation and have given more research grants, with an overall national result that is the exact opposite of what their own panels have called for. This NSF program finally makes this key recommendation for student-centered doctoral education operational. We hope it signals a breakthrough.

There is much to commend in the program guidelines. They emphasize the interdisciplinary nature of problem solving and call for innovative practices to produce "versatile" students. The program also calls on grantees to recruit a diverse cohort "from all sectors and groups of our society," to contribute to the public good. And grantees are required to collaborate with the private sector, as well as "nongovernmental organizations (NGOs), government agencies, national laboratories, field stations, teaching and learning centers, informal science centers, and academic partners."

The actual proposals appear to live up to these goals, at least so far. The examples of funded projects only increase our sense of the program's significance. An award to a group at Indiana University for "promoting Creativity . . . through Integration of Arts, Design, and Experiential Learning in the Curriculum" brings faculty in engineering and technology together with faculty in the fine arts to develop an experimental design track by which master's students "will acquire real-world problem-solving skills through short-term programs with industry and national laboratories." A project at Arizona State University, Citizen-Centered Smart Cities and Smart Living, takes up the urban challenges created by increasing populations affecting "issues of mobility, infrastructure, security, and safety, while enhancing the quality of life of citizens" of diverse backgrounds. Thirty-eight students (including 24 who are funded in the grant, together with 14 others) come from a range of fields such as human and social dimensions of science and technology, public affairs, computer science, and various engineering degree programs.[79]

Another funded project, at Stony Brook University, seeks to educate students in "the translation of complex data-enabled research into informed decisions and sound policies." The project focuses initially on environmental and energy sustainability, and will add population health in the third year. At Montana State, the Montana Partnership for Enriching Mathematical Knowledge and Statistical Skills will "broaden the training" of math and applied math students so that they may pursue diverse career paths and "recognize opportunities to apply mathematics and statistics to solve problems in a variety of settings." The project emphasizes both student learning (especially how to implement research) and team dynamics.

These typical examples collect students and faculty from varied programs into sensible collaboration. If we were invited to invent a reform initiative in the sciences, it would look a lot like this.

A Final Note on Recent Reform Efforts

There is a big difference between the reform efforts of the 1990s and early 2000s and those of the current time—and it is so obvious as perhaps not to be obvious at all. Without exception, every major national initiative since 2011 encourages careers beyond the professoriate. In the earlier era, career diversity was one idea among many, and sometimes it was not to be found. The titles of the books that arose from the earlier efforts (*Paths to the Professoriate*, *Preparing Stewards of the Disciplines*, *Educating Scholars*) are often at odds with their own recommendations for broadening career opportunities, and suggest a double-mindedness—or an ambivalence—absent from the more recent initiatives.

We welcome this evolution. But at the same time, we want to emphasize that many other aspects of doctoral education, like admissions; training in teaching; advising; and the structure of exams, research, and the dissertation, require thought and reflection as well. They matter not only because they shape graduate student experience but also because they affect student outcomes. We can improve the student experience then, but another reason to rethink program elements has to do with how they relate to the new PhD outcome—not merely replenishing the faculty but ensuring creative expertise throughout social sectors.

Reform has had an uneven career in the graduate school arena over the past 30 years, but the lessons learned provide ample resources. Major aspects of each reform initiative we have listed can be adapted to the needs of our times. We have good reason to hope that "we won't get fooled again" and that we'll get it right this time.

[TWO]

Purpose, Then Path

A Practical Guide to Starting the Conversation

Ramping Up

Once we review the recent attempts at doctoral reforms, it's difficult not to be discouraged. The defects of doctoral education have remained constant and have resisted any number of solutions. Given the lack of communication among all those concerned with graduate school (including the vacuum between the advisers and the eventual employers of students), few incentives or budget reductions based on performance, and little realistic information getting to the faculty members responsible for their own programs, past initiatives have largely failed. One effort (Preparing Future Faculty) promised too little to deserve the effort and time required by students, while another (The Responsive Ph.D.) asked for more kinds of change than any program might reasonably have achieved.

If the faculty are not fully consulted and enlisted (a major short-coming of the Mellon effort), suggestions proposed from on high will be first resented and then blocked. But even if the faculty engage (as with the Carnegie initiative), talk may lead nowhere but to more talk, and the "stewards" (Carnegie's flattering phrase for faculty) will become stoppers. We academics must be fully involved, but we're rather too good at blocking our own way forward.

Here's the good news. Given the right chance, we can do far better. These myriad past efforts shared a defect that hamstrung their process: they lacked a considered strategy for achieving consensus and for moving from consensus to action. They failed to offer a means for agreeing on final goals and a strategy for achieving them. That's good news because a diagnosis offers a possibility of cure. Earlier reforms had no strategy to use ongoing assessment as a means for enacting a plan that could succeed. We'll outline that strategy in this chapter.

To do that, we need to dust off the term "assessment." It's a dirty word to most academics because it is thought to objectify everything that properly resists objectification. Assessment also implies judgment by outsiders, especially negative judgment, and so becomes nearly synonymous with punishment. But the kind of assessment that we propose is largely qualitative ("Statistics are a wonderful servant and an appalling master," writes Michael Fullan)[1] and is defined and performed by the persons involved. Its criteria are not imposed from without but determined by those whom the assessment is intended to serve. Further, we suggest that assessment should begin not *after* an effort (performed by a scowling examiner) but *before* it begins (as a communal goal setter). The right kind of assessment is also *ongoing* (as a constant for corrections along the way) because no one can get it just right from the start. In fact, colleagues will be more willing to try something new if there is a guaranteed date by which the group can decide whether to maintain, expand, modify, or eliminate it. The kind of assessment we propose here is intended not so much to judge as to improve performance. In all, this version of assessment should be intellectually engaging and maybe even gratifying.

Ramping up will require several activities. They're especially necessary to overcome a difficulty well expressed by David Damrosch: "We academics are better placed to solve the world's problems than our own. It is hard to get an analytical purchase on the situation in which we are immersed."[2] To achieve that perspective, to move past defensiveness to an openness to change, requires a mood that is empathetic, experimental, and optimistic. Getting people ready to do the work together is a challenge that needs to be met with planning. Here's how.

Introduce Mission Time and Guard It

This is a major emphasis in David Grant's highly readable *Social Profit Handbook*, the best source we know for advice on setting group goals and achieving them.[3] Grant observes that the most important aspects of a program's success usually are not those most pressing at any moment. But those pressing matters don't allow time for any fundamental thinking, so it becomes easy to stay busy putting out fires while the house slowly floods. In the case of academic programs and departments, for instance, the annual budget may be due next week, but the quality of the student experience never is—and yet the latter is supremely important and, apart from ideals, may well affect future budget resources in a major way.

What is most important may not be most urgent and therefore can be overlooked or infinitely postponed. "How do people we know actually accomplish important, non-urgent activities on a regular basis?" asks Grant. "They schedule time for them, and that time is inviolate." There's an economy to this, he says: "Mission time calms you down and saves you other time in the long run." It's also a separate time to step back: "Mission time is where we can achieve thoughtful clarity about who we are, what we are going to do, what we do best, and how we will go about it. We can ask how the world is changing around us and reflect on how we will know whether we are being successful in it."[4]

Let's assume the department chair and graduate chair have determined, in discussion with colleagues, that the doctoral program requires a basic rethinking to change some of the questionable norms we listed in our introduction. These leaders bring the matter to the full faculty and graduate student body, to begin in the spirit Grant espouses. It well may be that a prime motivation for reform is negative—student enrollment or quality is declining, or academic job results for students have been disheartening, or students are reporting unhappiness and even anger. But while difficulties should be frankly acknowledged, the best way to take a fresh look at the PhD is through an appeal to individual and collective self-interest. Ease up on the threats to the current program, and emphasize the opportunities—like a more interesting experience for faculty as well as students, a more distinctive program, national leadership, a still more interesting student cohort, and so on.

The first mention of changing the doctoral program, then, should take place outside the shadow of a crisis. The chair and graduate chair can emphasize that the mission time now being carved out for possible reform will become a continuing norm, a periodic practice, for the department. If we do that, they'll affirm, we won't have to engage in this soup-to-nuts rethinking again because we will be doing it as we go along.

Accompanying that notion of continuing reassessment is the need to establish a will to action. Time in academia too often resembles a melting Dali clock, where long debate results in poor compromises just to get past an issue. Leaders therefore need to establish a timeline that assures decisions within a period of months and early implementations within a year, while at the same time guaranteeing opportunities for participation by all. To beat the clock requires naming a small committee of, say, six or eight faculty and two or four doctoral students (even numbers so that pairs can work together on specific tasks). They should be respected by their peers and should represent a diversity of interests and expertise, gender and race, and career stages. The committee may also require an outsider, either a consultant familiar with both curricular change and graduate education or a member of the university versed in consensus building. All will emphasize that there will be no secrets, that the members of this lead committee will be communicating regularly with all faculty and students.

To enable an economy of time and a sense of serious purpose, here's a simple four-part process. We will ask *what we know, what this information means, what we should do in relation to that meaning, and how that would look and feel.* While the best innovations may bump against institutional limits on resources and even space, we'll deal with that in stage four; at this point, we won't allow such concerns to interfere with the creative process of agreeing upon goals and best means for achieving them.

The committee will look at a range of concerns like those we list in our introduction, but one (or at most, two) must be chosen as central.

Other program features will receive attention and rethinking in relation to that top priority. For example, a department may decide to focus on diversifying the student cohort, but that will mean rethinking admissions, advising, and the curriculum—and emphasizing public scholarship and career options beyond the professoriate (since studies show both are of great import to students from underrepresented groups).

If the announcement of the project and the committee takes place in, say, March, the committee should be financed to work through the summer and report back at a September two-day retreat where faculty and representative students will engage in a wide-ranging discussion of the committee's report and early recommendations. That is, the summer will be for collecting information (increasing what we know) and the fall will be for considering what this information means and beginning a plan to act on that meaning.

Enlist Higher Administration and Gather Resources

Ideally, an entire graduate school led by an empowered dean would organize this effort and create networks so that programs could learn from each other across any number of disciplines. But if a program must go it alone, it should husband resources by letting relevant members of the administration—president, provost, dean(s)—know of your effort before you've identified your main emphases. Let them know you are engaging in self-examination with an eye to improvement, for we know of no administrator who would not encourage that. There's a good chance that the administration will support it with the modest finances it might require (such as summer stipends for the small committee that will lead the way).

Making key administrators aware serves another purpose: it encourages their own learning about the doctorate. Provosts in particular may tend to judge programs by counting traditional placements at high-ranking universities, with little awareness of the changed academic job market. Following faculty discussions, even at a distance via periodic reports, will encourage administrators to broaden their own perspectives while the faculty does the same.

Beyond the university, you should also let the national disciplinary association (and any other national organization or foundation that might be interested) know what you're embarking upon. Some of these groups have their own ongoing reform initiatives. The recent efforts, and lessons learned, by such organizations as the American Historical Association, the Modern Language Association, and the American Academy of Arts and Sciences (as well as the National Science Foundation) will add to the store of information you're gathering. And finally, if later you discover that your agreed-upon goals (say, to emphasize public scholarship or create internships at nonprofits and for-profits) may affect the community, then you can inform and engage local and regional organizations and politicians as well.

Increase the Knowledge Base

This is the key first challenge for the lead group. Gathering full knowledge (and chucking false assumptions) is the first task. It's a truism that the prior learning we bring to any discussion affects the quality of that discussion. Yet most of us have earned our PhDs without spending much time learning the history of our discipline, exploring its relation to other disciplines, or receiving even the briefest introduction to the historical development and landscape of higher education in the United States. Many of the senior professors who wield the greatest influence in a department sit furthest from current realities. Young or old, tenured professors in doctoral-granting universities are not normative or representative: they're special cases. But it isn't too late for them, or anyone else, to gain a wider perspective. Faculty members in a graduate program don't have to become education experts, but every member of a graduate faculty could read a historical summary of the major issues like the one we present in our introduction. (Of course, the lead committee of faculty and students should go into greater depth.) Many national disciplinary associations have published work or maintain websites on doctoral reform in particular fields also. Committee members should familiarize themselves with the most relevant ones. But most of the major challenges cross disciplines—as we do in this book.

It's about Students. Listen to Them

For this unlearning and relearning, we too often neglect a resource that is right in front of us. If you want to know what works and what does not, ask the people you're doing it for. It is worth reminding ourselves periodically that graduate school *is school*.

By first surveying current students, recent graduates, and (importantly) some students who did not complete the program, faculty will learn a great deal. In particular, faculty will see the aspects of their program that have not really been planned at all, but that students are experiencing vividly. One obvious example we treat later is the advising of students, the Wild West of the PhD.

The students themselves want and expect to be consulted more than ever before. That's one reason for the surge of graduate student associations in recent years. Centralized graduate student associations (or councils or congresses) have been around for decades, but lately they have grown and found a renewed purpose: to provide a unified voice demanding changes and improvements in graduate education, including better advising, more resources for wellness and particularly mental health, and wider avenues of professional development.[5] Students are strong advocates for change, and senior-level administrators may listen to students more than they listen to graduate school staff. The graduate student association at Purdue, for example, worked with the university's Graduate Council to develop and implement a Graduate Student Bill of Rights and a Mentor-Mentee Agreement that spells out obligations and expectations on both sides. It's worth taking the time to see what students want.

A thorough student survey was modeled impressively almost two decades ago by David Damrosch when he chaired the Department of English at Columbia. Damrosch and his colleagues composed a survey for their current students—80 questions in all, on every facet of the program and, importantly, on their life situation while in grad school. The results yielded many surprising discoveries about the actual circumstances of those students and, said Damrosch, "a wealth of statistical information and many thoughtful, creative ideas for change."[6]

Damrosch confessed that he "had no idea . . . how many hours a week the students in our 'fully funded' Ph.D program were working off-campus just to make ends meet (typically 15 and often more)." He was surprised as well by "a widespread dissatisfaction with the lack of advice on courses," which not one of 50 students described as excellent and only 9 characterized as adequate. The survey also revealed an unexpected dissatisfaction with curricular offerings and with the failure to ask students what courses they needed. (Not surprisingly, course offerings were determined almost exclusively by faculty research interests. We consider that problem more thoroughly in chapter 6.) Damrosch concluded that the students' survey responses helped to persuade both faculty and administration of the importance of change.[7]

We would modify Damrosch's survey (as he himself wished to do but could not) by including recent graduates—and non-completers—along with current students. Locating alumni may take some doing, as some programs haven't always kept track of their graduates. But in the age of social media, the job is much easier than it once was. (We suggest funding a graduate student or two for the summer to track down and survey the last 10 or 15 years of alumni—and also those non-completers, whose stories and choices will also prove valuable.) We would further echo Damrosch's insistence that junior colleagues take a major role in formulating the survey—and the entire process—as "they are the faculty most likely to retain a sense of the realities of graduate student life" and are "closest, as a group, to new directions in the field." In the end, said Damrosch, they are "the very real future of *our own* department."[8]

Create a Conversation between the Faculty and the World, Beginning with Employers

Grant insists that all stakeholders in an organization's work should be enlisted in the process of determining goals and strategies. And psychologists have shown, in the words of Steven Johnson, that "homogeneous groups" (and that would include faculty in one sense) "tend to come to decisions too quickly. They settle early on a most-likely scenario and don't question the assumptions."[9] That's why the inclusion of students in the survey (and in person) is important. But also, in the case of doctoral education, as the national convention of the Re-envisioning the Ph.D. initiative at the University of Washington group demonstrated more than 15 years ago, a discussion of the future of graduate school should include an especially vital group: the consumers of doctoral graduates, meaning the people who employ our students, both in and beyond academia. Much research on successful innovation shows, as Ronald S. Burt puts it, that "this is not creativity born of genius. It is creativity as an import-export business."[10]

If possible, the lead committee should consult a group of recent PhDs during the fact-finding process. These graduates should include not only professors but also (maybe especially) employees of small colleges, community colleges, research and branch universities, as well as nonprofits, corporations, tech fields, K–12, and government. "We need to broaden the conversation," says Damrosch, "intellectually, experientially, and even in basic personal terms."[11] Moving the conversation beyond the faculty lunchroom generally proves a friendly and eye-opening activity, and a few sessions can refresh thought and generate a range of perspectives. Pairs of committee members could interview these varied representatives, with the goal of bringing the most interesting of them before the entire faculty in the fall.

Other lead committee members could approach other PhD-granting departments in their own university. Processes vary greatly given the loose (we think too loose), discipline-local structure of doctoral education. That means speaking with colleagues both in neighboring disciplines and in disciplines further away. For instance, a history department may want to learn about how English or political science programs at their university shape and govern themselves, but it may be even more useful to learn about the experience of doctoral students in chemistry or biology. "An idea mundane in one group," Burt writes, "can be a valuable insight in another."[12] For example, the norm in the bench sciences of collaborative work may spark creative insight in disciplines where the lone scholar is the assumption.

As a final task, a pair of committee members can use the examples we sketch later in our book, along with disciplinary studies and higher education periodicals, to review successful reforms at other universities. Reform is a steep climb, and there is no disgrace in hauling oneself up by grabbing onto others' innovations.

Beat the Clock

We said this before, but it is worth saying twice. Time is your friend until it is your enemy. You need time to achieve these preliminaries, but don't let any part of the process drag on. There is no greater source of pessimism about change than endless bickering. Establish the goal of a process that begins in summer and ends the following spring. To do that, create norms of discussion that avoid pitfalls. Stay out of the weeds, embrace a details-to-follow process, and remind colleagues again of the four-part order: what we know, what it means, what we should do, how it looks and feels. Only in the final stages will a small group again fit the ideal within the limits of institutional resources.

Planning Backward: Creating a Culture of Yes

Equipped now with some preliminary knowledge of issues in doctoral education; a sharper, fuller sense of the real-life experience of students in your program; a broadened perspective achieved by a dialogue with those who employ doctoral graduates in different kinds of academic institutions and in other social sectors; and some encouragement and suggestions from within the university and from national and local organizations, you're now ready for the big discussion of goals. Almost.

Before a weekend retreat for the entire faculty and representative students somewhere off campus, it's worth issuing a key challenge to all participants. To examine our own practices and question our own assumptions, we must obey a difficult injunction to unlearn what we think we know. It wasn't really Mark Twain who said, "It ain't what you don't know that gets you into trouble. It's what you know for sure that just ain't so," but it sounds like him. Or again, Tolstoy: "The most difficult subjects can be explained to the most slow-witted man if he has not formed any idea of them already, but the simplest thing cannot be made clear to the most intelligent man if he is firmly persuaded that he knows already, without a shadow of a doubt, what is laid before him."[13] To change, we need self-skepticism. A key attribute of design thinking is to become a visitor from another planet who keeps asking, "Why is it this way?" especially when we've taken the way it is for granted.

This unlearning is especially important because most professors are motivated by a combination of intense interest in a subject and a sense that our earned expertise will add to the quality of others' lives. "Social profit" is Grant's substitute term for "nonprofit," and it's an apt descriptor for the motivation of faculty, because a redirecting of the doctorate into a truly student-centered degree stands to not only bring greater happiness to students but also provide greater benefits to the public. Yet somehow it is at the graduate level where academic people often forsake our liberal arts and social ideals for a certain rigidity. Explicitly encouraging and even modeling openness at the beginning and every subsequent stage of the reform effort is a way to show our students how to do the same.

It's worth pausing over this issue, especially when we recall the millions of dollars and untold hours spent in a previous era of reform that bore so little fruit. The elephant in the planning room is described by Clark Kerr in his second-edition amendment to his classic *The Uses of the University*. "It is remarkable," Kerr writes, "not how much has changed but how little has changed on so many campuses in those areas that are under faculty control." Kerr was speaking generally, but his observation aptly describes doctoral education. He continues, "The more the environment has changed, the more the organized faculty has remained the same. It has been the greatest single point of institutional conservatism in recent times, as it has been historically. Little that it has held dear and that it could control has been allowed to change."[14]

Damrosch applies Kerr's observation to PhD programs: "Tenured faculty are prime beneficiaries of the present system, profiting from graduate students' labor in many ways large and small." Not surprisingly, Damrosch argues, they have powerful disincentives to lead change. Instead, they're wrapped in a willful ignorance, with "little awareness of what the system's disadvantages may have been for the unlucky few—in fact, the many—who have dropped out along the way or who have failed to find a job they like."[15] Indeed, the tenured faculty at research universities is the academic equivalent of the now-infamous "1 percent."

Academic habits of thought add further incentive for resistance. Professors are not just expert critical readers; we are *very* critical readers. We (the authors of this book) often see this in ourselves. Even when we're almost lost in admiration of an argument, we find ourselves searching for a "Yes, but . . ." Such skepticism, essential for the ongoing life of the disciplines, can inhibit change, especially when it's coupled with a melancholy consciousness of academia's declining fortunes. When Groucho Marx played a college president in *Horse Feathers* (1932), he sang, "Whatever it is, I'm against it." We see that kind of negativity too often among graduate faculty. Academics who ponder reform sometimes resemble cars whose unbalanced tires steer skeptically toward the curb. We so fear an accident that we may permanently stall there, revving loudly, going nowhere.[16]

True, it's not always necessary to go somewhere. Academia is conservative (with a small *c*) for a reason, and upholders of academic tradition rightly observe that universities are one of very few institutions that have survived for centuries. The deepest values of the arts and sciences, rooted in the long history of human thought, deserve to be considered an eternal light. But in a changing world, their various applications don't. They are candles in the wind.

A further reason for professorial resistance to change has to do with conclusions. Put simply, we don't know how to end things in academia. Look at any university and you'll see any number of moribund practices (sometimes whole programs) that wobble on, supported by a few dedicated advocates, consuming resources that might be better expended to serve larger or needier populations. We are not good at pulling the plug. Or, to put it another way, once we start something, it usually stays on the curricular shelf long after its sell-by date. Which can result in conservatism at the planning stage: "Let's not start it at all, then."

Such resistance can sacrifice the qualities that have made American higher education so successful: seizing on opportunity, improvising in the face of necessity. Such pioneering spontaneity, David F. Labaree argues in his recent history of American higher education, shot us ahead of European systems burdened by their heavy backpack of history.[17] For doctoral education, we have arrived at a time when the risks attached to innovation are far less threatening than the danger of staying put. We can undermine our own static tendencies by becoming more aware of them. There always appear to be more reasons not to do something than to do it, but appearances may deceive. We're living in a changing climate, and as we contemplate what to do about that, we should keep in mind that one success can make several failures worthwhile.

Beyond a skepticism of our skepticism, a way to confront concerns about an innovative practice or policy is to lay them out in plain sight. Psychologist Gary Klein argues for what he calls a "pre-mortem." Klein asks planners to "imagine that it is months into the future and that their plan has been carried out. And it has failed. That is all they know; they have to explain why they think it failed." In this exercise, the subjects can then "plan around" or fix these shortcomings before actually undertaking the reform.[18]

Sharing this anxiety about inaction with faculty may seem unfriendly, but stated as a common problem (with everyone admitting it), it can raise collective awareness. Alacrity will be one of the ways the department will gain an advantage. We therefore propose the academic equivalent of a prenuptial agreement: establish a stop/sustain/spread date before the concept is launched, with rigorous periodic goals and evaluations baked into the proposal. In this way, David Grant's notion of mission time as a constant takes on the additional utility of an insurance policy.[19]

We're almost ready for the first retreat, but we urge a homework assignment beforehand for all participants. Grant lays out this important preparation for the general conversation:

We ask what it would look like to succeed in our mission, goals, and strategies. We ask if there is something that matters a lot to us that resists quantification. We ask if there is something we need to talk about that we haven't found a way to talk about yet. We ask if there is a key performance in the work of our organization, one that would benefit from being described more specifically so that people can get better at it. We ask if there is an essential question to our work, one we never get to the end of, where we need a vehicle for ongoing discussion and learning. We ask what is the social profit we are trying to bring about.[20]

While we earlier urged inviting the widest range of voices into the conversation, now it is time to listen with special care to the graduate faculty itself—listen, don't judge—so as to avoid those defensive attitudes of "You can't make me" and "I'm not doing it wrong."

In organizing the key discussion, Grant suggests posing three questions *in writing* to the participants, who will respond to them in kind:

1. Given your organization, with its particular mission, what would success look like for you in the next three to five years? (More playfully, imagine the lead paragraphs of a major story in the *Chronicle of Higher Education* or *Inside Higher Ed* that describes your program's success. What would you have it say?)
2. Whatever you just wrote, can you be more specific?
3. If you haven't already done so, would you give an example of what you've just written about?

Then Grant suggests returning to the first question to ask whether you can go further: "Now describe what it [the success you mentioned earlier] would look like at an even higher level." And again, he urges, ask the participants to specify and exemplify these ultimate goals even if they have to invent an example.[21] In this particular instance, participants might review the challenges to doctoral education that we described earlier. Again, while solving one or two will become ultimate aims, most of the others will function instrumentally as a means toward the goal. (That distinction will come in handy, for in planning backward, we'll ask what it would take to achieve the goal.)

Grant calls planning backward "the *sine qua non* of formative assessment." It's necessary to "identify what matters most to us" and "forces us to focus on our primary values and our highest aspirations for the impact of our work." In the end, planning backward "changes what we do. It changes how we perform."[22] So before you even examine your current program, you should describe your ultimate goals. We suggest identifying no more than one or two. Then make explicit the task at hand, to think of what few things would be necessary to achieve them, and what would be necessary to achieve *those* things, and so on backward, so that the group finally can identify a sound place to start.[23] And now, on to the first retreat.

The Fall Retreat

The retreat takes place over two days, and it begins with the three questions we just mentioned, posed to a panel composed of graduates who occupy a wide range of positions within and beyond the professoriate. For an hour or more, they respond to the three questions, after which the lead committee spokesperson carefully prepares and distributes a document summarizing their answers. Panel members are asked whether they would alter their responses in relation to the document, and all participants are asked the same.

These questions then engage the entire group over lunch. This exercise might produce some chaos, but part of the initial retreat should, we think, be devoted to listening to individual faculty. We've asked them to do a great deal of listening, sometimes to voices they are not used to hearing. Now they deserve to speak and be heard, generously. Here's a sample dialogue.

> Setting: Anywhere but on campus, a location large enough
>   for a faculty meeting of an ambitious academic
>   department
> Dramatis Personae:
>   Chair of the Department (CH)
>   Director of Graduate Studies, a senior faculty member (DGS)

Senior faculty member A
Recently tenured senior faculty member B
Junior faculty member C
Junior faculty member D
Very senior, distinguished, but crusty faculty member F

The lead committee spokesperson has just finished summarizing to the group of perhaps 30 professors and 10 students the main findings and results of their summer efforts. Now a free discussion ensues.

As we pick up the conversation, senior faculty member A, who has passed on reading even a summary, asserts confidently, "Our ultimate goal is simple, and I believe we'd all agree. It's to place the greatest number of students in tenure-track positions at good colleges and universities that value research."

"I don't agree at all," DGS responds impatiently. "What do we mean by 'good'? And what if some of our students want a position at a place that emphasizes teaching more than research? That greatest number, as you call it, in tenure-track positions at fancy schools is going to be a tiny number these days."

"Yes," adds junior faculty member C. "And some of our students would be better off in careers outside academia. Why would we not honor that? Our goal should be to maximize the number of our graduates who end up with satisfying careers of some import, period."

"Wait a minute," cries very senior, distinguished but crusty faculty member F. "We shouldn't think of ourselves as an employment agency first and foremost. Our goal should be to offer a superb set of intellectual experiences. The rest we can't control."

"But," C replies, "there is a great deal we can control in terms of outcomes. Are we preparing students to replace us at a university like ours? We'll almost always fail at that. But we can model and develop forms of interpretation and research that are widely useful. Can't we link best internal practices to desired outcomes?"

"That's awfully fuzzy," the department chair objects. "And I have a few more issues to raise. How about the fact that half of our beginning students don't finish?[24] Maybe our goal should be more modest, to ensure that they all do."

"But not all," DGS says. "Some people don't find a doctoral program to their liking and others may learn that they'd rather do something else besides graduate school. I like the issue, but perhaps we should set our completion goal at 75 percent."

"I have a further issue no one has mentioned," junior faculty member D says. "I've been reading a critique of graduate education that argues we only go deep and not broad, that we should, as Lee Shulman puts it, 'cross the T' and not just produce narrow specialists. 'T-shaped people' have specialized backgrounds that they build outward from. How can we do that?"

"Yes," adds politically minded and recently tenured professor B, "and that reminds me that one of my goals is to make our program respond more vitally to social challenges. We have a lot to offer to civil society, and this is the moment to think about how we can do that. I want to emphasize public scholarship."

The department chair is both encouraged by the richness of the discussion and worried by its growing diffusion. "Look," CH remarks, "we can't do everything at once. Can we choose one concrete goal—lessening time to degree or changing our notion of career outcomes? Or becoming more diverse in admissions and curriculum?"

"Well," A replies, warming to the task, "that sounds good to me. We need to succeed with something before we can tackle all things. But if we choose that one thing, we will find that at least a few of the other issues will connect to it. We'll have to solve multiple problems to reach the one we target."

"Yes," says B eagerly. "We might find that diverse careers and public engagement aid each other, and that focusing on both makes us more appealing to students of color."

"Exactly!" CH exclaims. "But we will need to see what we most care about and what comes first, what later. Now let's return to those three questions. What would success look like?"

And the participants end the day with a dialogue based on their written responses.[25]

On the second day, the participants move to another set of three questions, beginning again by writing responses. These are the three questions posed 15 years ago by the Carnegie initiative, which led to too much verbiage and too few concrete program improvements. But now, the meeting leader says, we can answer them with yesterday's responses in mind.

1. What is the purpose of the doctoral program? What does it mean to develop students as stewards? What are the desired outcomes of the program?
2. What is the rationale and educational purpose of each element of the doctoral program? Which elements of the program should be affirmed and retained? Which elements could usefully be changed or eliminated?
3. How do you know? What evidence aids in answering those questions? What evidence can be collected to determine whether changes serve the desired outcomes?[26]

These questions are well phrased, we believe. We challenge only the assumption, conveyed by the word "stewards," that all students will become steward-professors in turn, and so we suggest eliminating that sentence from the first question. Even with the change, that first question could lead to much back-and-forth over familiar ground, but sometimes it's worth rehearsing familiar performances to prepare for new ones.

Accordingly, the leader could allow that conversation to segue into the same question rephrased: "Given what we have learned from the lead group and given our discussion yesterday, how would we define the purpose of the doctoral program?" If responses cause some new differences of opinion to surface, then welcome that range and urge their coexistence for now, and remind people that it might be possible to design by "both/and" rather than "either/or," if we can find a way to do so that serves the interests of the students.

The third question may become unnecessary, given the student survey and other fact-finding efforts of the lead group. Or it could be altered to say, "How will we know whether any of our innovations are working well?" and thus point forward. But it is the second question that requires most attention, as it moves the department from redefining a general purpose to how to achieve it in specific terms.

Over the ensuing hours, any number of disagreements will likely emerge. Planners tell us there is an inevitable period of disorientation, when everything seems confused, but this constitutes an opportunity for reorientation. In particular, it provides an opportunity to take a fresh look at a problem and perhaps change its terms or to examine a silent habit. "What should we do with the dissertation?" might lead to the reformulation "What are some alternatives to the uniform dissertation model we now impose?"

It's useful to encourage disorientation in a bounded space and time: "trust-no-habit" questions unsettle, and that's why they're useful. Identifying and challenging assumptions either allows for bold change or else thoughtfully reaffirms a valuable status quo with new energy. Both are positive outcomes. When a degree of consensus is reached, it carries the assurance that comes from exposing the depths of the foundation of the attitudinal edifice.

At the end of the second day, the leader will summarize some reactions and ask participants to write down what the lead committee should plan next. By this point, a main goal or two should have emerged, and various parts of the program will have been discussed in relation to the ultimate goals. These goals and discussion will shape the lead committee's work for the next few months. An alternative is to spread that work and assign those aspects of the program targeted for change to a trio of additional faculty not in the lead group, so as to get more faculty and students involved. The lead committee itself will summarize the retreat in writing, including the evaluation by participants, and will continue to provide detailed minutes of its ensuing meetings, leading up to a second retreat.

Between the first and second retreats, the faculty will meet to discuss the program further. (Time can be set aside for this at regular department meetings. It's important to have such discussion time that isn't followed by a vote.) Perhaps more important will be something less formal but more continuous—namely, talk in the halls. The leaders of the department and the members of the lead committee should simply reach out to their colleagues for informal conversation. Have lunch, have coffee, stop in people's offices. Now is also the time for both written and in-person reports to the dean, provost, and perhaps the president. These meetings also offer a chance to raise important questions about available resources.

Breaking Better: The Second Retreat and Next Stages

The second retreat occurs in a single day, preferably at the same setting to suggest continuity. The participants will consider the recommendations of the lead committee, which will include reworking aspects of the program. Here we hope that the planning-backward process will prove a shortcut to action. We suggested earlier that guarding mission time will save time later, and this second retreat should illustrate that.

For example, let's imagine a department that wants to challenge itself with the goal of shortening time to degree without weakening the essential experiences of the program (which is a frequent objection to this intention). To determine what is essential and what isn't, the Carnegie initiative's second and third questions would come into useful play. The faculty could brainstorm means for streamlining the degree in ways that might actually add to the intellectual experience and to students' professional abilities, especially because real-life tasks in and beyond academia often have deadlines. The Mellon Foundation report on its Graduate Education Initiative provides a storehouse of ideas for programs seeking to shorten time to degree, from summer financial support to clear program guidelines with a strictly enforced timeline, to a comprehensive exam that includes the prospectus for the dissertation. Such possibilities arise when you start by planning backward.

In determining the changes that will inform the larger goal, the leader should insist that the plan must not become a Rube Goldberg contraption with impossibly intricate moving parts that all depend on each other. Here we invoke an admittedly awful planning neologism, "simplexity," which means keeping practice simple in response to complex matters.

Like everything else here, keeping it simple is a complex challenge. That's why, while we urge alacrity, we also suggest realism, a need to stay sensible about how much can be done at once. While the main goal(s) may require changes in several aspects of a program, these changes can be staged, with careful attention to how current students will be affected.

Most important, even if a major assessment has been promised for three years hence, continuing assessment—data, sure, but also regularly scheduled qualitative feedback from all participants—will allow for timely adjustments. We wrote earlier that no one gets it all right from the start, but we do need to start, and so an expectation of continuing adjustments may quiet panic and encourage boldness.

Even so, it is possible to reach a point of informed and honest conflict. At that crucial moment, the leaders will need to distinguish between bad compromises and good ones. A bad compromise weakens the innovation in a way that empties it of its potential for energy and action. (This frequently happens in negotiations of undergraduate core requirements, for example.) A good compromise, bolstered by the promise of continuing monitoring, says, "Let's try it." Strategic planners are unanimous in urging trial by experience rather than inaction through more and more talk. At the very least, allow for alternatives to be adopted, to be measured against each other as students choose to fulfill one or the other. Their advocates will then take them up with energy and spirit. In a bad compromise, everyone is dissatisfied and dispirited, and drained of the excitement that can fuel action. The second retreat should end with a sense of shared expectation in which participants feel heard and valued—and ready to move.

We've tried to write the rest of this book with an understanding that different programs in different disciplines in different universities will have their own best sense of what matters most. We don't want to dictate your priorities. But our title, *The New PhD*, suggests an overall redefinition of the degree's purpose, and so we encourage departure from a status quo that doesn't serve us anymore. As our review in the previous chapter shows, career diversity powers every single national reform effort of the last few years, and it represents by far the greatest number of institution-specific initiatives as well. Something is going on, and even if yours decides to take another path, every program needs to contemplate why so many academics consider a broadened sense of professional opportunity crucial to the future of the degree—and of our society.

THREE

Career Diversity

A Liberal Arts Approach to the PhD

Necessity and Virtue

"To maken vertu of necessitee" serves as the ruling principle of wise Theseus, Duke of Athens, in Chaucer's "Knight's Tale." Confronted with the inevitable foibles and conflicts arising from human passions—in his case, two quarrelling knights in love with the same lady—Theseus creates social rituals (a tourney) that order and resolve destructive passions in a manner that restores the dignity of the rivals and strengthens the community.

Our necessity centers on ending, after 50 years, the training of graduate students for jobs that don't exist—and teaching them to want those jobs over all others. Our necessary task follows from this fact: we need to broaden the career options of doctoral students beyond the academic job market. The virtue we can derive from our necessity is a more socially consequential PhD, one that can apply greater expertise and wisdom to different social sectors and human challenges. We understandably mourn the long-ago passing of a relatively brief era when graduate study was an insular apprenticeship for the professoriate. That was then. Now, we need a more socially responsive and engaged PhD, a degree that will return more to our students—and to the world—than the old, hermetic model.

Given the bizarre impracticality of the present norms, we might seek a fix in our own liberal arts credo. Colleges and universities have long asserted the versatility of a BA in the arts and sciences and based the undergraduate curriculum and requirements on attaining qualities of thought and communication that provide for all-purpose habits and capacities. Liberal arts colleges are currently being challenged to prove this contention by helping students to address career outcomes far more explicitly than in the privileged past—even though the employment markets have never failed to bear out the conviction that a liberal arts degree is both valuable and useful. We need to adapt both the liberal arts credo and the challenge of outcomes at the doctoral level too.

We have long been accustomed to viewing the doctorate through the lens of a narrow careerism: replenishing the faculty. This esoteric preprofessional aim has led to a soaring failure rate. Our collective failure to confront this fact both practically and emotionally has harmed the lives of many graduates. Council of Graduate Schools president Suzanne Ortega suggests that "we are not overproducing PhDs, but we may be underutilizing them." Ortega's insight situates the problem not only in higher education, for not preparing PhD graduates for career diversity, but also with employment outside academia, where the value of a PhD may be underestimated or simply overlooked.[1]

As we discussed in the introduction to this book, there is a deep history behind why we so compromised our liberal arts credo where it most needs to prevail. A new PhD calls for a different goal: not the cloning of professors but the development of widely applicable expertise. These certainly include academia and the professoriate but also other professional destinations, from industry to K–12 education, from media to government at all levels, from nonprofits to technology. This redefinition of the doctorate aims to develop not only scholars but also creative professionals who can work throughout society. The best argument for graduate school is made by people who take their training into the world where others can see it: a kind of practical, graduate-oriented application of the Jeffersonian notion that higher education benefits all of society.

The good news is that the "professorships or bust" idea "no longer receives the fierce pushback that it did even five years ago. We've gone from 'Why should we?' to 'How should we?' in a remarkably short time." If you google "beyond academia," you'll see a literally global range of offerings, from a graduate student organization at the University of California, Berkeley, whose mission is "connecting PhDs with the world" to initiatives, institutes, websites, events, courses, fellowships, publications, internship offices, and awards in the United States and elsewhere.[2]

In short, to speak of diverse careers is no longer a heresy. The subject was given a major boost in 2011, when Anthony T. Grafton and James Grossman, as president and executive director of the American Historical Association, published a widely noticed essay in which they said that many history PhDs will not obtain tenure-track positions and it is time to stop pretending otherwise. Instead, they wrote, "a Ph.D. in history opens a broad range of doors." They proposed a reorientation of doctoral education away from the long-prevailing attitude that imagines "the life of scholarship" as "somehow exempt from impure motives and bitter competition" and sees those who take nonprofessorial jobs as abandoning the virtuous life.[3] One year earlier, the Council of Graduate Schools and the Educational Testing Service had issued a report on the future of graduate education urging "increased emphasis on nonacademic career pathways" in doctoral education.[4] The same recommendation was elaborated more fully in the Canadian counterpart to this report in 2013.

On the national level, such recent initiatives as the Public Fellows Program at the American Council of Learned Societies, the Connected Academics effort at the Modern Language Association, and the especially ambitious and effective Career Diversity Program at the American Historical Association (outlined in chapter 1 and discussed in more detail later in this chapter and in our discussion of public scholarship in chapter 10) display this new level of interest. In 2010, only one of several respondents to a "What Should Be Done?" *Chronicle* set of interviews on graduate education in the humanities even mentioned careers beyond academia.[5] It would be a central topic at any such forum today.

The internet has aided this shift in emphasis as well. We noted in our chapter on the recent history of reform efforts that the American Academy for the Advancement of Science had in 2001 pioneered a website, myIDP, that matches the interests of science and engineering graduates with career possibilities, and that a similar site for humanities and social science graduates, ImaginePhD, has been created by the Graduate Career Consortium and released in 2017. (That such a consortium exists is in itself an important sign of change.)

But that doesn't mean we've reached a consensus—the national organizations appear to be far in advance of virtually all individual graduate programs—or that we've figured out how to contour graduate school to accommodate career diversity. Skeptics remain, especially in the humanities disciplines, and their skepticism is not always misplaced. Advocates for a new PhD need to answer their—and our own—reasonable concerns. Can a recognition of diverse outcomes be achieved without sacrificing the deep dive into a loved field, an exploration that carries its own value? How can our changed reality strengthen the life of the disciplines and allow academia a greater social influence without diluting the nature of research that is often necessarily highly sophisticated and specialized? How can professors defend the act of imaginative and critical discovery as a good in itself while also seeking a greater public consequence for learning? And how may this balancing act translate into the specifics of program elements? These concerns demand attention.

It's not an easy task to reengage the doctorate with the world. (Or vice versa: over many generations scholars have taught the general public to view our work as arcane and unapproachable. We will address that problem in chapter 10 on public scholarship.) Even so, this engagement must become our self-challenge. Beyond the question of numbers (to maintain the narrow goal of replenishing the faculty, we would have to cut our doctoral population by two-thirds), there is the historical fact that except for one postwar generation, the doctorate has never existed solely to fill professorships. Except for that one generation, PhDs and their teachers have always understood that graduates would work both inside and outside the academy. Put simply, radical doctoral birth control carries with it the danger of reducing expertise in a world that requires that expertise more and more.

We educators need to take the initiative. The welfare of our students is at stake. Individual departments and programs will decide what to do in their specific situations. As a matter of overall purpose, we second the plain statement of biologist Crispin Taylor: "Let us consider defining success for the newly minted Ph.D. as acquiring a rewarding position that offers legitimate opportunities for professional advancement, whether or not that job happens to be in academia."[6] As Merisi Nerad wrote after surveying PhDs in several fields 10 years after their graduation, "Rather than reducing the number of Ph.D.s produced, doctoral programs may want to focus on the kinds of skills developed during doctoral education and career guidance given to graduate students."[7] In sum, we urge that the PhD in all fields must open outward.

Surveys of graduate students suggest that many PhD candidates begin their programs with underinformed or even inchoate ideas concerning their career goals. Their ambitions become more precisely formed—and sometimes impractically narrowed—during the first years of study. Other surveys have shown that a large number wish to have the PhD look outward to a greater extent. Chris Golde and Timothy Dore report that over half of doctoral students want to provide community service, whereas fewer than one in five believe their education has prepared them to do that.[8] Similarly, when graduates of the six disciplines included in Nerad and Joseph Cerny's *Ten Years After* study were asked how their graduate programs could have been improved, they pointed to "the need for greater educational relevance to the changing world inside and outside academia and better labor market preparation."[9] That report included science disciplines as well, and in fact year after year, the National Science Foundation's survey of earned doctorates shows that just a bit under half of all newly minted PhD graduates throughout the arts and sciences take their first jobs in academia. That number has decreased further in recent years.

Cerny and Nerad studied the career paths of 6,000 doctoral graduates in six selected disciplines in the *Ten Years After* survey, and they discovered that job satisfaction among PhDs who found nonacademic employment was strong and even slightly higher than for the ones who stayed in academia. Moreover, those graduates who left by choice or necessity remain predominantly pleased that they earned the degree. "Despite the bias of graduate programs towards academic faculty careers," Nerad writes in an article on English PhDs from the survey, "respondents with nonfaculty administrative positions within academe and those whose career paths took them outside the academic milieu reported good salaries and overall job satisfaction." One English PhD described "a tiny mass psychosis going on among both the faculty and the students" in his or her department. "Everyone knew it was very difficult to get a tenure-track job," but even so, "anything less was considered a failure." Yet about two-thirds of those who left academia affirmed that "knowing what you know now," they would choose to do the PhD again.[10] More recent data, such as Katina Rogers's 2013 survey of humanities PhDs, support this conclusion.[11]

It's worth pausing a moment to reflect on this fact. It's certainly true that most graduate students in the arts and sciences want to become professors—just as it's true that most of them won't. Some critics of career diversity have argued that it's a self-serving excuse for professors to keep producing PhDs and sending them down a narrow alley leading to unhappiness. Apart from the historical sketchiness of the idea (because PhDs have almost always worked outside the academy), the criticism runs into the fact that *most PhDs who work outside of academia are happy.*

Nor should we lose sight of those who do not graduate. The attrition rate from doctoral programs in the arts and sciences is about 50 percent, with about half of those leaving later in their studies, abandoning a dissertation in progress. (We will discuss attrition further in chapter 4.) Barbara Lovitts, the leading scholar of graduate school attrition, found that a significant number of non-completers left because of a sense of irrelevancy. She warns that "losing students who have an interest in real-world applications means that important, socially relevant questions are not getting asked, much less answered," and this represents an intellectual failing as well as a detriment to career satisfaction.[12]

The difficulty in answering the "what's the use?" question greatly affects graduate students of color, many of whom wish to give back to their communities. A more socially responsive doctorate can serve as a worthy attraction for students from underrepresented groups. Study after study shows that minority students and faculty overall have a stronger desire than their nonminority peers to bring their learning into the community. Career diversity may also shorten time to degree, if it stops graduate students from clinging to their status as students to avoid what may appear to be a hopeless academic job market, and instead encourages them to look beyond that one goal.

In short, we professors and administrators need to stop sponsoring despair. That doesn't in the least mean encouraging graduate students to abandon scholarly pursuits, but it does mean integrating other skills and awareness that they will need outside of the university as well as within it. It means enabling students to understand better the full range of career possibilities opened to them by their graduate training.

We prefer to call this "career diversity," the term coined by the American Historical Association, rather than the older term, "alt-ac" (for "alternative academic"), because there is no such thing as an "alternative" career—and "career diversity" privileges multiple outcomes equally. (Today, says Kathleen Flint Ehm, who directs the Office for the Integration of Research, Education, and Professional Development at Stony Brook University, "the 'alt' career is to become a professor.")[13] Stacy Hartman, former head of the MLA Connected Academics initiative and now director of the PublicsLab at the City University of New York's Graduate Center, urges, "Don't take people out of their box. Smash the box."[14] Once we do that, the "too many students in doctoral programs taking too long" problems may well disappear. They will matriculate in timely fashion because they will have places they'll want to go.

The term "career diversity" should also remind us that colleges and universities don't have a monopoly on high-level thinking, and that a myriad of jobs across society offer intellectual interest and excitement. Until we honor—not just tolerate but actively encourage—the diverse career paths facing our students, we're not working on their behalf.

When we focus on the few who get professorships, we're telling a solipsistic and unsustainable story about ourselves, not them.

The Wrong Question—and the Right Response

"So What Are You Going to Do with That?": Finding Careers outside Academia is the title of a very successful guide first published in 2001 by Susan Basalla and Maggie Debelius, now in its third edition.[15] In itself, the title is natural and appealingly direct. But one might instead ask, "Is there anything you can't do with this?"

When Elaine Showalter of Princeton served as president of the Modern Language Association in 1998, she promoted the idea of nonacademic careers for English PhDs as a centerpiece of her agenda. Her efforts made scarcely a ripple in the prevailing stream of thought that led backward to the longing for the long-ago postwar generation of full professorial employment. Years later, Michael Bérubé recalls that the MLA Graduate Student Caucus at the time, led by Marc Bousquet and William Pannapacker, denounced Showalter's initiative as a disingenuous suggestion that people who had trained for a decade to be humanists could suddenly switch gears and become "secretaries and screenwriters."[16] Showalter proved prescient, of course, and her detractors now seem narrow minded in imagining life outside of academia in such demeaning and limited terms.

Recently, as part of a consulting job, we asked about 15 advocates for career diversity to nominate the most likely careers for majors in those humanities fields. We might have anticipated publishing, public humanities, library leadership, journalism and media, new media, and digital humanities. But the suggestions also ranged from data analysis and financial services to K–12 teaching and curricular leadership, from advertising, marketing, and public relations to civic and cultural institutions and academic administration. Government agencies figured prominently, and careers in medical humanities and teaching English language learners were included as well.

At a conference sponsored by the Woodrow Wilson Foundation some years ago, a corporate CEO said, "I can hire a typical MBA but it would take me years I don't have to teach this individual with only that narrow expertise how to write, how to present ideas, or in fact how to have an idea, how to bring a major research project to term, and how to teach fellow employees. On the other hand, I can hire a Ph.D. who knows how to do all of those things and teach this individual a particular task in hours. Why would I not hire your Ph.D. graduate?" He paused, and then answered his own question: "Because nobody like that ever applies."

The point is that the abilities of doctoral graduates are apt for just about any form of thoughtful employment. We don't need to create vocational tracks in a PhD program—and we should not. Instead, we need only train students to become aware of their impressive transferable skills and how to present them across a wide variety of job opportunities.

These capacities common to doctoral graduates in all disciplines—to manage a large project (think: dissertation), to engage in complex research, to think both critically and creatively, to speak and write clearly, to teach others (a constant in all work environments)—are highly sought after and uncommon. One of our recent interviewees said, "In financial services, when I interview a potential outsource, I certainly do the quantitative analysis, but it is my training in English and philosophy that gives me the greatest insight into the qualitative aspects. I effortlessly used that humanities advantage and advanced rapidly in the company."

Put simply, there is one challenge that is a mirage: whether doctoral graduates are valuable across the professions. They are, if they learn to realize it.[17]

What will it look like when graduate students appreciate their own skills and act on that awareness? The results will be, well, diverse, because students will be guided by their own particular interests. One may wish to work for a tech company while another may be drawn to a community organization. Another may want to teach and design curricula for a public school district, while her classmate may want to work with scientists in writing grants and conveying research results. One may become a journalist, while another may work in college administration. One may wish to serve as a historian for the National Park Service while another may choose museum work, and still another may look to a career at, say, Geico.

Each program needs to learn more about the career outcomes of its graduates and then plan backward from that information. What are they doing and what prepared them, however directly or indirectly, to do it? The answers will inform a general concept of preparation, not a curriculum of narrow career tracks. We will say again: we believe that the doctorate is and should remain a scholarly degree. But we are also saying that scholarship is more broadly useful than scholars may suppose.

If programs begin to track their graduates better, they may create, as Stanford has done in the humanities, a website for recording nonacademic outcomes. Such a resource can encourage students and perhaps change faculty attitudes too. But again, any such compilation should present itself as more suggestive than exhaustive. Instead, we need to teach our doctoral students to follow Emily Dickinson's example, to "dwell in possibility."

Challenges to a Multitasking PhD

A PhD intended for both future teacher-scholars and for disciplinary experts employed throughout society encounters three kinds of difficulties. Each of the three—attitudinal, institutional, and intellectual—requires direct engagement and effort.

The attitudinal challenge is vividly expressed by Simon Forde, the director and editor in chief of Medieval Institute Publications at Western Michigan University, following his participation in panels on career diversity at conferences for medievalists. He bluntly described the aim of these panels: "to break down the idea" that if you don't get a professor's job after earning the PhD, "you're a complete failure in life."[18] Another medievalist, Kristina Markman, says something similar. Markman is now assistant director of humanities at Revelle College at the University of California, San Diego. Earlier, while completing her PhD at UCLA, she worked on curricular development both at the college and at the K–12 level, while she also coordinated the university's Public History Initiative. "There seems to be an assumption among students," Markman wrote in a post on the AHA blog for career diversity, "that putting together an academic job portfolio is a noble task, while preparing for the nonacademic market is a debasing commercial venture whereby you sell your soul to enhance 'employability'."[19] In an interview, she added, "People say that those who don't want to become professors are 'stealing positions' in the graduate program from those who do," a sentiment wildly at odds with admissions practices that in fact privilege those who want only to become professors. It is equally at odds with the reality that many students who cling to this sole desire will be disappointed. "When you can't find a safe place" even with other graduate students, Markman continues, "it's really alienating." Those graduate students "who are willing to look at other careers don't say it."[20]

That silence replaces the conversations that ought to take place in faculty offices, student lounges, and around the proverbial water cooler. Instead, Markman uses the lexicon of the closet to describe choosing a career that fits one's personality: "When someone 'comes out,' that person risks criticism and even ostracism."[21]

Even those faculty members who consciously accept a career-diverse doctorate may unthinkingly carry forward old prejudices born of ancient assumptions. One of the volumes published by the Carnegie initiative of a decade ago contains several hortatory essays saying things like, "We ought to be thinking about how to develop doctoral programs that effectively prepare students for as many different career trajectories as possible." The author of those words, Crispin Taylor, further states that "the prevailing sentiment is that doctoral students are being prepared for careers in academia and that anything else is second-best." Yet the volume in which Taylor's essay appears is subtitled *Preparing Stewards of the Disciplines*, while its companion volumes bear the titles *The Formation of Scholars* and *Paths to the Professoriate*.[22]

That the curriculum in graduate programs in the arts and sciences centers on preparing all students to be professors at research universities is surely a problem simply because there are few such positions.

But it's an even bigger problem that graduate training persuades students that these are the only jobs worth having, and to work at anything else would be a betrayal, a comedown, and a loss. Of course we don't say these things from the front of the classroom; instead, we communicate them through the way we socialize students into our graduate programs. By showing them what we value, we teach them what they should value. It's not simply that graduate school prepares students too narrowly. It's that we teach them to *want* professors' jobs to the exclusion of anything else.

Let us put this in literally bold terms: we teach graduate students to want something that we know we can't supply except to a very few. **That means that we're teaching them to be unhappy.** That's a terrible thing for teachers to do to their students, yet graduate school in the arts and sciences has institutionalized it. Above all, that is what we must change.

Nothing we can say about graduate student career diversity is as important as the need for the students' actual professors to explicitly support nonacademic careers. This change is taking place, but it has been gradual and piecemeal, and generations of students continue to suffer from an unnecessary sense of failure, while society suffers from the squandering of human capital. Taylor suggests reproducing a tree diagram. The trunk has rungs denoting academic attainment, from BA through postdoc. (Remember that Taylor is a scientist, where the postdoc is tantamount to the final stage of the PhD.) The branches on the right represent academic jobs available at each rung. "On the left is everything else—industry, law, journalism, politics, government— similarly organized in relation to the rungs." He finds "particularly telling the far greater number of branches to the left."[23] The tree visualizes the point for skeptics.

But Taylor's diagram is just one example of the need for faculty (who are, after all, professional learners), to do some learning about these issues ourselves. The larger point remains paramount: Those of us who have spent our own careers within the professoriate may not be experts in advising students about possibilities elsewhere, but we don't have to do it by ourselves. We can and should involve the people both on campus and beyond who know more and can do this work. When we do so, we break a silence that implies disapproval.

Often forgotten in reform literature is the other half of the attitudinal challenge, which is to convince employers in business, government, media, technology, and K–12 of the value of doctoral graduates. The CEO may already understand this, but the human resources staff may not. Reformers too often imagine that their only challenge is to persuade the professoriate of the value of advanced study for nonacademic settings, but the people who work in those settings must often be convinced as well. This case needs to be made to the world at large. The initial stages of persuasion will often require locating middle managers closer to the hiring decision than is the CEO, but more aware than HR (which is more often tasked with saying no than yes) about the potential of PhDs.[24] Here is one of many places where alumni networking can achieve more than abstract claims. Show, don't tell—show that human resources officer or that management head an example of successful doctoral graduates in their type of workplace.

The institutional side of this challenge comes in two parts. Both invite a more concrete solution than simply persuading faculty or employers to question former attitudes. First, the fact that faculty often know very little about the world beyond academia requires the creation of new institutional links. Realistically, we can't expect all faculty advisers to take the time to become wide-ranging experts on careers—that's not how they imagine their jobs at universities with doctoral programs. Instead, university career offices need to create graduate divisions (if they don't exist already), and their graduate representatives should meet regularly with a range of faculty advisers as well as students. (We will have more to say about the specifics of advising in chapter 7.) Duke University's Versatile Humanists program, originally funded by a National Endowment for the Humanities Next Generation grant, provides one-on-one career counseling from professional advisers outside of the departments along with group-advising lunches, a weekly career newsletter, and a VH@Duke blog. More than 160 graduate students took advantage of the individual counseling provision during its first two years alone.[25]

Graduate school alumni, aside from serving as models of PhD versatility, ought to become a source of opportunities that extend beyond fundraising. Because internships offer great potential for preparing students for diverse career options, graduate programs should nurture connections with university alumni relations offices to generate such possibilities. Duke again serves as a model, where Ph.D. Advisor, an overall program, compiled information on more than 60 humanities doctoral alumni working beyond academia, conducted phone interviews with 20 of them, and launched a directory that includes profiles.

Such new intramural links are vital, for they reassure faculty members that their responsibilities are not being multiplied beyond their many current commitments. Even so, the new connections will require active coordination by a department leader. Most departments and programs have a few faculty members whose experience qualifies them to pilot these efforts—they're a good place to start. That liaison in each department will require support in the form of remuneration or a reduction of other duties. But this is a small-cost, big-gain trade-off.

The second aspect of the institutional challenge can also be handled directly and more quickly. But it is even more vital. Former MLA president Michael Bérubé has openly questioned higher administration's commitment to career diversity initiatives, especially "whether those careers will be honored and validated by deans and provosts, who remain likely to evaluate the success of graduate programs in the humanities by their placement rates," meaning professors' jobs only. He suggests that the embrace of career diversity may risk future funding.[26]

Bérubé's worries relate as well to disciplines in the social and bench sciences. But his concerns notwithstanding, we can't all just wait for each other to see the light. Leaders of graduate programs have the responsibility to educate deans and provosts and presidents on issues facing their disciplines. In fact, administrators already rely on them to do this. Any good administrator will welcome such a discussion, especially as it can now be informed by a considerable bibliography on career diversity (including this book!) and by the active support of many national disciplinary organizations, as well as leading academic philanthropies like the Mellon Foundation. So, get the administration involved in this rethinking with you, not just before or afterward but throughout.

If this initiative appears daunting, we ask faculty to remember that most administrators have fundraising responsibilities, and they should be reminded that many graduates who work outside academia may become potential major donors, or they may provide connections to major donors. More to the point, by urging a reconsideration of your program's goals, you provide your university's spokespeople—as well as your department—a chance to become thought leaders of a new idea.

By far the most daunting, but also the most interesting, challenge is the intellectual and educational one. A career-diverse doctorate carries with it a number of anxieties about curriculum, disciplinary integrity, student skill sets, and more. Many of these concerns are well founded. How can the changed employment reality for graduate students strengthen the life of the disciplines and allow academia to have a greater social influence without diluting the often necessarily sophisticated and specialized nature of research? How can professors defend the act of imaginative and critical and scientific discovery as a good in itself while also seeking a greater public stature for advanced learning? How can one integrate an enlarged notion of outcomes that might include work in anything from K–12 to data analysis to publishing, while still preparing this same cohort for lives as academic professionals? And how can we do so without simply multiplying required courses and experiences when excessive time to degree (which we'll consider in more detail elsewhere) is already a serious problem? Will these changes limit the deep dive into a discipline that distinguishes doctoral education and relegate doctoral students to the shallows? In short, can we achieve breadth without sacrificing depth?

To respond to that challenge, we need practical specifics, and that is the subject of the next section.

Practicing Career Diversity

Professors must instruct graduate students about the content and methods of their disciplines—that's what graduate school is. But we have to do that in a way that's consistent with the real-life outcomes that our students face. One education leader whom we interviewed about career diversity described digital analysis as "a form of interpretation that should be a natural for humanists and social scientists who are not afraid of numbers." But there is nothing "natural" about humanists considering data analysis jobs because graduate school teaches them that such positions are second choices at best. We're not saying that all humanists should become digital analysts, of course, but rather that they should know that they can be if they wish. We need to teach graduate students not only about the range of their choices but also how to be happy with the choices they make. One of the goals of this chapter is to show how we—faculty, administrators, and graduate students themselves—can do this.

Certainly it's a challenge to blend preparation for a professorship with preparation for other kinds of work. But the two are not really as separate as all that. A few years ago, the American Historical Association, as it was formulating its current proposals on career diversity, revisited a cohort of a dozen graduate students in history who, more than a decade earlier, had won summer fellowships for nonacademic internships as part of a far-sighted program sponsored by the Woodrow Wilson Foundation. All of these students were successful in their careers. Perhaps surprisingly, two-thirds of them had become professors, but they were as adamant as the others that their summer experiences off the pre-professorial career path had been not just germane but crucial to their success. It's a two-way flow. Just as research expertise gains value when viewed and practiced outside academia, so too the habits of workplaces outside of universities, and the wider view gained by work outside the academy, deepen the research of professional academics. Every graduate student is the CEO of her education and career, and she will do well to learn how the lessons of the nonacademic workplace powerfully complement the lessons of classroom, library, and lab.

Some critics of career diversity have raised the idea of dual-track doctoral programs with one path for scholars, another for everyone else.[27] We do *not* need to create specific extra-academic career tracks, and we do ourselves and our students a disservice if we do. Instead, graduate programs need only teach students to think of their abilities as variously applicable, to manage their priorities in relation to their career choices, and to describe complex ideas in the lingua franca (which after all is a basic virtue of good teaching). More specifically, the American Historical Association interviewed graduates working in and beyond academia and came up with five necessary skills that PhDs ought to possess regardless of career outcome: communication, collaboration, quantitative literacy, intellectual self-confidence, and basic digital literacy.[28] This is a reasonable agenda for the practical liberal arts, graduate division, and it's applicable to workplaces inside and outside of the university.

Or is it? How can such program elements be added without lengthening an already long time to degree? As we consider options here, we require that they be time neutral.

We have found many current examples on individual campuses. For example, a program run out of the Center for Humanities & the Arts at the University of Colorado Boulder places humanities PhD students in extramural internships. This program has enjoyed such success that it has now spread beyond the humanities. At the University of California, Irvine, the chemistry department offers an industrial recruiting program that engages companies in interviewing doctoral students for positions and sponsoring fellowships and symposia. And in a more general setting, Irvine offers a Career Seminar Series that includes converting a curriculum vitae to a résumé, developing a teaching portfolio, and becoming thoroughly acquainted with the resources of the career center. Similarly, at Arizona State University, students can meet with knowledgeable faculty and staff for career goal-setting PFx Workshops, an effort that has morphed into a two-credit course, Preparing Future Faculty and Scholars, with the term "scholars" construed broadly, not as a synonym for "professor." The course helps students learn to communicate their research to audiences outside the academy and to explore both academic and nonacademic pathways, with time devoted to each. Students create a digital portfolio, record a research pitch, and conduct an informational interview. In all, the program "supports an environment in which the diversity and variety of human experience are welcomed and valued." And at UCLA, a seminar on "the many professions of history" has students explore various career paths and provides "hand-on, project-based learning" focused on three of AHA's five skills: communication (with varied audiences in varied forms), collaboration (all students work in teams), and intellectual self-confidence (students self-assess their growth in key areas).[29]

At the University of Michigan, a two-credit course cotaught by English chair David Porter and the MLA's Stacy Hartman sought similarly "to empower students more actively and holistically to chart their own professional pathways both inside and outside of the university." First offered in spring, 2018, "Professional Humanities Careers" had some unusual assignments, which included

- writing brief organizational profiles of for-profit or nonprofit organizations in at least two social sectors;
- conducting and writing up three half-hour informational interviews with humanities doctoral graduates not teaching at colleges or universities;
- identifying three current job postings for nonacademic positions of potential interest in at least two different sectors and showing how a professional humanist might apply for them;
- preparing a cover letter and resume tailored to one of these positions; and
- composing a dissertation manifesto, "a 2–3 pp distillation of your training and expertise that captures what is unique and distinctive about them in terms that will be accessible and compelling to a non-academic audience" and "organized around a series of 3–5 Big Questions that . . . might plausibly resonate with problems of interest to non-academic organizations."[30]

The course, which Porter plans to repeat, proved an early success because it's honest about what it's offering. As with the historians who benefited from a Woodrow Wilson Foundation–financed internship outside the academy, students who plan professorial careers, not just those planning careers outside the academy, took Porter and Hartman's course, and valued it. In the same spirit, humanists at Emory University have developed a seminar course in public humanities that began in 2020. Open to students across humanities disciplines, the course combines readings and discussion with a different internship for each student, selected from opportunities curated in advance through town-and-gown partnerships with cultural organizations.*

A growing number of other campuses have also become increasingly active in generating hybrid possibilities for graduate students, but Duke University deserves special mention for its well-developed and sustained programs that promote career diversity. Versatile Humanists@ Duke, a program we flagged above for its bevy of counseling opportunities for students considering diverse careers, also features an initiative in which several students each year intern either with prearranged host partners or at self-created destinations. The initiative has also funded new departmental practices, such as a philosophy department seminar on digital publishing. And in a related, donor-funded program titled Bass Connections, graduate students work with faculty and undergraduates in interdisciplinary research teams.

Duke also offers a summer doctoral academy, a two-week program of short courses that help graduate students prepare not only for dissertation research and innovative teaching but also for leadership and public engagement. The courses are led by Duke professors as well as working professionals, with 16 offered in a summer. The menu includes such selections as "How to Build an App," "How to Launch and Scale

---

*Though the COVID-19 pandemic disrupted those internships, English Department chair Benjamin Reiss reports that students and their employers discovered novel means to work around the restrictions, and the course proved an exuberant success even on its maiden voyage. Benjamin Reiss, "Public Humanities versus Social Distancing," *American Literature*, forthcoming. Thanks to Professor Reiss for sending us an advance copy. The seminar was led by Reiss and Karen Stolley, the chair of Spanish and Portuguese. The graduate chair in history, Thomas Rogers, was instrumental as well in planning for the innovative offering.

a Business," "How to Work More Effectively in Teams," and "How to Communicate Science More Effectively." Each course meets for three hours a day for five days, so that a student may take four courses in the two weeks beginning right after the spring semester. This is not an advertisement for Duke as such (though there would be nothing wrong with one, if others may benefit from it) but to suggest how one university has found ways to provide a myriad of career-creative experiences without lengthening time to degree.

These formal career-diversity courses educate scholars, but more important, they express a liberal arts ethos rather than the monolithic goal of replenishing the professoriate. Nor do they lengthen time to degree. They might in fact accelerate it, if students see that they have good alternatives to remaining in school.

Internships

The hands-on aspects of these courses point toward the value of internships for today's graduate students. We've long assumed that graduate students should teach, and surely teaching can be an important part of their education. But why should teaching necessarily be the only work that they do? For some, internships may be more valuable—and may allow students to apply their teaching skills in a different setting. The program in American studies at Indiana University–Purdue University Indianapolis "closes the distance between academia and the world surrounding it" by making internships "the centerpiece of the program" and having them "replace the role teaching assistantships typically play." Students' internship work informs and intertwines with their dissertation research, with employers and faculty collaborating extensively on designing coursework and skills through the academic side of the program.[31]

Some (though not most) of these internships at IUPUI are offered on campus, and any campus likewise may serve as a key resource. Every college or university is a village unto itself, with any number of offices (student relations, development, university relations, publications, admissions, to name a few) that might provide positions. Staff pay might substitute for a TA stipend for a student's support during one or two semesters of the graduate experience. At this writing, few other graduate programs now encourage students to substitute an internship for a TAship, and it's an especially challenging exchange at state universities, whose rigid budget structures make such unconventional turns more difficult. But swapping a course for an internship could be revenue neutral in the case of paid internships off campus.

Viewed from a wider angle, the internship also suggests postgraduation career possibilities in which doctoral graduates may live an academic life, even teach sometimes, and meanwhile enjoy a rewarding career with leadership possibilities. Many graduate students who wish to live in an academic community can do so, often with comfortable salaries, in nonprofessorial positions in offices like development, publications, admissions, university relations, or the president's office, to name a few. Many PhD graduates already choose administrative positions rather than face the parched academic job market year after year.

Still, programs should not restrict themselves to the campus when they create internships, because the entire concept should connect academia to a range of social sectors. That range, in our view, should include businesses. Many humanists in particular distrust for-profit endeavors, but we suggest getting over that, if only to allow students to make their own choices. Is there really a great difference, say, between working for PBS (a nonprofit), as opposed to the History Channel?

Some reformers have begun to argue that site visits are more efficient than internships, which could occupy an entire semester or summer. We agree with Chris Golde, a consultant at Stanford and a leading voice in conversations about career diversity, that the two practices are helpful and complementary. She praises site visits—bringing students to the workplace—over campus panels featuring PhDs with careers outside academia (bringing the workplace to the students). "Site visits are like going on safari," she says, whereas the on-campus panel is like visiting a zoo. "The site visit allows a student to imagine what this kind of career life is like." But Golde argues for internships as well, "to provide a real working experience. The site visits are

So You Want to Start an Internship Program

We hope that you're now convinced that internships can help your PhD program. Maybe you've decided to start an internship program on your campus. As anyone who has run one knows, they're detail-intensive operations.

So that you can move smoothly from intention to reality, we offer a case study: the University of Iowa's Humanities for the Public Good internship program. As part of a program jointly funded by the Iowa's graduate school and a grant from the Mellon Foundation, the university's Obermann Center for Advanced Studies began offering internships to PhD students in the humanities and humanistic social sciences starting in 2019.

The program currently appoints nine interns (Public Good Fellows) each year. Internships last two months and pay $5,000. (Most students plan them for the summer, when funding can be hard to get.) The program also pays $3,000 to each site partner who takes on an intern.

The initiative has launched smoothly: both interns and partners describe rich and rewarding experiences. In particular, the students report a broadening of their professional horizons.

We see five main components to Iowa's success. We'll examine them here.

Thoughtful Advance Work and Design

When the University of Iowa received funding to start a graduate internship program, Obermann Center director Teresa Mangum sought first to build a solid foundation. She realized that "we needed to engage closely with partners to design and carry out meaningful, collaborative internships." This advance work is essential. Katina Rogers advises that for internships "to be mutually beneficial, strong and clear partnerships are needed between university programs and companies or non-profit organizations in the community. Taking on new staff with limited experience can be a drain on the organization," and it's important to recognize that the organization hiring an intern is giving as well as receiving something.[1] Those liaisons require advance planning.

Mangum and Associate Director Jennifer New decided to maintain a local focus—all of their partners lie within a 30-mile radius. New identified potential partner organizations. She looked for "missions grounded in the arts, equity and inclusion, education, and/or sustainability," says Mangum. (In a variation on this practice, Maria LaMonaca Wisdom, director of graduate student advising and engagement for the humanities at Duke University and coordinator of the graduate school's internship program, suggests that the student may gain professional development experience by taking part in this process of identifying where they want to intern.)[2]

New met with each site host "to discuss the goals of the Humanities for the Public Good and to outline expectations for the students, as well as our hopes for what the site will both provide and receive." The hosting organizations drafted descriptions of what they wanted their interns to do. Mangum and New paid close attention to what they were saying and worked with them. "It took a bit of back and forth," said Mangum, "to create experiences that would steep our interns in the culture, workflow, and habits of mind required to succeed in each workplace."

Ongoing Reflection by Students and Program Directors Cohort Consciousness

We're considering these two goals together because they're intertwined in practice. Mangum and New sought esprit de corps among their intern groups. Throughout their two months at work, the internship cohort met several times to discuss their experiences. They also maintained an online conversation, sometimes prompted by Mangum and New, sometimes by each other. "This process of ongoing reflection was critical," said Mangum, "as students moved through excitement, frustration, panic (as time grew short and projects expanded), insight, and ultimately immense gratitude and pride in their work." That reflection led to outreach.

Outreach

The reflection process extended through the students' final assignments. These were forms of public outreach: short video accounts of their work and brief written reports on what they learned for their departmental newsletters and websites. "We've also asked them to speak for us as ambassadors for the program at various public events," said Mangum.

If all of this sounds like a course—well, it should be one. Which brings us to the final important ingredient of the program's success, and its way forward.

A Strong Educational Focus

"We understand the internships to be an educational experience," said Mangum. As such, they demand "the same kind of careful design and attention to learning outcomes we would expect from a course." This priority came into play early: when Mangum and New were originally looking for organizations to partner with, they sought workplaces "where we knew staff members who would be gifted mentors." When the cohorts were in place, they conducted an orientation "to help students clarify what they wanted to learn and questions they would be exploring to connect their graduate work and their experience as interns."

The directors also invited their partners "to think of themselves as coteachers." That kind of pointedly educational partnership not only nourishes the relation between the university and the community organizations who take on interns but also gives unity to the students' experience.

The directors plan to stress this focus going forward. "The students are already clamoring for year-long internships," according to Mangum, which "could carry course credit rather than funding." But their future aim is for internships that take the place of graduate student teaching: "yearlong professional assistantships that carry the same funding and benefits as a teaching or research assistantship."

The outcomes point in that direction. Paul Schmitt, a fifth-year PhD student in English, credits the program structure (including the regular meetings and written reflections) with giving him a look at "what publicly engaged scholarship might look like." He found himself "thinking through personal questions of career diversity, the shape of one's research and its accessibility outside of academia, community building, and what constitutes meaningful work." Schmitt, whose research centers on environmental concerns, worked on flood preparation for a local community. The work ranged from digital mapping to door-to-door canvassing. In her oversight of Schmitt's work, New observed that Schmitt admired his site mentor's "ability to meet with a wide variety of community members and to gather stories; she was in awe of his ability to take what they gathered and present it in a coherent and engaging narrative." In the process, Schmitt "recognized—or perhaps relearned after years of doctoral work—the enjoyment I get from working in and with communities." He hopes to continue to do publicly engaged work.

Andrew Boge, a second-year student in communications studies, interned at the African American Museum of Iowa, where he worked on educational programs. "The museum has a longstanding Underground Railroad program aimed at elementary school students," said New, and it wanted one for high school students too. Boge researched and wrote a report for the museum on "the ethics of racial education." He wrote the report, he said, "as an educational praxis document for the museum," for staff to "inform their own pedagogy." He drafted several educational programs. His favorite "involved having students in an experiential learning scenario," based on primary sources, "where they are members of the American Anti-slavery Society."

Boge reports that he learned a lot, including about himself and his own goals. His internship showed him "that I have value outside of the academy," and that communities need his skills. He realized that he could make his own "connections between the academy and the community," and that he should make them a part of my scholarly and professional practice." What more could teachers wish to hear from their students?

---

1. Rogers, *Putting the Humanities PhD to Work*.
2. Maria LaMonaca Wisdom, email to Cassuto, February 2020.

appetizers while the internships are the main course." Extending Golde's metaphor, we would add that planning and clear expectations on all sides are crucial to ensure shared understanding between students, the program, and the internship hosts that the work will be filling and nutritious.

Sustaining such value is likewise important. The agreements between employers and programs and their students must not only be clear and detailed but also carefully assessed, maintained, and improved over time. And the agreements ideally should be written in such a way that they will withstand the departure of particular individuals on both sides.

General Principles

The specifics of the initiatives we've discussed here suggest some general principles of graduate student professional development.

First, we again emphasize that *these experiences are time efficient*, ranging from a one-semester course to a few summer weeks. Aside from lessening the time-to-degree worry, a program might well ask whether it truly dilutes the intellectual experience of students to substitute a single professional development seminar for a seminar in the discipline. In any case, professional development may be incorporated into existing courses, as well as internships that bear credit or replace teaching. (Collaboration, for example, is a skill valued both inside and outside of the academy. Lab scientists collaborate all the time, but team efforts are relatively rare in the humanities disciplines. It would hardly require a revolution to urge humanists to incorporate some collaborative work in courses already on offer.) Despite the ambition and persistence of the career-expanding efforts we've surveyed, they typically remain cocurricular add-ons. Career preparation is, as Rogers says, "needed at the core," not the margins.[32] This is everyone's business.

Second, many of those activities are perforce interdisciplinary. The examples we've cited here serve many programs at once, and in Duke's case, the entire graduate school. The University of Louisville's remarkable PLAN (Professional development, Life skills, Academic development, Networking) is a series of skills-based workshops that, because of the collective participation of students, departments, and the graduate school, constitutes an entire culture that supports graduate students as they pursue both careers inside and outside of academia. Developed from the top down and the bottom up at the same time, it's exemplary practice.[33]

The Duke and Louisville professional development programs model the creation of a porch society of continuing interchange and collaboration among departments—and with programs in professional schools as well as in the arts and sciences. Hence our advice to directors of graduate studies: *make new friends from other departments and build things with them*. It's enjoyable, provides a wider view of the university that can lead to new possibilities for your students, and creates a real and virtual common workspace for mutual benefit.

Third, *administrative units beyond the individual programs must sponsor these efforts*. That's part of the reason it's important to empower the graduate dean and the graduate school. (An engaged provost also helps.) It's past time to rethink the graduate deanship, to appoint dynamic and informed leaders, and to provide them with the resources required to motivate departments and individual faculty members. Internships in particular are difficult to establish without such guidance. They won't happen without appointing individuals to forge the necessary partnerships.

Fourth, these examples, especially Duke's, point to *the need for expert graduate career counselors.* Many professors excel at helping students prepare for a range of careers, but we more often encounter a fearful (and sometimes angry) FAQ: How can I help my students do something that I never learned to do myself? One answer: work with—and learn from—specialists at the office of career services on campus. Graduate career specialists are multiplying, and they want to—and should—work with professors to help graduate students prepare for their careers. Career counseling at Duke, especially for nonacademic careers, is conducted by professors within particular departments and also by expert counselors. In the case of graduate career counseling, it takes a village.

The overall lesson for advocates of a more dynamic PhD degree is a friendly persistence. Programmatically, this might mean offering opportunities to students rather than adding requirements. Politically, it means engaging as many faculty and staff colleagues as possible in the new initiatives. Pedagogically, it means ensuring that faculty frequently unpack for students the "learning objectives" of assignments—because if we can do that for undergraduates, we can do it for graduate students too. And we should, because it helps them understand what they're learning, which makes them into better decision makers about their own careers.

Fifth, *graduate programs need to forge productive relationships with the career services office and the office of alumni relations.* As we've said, alumni, including undergraduate degree holders, are among the most likely to offer internships to current doctoral students. It's a great deal easier when an alert upper administration forges these new links, but any program can create them on its own. In particular, it is past time for career service offices to provide specific counseling to graduate students; too many restrict their efforts to undergraduates. This is an additional expense certainly, but a necessary one that will also generate revenue from grateful graduates who will gain a reason to "give back." We encourage individual programs to take the initiative, but we also stress that the university administration has responsibilities here too. The doctoral universities that lead in career diversity initiatives have done so through a combination of approaches: bottom up, top down, both/and. At Emory, for example, where we have served as consultants, the collaboration between the dean of the graduate school, Lisa Tedesco, and the faculty and doctoral students in the humanities has led to valuable rethinking of degree goals and requirements.

To these insights that arise from current campus initiatives, we can add a few others. For one, programs should provide students with a synoptic view of higher education. Nancy Busch, former dean of the Graduate School of Arts and Sciences at Fordham, has said that graduate students should have a core curriculum that includes a course in the history of higher education. The point is that graduate students benefit from knowing about the system that they belong to. This too helps to make them into better decision makers.

And consider this large adjuration from one of the higher education leaders we interviewed: "The prejudice against government and business in some disciplines leads to the construction of irrelevance." We would push back halfway against this view. The tradition of the arts and sciences is to view our social surroundings rigorously and sometimes skeptically. But it becomes a disaster, practically and ethically, if professors allow their misgivings about government or business to limit the experiences of students in their charge.

Finally, a few suggestions for ways our doctoral universities can make life easier for faculty and for individual programs—and for themselves. First, groups of universities might renew an effort that actually matches students with specific employers. Nearly 20 years ago, in 2001, 22 major research universities created a virtual career fair for PhDs interested in work beyond the academy. According to Robin Wagner, an early advocate for diverse careers for graduate students while serving as associate director for graduate career and placement services at the University of Chicago, an impressive 77 employers posted 475 openings perused by 2,800 graduate students, 581 of whom submitted more than 3,000 resumes. Writing in the *Chronicle of Higher Education*

Michael Zimm, Tech Classicist

One of the participants at the Society for Classical Studies (SCS) career session was Michael Zimm, then a creative strategist at Digital Surgeons, a small company in Connecticut. Zimm got his PhD in classics from Yale in 2016, but he had "crunched the numbers," he said, and faced "the ongoing collapse of the tenure-track job market." He decided to leave academia for technology.

How did Zimm make the move? Through research. He burrowed in and learned about the tech field. PhDs are researchers, Zimm says. "We don't realize how good we are at it. I simply applied my research skills to tech."

As a digital strategist for a technology company, Zimm describes himself as "still an academic. I'm just *their* academic." He used his knowledge of ancient rhetoric to help twenty-first-century clients. "Data needs to be analyzed," he says. "Someone needs to synthesize it and tell a story based on the evidence. I'm pretty good at that." (Zimm has since moved on to become the marketing director for another tech company.)

Zimm's skill at his job arises directly from his graduate training. But employers need to be alerted and converted. Stereotypes proliferate. As Jason Pedicone, the organizer of the SCS session, put it, employers may wonder, "Why would I want some egghead around here?" Or, in the words of Alfredo Cumerma, a recent PhD in Romance languages and literature at the Johns Hopkins University recently, "Employers simply do not know what a PhD means or how it can contribute to their organization." That's where the local career fair comes in: it can effect two-way learning, for the employer as much as for the graduate student.

shortly afterward, Wagner could not document how many jobs were secured, but he saw that more than 20 of the 77 employers were looking for abilities appropriate to humanists and social scientists: "writing, oral presentation, foreign-language skills, and qualitative research methods."[34]

Wagner saw "great enthusiasm from graduate students and administrators around the country" for the event, and this leads us to propose that universities sponsor career fairs for graduate students, not just undergrads. Wagner reported on a virtual career fair, but we recommend a face-to-face version. In preparing one, university administrators will have to reach out to potential employers, but the benefits of doing so are obvious. When undergraduates look for work, their institution brings potential employers to the campus for students to meet with, formally and informally. Why can't we do that for graduate students too?

As a middle ground between field-specific on-campus programs and virtual job fairs, disciplinary associations have begun to provide such programs at national conferences. Both the MLA and AHA have staged such fairs at their annual conferences, where students move from table to table connecting with doctoral graduates in various nonacademic positions. In 2018, the annual meeting of the Society for Classical Studies began featuring a "networking session" featuring people who earned doctorates in the classics but are now employed outside of academia. The session's initial organizer, Jason Pedicone, recruited participants from a database that his company, the Paideia Institute, has been building over several years. (The Paideia Institute, which Pedicone calls a "humanities start-up," promotes the classics through different kinds of outreach and aims to interest people outside of higher education in the subject. Its Legion Project serves to "connect classicists working outside of academia." It's a website of personal narratives written by people who have taken their expertise in classics down different paths. There are lawyers and Latin teachers to be found, of course, but also data scientists and even a professional quilter. "Legionnaires" explain the role of classics in their nonfaculty lives.)[35]

The role(s) of the intellectual in society is a rich topic we can't fully excavate here. We acknowledge that many academics don't want to part with tradition—at least not too quickly. But we might also call forth some nostalgia for a time when graduate students could consider themselves apprentices and faculty members could feel they were helping to forward the next generation of both teachers and scholarly discoveries. But we can't refuse to confront not just present reality but a reality that has been with us for about half a century—half a century!

If we wish to commit to a more influential PhD, we need to map a route from the long-held, narrow goal of using the PhD to restock the faculty to a new PhD that will lend expertise to academia and other social sectors at the same time. That route, we believe, leads through the province of public scholarship. Public scholarship is no halfway measure—so we accord it its own chapter in this book. You may wish to move to that chapter now or first take a revisionary tour through the various components of doctoral education.

FOUR

Admissions and Attrition

When it comes to graduate admissions, faculty lead a largely unexamined life. When was the last time that a department had a serious discussion about graduate admissions among its members? Programs admit graduate students faithfully each year, but the only conversation that professors usually have about it is when we decide whose turn it is to be on the admissions committee each year. The members of the committee might talk about admissions criteria among themselves (or, more likely, not), but even such conversations will turn on details rather than the larger questions of whom we're looking for and why—and matters like diversity and the range of each applicant's experiences and interests. We would bet that most of our readers have rarely heard of a department coming together to do anything like that.

That's serious neglect of the garden. We have to think about who we admit to graduate school and why, how we admit them, what criteria we're going to use—and finally, how we can retain them once they arrive. That's what this chapter is about.

We aim most doctoral reform efforts at current PhD students, and that's reasonable. They're in school now, and they need the most valuable experience we can give them. But if graduate programs are going to do things differently, our attention has to extend past the students who are already there.

Dozens of books have been published on undergraduate admissions. On graduate admissions there has been . . . one, and it appeared only recently. That book, Julie R. Posselt's *Inside Graduate Admissions: Merit, Diversity, and Faculty Gatekeeping*, is fortunately an excellent study.[1] The last phrase of Posselt's title, "faculty gatekeeping," merits particular attention, because that's too much of what professors do when they practice admissions. Posselt, who embedded herself as an observer of the admissions process conducted by 10 programs in various fields at three different universities, demonstrates persuasively that when faculty undertake graduate admissions, we default to what she calls "homophily," or love of same. In other words, we seek to replicate ourselves.[2]

This "mini-me" phenomenon is not new, of course. Various commentators have deplored it in recent years, mostly as part of more general complaints about graduate education. Posselt finds that homophily starts during admissions, and one of her more interesting discoveries is that it goes on despite faculty's conscious attention to goals like diversity. In other words, professors admit people in their own image even when they're trying not to. Thus, what Louis Menand describes as "the production of the producers" starts early in the process.[3]

Professors say they want a diverse graduate student body, and they surely believe in the idea. But most of them don't want to change their admissions criteria in ways that might encourage diverse outcomes— or they don't even realize that they can. (Posselt points to the stubborn reliance on the Graduate Record Exam (GRE) as a cutoff tool as an example of this persistence of practice. We'll talk further about that below.) As for the idea of recruiting applicants from underrepresented groups so that there will be a robust and varied applicant pool, well, most faculty members consider that admittedly difficult job to belong to someone else.[4]

And it's an important job. Recruiting a more diverse cohort involves more than just targeted publicity or inviting likely looking undergraduates to a summer program. The data abundantly show that students from underrepresented groups especially desire socially connected work. There is, says Rogers, a "relationship between innovation, equity, and public engagement."[5] If we want diverse students, we need not just to admit them but to diversify our educational offerings also.

Everything connects, then. We will consider Posselt's important findings about racial and ethnic diversity, but they shouldn't distract us from the concept of diversity writ large: we should aim not only to admit students from a variety of backgrounds, but we should also aim to admit students who have a variety of goals. That is, we need all kinds of diversity, including the intellectual kind—while at the same time we need to accentuate, rather than blur, the traditional meaning of diversity as the goal of racial, ethnic, and gender representation. As we will show, intellectual and racial diversity tend to strengthen each other.

Consider the question of outcomes. Our students will work inside and outside of academia. The smaller number who get academic jobs will emerge from the ranks of today's graduate students (including recent graduates). But it's an unavoidable fact that most of our doctoral candidates will wind up in careers beyond the college classroom, with many outside of higher education itself. One of the main arguments of this book is that we need to prepare graduate students for the jobs that they're actually going to get, and that doing so will mean conceiving of graduate education in a different, student-centered way. Rather than treating graduate school as a largely unattended offshoot of faculty research, we need to think more instrumentally about what we're doing when we prepare graduate students for their diverse professional lives. When we do that, we also appeal more to students from marginalized backgrounds, for surveys have shown us that students of color have a particular interest in using their learning in their communities. As one example, James Soto Antony and Edward Taylor interviewed students in Education PhD programs several years ago and concluded that "research *must* be of service."[6]

It follows that faculty also have to think more mindfully about graduate students while they are admitting them. We're not telling faculty whom to admit. Rather, we want to show in this chapter what a mindful admissions practice might look like. We've organized the admissions thought process around a few big questions.

How Many Is Too Many?

Program size is the lightning rod for most arguments about all of graduate school, not just admissions. Some observers have suggested limiting the number of incoming students to those we can support through some combination of fellowships and a reasonable amount of teaching.[7] With the single exception of the part-time student (about which more below), we support this idea. No one should pursue a PhD in these times without a full ride.

Another argument for reduced program size arises from the brutal fact that doctoral education prepares students for jobs that don't exist, or more accurately, jobs that exist in vanishingly small numbers. As we've observed, the graduate curriculum is modeled on the career of a professor at a research university. That outcome is rare, but we hold it before doctoral students as the one true fulfillment of their education, and we teach them to feel like failures when they don't achieve it. (We have a lot to say about that problem throughout this book.)

From this disjunction often comes the call to admit a bare few graduate students, only enough to repopulate the academic ranks. The unhappiness of PhDs, according to this argument, arises from there being too many of them. Admit fewer students, reduce the size of the graduate enterprise, and supply will meet demand. All will be well— or at least better than before.

There's some sense to this idea, of course. If we decrease supply and demand remains stable, then we move closer to economic equilibrium. But the case is hardly as simple as that. First, we should point out that when professors retire, they're not necessarily replaced. (That's the whole nature of adjunctification: full-timers are replaced by part-timers—or in some cases, not replaced at all.) Though that inconvenient fact could short-circuit the whole argument, let's nevertheless table it for the moment and proceed.

Second, we should notice that many graduate programs are already reducing the size of their incoming classes, a trend that has been observable for at least a decade.[8] Most professors have seen this shift around them, and the numbers bear it out: the Council of Graduate Schools reports a small but steady decline in enrollment in doctoral programs in the arts and humanities over the past five years.[9]

This downsizing movement is not uniform across higher education. It's most pronounced in the humanities and arts, and more consistently visible at private universities. Some public universities have a harder time reducing their incoming cohorts because they need graduate students to teach introductory classes in order to make budgetary ends meet. (And amazingly, there are still institutions whose leaders believe that greater prestige comes from graduating more PhDs, regardless of those students' prospects.) Some programs use the for-profit master's degree (i.e., where financial aid is not usually offered) as a kind of audition for doctoral study, which leads successful applicants to enter their doctoral studies with a substantial debt load.[10] We strongly discourage this practice—because anyone who's willing to pay an opportunity cost to get a PhD shouldn't have to take on heavy debt on top of that.

Though there are few aggregated statistics to consult, it nevertheless seems clear that many, if not most, doctoral programs in the arts and sciences are shrinking.[11] The most prominent reason for that is the reduced number of full-time teaching positions in their disciplines. For years it was our entire vocational purpose to prepare students to fill those jobs; now that the workplace is contracting and changing, it makes sense for us to retrench and think about what to do, and for whom.

So how many students should a program admit?

If the goal of graduate programs were to produce only enough PhDs to fill the hiring needs of colleges and universities, then the answer would be very, very few. So few, in fact, that the method of delivering graduate education would have to change because classes could not gather enough enrollees to justify their existence. The alternative, perhaps, would be a tutorial system similar to the one used in Great Britain.

The academic job market for scientists is terrible, for example, so if educators' only goal is to prepare students to become science professors, then they should admit such a small number of them that labs would have to close or else be staffed entirely by paid professionals and not graduate students.

In the humanities, faculty would have to come up with an alternative to graduate seminars—or else run them with two or three students, who would have just two or three choices each term about what courses to take. That likely won't happen in straitened economic times, as already many universities have set higher minimum enrollments than that for graduate courses. More likely, departments with just a handful of graduate students at the coursework stage would need to move to some version of the British system.

None of these changes is automatically bad. In fact, we might say that anything that makes professors reflect on their graduate teaching is salutary.

But the real bottom line here is not a tiny class of entering doctoral students. Tiny programs are hard to sustain. If we conferred only enough PhDs to fill vacant professorial positions, the more likely outcome is that many doctoral programs would close. Some critics already think that should happen.[12] So what if it did?

Let's follow this thought experiment to its logical conclusion. What might happen if most PhD programs in the United States actually closed?

To begin with, let's identify the programs that would *not* close: the old, rich elites. In this scenario, that small group of universities would supply PhDs to the rest of the country. Of course these schools would be selective—they would be admitting a very small group of candidates from an entire national (and in many cases, international) pool. But in what ways would they be selective? We need not overthink this. In a constricted market, old and established gatekeepers would behave conservatively, in keeping with past habits, and in sober recognition of the present scarcity of positions.

Conservative admissions practices raise the problems of inbreeding associated with dynasties. There wouldn't be enough spaces to risk

What about Staggered Admissions?

John Guillory, an English professor at New York University, has proposed a thought experiment for a voluntary admissions moratorium by graduate programs in the humanities. Speaking at the Modern Language Association convention in 2020, Guillory suggested that the MLA should "coordinate a system-wide rotational moratorium on admission of graduate students according to the following principle: every year, one-third or one-fourth of the graduate programs in the country would not admit any graduate students at all."[1] Guillory's idea is that by admitting regular-sized cohorts for two years, programs would maintain a critical mass of students that would allow them to offer a coherent curriculum, and students would have a useful number of peers for cohort esprit. If all or most programs in a discipline participate (on staggered three-year schedules) and admit no students one year out of every three, then the total number of graduate students would drop by about a third. Guillory argues that this plan would ease the academic employment market.

Guillory first proposed his idea at a meeting of his own department. "Judging from the response of my colleagues to this proposal," he said, "my assumption is that it has no chance of ever being implemented." Certainly this response shows how attached faculty remain to their graduate seminars. It presumably came as no surprise to Guillory, who has studied the humanities as a profession for many years and has done much valuable work analyzing our professional practice.

We disagree with his prescription here, notably because it relies on two assumptions: (1) that graduate students are interested only in academic careers and (2) that graduate programs are capable only of preparing them for those careers. (We endorse another Guillory proposal that he delivered at the same time, for a professional development orientation. We'll take that idea up in chapter 7.)

Our position is on display throughout this book, but here we want to point to the implications for admissions. It boils down to this: if we believe that we can prepare students only to become academics, then we should admit only those students whom we believe can and will take this path. In most programs, that would mean slicing the number of admitted students by half or more. But more to the point, What about students with other goals? Should we not make a place for them in our graduate programs? Don't we want advanced learning to matter throughout society? We will consider how to do this as the chapter unfolds.

---

1. John Guillory, "Graduate Admissions: Remarks MLA 2020" (January 2020). We thank Professor Guillory for sharing his manuscript with us.

admitting an "interesting" or offbeat applicant, because that would mean rejecting a more sophisticated student, perhaps one who already has done some graduate-level work.

This squeezed version of graduate admissions would obviously work to the advantage to the wealthy, privileged, and connected. Students with the time and opportunity to work directly with professors (rather than, say, at work-study jobs) or to acquire languages or lab skills—these candidates would stand out in the applicant pool. And why shouldn't they? Such students display talent and ambition. And let's face it, many of them would also display undergraduate credentials from the same elite institutions whose PhD programs survived this hypothetical cutback.

This small, exclusive scale of graduate education evokes the old days of more than a century ago, when American graduate education was first taking shape. In those early times, formal application mattered less than what we now call networking: it mattered who you knew, because your undergraduate professor might recommend you to his (and we use the male pronoun advisedly) old graduate school professor and ask him to save you a spot. It was easier to be noticed from Princeton, less so from Pawtucket.[13]

Not until after World War II did graduate school admissions become routinized and bureaucratized in the familiar way, with uniform application paperwork and an admissions office to handle it. The larger numbers of incoming students after the war limited the inbreeding that went on when American graduate school was smaller.

So the thought experiment—What if there were many fewer graduate programs training many fewer students to become replacement professors?—might lead to a future that marches straight back to an elitist past.

But that unpleasant prospect is less likely than it might seem, and not just because universities don't like to shutter their graduate programs. Recall the initial assumption guiding the thought experiment: that it's the job of graduate programs to train replacement professors and nothing else. We already accept many of the trappings of that assumption. Consider how faculty still tend to define a "successful" job placement as a tenure-track professorship, preferably at a research university.

The assumption that the sole purpose of graduate school is to train scholars who will become tomorrow's professors dates from the postwar period of growth and abundance in American higher education that we discussed at greater length in the introduction to this book. For one brief generation, when higher education grew wildly, there was full employment for PhDs. The United States needed professors to staff new and growing colleges and universities that welcomed first an inflow of former GIs and then a generation of baby boomers. As historian Thomas Bender has observed, the powerful memories of that generation occluded the longstanding fact that, for many previous decades, PhDs did all kinds of work after they graduated.[14]

The PhD-to-professor career path is the relic of one prosperous moment. That moment proved an anomaly, but the anomaly was taken as the norm. The beneficiaries of that expanding academic job market are now in their 70s and 80s. It's long past time to change our baseline assumptions to reflect the realities of our students and not their grandparents.

What does all of this history have to do with admissions? First, consider that it grew out of a discussion of how many PhD students a program should admit. If we admit students in a way that is consistent with the endorsement of (not simply the acquiescence to) career diversity, then we'll need to open up the conversation about how we assess applications. The rationale for a new admissions practice lies in the Jeffersonian idea that society at large benefits from more PhDs in its midst—as long as they are there by choice.

Put simply, if we are to reconceive the guiding assumption that PhDs are supposed to become professors and nothing else, we have to do that from the bottom up. That means starting with admissions. When we open the field of possibility, we affirm the choices that our students already have to make in their lives. Most of them will try the academic job market, and we need to help them do that—but many won't get academic jobs. Some will never try the academic job market and will decide to do something else. Either way, we have to support them in their choices.

We should extend that affirmation to our students beginning at the earliest stage of graduate school. Professors already shape their students' expectations simply by standing in front of them and modeling their own lives. We're role models whether we like it or not.

So we need to use our position as advisers and guides to shape our students' expectations before they enter graduate school. We have to be transparent about their career options during the admissions process itself. That means sharing outcomes data (not just anecdotes about the students who got the "best" jobs). It also means frank talk about the realities of graduate school, economic and otherwise. Our applicants won't graduate into the same world that their teachers mostly did, and we need to alter their training accordingly to prepare them for the full range of jobs they will be able to get. At the same time, we can try to describe those outcomes by using examples that model their desirability.

The question of incoming cohort size finally has to do with teaching. We have to teach graduate students differently in these changed circumstances. With too few academic jobs out there, we have to prepare them for the jobs that they can get—and this entails more advising, more individual curricular planning. If we expect our students to plot an individualized path through a doctoral program, then they need help planning that path. Such advice is vital to the program's coherence, not a friendly add-on. And that means admitting only as many students as you can teach in this way.

So the answer to the question of how many graduate students to admit is, it depends. It depends on how much financial support is available for them, and it depends especially on advising, which is some of the most important graduate teaching we do. *Programs should admit the number of students whom they can advise individually.*

Tip O'Neill, Speaker of the House of Representatives during the 1980s, famously said, "All politics is local." He meant that you have to connect with your constituents and care about the issues that matter

Whatever Happened to the Part-Time Graduate Student?

One casualty of "rightsizing" graduate programs has been the part-time PhD student, a species once common in the humanities and humanistic social sciences. Part-time students made up the majority of American graduate students from 1967 until 2000 and amounted to about 55 percent of the total graduate student population through the 1960s and 1970s, according to statistics collected by the Department of Education. But there has been a marked shift since the millennium. Full-time students now make up significantly more than half of all graduate students. As of 2010, part-time students amounted to only 44 percent of the total, and that movement shows no sign of abating.[1]

The national shift away from part-time graduate school options has some reasonable motives. Many programs have eliminated them because they want to give full support to more (sometimes all) of the students they admit. They also don't want to overproduce PhDs for employment markets that can't accommodate them. But most part-time students already have jobs, so they don't necessarily need protection from a bad market. Many are secondary school teachers who would benefit from additional training. Some part-time students are willing to pay for graduate school because they enjoy it. Economist David C. Colander suggests that graduate schools ought to accommodate students who want to attend graduate school for pleasure.[2] Why should we deny such students a place if they are qualified? Part-time students need not make up a majority of American graduate students, as in times past, but we need not allow them to go extinct either.[3]

---

1. See National Center for Education Statistics, "Postbaccalaureate Enrollment," 2017, https://nces.ed.gov/programs/coe/indicator_chb.asp.

2. Colander, a professor of economics at Middlebury College, argues that graduate school ought to be presented not only as job training but also as a "luxury consumption good." Departments, he says, ought to distinguish between students who enroll in search of a job afterward and those who attend for the sheer love of the subject, a category that includes many part-time students. Colander focuses his analysis on English departments, but it's easy to generalize from his conclusions. Part-timers, he suggests, "might be organized into an 'Executive English Ph.D.' program" with "a more convenient schedule for working students, just as Executive M.B.A. programs have." See David Colander with Daisy Zhuo, "Where Do PhDs in English Get Jobs? An Economist's View of the English PhD Market," *Pedagogy* 15, no. 1 (2015): 139–56.

3. For more on part-time PhD students, see Leonard Cassuto, "The Part-Time Ph.D. Student," *Chronicle of Higher Education*, October 7, 2013, http://chronicle .com/article/The-Part-Time-PhD-Student/142105/.

Collaborative Admissions?

We're suggesting that all stakeholders—faculty, administrators, students themselves—reconsider their approach to graduate education, beginning with admissions. We're also arguing that everything is connected, meaning that admissions links to teaching, which links to career preparation. This new holistic approach—beginning with a reconsidered approach to admissions—will require creativity. In that spirit, here's an idea.

Why not admit some graduate students collaboratively? On the admissions level, departments might work together to admit a cluster of students into different departments who are all interested in, say, race- or gender-based inquiry. Departments could then plan to teach them collaboratively, across disciplines. They could offer interdisciplinary, team-taught seminars on those topics to appeal to these clusters. Because of their cross-disciplinary appeal, these courses would likely enroll healthy numbers and bypass concerns about low class enrollments that vex many graduate programs these days.

We offer this proposal for two main reasons. First, it's interesting and might work. Second and more important, we hope that just considering it might dislodge faculty and administrators from their perch atop a tower of ancient and unquestioned assumptions. Let's think about admissions differently and find some new ways to practice it.

to them. Graduate school in the twenty-first century needs to operate on the same principle. In terms of size, admit only as many students whom you can advise closely and personally as they design their own path through your program. If you have to wholesale your academic advice to students, you're probably accepting too many of them. Our students trust us with years of their time, the one thing that once you spend, you can never get back. The least we can do is invest some of our own to help them.

If programs open the admissions conversation not just to cohort size but also to cohort characteristics, then we can rightsize PhD programs at a level that is both viable and responsible. That level may be smaller than it has been, but not so small as to return us to an arrogant and privileged past that we left behind once already. And the country—not just the professoriate—will benefit.

What Are We Talking about When We Talk about Admissions?

Let's think about how a program's admissions conversation might go. We suggested in chapter 2 that a department open its own self-study by planning backward. In doing so, its members will have determined the most difficult and fundamental question: What are we here for? That is, what are our goals for students in this doctoral program? Once you have answers to those questions, then you can formulate an admissions policy that integrates these goals and centers on the most important question: What kind of students do we want and why?

Too rarely do programs reflect on graduate admissions in relation to their overall goals. Yet as we've pointed out, admissions has much to do with those goals. Graduate students are students and colleagues at the same time: fellow teachers (and people we train to be teachers) and researchers (and research assistants). Along with full- and part-time faculty, they shape a department's culture. The work that we ask graduate students to do should reflect their needs first, but it inevitably reflects ours at the same time. So we should think about what sorts of graduate students will fit best into a department's mission.

Posselt suggests that graduate schools practice holistic admissions. The idea of holistic admissions has been with us for a while, but primarily as part of undergraduate admissions.* The concept is familiar: consider the whole person—or as Posselt puts it, "evaluate students as individuals, in the context of their own opportunity and potential."[15] The undergraduate version of holistic admissions considers grades and scores as only one part—an important one, to be sure—of a whole application.

Holistic admissions has rarely been employed at the graduate level for two main reasons. First, graduate programs have traditionally con-

---

* Professional schools such as medical schools also employ versions of holistic admissions.

cerned themselves with scholarly potential, not the whole person. It might matter to an undergraduate admissions officer that an applicant is a cello virtuoso, but to a graduate program anywhere but a conservatory, that fact won't weigh heavily. Second, faculty engaging in graduate admissions—even in the humanities—typically try to avoid qualitative evaluation. Instead of reflecting on an applicant's entire file, they default into a "numbers game" in which, Posselt found, "numbers concealed underlying disagreements that faculty would rather not broach and buffered them from charges of unfairness."[16]

Posselt witnessed how numerical cutoffs push diverse applicants out of the pool of candidates before serious consideration begins about whom to admit. Foremost among these numerical tools is the Graduate Record Exam. There is little understanding of the predictive capacity of the GRE in relation to actual student performance, and ETS itself defines the test's predictive capacity as "modest" and warns against employing a minimum score as a gatekeeping device. (The board notes as well that undergraduate GPA appears to be a superior predictor of performance in graduate school.) Posselt found that faculty members in the varied departments she studied shared this skepticism of the GRE—yet they still employed it as a "magic bullet" to eliminate applications from consideration.[17] Those eliminated applicants can include many from underrepresented groups. Posselt recommends that a reconsidered admissions process treat issues of racial, ethnic, and socioeconomic diversity more integrally, not as token boxes to check off after the applicant pool has been reduced.[18] We'll consider those issues later in this chapter.

In this section, we want to highlight a different kind of diversity: a diversity of goals. Right now, the graduate school application process doesn't allow for any.

When students apply to graduate school, they adhere to strict and straitened conventions. Some of these conventions are obvious: applicants supply grades, scores, recommendations, and so forth, and they write a personal statement that ties everything together. Together, these amount to a self-presentation. It's a ritual dance, with prescribed steps.

The persuasive goal of that dance is understood on both sides: candidates should present themselves as prospective researchers. In theory, personal statements by graduate school applicants in the arts and sciences can contain anything, but practice is another thing. Faculty readers look for particular signals, and successful applicants supply them. Faculty readers especially want for candidates to demonstrate what kinds of scholars or scientists they will be. So applicants might describe archival or laboratory experience or a senior thesis. And they'll look ahead to describe what sort of research that they want to do. In the humanities and humanistic social sciences, they might describe a future dissertation topic.

On its face, the latter convention might appear silly. Applicants want to go to graduate school to learn to write a dissertation, so how can they describe what's in it ahead of time? But they're not really doing that. Instead, admissions committees ask applicants to present a plausible thesis topic. When applicants do that, faculty readers get to watch the minds of potential doctoral students at work on a revealing task. Everyone understands that the exercise is a fiction, but it's a useful fiction.

Or is it? The problem here is not the possible dissertation but the assumption it conveys—and that assumption underlies the whole application process. We're asking all of our applicants to imagine themselves as research scholars, and we're asking them to come up with a set of research ambitions that might lead to a teaching job at a research university. In other words, we're asking everyone to pretend that they want to be professors just like the ones who will read their applications. It's flattery by command performance.

The problem is that not all applicants want to be professors at research universities. And of those who do, most of them won't get there. So if we continue the dance metaphor, it's as though the heads of a dancing school that teaches all styles of dancing requires all applicants to audition by doing only specific ballet steps.

Applicants to graduate school weren't born yesterday. They have eyes and ears, and most of them know something of the desiccated academic job market. They might believe that they will be among the lucky few who will grab the brass ring of an academic job, but they know it's a long, difficult, and uncertain road. Some are ready to veer off that road toward other alternatives. But they're effectively not allowed to say that when they apply, because the conventions dictate that they present themselves as laser-directed scholars.

If doctoral education results in a range of outcomes for its students, then why do we require that students dress themselves up in the same outfit—as prospective research university professors—in order to pass through the door? Reformers (including us) talk about the importance of career diversity throughout graduate students' time of study, but here we suggest that *meaningful reform begins before they even arrive*. If career diversity is to become the new norm, we're suggesting its inclusion at every stage of a graduate program. We encourage schools and programs to consider this fact as a first step toward a full assessment of their admissions practice.

That doesn't mean ignoring the aspiring professors, of course. One vital goal of graduate admissions ought to be to identify future academic researchers and future college teachers. Preserving the disciplines by this reproductive mold has a necessary and positive function. But as it's now conceived, that mold can block applicants who don't fit within its confines. In particular it can discourage original thinkers from even entering doctoral programs. As just one example, we know of a lawyer who was simultaneously earning her law degree and a doctorate in women's studies—until she experienced skepticism from humanists toward her dual aim and left her doctoral program embittered. For her, as for all those who want a doctorate but who do not wish to join the professoriate, the message is clear: stay away.

And sadly, that message remains the same even in fields where extra-academic employment is more a traditional norm. Biologist Peter Bruns concludes that "in most cases, the goal in the sciences and engineering has been to produce researchers in the mold of the current faculty." This goal persists even though more than half of all doctoral students in many science fields do not expect to pursue academic careers. For example, a 2012 survey found that only 35 percent of PhDs in chemistry are employed at four-year colleges and universities, while 45 percent are in the private sector and 20 percent in governmental and nonprofit organizations.[19] In physics, 62 percent of graduates took a postdoctoral position after obtaining the degree, but a recent survey of PhD graduates 10–15 years later revealed dramatically different proportions: 45 percent remain in academia while the others have moved to government agencies or the private sector.[20] And with so many humanists who have not secured academic positions added to the perennial 20 percent who have other plans, about 50 percent of all PhDs across these disciplines will not become professors. (Downturns in the academic job market after 2008 suggest that the next updated percentage of those who do remain in academia will be lower, and the prospects of a post-COVID-19 academic job market inspire anything but optimism.)

Such data should surely inform the policies of programs, including admissions. But there appear as yet no innovative alternatives to the prevailing homophilic cloning culture in this first stage of graduate education. It remains all too predictable how a typical selection committee would view a PhD applicant in philosophy or English who states explicitly that her career goal lies outside the academy, or how a chemistry program would respond to an applicant whose stated goal is to teach at a small liberal arts college.

And what about community college? Faculty at four-year institutions have for years held community college professorships at arm's length, as less-reputable versions of themselves. Only recently—and driven by necessity—have decisions by new PhDs to work at community colleges even begun to approach respectability.

To work at a community college is to teach beginning college students. The negative associations that attach to such a job arise, of course, from the high teaching load and consequently reduced time for research that community college professorships entail. (The reality, as community college professors will point out, is more complex; we speak of the stereotype.) Here, at the end of graduate school, we see the same assumption in practice that guides admissions: our graduate students should be researchers, with any other choice second best (or worse). We're supposed to be training teachers, but when our students take jobs that center on teaching, too many "real" professors think they're slumming.

Our biases lurk throughout graduate education, beginning with admissions, usually hidden from view. One of us (Len) tells a story of his time as graduate director of his department. He accepted an applicant who wound up writing her dissertation under his direction. Just before she went on the academic job market, she told him that she wanted to look exclusively for community college jobs. This news he received with equanimity, but then she said further that this had always been her plan, since before she applied to graduate school in the first place. He then recalled reading her application—which revealed nothing of this ambition—and realized that if she had been up front about her goal in her personal statement, he might have viewed her application differently.[21] Sometimes our professional socialization betrays itself in sneaky ways.

What about those who don't necessarily want to teach at all? We might take a few lessons from economics departments in this respect. Economics is an outlier with respect to the issues we've raised in this section. Economics PhDs graduate to a myriad of careers, academic and nonacademic, public and private. The professors who train these graduate students accord respect to the full range of outcomes. One might argue that these careers deserve respect because they're prestigious, but that argument is ultimately circular: these positions have respect and prestige from professors because the professors esteem these outcomes in the first place. They're prestigious because they deserve respect—and vice versa.

Therefore, when economists admit new PhD candidates, they aren't looking only for the next generation of professors. They're fully aware that their PhDs will populate a variety of workplaces. The rest of us might adopt that point of view too. What about applicants who want to do public humanities, or who want to be activists? We don't have to view all career goals as equivalent, but our students benefit when we welcome a range of career possibilities.

We suggest that programs reexamine their admissions policies from the buried roots upward. So much of what we do has been unquestioned for so long. The academic landscape has changed in that time, and so have our students. Change what you will—and don't change what you want to keep. But either way, we invite you to reflect, so that you can craft an admissions policy based on goals that match the reality that our students already face.

Diversity Matters

When it comes to diversity, graduate schools talk a good game. Well-intentioned professors and administrators want a graduate student cohort that looks like America, but one glance at the demographics shows how far we are from that goal. In 2016 only 15 percent of all doctorates awarded by US universities went to African Americans, Hispanics, and Native Americans, although those three groups together represent more than 30 percent of the US population, and about 35 percent of the population that might be considered of doctoral-graduate age.[22]

Clearly, the obstacles facing those students are high and daunting. Students from disadvantaged backgrounds may never learn about opportunities available to them at the graduate level. If they do go to graduate school, many feel isolated in a community where few others (if any) look like them or share their experience. Undergraduate diversity efforts face well-publicized legal and social trials, but diversifying the graduate student body might be even harder, from the point of recruitment through retention to degree completion.

The best prepared are often the most traditionally prepared. But as we know, admissions standards don't end with traditional preparation. The general notion of "distance traveled"—that is, the level at which an undergraduate began compared to the level she or he reached upon graduation—seems more likely to predict future progress, and it's a measure that does not penalize students from underrepresented groups. In all, graduate programs should learn from the assessment revolution that is occurring.

But it's not enough to address your standards so that you can admit a graduate class that looks something like America. The applicants have to be in your applicant pool in the first place. Racial, ethnic, and socioeconomic diversity really centers on recruitment and retention.[23]

Both recruitment and retention require thoughtful commitment. In chapter 1, we cited the Mellon Mays program, which awards fellowships to gifted and motivated undergraduate juniors from underrepresented groups and funds them all the way through the PhD. Seeding interest early is the only way to enlarge the minority cohort, not fighting with competing programs to attract the limited number now motivated to apply.

One excellent example of recruitment is Target Hope, a nonprofit, Chicago-area college preparatory program that recruits high school students of color and places them in undergraduate programs with which it has partnerships around the country. In addition, the program has a "collegiate component" that introduces the option of graduate school to undergraduates from underrepresented racial and ethnic groups.

The magnetic center of the program is the Conference on Graduate Education, held at Washington University in St. Louis. Conference participants are alumni of the college preparatory program who have either graduated from college or are currently enrolled and are interested in learning more about graduate school. Conference activities include an overview of funding for graduate school, a panel discussion by graduate and professional students, lectures from faculty on the benefits of graduate school and how best to prepare for it, and school tours. Chancellor's Graduate Fellows—participants in a program aimed at increasing the number of graduate students who contribute to diversity in graduate education at Washington University and who are seeking faculty careers—assist at the conference as hosts and presenters along with other graduate students each year. The conference enables formal and informal contact between graduate students and conference participants, and formal interaction with faculty of color whom participants view as role models.[24]

Such conferences matter because, as Rafia Zafar puts it, young people know the difference between talking the talk and walking the walk. Zafar, a professor at Washington University and faculty director of the Mellon Mays undergraduate program there, stresses that recruitment goes beyond "sending letters to the chairs of departments you know saying 'send me your bright diverse students.'" You have to go to where your applicants are, or else bring them to you. "Is there a Mellon Mays regional conference near your school?" she asks. "Does your school host one—and if so, have you considered going to some of the panels?"[25]

Target Hope may or may not last as an individual program, but its years of success showcase a general principle of outreach.[26] Graduate schools in search of diversity need to go to places we mostly haven't been. Universities should ally doctoral education with K–12 reform efforts, and with community colleges, which serve a large population of students of color.

Such partnerships help students learn early about advanced degrees. For example, up to 70 percent of Latino students who attend college begin in community college (and often do not go on to four-year universities).[27] Graduate programs seeking diverse populations need to go where the students are and make a connection.

It comes down to this: the graduate school enterprise cannot survive on undergraduates alone. Not just for diversity's sake must we participate with earlier stages of education to enlarge the eligible cohort.[28] There's an even broader general principle at work here too: just as graduate school needs to stop isolating itself, colleges and universities need to get more involved with K–12 education in the United States. It's hard to find any industry that treats its main supplier with greater indifference than higher education treats the K–12 school system.

Diversity recruitment at the undergraduate level also has its value. The Graduate Research Internship (RI) at the University of Texas at Austin gives control over fellowship awards to individual faculty members, who use them to recruit outstanding graduate students to their departments. Well supported at the institutional level with good advertising and a healthy budget, the program invites faculty members to compete for 1 of 30 RI awards. The program thus attracts active research faculty who are also committed to student learning, and it's particularly appreciated by professors in fields where external funding is not readily available (such as the humanities and humanistic social sciences). Each faculty award winner identifies potential internship candidates among new graduate applicants, then attempts to recruit these students with the offer of the RI position. The faculty member mentors the RI during the student's first year and introduces him or her to methods, problems, and professional development opportunities in the discipline.[29]

At Vanderbilt University, the master's program plays a key sourcing role. That's a sensible focus, as students from underrepresented groups are significantly more likely to enroll in a master's program on the way to a PhD compared to the graduate student population at large. The Fisk-Vanderbilt Bridge Program, started in 2002, aims for students to make a smooth transition from a master's program at Fisk University, a historically black university in Nashville, Tennessee, to a doctoral program at nearby Vanderbilt (though a few attend universities elsewhere).[30] The program focuses on scientific fields and targets students "who genuinely need us," says its executive director, Dina M. Stroud. Once accepted into the bridge program while at Fisk, students gain a higher level of funding, access to labs at Vanderbilt, and support from faculty committed to the program. As important, the students are introduced to a range of support services, starting with "intrusive mentoring" ("you don't wait for students to come to you," says Stroud) by peers, faculty, and program staff. Students also gain access to Vanderbilt's counseling services. The results have been excellent so far, with high completion rates and low attrition.[31]

Such enrichment is a common and essential feature of effective diversity initiatives. The Summer Multicultural Access to Research Training program (SMART) at the University of Colorado at Boulder aims to increase the diversity of doctoral graduates and future faculty members through a 10-week, faculty-mentored research experience for talented undergraduate interns interested in pursuing graduate education. Intensive research training and a workshop series prepare students for graduate school and the professoriate. At an annual year-end symposium, interns present their research to the university community.

Funded by the National Science Foundation to increase diversity in STEM fields, the program is a component of the NSF's Alliance for Graduate Education and the Professoriate (AGEP).[32]

At the University of Washington, the Student and Faculty Advisory Boards support the Graduate Opportunities and Minority Achievement Program (GO-MAP). It's a comprehensive unit within the UW Graduate School dedicated to recruiting and retaining graduate students from underrepresented groups. The Faculty Advisory Board and the Student Advisory Board work both independently and together on activities, events, and programs that further GO-MAP's goals. This work improves the campus climate for all students through the asset of diversity. Faculty board members either volunteer or are invited to serve based on their reputation for understanding minority recruitment and retention. Members must attend one of the four GO-MAP signature events, participate in an additional GO-MAP planned activity, serve on an ad hoc subcommittee as needed, and identify colleagues to participate in the program. Two graduate student assistant coordinators who assist with the signature events also convene and manage the board meetings. In addition to planning and participating in GO-MAP events, the board creates opportunities for networking across departments and connecting with minority communities outside the university.

GO-MAP centralizes diversity efforts within a larger decentralized graduate school culture. Students, who are enlisted through email invitation, demonstrate commitment before they even start, and board members engage them in professional and leadership development on campus and in the community. Like the other examples we've cited, GO-MAP depends on coherent advising for a group of students who are encouraged to form a cohort community.

The Problem of Attrition

The need for a supportive community for graduate students—especially those from underrepresented groups—leads us to the related subject of attrition. Attrition is the corollary of admissions, and retention is its positive expression. Retention matters for the whole graduate student population, but it's especially important—and challenging—when it comes to underrepresented groups. As the foregoing examples suggest, successful diversity initiatives merge recruitment and retention in practice. Without recruitment, there's no one to retain. Without retention, recruitment becomes a Sisyphean pursuit.

Attrition is disturbingly high among doctoral students in the arts and sciences: it stands at about 50 percent. Equally disturbing is the general lack of awareness of this fact. Who ever heard of another training program that discards half of its trainees? Recall the hypothetical seminar of eight students that we discussed in the introduction. We should expect only four to finish.

That about half of all entering doctoral students do not complete the PhD has often been cited as evidence that something is wrong with the degree. We agree: that high figure certainly suggests that something is amiss with the training for it. As Derek Bok observes, professional school students are much more likely to complete their graduate degrees, in painful contrast to doctoral pursuits.[33]

The familiarity of high graduate school attrition rates may be a reason that so many of us aren't aware of them. They've been part of the graduate school landscape for so long that they just blend in and inspire no administrative or faculty alarm. Deliberately high attrition in doctoral programs in the arts and sciences is a practice that dates back many generations, in fact. For years the pruning of large cohorts was employed as a lucrative alternative to turning away applicants at the door. (The lucre comes from the students' tuition.) In effect, that Darwinian weed-out was (and is, in the few places where it's still practiced) a cynical extension of admissions: students pay while faculty continue to decide whether to let them in. It's entirely consistent with these bad ethics that many faculty members, when they think of attrition at all, blame the students themselves for leaving.[34]

A certain attrition rate is healthy. Some students will try doctoral study and conclude that it's not for them, and they need a smooth exit path. But an attrition rate of half of all beginning students is clearly too much, probably twice too much.

Perhaps the important question about attrition is when it takes place. The Mellon Graduate Education Initiative emphasized the desirability of early attrition, which corresponds to students' changes of heart after they try graduate school. The study commendably distinguishes early exits from late attrition, which follows years of drift at the all-but-dissertation (ABD) stage. "High attrition rates and long [time to degree] clearly countered the interests of degree seekers," writes the Mellon group. "It was less often recognized that they also countered the interests of universities," argue the authors of the study. Late attrition costs students and schools alike large investments in time and funds "that were not yielding their desired outcomes."[35]

But this description, while accurate, elides the human factor. For students, the emotional cost of late attrition is virtually incalculable. For many late non-completers, the sense of failure resembles the wound of Philoctetes from Greek myth: a source of constant pain and stigma.[36] Costs are important, but the human suffering alone ought to motivate us to reduce late-stage attrition.

Attrition timing varies by field. The Mellon figures from entering classes of the early and mid-1980s for humanities students in its target departments show that a little under half of those who depart programs do so in the first two years and a bit under 60 percent in the first three years. About a quarter left as late as the sixth year and after, and 15 percent in the eighth year and after.[37] By contrast, most science and math students who depart leave by year three, according to the Council of Graduate Schools.[38]

The Mellon researchers discovered that their initiative scarcely reduced attrition, but programs that introduced clearer timetables "and encourage[d] students to finish their dissertations as soon as possible" made some progress. Interestingly, quick completion reduced attrition. Less surprisingly, skillful advising mattered greatly.[39] Barbara Lovitts, who has studied attrition closely, concludes from her interviews with more than 300 students who left programs at two different universities that student background affects student attrition less than "what happens to them after they enroll." When it comes to attrition, the present outweighs the past.[40]

Why, then, do students leave? The answers vary. In Lovitts's study, the deciding factors proved to be the quality of the adviser, the departmental culture, the inequitable distribution of resources (both financial and interactive), and a disregard for students "who have an interest in real-world applications."[41] To these reasons for student departure, we might add their programs' lack of concern for retaining them. Consider that these causes were discovered by Lovitts, not the programs themselves. This absence of intramural curiosity is conspicuous.

Given this inertia, it's not surprising that suggested remedies to attrition have been few. We offer some ideas here, but there's room for further creative thought about this problem. We suggest exit interviews of departing students (after the fact, if necessary). If programs learn why their students leave, then they can do something about it. Before then, we suggest that faculty from outside the department (mutual courtesies may be extended) and administrators periodically visit current students. Graduate cohorts are not so numerous that we can't sit down with our students and find out what didn't work—and what isn't working. (It's also worth talking about what does work—so we recommend exit interviews with students who graduate, not just the ones who fail to complete.)

Among other solutions, Derek Bok suggests a zero-sum admissions game in which programs with higher late-stage attrition (and/or high time to degree) receive fewer slots for new students.[42] Chemist Angelica Stacey extends the principle to individual faculty: "What if faculty members were evaluated and rewarded, in part, on the basis of completion rates (how many of the students in your group complete the program)?"[43] These measures may be rigid, but they also may hold promise.

We'll soon see just how much promise they hold. The University of Chicago announced a wide initiative in 2019 along just these lines. It applies to doctoral students in the humanities, social sciences, divinity studies, and social service administration. Aimed at late-stage attrition, the program promises full funding to graduate students at the dissertation stage for as long as they need to finish the degree. But this unlimited funding for individual students will be linked to a department-specific cap on the number of students in the PhD program. In other words, faculty won't be able to admit new graduate students until the old ones finish, an almost literal application of Bok's one-out/one-in proposal.[44]

The CGS Degree Completion initiative takes a more consultative, several-stage approach. It recommends thoughtful admissions based on the fit of the student and the program, more frequent and thorough early-years assessment and advising, and reasonable financial support. This integrative, student-centered approach to retention is consistent with our overall approach in this book. But the Chicago initiative may address the accountability gap in doctoral education: we need to take more responsibility for attrition, along with many other program features and outcomes.

Attrition poses a particular threat to members of underrepresented groups. In her study of attrition based on several years of data, Barbara Lovitts writes that for diverse populations, wider career options and an interest in real-world problems "are of special concern because women and minorities often have a style of interaction and an interest in research questions that do not conform with prevailing norms, and they leave their graduate programs in higher numbers than men and members of majority groups."[45]

The Summer Institute for New Merit Fellows (SI) at the University of Michigan shows how retention efforts might work preemptively for these populations.[46] As a diversity initiative, the SI works with new doctoral and MFA students from groups that are historically underrepresented in their disciplines. The optional eight-week program, which annually accepts up to 50 students in the summer before their first semester of graduate school, helps prepare participants for the intellectual, professional, and social transition into their degree programs. Beginning in late June and ending in mid-August, the Institute enrolls fellows in an advanced language preparation study (for humanities majors), research methodology course (for social science majors), or a science ethics course (for science and engineering majors). In biweekly seminars and activities, fellows cover such topics as financial survival, career planning, diversity and affirmative action issues, and the basics of academic writing. Each student participant receives a stipend, health insurance, and tuition waiver.

Paid graduate student coordinators manage the Summer Institutes, and one faculty member serves as the faculty coordinator and adviser to the program. A committee composed of the program director(s) and past SI student coordinators hires the graduate student coordinators through a formal application process, so program history is preserved. Similarly, the faculty coordinator recruits other faculty members to serve as discussion facilitators, directs the staff in the design of seminars, advises SI participants, participates in weekly SI staff meetings, and fosters relationships with departments.

The rational structure of Michigan's SI program contributes notably to its effectiveness. The program demands a contractual commitment from participants that requires consistent participation (including attendance at all SI sessions), for example, and such contracts have demonstrated effectiveness in compelling student performance.[47] Meanwhile, a program template creates continuity from director to director.

Like certain kinds of admissions practice we discussed earlier, successful retention has a holistic quality. Partners for Success, a voluntary diversity initiative at the University of Wisconsin, demonstrates this holism particularly clearly. Partners identifies six stages of a graduate student's career for specific focus: recruitment, admission, academic advancement, retention, exit, and reaffiliation as an alumnus. The program begins by matching new graduate students of color with continuing graduate students, as well as some faculty and recent alumni, who serve as mentors. (Mentors receive their own dedicated training and meet periodically. That many students who go through the program become mentors later on demonstrates the kind of commitment it generates.) The program provides professional, social, and educational networks that support the students' transition to graduate school. Programming includes monthly workshops, formal and informal social activities, and large group outings that help acclimate students. A doctoral student serves as project assistant and coordinator.

Case Study: How the CUNY Graduate Center Increases Diversity the Right Way

In this final section, we look closely at an exemplary institutional case study that integrates recruitment and retention of diverse populations. Focused on the humanities and social sciences, the Pipeline Fellows Program at the City University of New York (CUNY) Graduate Center begins at the undergraduate level and continues through the PhD. It's a remarkably economical, streamlined program whose ambit extends from admissions to graduation. These concerted efforts enable the institution to fulfill the mission of an urban public university—and meet the ethical imperative of inclusive graduate admissions.

Two Pipeline Fellows Programs, undergraduate and graduate, dovetail at CUNY. The undergraduate program recruits promising students from the system's many branch campuses and exposes them to graduate school as a next-step possibility. The idea is not so much to get them to go to CUNY's Graduate Center (though some undergraduate fellows do) as to give them background knowledge and preparation for wherever they land after the BA. The graduate pipeline program recruits and admits diverse candidates to the university's one graduate school of arts and sciences. The two pipeline efforts are separate but connected, both housed in the graduate school's Office of Educational Opportunity and Diversity Programs, and encompass outreach, recruitment, admission, and retention.

The architect of this combined structure is Herman L. Bennett, a professor of history at the Graduate Center. His successes are instructive. Bennett didn't invent any new programs; instead, he changed how the existing ones operated and, in so doing, raised CUNY's diversity numbers. More important, his work helped change the collective understanding of diversity in the graduate school.

Both pipeline programs date back to the early 1990s but had underperformed for years. Three years after Bennett joined CUNY's faculty, he took on the position of executive officer of the graduate school's diversity office. During his six years at the helm—through 2019—he has unified and modified the two programs and in the process unlocked their potential.

Bennett started small. His work began in his own department, where he tried to cultivate what he calls "a culture of advising." Students "weren't being properly prepared," he said. "They came to me because I was pushing them." He spent his own research funds to send graduate students to archives abroad. "They came back and talked about it."[48]

When Bennett was offered the graduate school's top diversity job, there wasn't much to it at the time. "They gave me keys to an empty office," Bennett said, "and told me that I had to hire an administrative assistant and staff the place"—all while teaching his regular course load.

The programs themselves were hollow shells, languishing from lack of care. University-wide, there were just eight graduate fellowships designated for minority candidates. Applicants had to apply for admission to one of CUNY's doctoral programs and then attract the attention of that program's admissions committee. Only then could the PhD program propose the candidate for one of the eight diversity fellowships. At the time Bennett took over, many of the graduate programs—the CUNY Graduate Center has 32 in all—had never admitted a diversity fellow.

Bennett converted the program from eight full fellowships to 18 "top-ups"—that is, awards of $10,000 a year that were added to a student's initial offer of admission. The change not only increased the number of diversity fellows; it also aided the university's recruitment. "More students started applying and getting in," said Bennett, and graduate diversity at CUNY gained critical mass. And at the undergraduate level, 30 students, mainly from underrepresented groups, were chosen each year for the expanded program.

Bennett also gave the two pipeline programs substance and coherence. For example, he scheduled monthly gatherings of the fellows for mini-conferences devoted to career-development tasks like grant writing and publishing articles. These meetings contribute to "a culture of professionalization," said Bennett, in which the students learn about their place in the academic profession—or in professional life more generally.

The meetings also allow the fellows to see each other regularly, which strengthens the bonds between them. "I feel like I'm among colleagues," said Robert P. Robinson, a PhD student in the urban-education program. "It's a beautiful thing." Ashley Agbasoga, a PhD student in anthropology at Northwestern University who was in CUNY's undergraduate pipeline program, said it "felt like a family."[49]

Not surprisingly, attrition is not a problem among the graduate fellows. "Since I've been in this program we haven't lost a single grad student," said Bennett.

The commitment to professionalism is matched in the undergraduate pipeline program, which brings the group of 30 to the Graduate Center to introduce them to the world of graduate study. The undergraduate experience stretches over a year—from spring through the following fall. Before Bennett took over, "it was run as a place of occasional lunches," but "we reoriented the program around a summertime core," he said. Undergraduate fellows now attend a six-week, intensive summer introduction to graduate school. They take a humanities or social science course (depending on their interests) and a GRE preparation course. They also attend numerous meetings with experts that Bennett brings in. These commitments fill every day, from 9 a.m. to 6 p.m. And he instituted a practice of personally meeting with each student two or three times over the course of the summer.

The program supplies breakfast and lunch to the undergraduates, and they eat together. This promotes esprit de corps. The meals also supply simple nutrition for students who are, said Bennett, "overwhelmingly poor." Attendance went up when the program started providing meals, he recalled. "It changed the whole dynamic."

Student poverty requires alertness to other problems, too. Many Pipeliners live in households earning less than $30,000 a year. Many are responsible for contributing to their household income. Some are independent minors. "Every year," Bennett said, "there has been at least one student who is homeless." Graduate school does not usually contemplate, let alone anticipate, such acute levels of need. Bennett said simply, "We try to reach out as best we can." (The program pays them a summer stipend.) As a result, students emerge from their pipeline summer "fully charged. They know each other and themselves really well."

These ties cross the graduate-undergraduate boundary. Undergraduate Pipeliners are matched with graduate fellows in mentoring relationships, and many graduate student Pipeliners work in the summer program. There's also "quite a bit of peer mentoring going on," said Ethan Barnett, who was a Pipeliner at CUNY and is now a PhD student in history at the University of Delaware. The students serve each other as advisers, editors, counselors, and simply as narrators of their own experiences. In that way, said Bennett, "the students perpetuate their own culture." Many undergraduate Pipeliners apply to graduate school, and while they scatter around the country, a few always enroll at the CUNY Graduate Center.

Students relax and thrive in this culture. The program "gave me a space to sound like myself," said Michael Mena, a pipeline fellow and a PhD student in anthropology at CUNY. Without it, he said he "would have returned home." Sheneque Tissera, a former undergraduate Pipeliner, said the program helped her "understand who I am, and what I need to do to succeed." Tissera left graduate school with a master's degree in geography to pursue a career in entertainment, but she nevertheless credits the program with pushing her "to follow my dreams."

It's hard to overstate the importance of this work. On one hand, it's an extraordinary instance of, as Bennett put it, "being present and offering them the resources that we can." On the other hand, it's the creation of what he described as "both a culture of diversity and a culture of inclusion." The creation of such a "cohort effect" is the point of important philanthropic diversity initiatives like the Mellon Foundation's Mellon-Mays Undergraduate Fellowship Program, which funds similar efforts at dozens of campuses nationwide and abroad.[50] At CUNY, it's nurtured a culture that Tissera described as "totally geared toward the student."

Bennett's exemplary work offers his institution—and all of higher education—a chance to "rethink what we mean by the public interest, what the university is, and how underrepresented people fit into it," and something more: "how they're constitutive of it."

The CUNY example, along with the others we've cited in this chapter, shows how admissions is more than a student gateway to graduate school. For faculty and administration, it's a gateway of a different sort, an entrance not just to guard (or gatekeep) but to reflect on. When we think about how we do admissions, we necessarily have to think about how we do graduate school as a whole.

We end this chapter by stressing the need to uncover and question assumptions. The GRE is only one example of an unquestioned assumption enshrined in the form of a highly consequential procedure. We therefore ask how a proposed revision of a doctoral program could be reflected in the application evidence that faculty members consider. These are questions of diversity of different kinds—including intellectual—and of scholarship itself.

[FIVE]

Student Support and Time to Degree

Today's critics of doctoral education aim their rapiers in many directions, but most of them are pointed at three hard facts:

1. It takes too long to get a PhD.
2. There aren't enough professorships for those who do.
3. And a corollary of the first two: for those willing to brave the gantlet, graduate school costs too much.

We need to face those facts two ways. First, we have to consider them as related parts of a larger whole, a greater graduate school reality. Next, all stakeholders need to get on board. That is, these facts need to be taken up by faculty, administrators, and students together.

For years, says John McGreevy, former dean of the College of Arts and Letters at Notre Dame, "there was the sense that 'it's fine, no problem' for graduate students to stay seven or eight years—and then not get an academic job."[1] That belief is changing, but slowly. And the facts that drive it aren't changing much at all. How can we build a graduate program in which students can finish their doctorates without enormous opportunity cost and significant debt before they reach middle age, and also prepare themselves for the diversity of careers before them (including academia) when they reach the finish line?

The urgency of these questions comes down to ethics. We have no right to claim nearly a decade of our students' lives, or any of their time at all, without giving them something useful in return. Once upon a time, long ago, the question "What is graduate school for?" had a simple answer: it was an apprenticeship. Doctoral students put in their years (fewer years then, it turned out), received a specific training, and in exchange they were given a likely ticket into the professoriate.

That bargain lasted for a short postwar generation. Graduate school cannot legitimately be considered an apprenticeship anymore. There's no promise of a pot of professorial gold or indeed, much promise of anything specific at all—and the COVID-19 pandemic will only worsen the situation. The bankruptcy of the apprenticeship model has contributed to the rise of the graduate student labor movement—and understandably so, because if graduate students aren't apprentices, then they have to be workers, and workers have rights. The purpose of graduate school has become more complicated, and it's past time that we contoured it to meet those complications. We can't afford to fall asleep at the pedagogical wheel, and neither can our graduate students.

Time to Degree—a Calendar for Sanity

Consider the shared expectation in the United States that a college degree will take four years. Lots of people share that expectation: not only faculty and administrators but also (and especially) students and their parents. But what if undergraduate programs didn't begin with that norm? What if colleges simply listed all desirable achievements for undergraduates, with the assumption that when their professors thought the students had attained enough of them, they would confer degrees upon them? College might then take 8 or 10 years, and it's hard to imagine that students and their parents would stand for it. But that's essentially what we have done with the PhD. Let's start there.

The problem of a ridiculously long and costly number of years to earn the doctorate has many components. Expected time to degree has become more and more vague, and demands for achievement have multiplied. Perhaps the most concerning is a deadly inertia that has led us to require more and more of graduate students, as if the doctorate were the last stage of knowing, rather than a moment that leads beyond itself.

It is also the case that time to degree is longest in those fields where academic job prospects are poorest. In disciplines like history and English, typically only a few PhD recipients will end up as permanent faculty at research universities or colleges. Which raises another reason for protracted progress: Why leave, if students see nowhere to go?

Yet there are plenty of places to go if doctoral graduates are encouraged to interpret their abilities differently, and if faculty can reward the success of students who don't necessarily become professional clones of their teachers. Graduate students won't want to linger in a safe but low economic and professional stratum if they perceive a next place to go. A differently conceived graduate school, working with the university career center, alumni office, and regional organizations and businesses, can help them draw a map to get to the destination they choose.

Time to degree, even when calculated most conservatively (as actual years when a student is actively engaged in pursuing the doctorate, as opposed to a master's at the outset), yields troubling results. Most data shows that eight years is the norm in the humanities and six to seven in the sciences. But as is well known, scientists instead face an indefinite series of postdoctoral years in addition. In a field like neuroscience, that postdoctoral period "stretches to four or five years."[2] For many scientists, a postdoctoral living on "soft money" has become the equivalent of the professional adjunct in the humanities and the humanistic social sciences. But even without postdocs, the median age for graduates in the humanities is 34.2 as of 2014, surely one of the world's longest periods of adolescence.[3]

Time to degree pressures graduate students. We're suggesting that it should also pressure faculty and administrators. Moreover, in ways that are too easy to overlook, time to degree also matters to people who aren't in graduate school at all. When a doctorate takes so many years to complete, many students, especially the less well off, are discouraged from going to graduate school in the first place. "The result," writes Louis Menand, "is a narrowing of the intellectual range and diversity of those entering." That's bad enough by itself, but as Menand says, it gets worse, because this lack of intellectual diversity widens the "philosophical and attitudinal gap" between academics and "nonacademic intellectuals" and so contributes to the national town-and-gown problem that has fueled so much public misunderstanding—and caricature—of higher education.[4] So time to degree is not a niche issue. It affects everyone who cares about graduate school.

Because of the perpetual shortage of academic positions and a general resistance within the university to embrace the roles of intellectuals beyond the academy, the competition for those few academic jobs has sharpened to an almost unbearable edge. Consequently, we have witnessed greater and greater demands upon doctoral students to publish while in school, rather than work directly toward graduation. In other words, the situation of an absurdly protracted, economically and emotionally stressful adolescence has become much worse.

We're aware that some of the adjustments that we are urging in this book have the potential to add new demands that could lengthen the PhD. Our intent, instead, is to help programs abbreviate time to degree and provide a consistent and livable level of financial support to students as they pursue it. We'll talk about the faculty's responsibility presently, but let's start with encouraging student accountability.

The balance between carrots and sticks is central to this question of shortening the time to degree, and that balance proves surprisingly complex. To begin with, time to degree is not a problem that we can simply throw money at, even if there's money available to throw. We've known this for a while. The Ford Foundation Graduate Program, instituted in 1967, offered generous stipends to graduate students in the latter years of their studies. The goal was to hasten their time to degree. The result? The opposite. Students used the money not to get out faster but instead to stay longer and do more. The program folded after seven years.[5]

The well-funded Mellon GEI initiative (which we outlined in chapter 1) similarly aimed to lessen time to degree. That effort didn't succeed either. It did generate important findings, such as that "slower completers had significantly lower numbers of publications" and "less success on the [academic] job market."[6] At first glance, this finding suggests that the publishing "arms race" may not extend time to degree greatly; this outcome seems to counter common wisdom. But we would suggest that the Mellon result argues instead that programs that encourage timely completion instill a professional and energetic attitude in students that results in quality work. And to generalize from that finding would elide the salient fact that the Mellon study encompassed only programs that can support students more generously than most.

Early completion—with or without published work—should obviously be tied to financial support. The question is how. Since Mellon's disappointing GEI results, several examples have shown that financial rewards can actually help reduce time to degree, but only if the money acts as an incentive. The geography department at the University of Minnesota, under the chairship of John Adams, introduced three tiers of pay for graduate students, one for new students, a second for holders of a master's degree, and a third for ABDs. "The differences in pay were not great," says Adams, "but to the students the differences were a significant motivator."[7]

Brandeis University employed a contractual agreement between adviser, student, and university as part of its dissertation completion fellowship program. These fellowships, also funded by Mellon, carried a large final-year stipend and teaching release, but with the important difference that students needed to sign a contract before they received the first check that recorded their vow to finish the degree within a year. Results were encouraging: students adhered to the terms of the contract and finished on time.[8]

The incentive can also take the form of an extra year or two of funding of a different sort. Notre Dame offers a carrot-and-stick combination that they call a "5 + 1" program. The carrot: students who finish in five years get an extra year of full support at a regular salary, with benefits. The stick is that if students don't finish in five years, funding for the sixth year is by application. It isn't guaranteed. (We'll discuss the Notre Dame example at greater length later in this chapter.) Vanderbilt University similarly provides a one-year, full-time lectureship to students who finish in five years, and the University of California at Irvine has a 5 + 2 program, also funded by Mellon, that offers a two-year term as a clinical (i.e., teaching-centered) assistant professor to graduate students who finish in five years.[9]

Even if programs gain new efficiency through these strategic incentives, difficult decisions remain: Which present requirements and practices should be eliminated, or else streamlined, to speed students up? It's far easier in academia to add than to subtract, but there's a limit to what programs can hold, and especially to what students' lives can bear. Here we return to one of our consistent themes in this book: that programs reflect on their practice. Consider each program requirement in terms of how much student time and faculty effort it requires in relation to its importance. Such a review may result in doing away with some program aspects—or not. More likely, the review will encourage different, more efficient ways to achieve the same ends.

Time to degree is the arena where reformers and traditionalists most often contend. George Walker, writing for the Carnegie Initiative on the Doctorate, calls attention to evolving standards for entry-level academic jobs. "Where the gold standard for newly minted Ph.D.s twenty-five years ago was likely to be the promise of significant research productivity," he said, "today's job postings . . . are likely to call for 'a proven record of success,' a 'history of publication' and 'demonstrated facility' in the teaching area."[10] Walker wrote those words almost a generation ago. As academic jobs have become harder to get since then, "new elements" have been added to programs, and old ones have rarely been excised to make room. More and more demonstrated achievement is now required, when potential was once sufficient—and achievement takes years.

Clearly, the cost (including opportunity cost) of the lengthy doctorate to institutions and individuals is exorbitant and may push any number of talented students away from the PhD. It also reduces the time of what chemist Alvin Kwiram terms "the window of creativity"[11] when scientists finally can propose their own programs of research. At an opposing extreme to the status quo, Menand urges a three-year doctorate with a publishable article substituting for a dissertation in nonscience fields. Kwiram notes that "students in the United Kingdom are expected to complete their Ph.D. studies in three years" with exceptions made only reluctantly, while students in Germany typically take three years after earning the equivalent of an master's degree, thus five years overall.[12] The implication is that the United States ought to be able to follow suit.

Many faculty members nevertheless see their program requirements as utterly necessary. We ask that programs consider such practical matters as their students' finances and timely progress in life. Here we want again to invoke an ethical imperative. Graduate students trust faculty with their time, the one thing that once they spend, they can never recover. When professors accept students into a graduate program, they accept a responsibility to honor that trust. Practical concerns obviously matter to students, but they ought to matter to their teachers as well.

The Mellon Foundation Graduate Education Initiative researchers finally surrendered to faculty opinion, admitting that professors simply did not see time to degree as an important concern. "Insisting on 'fast' degrees," they concluded, "is likely to evoke resistance from faculty members, whose role in graduate education is central."[13] The GEI goal for a "fast" degree had been six years. That a six-year norm should seem radical suggests how extreme the situation had become—and remains. The Mellon researchers started out favoring "incentives and deadlines for satisfactory progress." They also observed that "those who took eight years or longer to complete their degrees (about half of the sample) were less likely to find jobs on the tenure track than their counterparts who finished more quickly."[14]

Delivered in dispassionate prose, these findings from the Mellon study remain trenchant. Faster completion helps students. We hope that such findings will ready institutions to confront resistance to a faster path. Without one, would-be guardians of the integrity of their discipline may find that they will cripple its viability. This is an unexamined idealism that loses gifted applicants to the professions and harms those it may still attract.

The Mellon researchers identified three factors as most crucial in shortening time to degree: clear expectations, better advising, and better financial support tied to requirements for timely progress.[15] They may not have succeeded in shortening time to degree at their target programs in the GEI study, but we believe they failed because the programs themselves did not subscribe to these guidelines, and Mellon lacked an enforcement mechanism. In other words, the ideas were good, but they weren't matched by good execution. The more recent results—some also supported by Mellon—at Brandeis, Vanderbilt, Notre Dame, and Irvine suggest some possible ways forward.

Other suggestions to decrease time to degree include streamlining predissertation examinations. Programs can do this either by offering summer courses to prepare students or by including the requirement of a dissertation prospectus as a part of the exam. (We'll consider these options more fully in chapter 6, on curriculum and exams.)

But for all of that, not every student will finish the PhD. We've considered ways to limit attrition to acceptable levels elsewhere in this book (see chapter 4), but educators also need to pay attention to the actual people who don't finish and learn from their experience.

Some have suggested terminal MA degrees that would serve as an early off-ramp to careers outside the professoriate. That's more complicated than it sounds. For one thing, the master's degree in many arts and sciences fields has no clear purpose, and accordingly, many universities have eliminated it entirely. Some struggling graduate schools have sought money-making possibilities in master's degrees of different kinds, from international politics and economic development to health care ethics. We believe that master's degrees in the arts and sciences are worthwhile as long as they lead somewhere. That is, they must have value for the student, not just to the graduate school's bottom line.

Some doctoral students might choose instead to exit with a master's degree if that degree meant something, and if it were a credential with clear use. However, in most fields it possesses neither attribute, and that fact is our own sad legacy of negligence toward the degree. Historically, the rise of the PhD came at the expense of the master's. We have denigrated the master's degree for so long that its rehabilitation will be difficult.[16]

Yet the professional master's program in various scientific fields has proven remarkably attractive and successful. It's plausible to consider professionally oriented MA degrees in the humanities and social sciences as well, especially given the emphasis on career diversity and the goal of ethnic and racial diversity of students. We recognize that this will be a long and hard row to hoe because we academics have done so much historically to make the land untillable. But the recovery of a viable master's degree is a worthy goal, as it may participate in the creation of better outcomes for doctoral and master's students alike.

A professional master's degree in a nonscience field would require careful design and most likely, foundation support to prepare for its launch.[17] Such programs would have to make money from students paying tuition (fellowships being unlikely at that level), so the degree would have to be worth something to its holders. Starting a professional master's degree in the sciences entails meetings between faculty and employers to establish an understanding of what sort of preparation students should have. Professional master's degrees in the nonscience fields would have to do the same. And it seems clear that a professional master's degree in a nonscience field should include an internship of some sort to emphasize its professional status. We will consider this prospect further in chapter 9.

Professional development finally unites the issues here. Whether graduate students are studying for a master's or a doctorate, for a professorship or a different career, graduate programs have to prepare them for their possible outcomes, and we have to do it in a reasonable and responsible period of time.

What's the takeaway, then? We suggest that clarity of program requirements should include a timeline tied to continued aid and that aid should encourage completion. Summer stipends and internships, along with focused and continuous mentoring, all matter here. We'll address these more fully in the last section of this chapter, on student support.

First, we present a case study for discussion.

5 + 1 at Notre Dame

The example of Notre Dame deserves attention because the university is trying to create a culture of early PhD completion. We've already mentioned how the institution offers an extra year of funded support to PhD students who finish the degree within five years. Students who fail to finish in that time have to apply for a sixth year of funding, which is likely but not guaranteed.

Let's look closely at that carrot-and-stick combination. By themselves, threats of punishment usually fail to speed graduate students' progress, and faculty and administrators have proved understandably unwilling to ratchet up the penalties. Who really wants to expel students who are stuck after they've already invested so much sweat and treasure? Better to try to help them—and to give them real incentives.

Notre Dame's 5 + 1 program, led by John McGreevy, then the dean of the College of Arts and Letters, tackled the problem in that spirit. The 5 + 1 program advances a solution grounded in pedagogy. It's a worthy and promising attempt to meet one of the most vexing educational and, as we've said, ethical challenges facing every graduate school.

We've mentioned programs at Vanderbilt and Irvine that also offer incentives for early completion. We endorse the incentive model generally; it's one of the few strategies that has shown signs of budging the stubborn time-to-degree figures. What distinguishes Notre Dame's version is that it privileges professional development. The extra year's salary is important, of course, but more crucially, students get a university-supported year of career building, enabled by a reduced teaching load and a special professional development budget for each graduate.

At Notre Dame, then, the extra year isn't so much a teaching job as an invitation to the newly minted PhD to think about what comes next. If the new graduate is looking beyond academia, an off-campus internship—in a different city or a different country—can replace half a year's teaching. And graduates can apply for academic jobs at the same time as they test these alternatives. The goal is bridge building, not bridge burning.

Second, the Notre Dame program is remarkable for its integration. The five-year goal—marked from the point at which students begin graduate study—applies to all arts and sciences disciplines. The university's graduate students are socialized to expect to finish in five years, and faculty teach toward that goal. The 5 + 1 goal is for all students, not just the exceptional or the precocious. For McGreevy, the guiding question to departments was, "Have you built a program so that a student who's good, but not unbelievably good, can finish in five years?"

A five-year degree starts with annual funding packages that cover students for 12 months at a time, not just the nine months of the academic year. Year-round support is commonplace in the sciences but not in the humanities and humanistic social sciences, yet the Mellon GEI researchers emphasized how important it can be. If graduate school is to be a time-limited, end-focused pursuit, then programs have to free their students from the annual scramble for summer money. Twelve-month support especially helps students who need to develop language proficiencies. They typically use the summer funding to do that.

But a five-year PhD requires more than committed graduate students. It demands commitment from professors, too. Perhaps the most important ingredient of Notre Dame's 5 + 1 program is the faculty commitment to marking students' progress—and helping them reach the benchmarks on the way to the degree. Graduate programs at Notre Dame aim to get students into the dissertation by the halfway mark. "A lot of the planning went into this part," said McGreevy.

Before the program became policy, departments reflected on their predissertation requirements. They became "more intentional" in their course offerings, McGreevy said, and experimented with linking and sequencing courses in rotation. Some have also encouraged team teaching of larger-scoped topics (for example, a course on colonialism instead of the colonial stage of a given country).

The 5 + 1 program was formally instituted at Notre Dame in 2016. In the planning phase, the dean's office asked programs to examine their requirements during the comprehensive exam year, including the teaching requirements students face. Some departments rethought the structure of their comprehensive exams. The English and history departments reduced the number of required fields to be covered. At the same time, they each added one field specifically linked to a student's proposed dissertation topic and another section based on teaching, in which candidates present a syllabus and defend it.

The last mile to the five-year degree is the steepest, because it contains the dissertation. History departments nationwide have engaged in particularly fractious debate around the shape and scope of the dissertation in recent years, so we were particularly interested in how Notre Dame's history department was handling the challenge. The solution, said department chair Patrick Griffin, is "pretty simple," but it's pretty demanding at the same time.[18]

"We work on teaching students how to work," said Griffin. The program focuses on "a few key points" in each student's course of study. "The first is getting the proposal done and defended. We keep a tight rein on deadlines." (The proposal is due in October of the third year.) "We then focus on how to do the research," said Griffin. Students "start in the library, so the archival visits can be as productive as possible." Next comes "the transition from research to writing," said Griffin. Professors encourage students to write—"even before they feel ready to do so," he said—because that strategy avoids the pitfall of perfectionism and "gets them thinking early on about broad themes and narrative structure."

"We also tell them that writing is a daily discipline," Griffin said. "Advisers let students know that they have to hold themselves accountable on a daily basis for pages and word counts, and that this discipline can stand them well throughout a career." None of that discipline is necessarily obvious to graduate students. "They see unlimited amounts of time—time that can suck away tangible goals," Griffin said.

Detail- and deadline-oriented advising continues for doctoral students in history right through chapter and draft deadlines and through that key fifth year. "It means," said Griffin, "that advisers have to be more engaged." Indeed. We've described the department's process of dissertation advising in some detail because it's critical to bringing students' dissertations into port by year five, and because it's so different from the usual solitary practices of advisers. (We'll discuss that issue of advisers working in isolation at greater length in chapter 7.)

Consider the steady repetition of the word "we" in Griffin's description. When professors work together to develop a course of instruction, students get a more coherent picture of what they need to do. Such collaboration among a community of teachers happens often enough at liberal arts colleges, but it's a rare thing at universities, especially at the graduate level. Its rarity stems from the idealization of graduate school as an individualistic pursuit for both the students (who design their own specialized projects) and the faculty (who advise "their" graduate students). That cubicle-oriented thinking, in which intellectuals labor in isolation on what ought in every way to be a common mission, is hurting graduate education and the image of the university generally. A coherent sense of faculty community helps each individual student and the whole at the same time.

With a plan like this, Notre Dame spotlights the "school" part of graduate school. The 5 + 1 program depends on more than setting deadlines; it requires hands-on teaching by professors who seek out students instead of waiting for them to drop by. Yes, Notre Dame is rich. (The university ranks in the nation's top 25 in endowment dollars per student.) The institution's wealth surely helped it to build this model. But the program's value depends not so much on dollars as on attitude. What separates Notre Dame's 5 + 1 program from its competitors is the active and concerted commitment to teaching that's built into it. If we want graduate students to finish sooner, we have to teach them better. We can do that better if we approach the task together.

Notre Dame's 5 + 1 program certainly isn't perfect. The program was devised without graduate student input and introduced suddenly. The enthusiasm of administrators to roll out the program as quickly as possible led to some anxiety and resentment among graduate students who were admitted under one regime and suddenly shifted to another. The lack of transparency, combined with the rapid pace of the changes, created friction that might have been avoided.

A practical concern of 5 + 1 at Notre Dame is that one size has to fit all. That is, the 5 + 1 program makes no distinctions between the demands of different disciplines or fields within a discipline. Students in medieval studies, for example (which is typically a large specialty at Notre Dame and other Catholic universities), need to acquire more languages than, say, students of contemporary British history—but it's 5 + 1 for both. (This difference may have ramifications for admissions: if medievalists have to finish in five years, then Notre Dame might have to consider admitting into those programs only students who have some languages already and be less willing to take a chance on a more interesting but less well-prepared applicant.)

Similarly, the pressure to finish in five years affects the sorts of dissertation topics that students may choose. Should graduate students be encouraged to write expansive dissertations? Maybe or maybe not, but immovable 5 + 1 deadlines will make it hard to do so at a place like Notre Dame. These concerns segue to the topic of student support, which we will consider next.

Student Support: The Answer Is Not Just Money, but What Exactly Is the Question?

Graduate student support begins with money. When a student is admitted to a doctoral program in the arts and sciences, admission is usually accompanied by an offer of financial aid, consisting of some combination of fellowship support, teaching stipends, research assistantships, and benefits such as reduced-cost health care. An obvious and continuing challenge for many institutions is a scarcity of funds.

Let us begin our discussion of support with a postulate: *graduate programs should pay their students enough for them to live reasonably while they study*. More precisely, students should receive a level of financial support over a period of time sufficient for completion of the degree. And it should be enough money to allow a student to live modestly but not meanly, without going into debt. Graduate students in the arts and sciences typically do not chase the kinds of jobs that would allow them to pay off large amounts of student debt without pain. Let's set their pay at a level that will allow them to avoid borrowing in the first place.*

All PhD students should receive this financial guarantee. It's widely and generally understood—in academia, at least—that doctoral programs in the arts and sciences are not expected to make a profit; they represent the university's investment in itself as well as its students. (Master's programs are another story; we'll take those up later in this section and in chapter 9, on degrees.)

Graduate students represent that investment in visible and valuable ways. They represent the university wherever they go not only during their graduate careers but also, and more importantly, afterward. They require a baseline level of financial support. We're deliberately avoiding specific numbers here. Cost of living varies widely from place to place and over time. Instead, we call on graduate programs to allot money to meet a standard that reflects the difficulty, length, and uncertainty of the doctoral mission in these challenging times.

As we discussed in chapter 4 on admissions, the widespread downsizing of doctoral cohorts in the arts and sciences has generally increased levels of support for the smaller number of students who gain admission to PhD programs. But is it enough?

At most programs, the answer appears to be, not yet. Funding of graduate students varies widely from school to school and field to field, but it remains low, considering the time to degree—which is itself affected by the amount of teaching that graduate students do to support

---

* Full support for full (though smaller) student cohorts has become more common in the past decade, since the 2008 economic downturn led to a jobless nonrecovery for academia. A few years before that, the Mellon GEI researchers observed that while such support may attract talented students to graduate study and improve their lives while in school, "fellowship recipients did not have appreciably higher rates of completion than their classmates, nor did they have substantially shorter [time to degree]." They argued that "students with guaranteed funding stay longer and drop out later than they would have done" without any guarantee. The original intent of the initiative had been to make funding in the selected programs conditional upon "achieving specified steps toward the degree," but this never happened.

In these times, we might view the Mellon findings as an indication that more aid without more planning and program reform is not a good bargain for institutions, other than as a recruiting method.

themselves in the humanities and humanistic social sciences. Stipends have risen, but not always with the cost of living. We mentioned earlier the surprise of the English department chair at Columbia who learned from a student survey that most of the students that his department considered fully funded needed outside jobs to support themselves.[19] Furthermore, graduate students, like undergraduates, take out loans to finance their degrees. Students borrow an average of $25,000 for graduate study, and their degrees do not necessarily lead to the jobs that they expect.[20] Further, health insurance for graduate students has become a major source of campus tension. As graduate students have lost benefits, we should hardly wonder why they've turned to labor activism to protect their entitlements.[21]

The Graduate Funding Initiative at Washington University in St. Louis is a good example of how centralized funding can result in thoughtfully considered student support. All students admitted to a PhD program at Washington University receive some kind of stipend support (fellowship or assistantship) for a maximum of six years, provided they remain in good academic standing. Faculty are strongly committed to this approach, because new student admission is linked at Washington University to completion of the doctorate by currently enrolled students.

Key to the Graduate Funding Initiative is that a central authority (the graduate school) allocates resources to programs. Each year, the overall number of graduate students admitted is based on the division of money into tuition remissions and stipends for graduate students. Each year, individual departments submit requests for teaching assistants needed for the year, along with written justification for any increase in number over the previous year. Departments are then allocated resources according to disciplinary and market standards; the hiring process of placing students in the actual positions is handled at the program level.*

---

*This is just one example of how a centralized graduate school with an empowered dean is crucial to the quality of programs and the well-being of students.

When it comes to funding graduate students, the sciences have specific issues that differ from those in non-laboratory disciplines, and we pause here to discuss the economics of science degree programs generally.

Science and engineering have been the fastest-growing PhD areas. For a decade beginning in 2002, while student enrollment in other fields declined slightly (by 1.5 percent), science and engineering grew by 45 percent. These days, science and engineering students receive around 70 percent of all PhDs awarded in the United States each year.[22] Their programs resemble those in other fields in that they're primarily faculty centered, but they rely less on institutional infrastructure.[23]

Much of the student funding in the sciences, far more than in the humanities or humanistic social sciences, is external to the university. It takes the form of research assistantships, training grants, and public or private fellowships. The need for external support has often contributed to, and in some ways determined, the specific design of programs in the bench sciences. The laboratory lies at the center of graduate student experience in these fields. Accordingly, doctoral education in the bench sciences has generally been characterized by some course preparation, but mostly by apprentice-type research experiences directed by a single faculty member who runs the lab that the student joins early on. Once the student joins a professor's lab, that professor—now the student's adviser—pays the student's stipend out of the lab's budget. As part of the same economic logic, the student's subsequent work is tied strongly to that faculty member's research interests.

The university contributes a portion of the lab's budget, but the enterprise requires grant support to run, and a significant chunk of the faculty director's time is spent applying for these grants. The largest number of available grants are research grants—that is, grants to fund particular scientific projects. By contrast, training grants—which are much scarcer—privilege the student's own research questions and learning. We've discussed the predominance of research grants over training grants in previous chapters—it's one of the parts of science graduate education that doesn't work very well.

Teaching is too often an afterthought in science graduate education. For science students, support through teaching is seen as a consolation prize for students not included in research grant support. The result is an underemphasis on pedagogical training. (We will take up that issue further in chapter 8.) As competition for outside grant support ratchets ever tighter, it exacerbates the long-standing issue of the predominance of research assistantships in the sciences.

The example of graduate students in the sciences laboring on research grants shows that money is only one form of graduate student support. Enough money is important—hence our beginning postulate—but when it comes to support, money is a subset of something larger.

So here's a second postulate: *student support is more than a matter of money*. It's necessary to pay grad students adequately, but it's just as necessary to help them design the jobs that we're paying them to do.

Because graduate school is, after all, a job. Graduate students inhabit the academic workplace as colleagues as well as pupils. Faculty encourage them to acquire and hone professional skills and expertise related to their disciplinary specialty. Their workplace should make sense to them and to their teachers.

Here too, an ethical imperative underlies the faculty's role. To help students complete their degrees with productive alacrity, professors have to involve themselves in their students' work. Graduate students deserve a coherent education in terms of both curriculum and professional development. The troubles facing doctoral programs in these times make that coherence difficult to achieve but hardly impossible. Consider the example of Notre Dame: the administration and the faculty got together and designed a template for graduate study that weaves together curriculum and professional development. Doing so required—and still requires—ongoing faculty collaboration and open partnership with students. These things require time and effort, not necessarily money.

We detail practices throughout this book that aim at the kind of coherence that we're describing here. A thoughtfully designed, student-centered graduate program is, in the end, an important form of student support.

Graduate Student Internships at Lehigh

The Lehigh English department's analysis of PhD career outcomes showed that doctoral students benefited from gaining work experience outside the discipline, so professors built that option into the curriculum revision that they undertook beginning in 2013.

Along with the usual teaching assistantships, the department established graduate assistantships outside the undergraduate classroom. "We saw that some of our students who got tenure-track jobs worked in the Global Citizenship program," said graduate director Jenna Lay. Helping to supervise a study-abroad trip "expanded their professional capacity." So the faculty planners generalized from that finding and arranged internship opportunities with other offices across the campus. English graduate students may now—as a substitute for a TA stint—choose to work for a year at the Office of First-Year Experience or the Center for Gender Equity, among others. Lay described such jobs as "super-GA positions." The students do programming, public teaching—"whatever needs doing"—and gain different kinds of professional experience.

Sarah Heidebrink-Bruno, an advanced doctoral student in English at Lehigh, recalled that her GA work at Lehigh's Women's Center (now the Center for Gender Equity) "taught me to appreciate all of the different kinds of educational work that happens at a university, not just from the faculty side." She subsequently undertook another GA-ship working to train undergraduate writing tutors. "I would love to continue to work with students in some capacity," she said, and may pursue a career in student affairs.

Heidebrink-Bruno's GA work has also affected the direction of her dissertation research. Her project now "blends more traditional literary analysis and applied pedagogical practices that foster social justice in higher education." Most important, Heidebrink-Bruno is glad and grateful for this evolution of her work and goals: "I guess you could say that I fell in love with books first, and books brought me to graduate school, where I then fell in love with teaching. Then having a GA-ship broadened my understanding of teaching and education, and I realized that what I really love is talking about big ideas and working with young people—and if I had the chance to do that kind of work in the future, I think that would make me really happy."

Jimmy Hamill, a doctoral student in English at an earlier stage, worked as a GA at Lehigh's Pride Center. "Seeing some of my colleagues and mentors take on GA-ships communicated to me that there were options beyond the traditional tenure-track path that were just as valid and important in higher education," he said. The job itself "has allowed me to explore my own interests as a scholar-activist." Like Heidebrink-Bruno, Hamill has found that his GA work is shaping his intellectual identity and goals. "Theoretically," he said, "the GA-ship has challenged me to consider how intersectional methodologies and theories inform the kinds of questions I may want to answer on my comp exams." As he eloquently put it, he has gained "a clearer understanding of my 'why?'"

That's exactly the kind of takeaway the professors were hoping for. "We want our students to have a capacious understanding of the possibilities available to them," Lay said. We want to emphasize this critical goal of self-aware understanding. It means nothing to equip someone with tools if they don't realize that they have them. Likewise important is the pleasure that comes from knowing that you have options.

"We don't really have a lot of opportunities to speak about what genuinely brings us joy in graduate school," Heidebrink-Bruno said. Lehigh's GA positions "help us to think about all of the skills and talents we've gained from our program." In that light, she said, a nonfaculty career path appears "not as a cop-out, but as a viable choice that could also make us as happy."

The department's goal is to stay attuned to what students are experiencing in their GA positions and to the "individualized pathways" they are following to the PhD. Because doctoral education, carefully curated, takes time and attention, the department has reduced its PhD admissions from four to six students annually to two to four a year. (It also increased the number of master's students—fully funded—from 5–6 a year to 8–10 a year.) It's easier to keep tabs on a smaller graduate cohort and use the information collected about them to make further adjustments in graduate training. In that way, Lehigh's English department has changed not just its curriculum, Lay said, but its "ways of thinking about graduate education."

Programmatic support is especially needful today because doctoral education in the arts and sciences is now a 12-month a year job. Graduate students in some fields once shifted into a lower gear in the summertime. Many (especially those in the humanities and humanistic social sciences) needed to work for extra money at jobs unrelated to their studies. No longer can they afford to do this. Interdisciplinarity, a growing aspect of graduate education, takes time, for example. If programs are to encourage their students to work across disciplinary boundaries, says Kenneth Prewitt, such a move "requires equally ambitious changes in administrative and budgeting strategies," including student support.[24]

For this and other reasons, year-round professional development is a must for graduate students now. An important Mellon finding from the GEI study emphasizes the importance of summer support. "Targeted funding during the summer has great potential to improve both the efficiency and the quality of the education of scholars," write the researchers. "It requires modest resources and permits students to focus on graduate study."[25] We see a growing realization in the years since the GEI that graduate students need support all year long, but implementation of this awareness remains difficult. Some programs have succeeded at it. Beginning in 2019, the Graduate Funding Initiative at Washington University extended graduate stipend support to 12 months. And here too, we can look to the Notre Dame example: their program incorporates summer funding into its design.

The reality of career diversity likewise calls for expanded student support, and not necessarily of a financial variety. In particular, we encourage programs to expand opportunities for graduate student internships. Instead of a teaching assistantship one semester, a student might intern in an off-campus workplace or intramurally, in an office of the university itself, such as publications and media, student affairs, or development. At the University of California, Davis, a year-long Professors for the Future fellowship allows graduate students to work on a project that will enhance their peers' graduate or postdoctoral training. And the University of North Carolina's Royster Society of Fellows provides mentoring and professional development opportunities to selected students. Lehigh University's English department has developed a suite of on-campus opportunities during the past decade.

The example of internships shows particularly clearly how the issues we have been considering (money, summer support, career diversity) come together under the larger rubric of student support generally. We call in this book for a student-centered vision of graduate education. When we consider the meaning of student support, we can answer the question by asking what students need.

With need in mind, we close this chapter with a question. Financial need is rarely (and barely) considered in funding decisions for graduate programs, a practice that favors students from affluent families. Here as with many current practices, we need to ask, simply, why?

[SIX]

Curing the Curriculum and Examining the Exam

An Outcomes-Based Curriculum

There's an old Jewish folk story about a man who lives with his family in a one-room house that's crowded and noisy. He goes to the village rabbi for advice, and the rabbi suggests that he move his farm animals into the house with his family. The man is puzzled, but he complies, and the noise and disorder multiply. Now distraught, the man returns to the rabbi. At this point the rabbi advises the man to move the animals back outside. Before long, the man comes back to the rabbi. He gratefully reports that with just his family in the house, all is now quiet and peaceful.[1]

Let's begin this discussion of curriculum with a thought experiment in the spirit of the story. Imagine an inventory-reduction sale on program requirements. In *The Marketplace of Ideas*, Louis Menand argues for a three-year PhD. Maybe you don't agree with Menand on a three-year limit in the doctorate, but pretend that you do. Have four varied but highly respected faculty members with administrative smarts and empathy for students each design a three-year doctorate adapted from your current program design. Then have them meet as a subgroup to agree on a best proposal.

You need not consider that proposal in total. Instead, focus on what it eliminates from the current doctoral program. We know we need to add some elements to create a more student-centered and effective PhD. But we can't just lengthen the already overlong timeline. So what goes away?

For each member of this little task force to do his or her work, we might suggest looking to our earlier chapter on "planning backward." To reverse-engineer the curriculum, we can focus on a single question: What do we expect every doctoral graduate of our program to be good at? (We choose this phrasing because the alternative of what each graduating student should "know" would emphasize content at the expense of abilities, and we want room for both.)

There may be a faculty member (or several) who finds even the idea of encompassing "every student" an imposition on individuality. But the definition of "curriculum" implies a plan, and if we give up on that, it eventually becomes impossible to argue for a "program" or even a "discipline" at all. Short of anarchy, we need agreement on a set of core capacities.

The sciences—both in the dicta of their national disciplinary associations and in the norms of individual faculty—are less skittish than the humanities about this, and the 2018 *Graduate STEM Education for the 21st Century* report provides a list of 10 "core elements of the Ph.D. degree" for all science disciplines. This list can serve as a helpful starting point for other disciplines as well. Developed out of a "Call for Community Input" effort, the 10 elements are divided into two groupings, with seven under the heading "Develop Scientific and Technological Literacy and Conduct Original Research" and the other three under a second heading, "Develop Leadership, Communication, and Professional Competencies." The two lists reflect the same dual but intermingled and complementary purpose that we espouse.[2]

The first category, on scientific literacy and research, contains these seven items:

1. Develop deep specialized expertise in at least one STEM discipline.

2. Acquire sufficient transdisciplinary literacy to suggest multiple conceptual and methodological approaches to a complex problem.
3. Identify an important problem and articulate an original research question.
4. Design a research strategy, including relevant quantitative, analytical, or theoretical approaches, to explore components of the problem and begin to address the question.
5. Evaluate outcomes of each experiment or study component and select which to pursue and how to do so through an iterative process.
6. Adopt rigorous standards of investigation and acquire mastery of the quantitative, analytical, technical, and technological skills required to conduct successful research in the field of study.
7. Learn and apply professional norms and practices of the scientific or engineering enterprise, the ethical responsibilities of scientists and engineers within the profession and in relationship to the rest of society, and ethical standards that will lead to principled character and conduct.

A social science program might adopt these desiderata with little change, while a humanities program would find the first four easy to adapt and the final three perhaps less so—though after a cross-disciplinary translation, they would be suggestive.

Here's the second set of three elements, which looks ahead to career responsibilities:

1. Develop the ability to work in collaborative and team settings involving colleagues with expertise in other disciplines and from diverse cultural and disciplinary backgrounds.
2. Acquire the capacity to communicate, both orally and in written form, the significance and impact of a study or a body of work to all STEM professionals, other sectors that may utilize the result, and the public at large.

3. Develop professional competencies, such as interpersonal communication, budgeting, project management, or pedagogical skills, that are needed to plan and implement research projects.

The first criterion in this second set might easily translate into a consideration of behavior in seminars and other public fora, including written media. The second would require only the removal of the STEM acronym to be applicable across disciplines, while the third might not survive in a nonscientific setting, though grant writing matters in all fields. The list may generate a high number of desiderata. In setting student-centered goals for all graduate students, one might do better to limit the list to five or fewer items, to promote sustained focus on each. Contrary to much graduate school practice, more is not necessarily better.

Figuring out what students need is bound to be challenging work. Each program, each discipline, must come to comprehend that its traditional practices are a matter of choice rather than of nature—and at the same time, respect the wisdom of past choices and the practice that has arisen from them. Current norms, after all, are the past answers to similar questions of need and purpose, whether articulated or not. But every discipline has its own culture, its own tribal traits, and a program in that discipline can fully comprehend itself only by seeing itself in relation to other tribes, a point we've already made about the polar differences between the advising of dissertations in the sciences and the nonsciences. Here, as elsewhere, we urge making friends across the university—actually visiting with leaders of doctoral programs in several other disciplines and bringing back the news to colleagues in the program, along with a capacity to help them imagine alternatives.

Having performed this task (which need not take months), the participants can now move to triage. Still using that three-year time to degree as a goad, they determine which program elements are more or less germane to the student development viewed as ideal or at least requisite to earn the academy's highest degree. Finally, at this point, just as the man in the folk tale finally banished the animals from his house, you can relax the three-year limit and extend it (but not too far) and add program elements to ensure a new, student-centered PhD.

We're going to make a major assumption here that the most audacious change agents may forgo: that the means for delivering these PhD program goals will include courses, a pre-dissertation assessment, and the dissertation itself. These time-honored teaching tools are not necessarily required in their ancient forms; in fact, shrinking student cohorts, a goal of shortening time to degree, or advanced considerations of student learning may require new designs. Other means of achieving educational goals through the curriculum could include individual or small-group tutorials or even lectures rather than seminars to cover major areas, modules that take up less than a full semester, collaborative research projects that might even be student led (in the humanities, a growing number of programs now adapt the science model of a laboratory for work by teams),[3] online offerings that might be provided for a number of programs in the same discipline at different universities, and cross-disciplinary offerings including collaborations between disciplines in the arts and sciences and disciplines in professional schools of the same university. Ambitious portfolio writings or an experiential set of scholarly criteria might substitute for the ubiquitous exam, and relevant work internships or forms of public scholarship could become alternatives or additions to courses, the exam, and the one-size-fits-all dissertation. (We offer examples of cocurricular possibilities in chapters 3 and 10.)

But for now, let's talk about courses and then the big exam, while including possibilities for promising supplements to, or substitutes for, each.

Courses versus Curriculum

There's a sleight of hand in the *21st Century STEM* report listing of desirable student outcomes. "Specialized knowledge in a particular discipline," is merely the first of 10 items in the report's listing. Yet for many doctoral programs, it's the one and only. The report makes a crucial correction. While disciplinary content knowledge rightly deserves its place at the top of the list, the list shouldn't end there. Fulfilling the need for content knowledge begins with a curriculum, and about that we have something disconcerting to suggest.

Many doctoral programs do not provide a curriculum. They have requirements, of course, but a curriculum is a course of study, not just a set of requirements. Onetime graduate school classmates Eric Wertheimer and George Justice together recall "a curriculum that failed to cohere or mark an identifiable starting point." Their graduate coursework "energized our aspirations with its intellectual content," but "in only a few instances did we understand it as part of a coherent program," they recall. Their courses didn't "come together" by themselves, and they rightly believe that "this gap is, unfortunately, status quo in our profession."[4]

A thoughtful curriculum design starts with a coherent set of courses. "If you really want the students to take their general exams, and soon," remarked Russell Berman, a former president of the MLA and a professor of German and comparative literature at Stanford, "then offer them the courses that prepare them for it."[5] But smaller student cohorts preclude comprehensive course offerings. And especially in the humanities, faculty frequently don't want to offer foundational courses anyway. At too many programs, the consequence is a restricted menu of individualized, hyperspecialized seminar courses.

Professors love their seminars dearly and all too well, and they like to enjoy them privately—which is to say, without conferring about them with their departmental colleagues. Drawing on her experience as a college and foundation president, Judith Shapiro argues for a communal approach to teaching.[6] It is, after all, collective work: The faculty share the instruction of their students, so why should they not talk about their courses together? Graduate teaching is particularly resistant to this sort of approach because of the European legacy of the charismatic master who designs his own miniature educational culture for "his" graduate students. (We use the male pronoun advisedly here.) On the level of dissertation advising, the result is the familiar tradition of an adviser-student dyad that is ill suited to the needs of the present day. We consider that problem in greater detail in chapter 7, on advising.

In the case of curriculum, the frequent result of this balkanized approach is an atomized teaching experience (each graduate course becomes its own universe), and in the humanities fields, where the national disciplinary associations lack the authority to set criteria, this random collection of highly specialized inquiries leads to curricular incoherence and a paucity of the sort of fundamental instruction that we claim to want for our students. Such practice increases time to degree (for how are students to acquire basic knowledge except on their own time?), and as important, it conveys the implicit and explicit lesson that hyperspecialization is better than broad learning, a message underscored by the benefits of publication that such a deep-but-narrow approach may allow.

At the root of this incoherence is a lack of communication—of community—among faculty. If doctoral education is often the beneficiary (or victim) of administrative laissez-faire, the subsequent lack of organizational oversight extends to the individual graduate faculty member. The lack of a teaching community in most departments and programs leads to a neglect of curricular planning, let alone discussion of actual teaching. The kind of cross talk that often informs undergraduate instruction (especially at liberal arts colleges) is rarely sighted at the graduate level. And such talk is all the more necessary to rethink the possibilities of the doctorate. Collaboration is not simply important; it is necessary.

Most graduate faculty don't have the time to become educational theorists or cognitive scientists, but they can, as a community, learn more about the ways graduate students learn. The teaching of undergraduates constitutes a field of study. Books and articles on undergraduate teaching—both in general and in relation to particular fields—keep researchers busy. By contrast, we know of no books on graduate teaching in the arts and sciences (unless you count volumes like this one) and a scant number of articles. That's because graduate teaching has traditionally been viewed as a dependent variable—an offshoot of faculty research—rather than a pursuit in its own right.

That's an unsustainable model in these times. By learning about learning, graduate faculty may not only improve their curricula, but they can also model anew for their students the full meaning of "scholar-teacher." That balance does not exist in doctoral education right now.[7]

Less formally, graduate faculty need to think about how their students learn and what they need to learn, and then they need to plan their offerings accordingly. Graduate students face difficult choices, and their professors need to teach them with their futures in mind. Put simply, graduate education needs to become more student centered—if for no other reason than it is about educating students.

But that newly collective curricular conversation among colleagues is going to occasion a strenuous dialogue. It certainly did so in North Dakota State University's microbiology department. But that's the sort of lively back-and-forth we should expect of a community of teachers working together on the common goal of curriculum development. It's hard work, and it requires attention to civil exchange, but it's worth doing—and necessary.

In the humanities in particular, decades of arguments about canons and methods have tattered any consensus about what constitutes core knowledge. That's one reason professors default to hyperspecialized courses and an increasingly indifferent attitude toward requirements. There is no benefit in continuing to elude disagreement by neglect of a curricular plan. An ongoing debate about the nature of a discipline can be important for graduate faculty in forming a teaching community, and beneficial for graduate students to see issues elucidated rather than hidden.

Here too, outcomes-based conversations can help. To start with, they focus on the students' needs, which naturally have much to do with student outcomes. Thinking about curriculum in terms of a degree that will help students usefully centers the discussion. The graduate curricular reform process undertaken by the Lehigh University English department illustrates this practical virtue particularly well.

Outcomes-based curriculum is no panacea, of course. A range of practical problems remains. Many graduate programs have restricted enrollments and eliminated the master's degree and its student cohort. That scarcity of students makes it difficult to mount a curriculum,

Outcomes-Based Curriculum in the Sciences

At North Dakota State University, a combination of curricular and cocurricular changes has catalyzed a cultural shift in doctoral training. As associate dean of the College of Graduate and Interdisciplinary Studies, Brandy Randall has been helping graduate programs move to outcome-based planning. Such planning starts with the question of what faculty members can do for students, not the other way around.

The curricular changes at North Dakota State take place mostly at the departmental level, with guidance from above. In the microbiology department, the outcome-based reforms are a case in point. As a young doctoral program—it's less than 10 years old—the department encountered problems large and small soon after its inception. In the early years, "there was no culture of information," said Peter Bergholz, an assistant professor and the microbiology graduate program coordinator. "Very few people were communicating what students should expect to do in graduate school. Students weren't talking to their advisers about their futures."

Some urgent problems demanded immediate attention. "There were enormous disparities from lab to lab," said Bergholz, and too many students were failing their comprehensive exams.

Professors in the department decided "to formalize what the program should be," Bergholz said. They wanted to create a "road map to success." So they talked with one another, and to their students, and eventually brought administrators into the conversation. After almost two years, the department arrived at new goals for the graduate program, adopting them by vote in 2017.

Some of the goals are the usual content-based ones: knowledge and skills that students need to become microbiologists. But other goals reflect the kind of work that most of the program's PhDs actually pursue: not tenure-track jobs but positions in the private sector at biotechnology companies. (Occasionally some of the department's PhDs do seek teaching jobs, but mostly not.)

The reforms streamlined and reworked coursework so that it more explicitly targets the skills and knowledge that microbiologists need to succeed as scientists. The content knowledge (that is, foundational microbiological facts and principles) is the focus of the first year, culminating in an oral comprehensive exam. The students start preparing for the doctoral candidacy exam in their second year.

The "programmatic learning goals"—skills such as the ability to formulate scientific hypotheses and to design and carry out experiments to test them—are a continuing focus. The department measures student progress toward the programmatic goals annually. Students submit an electronic portfolio each year as part of the Doctoral Portfolio course. Every student has an individual research committee whose members assess the portfolio and meet with the student to talk about it. The committee also writes an assessment letter that includes specific recommendations for how to make progress in the coming year.

Such individual attention allows students to plan their own ways forward. "We do our best to set students up with internships in their chosen field," Bergholz said, citing a student who recently worked at a US Department of Agriculture lab and "returned with two publications' worth of data" that led to a job offer from a private company. Another student in the program got a job working part-time locally as a histotechnologist—that is, a specialist in preparing tissue samples for microscopy—that moves her toward her goal of running a research program in clinical diagnostics.

That sort of flexibility prevails throughout the program now. "With outcomes and an assessment plan," Bergholz said, "we can assign the course training we want." That training now centers on a newly designed first-year required course, Foundations in Microbiology Research. It's a team-taught series of modules that cover fundamental knowledge in the field as well as key research concepts.

The road has not been without potholes. The assessment of outcomes (both their appropriateness and whether students are meeting them) has proved "more work than people thought," Bergholz said. Some professors were also taken aback by the workload that accompanied the new Foundations course. "Everyone had some gripes" about this centerpiece course, said Bergholz, but the professors have worked together to smooth it out.

For their part, the students have thoroughly benefited. "They feel that they know what's expected of them now," said Bergholz. Their performance has improved, and so has their morale.

Autumn Kraft, a fourth-year PhD student in the department, praised the changes. In concrete terms, the new program gave her "a focused path" to her comprehensive exam, the first of two that students take before they move to the dissertation. The first exam is content based; the second a defense of their dissertation proposal.

The program created a peer-and-faculty mentoring plan to help students prepare for the second exam, which helps shape the methodological basis for the student's thesis. Reed Hawkins, a second-year student, said that the proposal exam pushes students to "a clear idea of our research plans and direction. It's amazingly helpful to have this sort of long-term planning in our minds throughout our second year." Such planning is "super motivating," he said.

Motivation produces results. Even at this early stage in her research, Kraft said, she is making progress on her dissertation because she has been asked to think ahead toward her research and not just to the next exam hurdle. The program's new attention to "goal planning and committee feedback" allowed her to "focus on my research" early on, and not just on fulfilling "explicit course/credit requirements." As a result, she was already working on her dissertation, "writing and all, even before I had passed my exams," she said. Kraft credits the program's new structure for her rapid progress.

The transparency of the new requirements also helps counter the typical anxiety that many students experience in graduate school. ("Is there some expectation I'm not meeting? Am I somehow a fraud?") In other words, the new environment promotes not only better learning but also better mental health. And a better bottom line: Students are passing their exams and progressing through the program more quickly.

The goal of microbiology's curricular reform, said Bergholz, was "to make sure we were developing scientists who could do well in a variety of fields." So far, it looks like they are.

In the Doctoral Portfolio course, Kraft and her cohort "review what we've done in progressing toward our doctorate and reaching the necessary milestones," and the students' committees evaluate their work at the same time. "We then work together to set new goals and how I can continue to progress in the program," she said. "This method forces me to spend time explicitly laying out my goals, communicating them with my committee, and focusing on my future."

That sort of productive reflection by graduate students would be exemplary at any time, but it's especially welcome at a time when academic jobs are scarce. Kraft and her peers are taking the initiative in their own professional development. What more could their teachers wish for?

Outcomes-Based Curriculum in the Humanities

At the Lehigh University English department, the numbers tell the outcomes-based story. In 2013, 39 percent of the department's PhDs found work only as contingent instructors. By late 2018, that figure had dropped to 9 percent. Instead of dead-end adjunct work, 46 percent of the university's English PhDs now enter humanities careers other than college teaching. Equally striking, however: the number of the university's English PhDs who find tenure-track professorships also went up—from about 18 percent in 2013 to 27 percent five years later.

What happened? In short, the English department at Lehigh used data-centered, outcomes-based planning to assess and overhaul its doctoral curriculum in line with what made sense for its graduate students. In 2013, Jenna Lay, then the English department's director of graduate studies, began compiling data on the department's graduate student outcomes. She focused on career trajectories for the department's PhD graduates going back to 2000. In keeping with the humanistic conviction that the truth doesn't lie entirely in numbers, she also collected the students' stories. "The combination of data and narratives," she said, is "very important."

The data revealed where Lehigh's English graduate students had been getting jobs. Between 2000 and mid-2009, nearly 60 percent of Lehigh's English PhDs found tenure-track professorships, mostly at teaching-intensive institutions. You can't call it a wonderful result when 40 percent of academic job seekers encounter disappointment, but it is notable: Lehigh's percentage exceeded the national average in that period for English departments, and for most humanities disciplines generally.

Things got a lot worse for Lehigh's English PhDs after that, mirroring a national trend. Between 2009 and 2013, the proportion of students who found tenure-track jobs dropped by more than two-thirds, to 18 percent. The numbers "confirmed what we were hearing from graduate students," Lay said—namely, that the market for professorships had withered. In a parallel finding, the number of Lehigh English PhDs who wound up as adjuncts—previously a minuscule 3 percent—shot up to 39 percent.

With fewer than one in five graduates landing on the tenure track and nearly two in five paddling desperately in the contingent labor pool, Lay and her colleagues recognized this as "a crisis for our students." The situation had "crept up" on the department, but professors now realized that they "needed to make changes," she said. The data "helped us make decisions about how to prepare students to think more broadly" about career options for PhDs. (Very few programs gather such data, yet keeping track of student outcomes is a sure lever for program improvement.)

Lay and her colleagues proceeded in their decision making in much the same way we suggest in this book. They began with emotions—specifically, their own "fears and anxieties" surrounding reform of their graduate program. Then they proceeded logically: they "drilled down" and analyzed the data. In particular, the faculty looked at students' career outcomes and asked, "What was helping them?" For example, professors saw that the successful academic job seekers among the department's pool of PhDs had certain qualifications in common. Most had additional training in teaching composition. Some had an additional degree, such as a teaching credential. And most had nonacademic work experience on campus, such as time spent working in the university's Global Citizenship program.

Professors recognized, Lay said, that "we needed to do more" to help students develop—and demonstrate—such competencies. Looking at which skills were helping students the most on the job market, the department devised various certificate programs, including a particularly successful one on teaching composition and rhetoric.

English graduate students at the university can now opt to complete an additional certificate (or just take a few courses) on the way to either an MA or a PhD. While the department has expanded its graduate curriculum, it hasn't burdened students with additional degree requirements. "The certificates don't add onto students' time to degree or time in coursework," Lay said. "Instead, they serve as optional pathways through the program and count toward the required courses for the PhD (a number that has not changed). The certificates, in other words, help students to identify areas of focus earlier in the PhD."

On the faculty side, the certificate program in writing instruction "revitalized our graduate coursework in composition and rhetoric," said Lay. The certificate requires 12 credits, three of which students already have to take in order to teach in Lehigh's first-year writing program. The nine other credits come from new courses developed for the purpose, including Rhetoric and Social Justice (a topic consistent with the department's social justice mission)[1] and a course in public rhetoric in which students study the "civic turn" of composition studies (in which composition instructors have students get involved in local projects and then write about their experiences). Professors also devised practical one-credit courses aimed at developing writing pedagogy, like Teaching Developmental Writing in College, which prepares students for community college job opportunities.

Of course professors are better at adding programs and requirements than at eliminating them, and the department tried to keep that academic truism in mind. "We don't want to add on extra work for our students," said Lay. Instead, the faculty aimed for a "cohesive and integrated" curriculum that gives the students more freedom to string existing (and some new) courses into sequences that will give them an additional credential, such as the certificate in writing instruction. The department's analysis of PhD career outcomes also showed that students benefited from gaining work experience outside the discipline, so professors built that option into the revised curriculum, too. (We discuss that cocurricular aspect of the program in chapter 5, on student support.)

---

1. Lehigh's English department decided to "brand" itself in 2009. See Lehigh University, College of Arts and Sciences, "Literature and Social Justice," https://english.cas2.lehigh.edu/content/literature-and-social-justice-1.

especially one that insists on foundational knowledge rather than faculty-favored topics. Together with an increasing tendency toward canceling courses that fail to meet minimum enrollments, it's clear that the national trend is toward fewer graduate courses.

We believe one best alternative is renewing the master's degree, as we discuss in chapter 9. We seek a new kind of professionally oriented master's, not a cheapened version of the doctorate but a degree that would still require substantial disciplinary course work. Some programs have also had success with 4 + 1 dual-degree options that allow talented undergraduates to start taking graduate courses in their senior year and earn a master's in one additional year. (Such a format, if coupled with a professionally oriented view of the master's, has the additional virtue of encouraging undergraduates to major in fields suffering from a reputation for poor career outcomes because, as the word on the street goes, the master's is "the new BA.")

Multidisciplinary offerings may provide students in smaller cohorts with a greater range of course opportunities than any single program can provide. We'll take up inter- and multidisciplinarity in our next section, but for now, we should point out that many of the desired student outcomes enumerated in the *21st Century STEM* report and elsewhere can be achieved through courses that cross traditional departmental boundaries and enroll students from multiple disciplines. For example, a course on the broad theme of empire and colonialism might draw on students from literature, history, and racial/ethnic and area studies, to name just a few possibilities. (Notre Dame is one university that has revised its graduate offerings in this way.)

Another option goes in an opposite direction: to adapt the British doctoral mode of individual tutorials (perhaps in addition to a reduced menu of courses), with a new workload system. How many tutorials would equal a course? That would be worked out in practice. Given the prevailing trend toward lower graduate enrollments in the arts and sciences, it seems only a matter of time before a thoughtful program tries this out.

One solution does not preclude others. For example, a department might invite other departments into discussion of mutual interests and potential offerings, with the possibility of offering broadly scoped courses to advanced undergraduates or honors students, and also to MA and doctoral students on a selective basis, while providing a tutorial system that makes professorial workloads more versatile. Or again, common interests and complementary expertise may lead to collaborations with professional schools on campus—law, education, business, media, and public health most obviously—but these connections need to be sought out. The recent pandemic has made many faculty newly competent (and some enthusiastic) about online learning. One virtue of the virtual is that it may enable team teaching not only across schools but even coordinated among several universities.

Of all the curricular things professors need to make, sense is the most important. Graduate students need a sensible curriculum that encompasses the needs of disciplinary learning and outcomes together. Not every change will work, but it will be easier to adjust if faculty work together in a doctoral teaching community. Collaboration will ensure continual conversation while everyone learns from experience—including the students, who will benefit by emulating their teachers' example of community, wherever their careers take them.

Life beyond the Discipline

The great challenges that face societies and individuals don't come in little packets marked "Political Science" or "Chemistry" or "Philosophy." We might also recall that the first philosophers are literally indistinguishable from the first scientists. There's a reason the various disciplines are gathered on a campus rather than existing—as it sometimes seems, even on that campus—on different planets.

Curricular planning also benefits when we take it beyond the boundaries of individual programs. Multidisciplinary offerings may provide students with a greater range of course opportunities than any single program can provide. The President's Council of Advisors on Science and Technology recently called on universities "to go beyond training within traditional disciplines and to institute or expand the scope of project-based, multidisciplinary learning."[8] The sciences have adapted readily in the sense that many young scientists work across field boundaries, but this adaptation remains within their grant-fueled organizational scheme, and it may encounter limits as funding has become scarcer.

The nonscience disciplines have also challenged disciplinary boundaries. Historians of education like Douglas Bennett identify a drive toward the interdisciplinary and an accompanying interest in collaborative learning as two of the major trends in the past few decades.[9] But doctoral education is playing catch-up and has been for a while. Golde and Dore found that 60 percent of graduate students in their 2001 survey desired collaboration across disciplinary lines, but only 27 percent believed that they were getting it or were prepared for the possibility.[10] Nowhere is this clearer than in the academic job market in the humanities and humanistic social sciences, which is still organized almost entirely around disciplines and subfields. The disjunction between interdisciplinary inquiry and traditional job categories has vexed these fields for generations. The problem will persist unless we change the way we hire. Ironically, the post-2008 job squeeze has helped to drive this change. The COVID-19 pandemic will likely accelerate it. With job openings so scarce, most programs can't afford to design new faculty positions to cover the usual curricular real estate—so when a department has been able to offer a job opening, it may now straddle or even go beyond traditional categories.

Despite widespread praise for interdisciplinary research and teaching, it remains underfunded. Departments and interdepartmental programs battle over rights and faculty. How a university administers the interdisciplinary in relation to the disciplines remains a fraught problem that is economic and academic at the same time.

The disciplinary-based counterargument, of course, is that breadth sacrifices depth. When we advocate for breadth with little sacrifice of depth on the graduate level, we also raise the practical concern of a time to degree that already borders on the interminable.[11]

Perhaps one way to give greater academic standing to interdisciplinary study is to acknowledge that it's difficult, even controversial. The deeply contentious nature of the interdisciplinary—it seeks, after all, a reorganization of knowledge—should lead to thoughtful debate that might allow a new understanding of traditional disciplines in the process. Today's doctoral experience requires both.

Current models of interdisciplinarity in doctoral education do not much challenge the organization of the university or of knowledge itself, but they do usefully remind students of a wider intellectual world than a single discipline can provide. Among many such examples, the University of Michigan May Seminars bring together students and faculty on a common theme that crosses the disciplines. At Washington University in St. Louis, dissertating students meet through the summer on a multidisciplinary basis.[12] (A Student Lecture Series at the University of Pennsylvania brought graduate and professional students to the campus-wide Graduate Student Center to present their research to an audience of their peers. Students could present current research or practice a job talk or conference paper. This program is no longer extant, but it looks worthy of revival at any campus.) The Intellectual Entrepreneurship teams at the University of Texas were almost always drawn from several disciplines, and this remains true in the current undergraduate version of the program there. Duke encourages students to take courses toward a cognate master's degree, and Brown has recently inaugurated a program that sponsors students to do the same.[13] Arizona State, as part of the Responsive Ph.D. initiative, had offered special fellowships to students attempting interdisciplinary dissertations, and certainly financial support is one requisite for transdisciplinary encouragement.[14]

In the sciences, a private foundation, the Howard Hughes Medical Institute, provided initial private funding for a Biomedical Imaging and Bioengineering Interdisciplinary Graduate Research Training Program. The National Science Foundation has provided public funds to sustain this private/public partnership so that it may achieve ends neither public nor private institutions could reach alone. The exemplary partnership has funded a number of ventures, including a program at Brandeis in quantitative biology linking physical and biomedical sciences, another at Johns Hopkins in nanotechnology for biology and medicine, a program at the University of Pennsylvania in clinical imaging and informational sciences, and a program in biophysical dynamics and self-organization at the University of Chicago. And finally, the groundbreaking NSF program in research traineeships (the final program described in chapter 1) requires a thorough mingling of disciplines for every chosen proposal and matches pairs to combine technical discovery with public collaborations and concrete outcomes.

In truth, the most practical and far-reaching organizational change that can accommodate and enable the transdisciplinary mode—and student—is to make the graduate school a more dynamic and autonomous (and better financed) body in every university, a case we make more fully at the end of this book.

Examining the Exam

What should the doctoral qualifying exam look like? Should there even be one? We start with these first principles not because we want to keep or do away with exams. That is the decision of each program. Instead, we're looking to clear the table to begin a discussion. We encourage programs to begin their own discussions at the beginning too.

Our students spend a lot of time preparing for their exams—generals, qualifiers, or whatever they may be called. That's not a bad thing in itself, but it's a fact that requires periodic reflection because we need to make sure that their time is being well spent. Historically, we haven't been doing enough of that reflection, and lengthy time to degree is one consequential result. General exams evolved as graduate programs grew during the middle decades of the twentieth century, especially after World War II. They're an outgrowth of a bureaucracy that necessarily came into being when students were being admitted in numbers too great to advise and assess personally at the early stages.[15]

Perhaps "barrier exams" made sense as a way of coordinating the graduate education of large numbers of students during those times, but our times are different. Most fields don't admit large numbers of PhD students and cull them anymore.[16] We should therefore ask what value a qualifying exam serves in today's smaller graduate school environments. As a first postulate, we could say that the value of the exam lies in its relation to the progression of a student's graduate career. Put simply, *the exam needs to make sense in the context of a student's education as a whole.* It can't be just a hazing ritual. What kinds of sensible purposes might general exams serve? There are two main possibilities: the exam can look forward or back. (Or a third possibility: both, as at North Dakota State's microbiology program.)

A backward-looking exam requires a student to demonstrate basic competencies. Doctoral students need certain skills and knowledge to research and write a dissertation in a field. The notion that graduate students should possess broad knowledge of their discipline is surely sensible. The qualifying exam serves as a check, to spot those students who are unprepared for the dissertation, saving them some years of frustration. The system of qualifying exams promotes both earlier attrition and academic breadth.

Yet the comprehensive exam often delays progress toward the degree. This tendency is most noticeable in the humanities and humanistic social sciences, as students cram to "cover" their fields. We want students to be independent learners at the exam stage, but would we not rather have them delving rather than skimming? What literature PhD doesn't recall skimming through one novel after another in a period of intense cramming for The Test? (One senior Harvard professor confessed to Len years ago that when he was studying for his comprehensive exams, he would blast through novels by reading just the dialogue. Bob confesses to having resorted to plot summaries in his time, a spirit-killing, self-shaming exercise.) This coverage model, as William James so long ago noted, may well "divert the attention of aspiring youth from direct dealings with truth to the passing of examinations."[17] A century later, the Carnegie leaders acknowledged that "the educational purpose of the exam is often unclear to students."[18]

So it's reasonable to test student competencies through a Big Test—but only if the preceding curriculum (mostly coursework) helps them prepare for it. If the courses don't develop core knowledge and skills, then that lack of coherence interrupts students because they have to acquire them from scratch. This kind of studying—building a building rather than adding onto one—extends their time to degree. But if coursework leads harmoniously to the exam, we can imagine the barrier exam playing its role as the final and highest hurdle for a student to clear before the final stage.

A forward-looking exam points the student toward that final stage: the dissertation. In this scenario, the exam serves as an on-ramp leading to the dissertation highway. It can do this in a number of ways. A student might choose examination fields that relate directly to a dissertation in the offing or even defend a dissertation proposal as part (or all) of the exam itself. In these scenarios, the exam launches the student into the dissertation to follow. (It can also look toward a graduate student's teaching. Students might submit to the exam committee an annotated syllabus for a course in the student's major field.) The forward-looking exam is not so much a barrier as a gateway.

The creative possibilities inspired by the forward-looking exam inspire their own question in turn: Does this gateway need to take the form of an exam at all? We need to think of these exams as a kind of teaching. Because they're a part of the curriculum, that's what they are—or at least what they can, and should, be.

So we might ask: How might a program best use the moment now dedicated to comprehensive exams? If a moment of assessment is called for, what needs to be assessed, and what is the best way to assess it? We seek to promote the creative, problem-grappling, adventurous attitude that a strong dissertation requires.

We recommend that programs consider complements or substitutes to the traditional exam. Even if you don't adopt them, the act of considering such possibilities and the discussions you have will strengthen your sense of curricular purpose. These conversations provide another example of the reflective practice we have encouraged throughout this book. David Jaffee has suggested that faculty design into the big exam tasks that would allow students "to use the repertoire of disciplinary tools . . . to analyze and solve a realistic problem that they might face as practitioners in the field."[19] This "response and transfer" model holds greater potential than having students rush through a stack of readings to make up for the coursework the program failed to provide.

Many biology programs now require students to develop and defend a research project of their own invention as part of their advancement to doctoral candidacy. We suggest that the humanities emulate this model and replace coverage-based exams with task-based examinations that look toward the dissertation to come. In this way, the exam plants the seeds for dissertation work rather serving as a barrier that separates the student from it.

Integrating preliminary dissertation work into the qualifying examination is also becoming more common in the humanities. Examples include an interdisciplinary research paper at the American studies department at the University of Maryland, an exam based on the student's dissertation reading list in English at West Virginia University, an early written exam followed by a research paper of publishable quality and an exam in three fields related to the proposed dissertation for the American studies program at St. Louis University.[20] Other programs have experimented with reading lists tied to the dissertation, or capstone projects in which student write or revise two papers to demonstrate methodological competence across some range of the field.

Likewise worthy of consideration is the substitution of a portfolio for an exam. In the history department at the University of Kansas, the "data-dump exam" stalled students for so long that the faculty decided to substitute the professional portfolio, "a collection of artifacts designed to help students document their own histories as emerging scholars": a CV, all seminar papers, any published works, "a 15–20 page professional essay explaining why the student selected his major fields, how those fields might be integrated and related to one another, and what he understands to be the leading research issues." A dissertation prospectus is also included, along with materials about teaching.[21] The Carnegie team observed that such a portfolio format provides ongoing self-assessment, gives the student greater responsibility and control, develops documentation habits relevant to any historian, and creates "habits of mind that will stand graduates in good stead in their future workplaces."[22] This set of attributes might serve well as the goal for the exam in any program in any discipline.

The substitution of a student portfolio for all or part of a comprehensive exam has become something of a trend. Edward Balleisen and Maria LaMonica Wisdom cite 20 different programs that have adapted the portfolio model, each in its own way, including six in history (Duke, Kansas, Colorado, Emory, Tulane and New Mexico), three in English (Emory, Iowa, and the University of California, Riverside), three in anthropology (the University of Virginia, Carleton University, and Duke), three in philosophy (University of California, Irvine, the University of Pittsburgh, the University of Tennessee), and one each in French (Johns Hopkins University), computational media, arts, and cultures (Duke), American studies (the University of North Carolina at Chapel Hill), Romance studies (Duke), and science and technology (Rensselaer Polytechnic Institute).[23]

In their way, comprehensive exams reflect a program's mission. Here too, we recommend planning backward, from an outcome you design. By planning backward, programs can ask themselves how the student outcomes they have agreed upon can best be achieved, and a formal exam may prove less efficacious than any number of alternatives. If you decide that the test has aged past the possibility of use in your program, then put it out to pasture. There may be value in an intermediate rite of passage on the way to the dissertation, but it doesn't have to be a traditional written or oral exam. A portfolio of coursework, occasional reflections, and a prolegomenon for the dissertation could also serve.

When departments reflect on specific program requirements in this way, they alter—or renew—the norms of their disciplines. That's because what happens in PhD education never stays confined to those precincts, but instead informs the nature of the field all the way down. So look, listen, reflect—and change what you will, with the knowledge that your work is bound to ripple outward.

SEVEN

Advising

Graduate advising is institutional. That's definitionally true: students get their degrees from universities, not advisers or committees. Yet in practice, we academics treat graduate advising as personal—the private property of the individual professors who do it. That combination of the personal and the private makes graduate advising a potential tinderbox.

That tinder burst into flame in the fall of 2018, when graduate student advising made the front page of the *New York Times*. The reason, not surprisingly, was a prurient case of misconduct. Avital Ronell, a professor of German and comparative literature at New York University, was suspended from teaching for a year for the sexual harassment of Nimrod Reitman, one of her recent PhD advisees. Reitman, who brought a Title IX complaint against Ronell after he graduated, further claimed that Ronell's lukewarm recommendations hindered his search for an academic job. Ronell disputes all charges.

The case turned into a sensation for many reasons. One is that Ronell is a woman and Reitman is a man—an inversion of the usual pattern for sexual-harassment cases. Further, Ronell is a prominent scholar. And the kicker: Ronell is lesbian and Reitman is gay. The two flung he said/she said barbs at each other for weeks after Reitman's

accusations went public. More than 50 scholars signed an open letter of protest of NYU's investigation, an action meant to defend
Ronell, but that also generated its own controversy. And once the university found that he was sexually harassed, Reitman sued NYU for
damages.

"What Happens to #MeToo When a Feminist Is the Accused?"
asked the *New York Times*. "Groping professor Avital Ronell and her
'cuddly' Nimrod Reitman see kisses go toxic," said Britain's the
Times. The public fascination is no wonder. This is bizarre stuff.[1]

It shouldn't take a salacious case like Avital Ronell's to make us pay
attention to graduate advising. The case at first seems like an extreme
outlier in the world of dissertation direction, but there are ways in
which it's not an outlier at all. It illustrates the typical structural problems that attend graduate advising, especially of the doctoral kind.
Teachers of graduate school don't talk enough about those problems.
Even when they flare into view, as in this incident, we educators join
the general public in gaping at the burning tree rather than considering the parched, crackling forest it's part of.

Now consider a deliberately unsensational scenario. Let's say a professor is engaging in questionable advising practice—like putting a
student through 18 drafts of a dissertation proposal that was ready to
be submitted for committee approval months ago. If a colleague in the
same department read the manuscript and saw the student losing traction, do you think that colleague would take the professor aside and
offer some friendly suggestions? In practice, that conversation rarely
takes place. Usually the colleague decides to mind his or her own
business.

But whose business is it, really? Graduate education is the responsibility of the entire department—or even, on a wider scale, of the university itself. When a student chooses an adviser, it's not as though the
student is withdrawing from the department's common culture to enter the adviser's private world. So why do we act as though that were
the case?

The roots of this habit of thinking—and the resulting practice—lie in
the American university's European past. The founders of American

research universities were mainly inspired by German models. And in German universities during the eighteenth and nineteenth centuries, the learned professor radiated power and intellectual allure, an effect that the historian William Clark calls "academic charisma."[2] The charismatic professor was more of a master instructing acolytes than a mere teacher advising students. He was also an overbearing intellectual father figure who encompassed his students' professional world. In fact, the German word for graduate adviser, *Doktorvater*, literally means "doctor-father."

American research universities imported this straitened and hierarchical worldview when they were founded in the decades around 1900, and early American university professors wove it into our common culture. Historian Laurence Veysey points out that the rise of "cults" around "magnetic" professors in the United States coincided with the general withdrawal of these "investigators" (and their students) from the public sphere, to labor behind ivied tower walls.[3] As American academia expanded and flourished in the mid-twentieth century, the role of the *Doktorvater* professionalized while remaining, in the words of James Grossman, "clearly defined, intellectually magisterial, and blatantly hierarchical." The modern *Doktorvater*, says Grossman, might provide a recommendation to admit a student to an archive, or "he might assign a dissertation topic outright. Pathways to career success were generally narrow, sharply defined, and marked by footsteps to be followed." When the student finished the degree under his direction, the *Doktorvater* would make a few calls and get the new graduate a job as an assistant professor. For graduate students, this paternalistic practice marked their admission to full membership in a hermetically sealed academic world.[4]

The opposite is true today: graduate students have to think about jobs outside as well as inside academia and the "old boy network" has gone the way of crewcuts. But the personal and private view of advising has persisted even so. Graduate students have dissertation committees, it's true, but many (if not most) committee members do little and defer to the main adviser in charge. In the sciences, this situation is still more extreme, committee or no. The research adviser is also the laboratory boss, and while collaboration in writing up research ideally starts a graduate student on the way to professional esteem, intellectual property disputes end up in the graduate dean's or provost's office all too often.

Given the institutional conservatism of American academia, we shouldn't be surprised that this old, insular model persists. David Damrosch has written, "The heart of Ph.D. training is the relationship between mentors and students."[5] That's surely true. The question is how that relationship should be structured.

The Ronell-Reitman affair "may be a weird case," as one scholarly editor put it, but by glaring omission, "it highlights the fact that the professional duty of a professor is to prepare grad students for their careers and help them get jobs." That instrumental view makes sense, of course. But for advisers to prioritize that student-centered goal, we need to work together and in the open. Graduate advising is, after all, a form of teaching, and teaching is inherently public work.

With the public face of teaching in mind, we need to escape the thrall of the European past and remember what we're supposed to be doing here and now.

How to Build a Collaborative Advising Culture

We should develop institutional—not personal—models of advising. This is especially necessary at a time when the implied idea of replication (that the student will get a job like the adviser's) holds less true. In the words of historian Thomas Bender, the "master" and "apprentice" model "needs ventilating."[6]

What's the best way to open the vents and let some light into the black box of graduate student advisement? The literature that analyzes graduate student advising is scant. This absence is telling in itself. In contrast to the large body of scholarship on undergraduate teaching, there's very little in the way of studied procedure, of intellectual exploration of an activity that arguably defines graduate study. Instead, there's plenty of lore—which is of limited value.

We therefore offer some practical recommendations. First of all, advisers need advising themselves. We suggest more standardized practice within programs. Advising has a deserved reputation as private and idiosyncratic, but even so, all departments have norms and standards, such as comprehensive exams and dissertation proposal formats. So we're not starting from zero here—there are some shared assumptions about what this thing is supposed to look like. To begin, we need to acknowledge and expand them.

Some graduate schools and programs have published guides to advising practice. Such documents aim to structure advisement in the humanities and humanistic social sciences, where there can be too little supervision and not enough checkpoints or agreed-upon intermediate goals during the process. Among the current models for this practice is Duke, which provides resources on mentorship to faculty. Their website has some self-help advice for mentors and a reading list.[7]

Written guides can help faculty members comprehend and value their advising responsibilities more fully and help to build social norms within a department, but only if people read them and take them seriously. Organizing your department's (or institution's) advising practice in an open and thoughtful way involves more than posting some instructions on a website. Collective ownership is the aim here. Faculty members need to identify the goals of advising and then set up a collectively maintained structure to meet them. Talking about those assumptions helps keep them visible and vital within a department's culture.

Here we note a basic difference between the bench sciences and other disciplines. In the bench sciences, a faculty member directs a lab and uses grant money to fund PhD students. Under this model, the students' work is expected to further the faculty member's research program, and the student's publications (with the adviser as a listed coauthor) bolster applications for further grants that continue the funding-and-labor cycle. In this situation, student supervision comes to resemble an employer-employee relation, leading chemist Angelica Stacy to describe advising as "really about power."[8] Some observers of the Ronell case have drawn a similar conclusion.

When it comes to power in the advising relationship, graduate students need more of it. After all, they're the ones who must plan their own futures, and they need more self-determination to be able to do so. Here too, some exemplary practices in the sciences—modest efforts to make advising more flexible and student centered—offer a way forward for other fields. The National Institutes of Health has called for the creation of individual development plans (IDPs) for all NIH-supported grad students and researchers. Though IDPs are a recommendation rather than a requirement, NIH does require grantees to say in their progress reports whether the institution uses IDPs and how they are employed to manage the training and career development of students. This is friendly persuasion from an important income source. IDPs provide a formal structure for the mentoring process, and a large number of schools now offer students assistance in developing them. Iowa State University currently provides a framework for students to create an IDP simply by referring students to the myIDP and Imagine PhD online resources, and appointing a specific career coach in the graduate school to aid any student in developing one. The University of Nebraska has its own website for advising students on how to create an IDP. Brown University's Division of Biology and Medicine goes furthest: the program requires all incoming students to complete and submit a draft IDP to the graduate school by the end of the first semester and to update it before the end of four years. Brown also developed its own self-assessment guidelines to prompt students to reflect on their goals and accomplishments, and then they develop a plan with their adviser.[9] Without similar pressure from a key funding source, the humanities and social sciences rarely offer the same opportunity for such self-examination by students, but there is no reason, especially now that there is a helpful website as an aid, not to institute the practice.

If power is an issue too often elided when we talk about advising, so is the need for comprehensiveness. These student-centered IDP models convey the understanding that advising comprises, or should comprise, more than just dissertation direction. Right now, too many graduate programs offer perfunctory check-the-boxes advising to students in their first years, with the understood assumption that the "real" advising starts when the student chooses a field of specialization, a dissertation topic, and a professor to oversee the project. That model has a provenance that goes back generations, but it doesn't meet the needs of today's doctoral students.

We need to reconceive advising to include all of the communication between faculty and students from orientation through graduation. Beginning graduate students need clarity about the education they are embarking upon and the outcomes that await them. They have important choices to make, and it's the job of their advisers to help them make informed decisions. This need for clarity is all the more important because student outcomes are so diverse.

One historian told a Carnegie survey that "intellectual community is the most important facet of any doctoral community. Students need a supportive community among themselves and collegial relations with faculty."[10] That's obviously true, but the key word is "supportive." Advising should include students' socialization into their discipline, and that includes presenting to them the diverse options they have as professionals. Put simply, departments—and their faculty—need to advise students as human beings, not larval professors.

Along with clarity, graduate students need trust. They already trust the faculty with years of their lives. With that much on the line, we have to advise them with thoughtful care, and with openness and honesty.

To promote openness, we recommend a cohort seminar in professional development for doctoral students in their first or second year. Earlier is better because students need to understand the intellectual and practical sides of their work as soon as possible. Earlier is better also because it guards against the unconscious biases of some faculty toward cloning themselves. A professional development seminar might cover the intellectual history of the discipline and its methods. It might introduce graduate students to the mechanics of conference presentations and publication. A professional development course in the geography department at the University of Minnesota not only took up those topics but also brought in a series of professors to talk to the students about career choices, work-life balance, and other real-life topics.[11]

A Case for Professional Development Orientation

Graduate students need to know what to expect. John Guillory suggests that we enlighten them right away. We have to teach them what they're facing as soon as possible, he said in a talk at the 2020 Modern Language Association convention. "The moment to prepare them is when they arrive to begin their studies."[1] They need a workshop on the job market—not just the academic job market—as soon as they walk in the door.

The need is immediate because we start socializing graduate students immediately. Honest career counseling needs to be part of that socialization. Usually, Guillory said, "career counseling for graduate students is something that is left to the end of doctoral education, when the student is approaching the market. By that time, students have been thoroughly set in their ways."

Consider, said Guillory, "how difficult it is to disabuse prospective or incoming graduate students of the notion that they will be the exception, that they will be one who gets a job." And the longer we wait, the harder it gets—because meeting with their dissertation advisers naturally reinforces the focus on the academic path that the advisers know best.

What results is not so much determination as rigidity. "It does not serve students well," said Guillory, when they "are inadequately prepared for the most probable outcome" of their PhD studies. In fact, they can become permanently embittered: "They become our enemies in their later careers rather than our friends."

Guillory proposes a professional development workshop run by the graduate school, not by each individual program. Every incoming graduate student would get the same information from the same source. Centralization would create consistency at this early moment. It would also send a caretaking message that concern—and responsibility!—for graduate students' professional development extends beyond the adviser and the program to the whole graduate school. After this initial graduate-school-centered moment, the responsibility would fall to departments.

This initial, school-wide stage would aim to establish a broad—not field-specific—orientation to the professional realities of graduate study. Here is how Guillory envisioned the workshop:

- First it would lay out the bald truth for students, speaking "honestly and fully about their prospects upon completion of the Ph.D."

- Second, it would "begin to instruct students about the types of jobs that Ph.D.s do attain" and the job satisfaction that comes with them.
- Those assessments of job satisfaction should come from the source: PhD alumni employed outside of academia. The graduate school should, Guillory said, "invite them to campus to speak with new doctoral students, pay them for their services, and take the opportunity in the meantime to reconnect them" with the university. PhD alumni from nonfaculty professions "should be feted and celebrated, invited to speak about their scholarly work and the work they currently do. They are, quite literally, our future."

We think Guillory has this just right. If the university honors diverse career paths from the beginning, graduate students will be far less likely to feel stigmatized—as so many now do—if they decide to look for such jobs themselves.

---

1. John Guillory, "Graduate Admissions: Remarks MLA 2020" (January 2020).

Professional development seminars might also focus on diverse career options. Professional Humanities Careers, a recent cross-disciplinary humanities professional development seminar at the University of Michigan, included site visits to nonprofit organizations and required students to interview PhD-bearing professionals outside the academy.[12] As these variations suggest, there's no single way to run a professional development seminar. Instead, think of it as a reverse-engineering problem, in which you work backward from the endpoint of socializing graduate students into their discipline.[13]

Professional development seminars introduce a more flexible advising model that's badly needed in the humanities and humanistic social sciences. The exposure that such seminars give students lays the foundation for students and professors to join in shaping individual students' curriculum to meet students' needs. The cohort seminar thus welcomes students into a long professional development conversation that extends throughout the graduate years.

"A Plurality of Advisers"

There are myriad ways to open doctoral advising outward. We already do it at the job-market moment, when students typically enlist the help of a department "placement director." But we need to lift advising out of its black box well before that point. We second Thomas Bender's call for "a plurality of advisers at all stages."[14] Columbia's English department, to name one example, relies on three-member dissertation committees in which no one faculty member is the student's primary adviser. In practice, a de facto go-to person may emerge, but power is shared, and access is supposed to be equal.

This good idea begs for expansion. We suggest a committee of flexible size whose membership goes beyond the usual suspects. For example, in the case of a political science student who wants a job in government, her committee might include an outside member from a public policy program. Graduate students have different professional needs. To require that everyone's committee be the same size imposes a procrustean restriction.

Once that committee is in place, it needs to be more than a symbol. It should meet regularly. Even now, graduate students may meet a member of their committee for the first time at the dissertation defense! We recommend that departments mandate regular meetings of student advising committees. (We say "*advising* committees" because a committee should be in place before the dissertation phase. When the student chooses a dissertation topic, membership of that committee may change.) One good reason for regular meetings is obvious: to discuss a student's work often. In the case of dissertation committees, a department might agree that when a graduate student completes a draft chapter, all members of a committee will meet in person to discuss the manuscript with the student within some set period (a month?) after submission. Institutionalizing such a practice within a graduate program creates accountability for teacher and student alike.[15]

Regular progress reports have numerous virtues. They promote accountability for both students and faculty. They keep all members

The Case of Time to Degree

Let's imagine a hypothetical department that prioritizes swift time to degree. Frequent meetings between students and advisers will be crucial to meeting this agreed-upon goal. The faculty of this time-to-degree-focused department might agree that each student should be assigned a faculty adviser at point of entry into the program. (The students would choose their own advisers when they decide upon a specialty.) From the beginning, advisers would agree to meet with their students on a biweekly basis. This practice would not only establish professional relationships but also keep the students on track.

of the committee in the information loop. And they show students that the program takes an ongoing interest in their work. This regular interest demonstrates ongoing commitment, so it builds trust. Progress reports amount to a bureaucratic expression of caretaking. And care helps to inhibit attrition, a problem we discussed in chapter 4.

Accountability in advising also helps to speed time to degree. As chair of the geography department at the University of Minnesota in the first decade of this century, John Adams did a study of his own student body, past and present. He looked for "the various attributes of students entering our doctoral program in the period 1981–2006 (almost 500 students) that were statistically linked with successful completion of the Ph.D. The attribute most highly correlated with prompt and successful completion was who 'was the student's Ph.D. adviser.'"[16] Good advisers help students finish faster—and accountability through regular meetings helps more faculty to become good advisers.

But an equally important reason for such meetings is for student and committee to discuss the student's larger goals, not just her current work. Following a plan developed at Stanford, all graduate students might have a formal meeting (something more than a regular check-in) with a faculty committee after two years of study to discuss the student's prospective career choices. (If the student has identified specific career fields that lie outside of the university, an authority on those fields should attend also.) The goal of such a meeting (or series of meetings) would be to design a curriculum for the remainder of the student's course of study that is contoured to meet those goals. In this way, dissertation advising harmonizes with the larger objective of career diversity that we discussed in chapter 3. For example, if that graduate student in political science we mentioned a moment ago decides to pursue a career in government, then she should write a dissertation that relates to that pursuit—and perhaps instead of teaching, she should intern in a government office for a term or a year. Such moves need planning—and when the program and the student plan together, the results are both more thoughtful (great minds working together) and more efficient (which can reduce time to degree).[17]

Many PhD students still believe that their advisers will disown them if they admit to an interest in a job outside of academia. Some are giving their advisers a bad rap, but even in these cases, we might ask why these students are so quick to jump to a mistaken conclusion. (One answer might be found in the larger culture of the program.) Other students are not mistaken about this bias: even in these times of change, there remain too many advisers who disrespect the choice not to pursue a professorship. (Bob confesses that some years ago he told a student planning to teach high school, "This isn't why we gave you a fellowship." Now, he considers this student a model.) Either way, we need to recognize that academic culture still stigmatizes nonprofessorial outcomes. We have heard so much testimony from nervous graduate students in our own travels that this concern cannot be ignored.

Advisers need to show, not just tell, graduate students that nonprofessorial work is not a failure. It's a real and legitimate outcome that graduate school teachers need to respect, and it's part of the adviser's job to communicate that respect. If a program introduces its graduate students to the office of career services early on, then the office can intertwine its work organically with the department's offerings as students progress through the program. (Here we assume that the university has joined the burgeoning trend of hiring one or more graduate student career experts.) Orientation is not too soon to begin. James Grossman, the executive director of the American Historical Association, imagines a future presentation to entering graduate students in history at their orientation in 2022 (five years from when Grossman was writing). Grossman envisions the students being addressed there not only by the department's chair and graduate director but also by a graduate student career specialist from the office of career services, who will describe how the office works for graduate students "and how it collaborates with individual departments and the alumni office to identify employers, locally and nationally, who appreciate the value of a humanities Ph.D."

It's difficult to overstate the importance of representing the office of career services at a graduate orientation. The presence of the graduate student career specialist acknowledges the reality that many, if not most, of the students in attendance will seek careers outside of the academy. As important, the place of the career services specialist on stage communicates the message that the department does not simply accept that reality but also *honors* it.[18]

In the same spirit, the graduate student career specialist should visit the department's cohort professional development seminar.[19] He or she might work with the graduate director to coordinate periodic presentations to graduate students at different levels during each year—one for students taking courses, another for ABDs, and so on. Graduate students at both the master's and doctoral levels ought to see graduate career specialists in their halls often enough to get to know their faces. The familiarity promotes ease of access, and it inhibits stigma.

In the same overall spirit of holistic advising, programs should bring alumni back to campus regularly to tell their stories. Former graduate students make the best ambassadors for their own careers, and most are eager to return to explain what they do. (Apart from the nostalgia coupled with their return to campus, the invitation helps confer that legitimacy on *their* career choices.) And an alum might become an informal adviser to a student when they meet in this way, thereby increasing the students' advising resources.

Professors should also attend these presentations. Apart from the possibility that they might learn something useful, their presence visually symbolizes their commitment to their students. Again, when we show our students that their teachers value the diverse range of careers, we invite them to value their own choices. This too is a form of advising. That commitment begins with the career services officer's presence on the orientation stage, and it continues through the students' progress through the program.

All of this counts as advising, and it all takes place outside of committees. It manifests the collaborative advising culture that we started outlining earlier. The ingredients of such a culture will vary according to the needs of the cook. They can encompass faculty training, as at the University of Tennessee, which operates an Office of Graduate Training and Mentorship with workshops on mentoring. The office provides faculty training workshops and workshops for compliance with various research regulations.[20]

An advising culture can also offer less formal contacts. For more than 20 years, Yale University has staged a Feast (Free Eating Attracts Students and Teachers). The mechanics of the program are simple and inexpensive: free lunch for a graduate faculty member who meets with one or two graduate students in the graduate school's dining room. Feast encourages informal interactions in which students talk about their work with different professors, so the program creates an advising community that implies something more than the traditional adviser-student dyad.

But a culture of advising hinges on what it offers students. In one of the best examples that we've seen, the School of Interdisciplinary and Graduate Studies at the University of Louisville runs a comprehensive professionalization program for all graduate students called PLAN (Professional development, Life skills, Academic development, and Networking).

Appropriately, PLAN, which premiered in 2012, emerged from a collaboration between the graduate school dean, Beth A. Boehm, and a graduate student, Ghanashyam (Shyam) Sharma, who was then an intern in Boehm's office. (Other members of Boehm's office did an enormous amount of work to launch the program as well.)

PLAN is one big professional development program that runs as a coordinated series of workshops, about 20–30 each semester, sponsored by different departments, programs, and offices throughout the graduate school. Together, the workshops form a cycle that covers the whole graduate student experience, from teaching (The Teaching Toolbox, to pick one of many examples) to dissertation-writing skills (Writing a Literature Review), grantsmanship, or the job search (from The Academic Job Talk to Leveraging LinkedIn).

Boehm and Sharma designed PLAN with the idea of allowing graduate students to acquire the tools to get through their PhD programs, but also with an eye to what happens afterward. The program, they said, was meant to help graduate students take responsibility for their careers.

The means to that goal, according to Boehm, was "to create a culture" that encompasses both graduate students and faculty. PLAN doesn't cost much money because everyone takes responsibility for it together. Graduate students, faculty members, and staff administrators all volunteer to run the workshops, which Boehm called "a miracle." But it's not miraculous so much as demonstrative of the power of community advising.[21]

In the end, community offers an escape from the hermetically sealed advising practice that promotes problems and limits growth. The Avital Ronell case merits our attention not because of its gossip quotient, but because it shows the decidedly uncommunal model of advising we must escape.

When professors work openly and together on advising, their collaboration inhibits eruptions like the Ronell case. But more important, collaboration harnesses our collective expertise to help our students advance toward their professional goals. A graduate student can still have an adviser—but that central professor should be part of a team, not a lone wolf who separates the student from the pack.

In the end, students benefit from our mindful consideration of their needs in the workplace. The day has long since passed—if it was ever here—when one adviser could meet all of a graduate student's professional needs. It's time that we, their teachers, acknowledged that fact. If it once took a doctor-father to advise a PhD student, it now takes a village.

EIGHT

Students as Teachers

Status and the Status Quo

Most students begin graduate school brimming with enthusiasm for becoming teachers. Whether they plan an academic career or not, whether they see teaching as an immediate or lifelong endeavor, it's a goal. Most have arrived at graduate school, after all, because they were inspired by teachers they had as undergraduates. Their instructors compelled their interest in the subject, and many of these students now hope to do the same for their own students.

Many, perhaps even most, beginning graduate students see their undergraduate teachers as role models. It may be that some of their best teachers were also renowned scholars, but it was *as teachers* that they affected their students, and it was their pedagogical excellence that led these undergraduates to pursue the doctorate.

What if these beginning graduate students were told at the outset of their doctoral studies that teaching is far less important than scholarship in an academic life? What if they were told that their desire to be teachers was something that they should cultivate only if it didn't interfere with their research? Well, that's just what we do say. We don't always say it explicitly, but it's clear all the same. We deflate the status of teaching via our values and our lived practices. The message that teaching is secondary lies at the very heart of our students' graduate training.

Most graduate programs require about two years of coursework. A growing number require a single course in pedagogy, but many offer none at all. The message is clear enough. The implied belief (though "belief" gives too much credit to an unconscious acceptance of the status quo) is that teaching is a mostly accidental mix of personality and experience unworthy of formal consideration.

Has any student ever been asked (because of failure) to repeat any such pedagogy course? Has any doctoral student ever failed to receive the degree because of a poor performance as a teacher? We know of none, and we'll bet you don't either. What's the message there?

Nor do programs construct an intentional sequence of teaching opportunities for graduate students. Instead, we simply assign them to courses that professors don't want to teach, or to grading or lab tasks professors don't want to perform over and over again.

Graduate students hear the message of these practices loud and clear, and they've known for a long time that something is wrong. In Golde and Dore's student survey published in 2001, more than 4 in 10 students felt unprepared to teach discussion sections, 55 percent of science students felt unprepared to teach lab sections, and nearly two-thirds of all doctoral students felt unprepared to lecture.[1] The next year, the National Doctoral Program Survey found similarly that "students were concerned about not being adequately prepared and trained to fulfill their roles as teachers."[2]

Two decades later, we might expect that students would be somewhat more affirming, and they are—but not nearly to the extent one would wish. A 2014 Modern Language Association Task Force report decries a "tendency to devalue teacher preparation in parts of doctoral education," which is at odds "with the ever growing national pursuit of effective teaching."[3]

Even if graduate students may come to wonder where the pedagogy went, new students are most often unaware of the message they are internalizing. Their professionalization happens on so many fronts—learning new research techniques, attending classes, and working in labs with students as passionate and talented as they are, acclimating to a new social and intellectual environment at a new university. The intellectual and emotional energy required in this new environment understandably occupies a lot of attention.

But there's nothing new about the message that teaching doesn't matter much. Graduate teaching has never received sustained attention from anyone, and there's a historical reason for that. The first research universities were founded explicitly to create knowledge. William Rainey Harper, the first president of the University of Chicago, said as much when he declared that his institution's primary mission was to promote "the work of investigation." ("Investigation" was the popular term for research.) "The work of giving instruction," said Harper, was "secondary."[4] There is a large literature devoted to undergraduate teaching at different levels and in different disciplines. Some professors devote their working lives to the study of college pedagogy. Meanwhile, graduate teaching gets ignored. The reason, rooted in history, is worth highlighting: *graduate teaching is seen as the byproduct of faculty research.*

That truth explains a lot, including why professors prefer to teach graduate seminars (where they can bring their current research into the classroom) and not introductory courses. And because the disrespect for teaching pervades the graduate student's workplace, we shouldn't be surprised when our students adopt our values, look down on the teaching that they're given to do, and chase the jobs that look like the ones that their professors have. Those jobs, after all, would allow them to toss those service courses to graduate students of their own.

Let's rewind a moment to recall that exemplary and committed undergraduate teaching is what inspired most graduate students to enter doctoral programs in the first place. When graduate students enter a workplace that scorns the work that they start out wanting to do, they take on the attitudes of their role models and transform themselves accordingly, from the inside out. They have been successfully and silently enlisted in a folly—that good teaching is merely an offshoot of scholarship, that good teaching can't be taught.

It is from us that graduate students learn to describe teaching as a "load," while research is an "opportunity."

This is a grotesque misshaping of a foundational truth, that an active thinker in the ongoing life of a discipline brings the spirit of discovery into the classroom. We certainly do not see scholarship as the evil empire; no one should ever be made to apologize for wanting to learn new things. But graduate school isn't just the place where you learn those things. It's also the place where you have to learn to communicate them.

Nowhere are the stated values and the actual practice of higher education in greater conflict than in the training of academics as educators. Our institutional neglect of pedagogy wastes the potential interplay between scholarship and teaching. It's a measure of the low respect that teaching holds that so many of us speak of "my own work." If teaching isn't our own work, whose work is it?

There are capacities that belong to teaching alone, just as there are capacities exclusive to scholarship. Research alone can't engage the interest of others less experienced; and being helpfully explanatory up close and in the moment, an ability solely and crucially relevant to teaching, requires intentional development every bit as much as techniques of research and sustained reason.

The general public has never seen teaching, or professors, the same way that professors see themselves. Higher education in the United States has always held a place for teaching because the people who send their children to college expect that. In the current era of diminishing resources, patience has been wearing thin. As a result, new forms of assessment have arisen that challenge views of how much and how well students learn in their college years.[5] College and university presidents speak often of faculty dedication to teaching, but structurally speaking, little has changed: faculty status and prestige depend almost entirely on publication.

It's a saving grace that faculty often embrace teaching with authentic passion and enjoyment. But these same faculty members often speak cynically about thinking, testing, and discussing pedagogical strategies, as though it were all a mystery or an accident of personality. Consider how rarely faculty members visit each other's classes. Unless one's performance is being reviewed, one teaches in the company of one's students alone.

The impression conveyed by such practices is that one's teaching is one's private business, yet teaching is the most public activity that most professors engage in. (As Gerald Graff has said, if academics want to make a difference, we should consider that our students spend more hours with us in the classroom than anyone spends reading our writing.)[6] Once we start treating teaching as somehow private, the classroom becomes a walled enclave.

All of this hypocrisy gets codified and enacted in doctoral education. There is no more important aspect of graduate training than developing skilled and confident teachers, but there may be no other aspect of graduate education in which the academy claims so much but does so little.

In the sciences, graduate students teach when they fail to receive a fellowship to work in a lab. Teaching becomes a booby prize. Outside of the sciences, graduate students typically teach the so-called service courses—introductory composition and languages, intro to everything—and they do so over and over again. Rare is the graduate program that assigns its students to teaching to develop their abilities through a sequence of different class assignments, and it is rarer still for graduate students to be provided any instruction whatsoever in the history of their chosen discipline, or in the history and current landscape of higher education, or in the study of student learning. With our highest degree, we graduate only casually literate educators.

Because the PhD is offered at research universities—focus for a moment on that term—students quickly observe that tenure is granted primarily on the basis of published research, with teaching clearly secondary and service a poor third. It's a bad object lesson, especially when most of the graduates who do get full-time jobs teaching at the college level will work not at research universities but at institutions that weigh teaching more heavily. Because of this neglect, they may bring to their new jobs not only a lack of knowledge of what it means to be an educator but even a jaundiced view of their actual students.[7]

At the most pragmatic level, most doctoral programs are not training teacher-scholars to compete for jobs at the majority of colleges and universities.

According to Sidonie Smith, only 15 percent of undergraduates fit the traditional demographic of 18–21-year-olds living on a campus studying full time.[8] Smith lists the challenges involved in becoming an educator at this cultural moment: "New kinds of students. New dynamics of subjectivity" (by which she means the changes in cognitive attention created by new media and technology). "And third, new relationships of students to delivery systems of higher education" (such as online courses, now a commonplace in the post-COVID landscape, and other means of distance learning, as well as techniques for employing teaching technologies locally).[9] Smith's solutions emphasize digital learning, but the basics—course design, responding to student work, classroom techniques—also matter. As a graduate student said at a Woodrow Wilson Foundation panel several years ago, "It's as if my program spent years training me to know everything about the roller coaster. But now I'm in charge of the whole amusement park. I need to know about safety and publicity and all the other rides. No one has taught me about them. No one had even told me they existed."[10]

We also need to consider the large number of doctoral students who do not become professors at all. We have been emphasizing the fact that a majority of PhDs will not enter the professoriate and that a great many will seek positions outside of the field of education. Why should those people care about teaching?

The obvious first answer is that most skilled endeavors involve teaching in one form or another. Professionals need to know how to explain what they're doing, to both nonprofessionals and their own apprentices. Further, teaching beyond the traditional classroom might give life to the notion of service. (And students want the opportunity. Among those attending the 2003 National Conference on Graduate Student Leadership, social responsibility emerged as the top agenda item; and Golde and Dore documented that over half of doctoral students want to provide teaching and other forms of community service, but "this positive news was offset by very low proportions of respondents reporting that their programs had prepared them for service roles. Indeed, this aspect of preparation is nearly absent.")[11] If we are to believe that scholarly training benefits all graduate students regardless of career choice, that should go double for teaching and especially for forms of teaching beyond the campus.

In fact, many nonacademic social sectors train skilled teachers far more intentionally than graduate schools do. The military is one. People generally don't think of the armed forces in this way, but that's because most of us recall the caricatures of military training, like the vividly foul-mouthed drill sergeant in Stanley Kubrick's *Full Metal Jacket*. Former marine helicopter pilot Samuel Grafton emphasized that, beyond basic training, the military ensures a staged educational process that begins with memorization of such matters as "force vectors on outer blades" and on the workings of their equipment. Then comes practice and evaluation, with "feedback and techniques to do each maneuver correctly" along with the opportunity to repeat the procedure for improvement. Only then do helicopter pilots graduate to "tactics and mission planning." And finally, successful pilots make the transition to become teachers themselves.[12]

We're not suggesting that college teaching and flying an aircraft are entirely comparable. Getting it just right, for instance, makes more sense in relation to a piloting procedure than it does in terms of teaching a class. The real difference between the two does not flatter professional college teachers: military training is planned and then enacted with sharply etched goals in mind, while the training of future teachers in graduate school is generally limited in planning and unambitious in execution. Who would want to fly in a helicopter piloted by someone who had been taught as much about piloting as students are taught about teaching in graduate school? (That's okay. We'll ride the bus, even if it does take three days.)

There is a history to the startling neglect of pedagogy in doctoral programs. The tensions of the Cold War contributed to the growth of higher education to its present scale, with research driving the change along with increased student population.[13] As Richard Lewontin documents, the university became the research and development lab for the Defense Department, and indeed for the whole country, as the government took to funding the STEM disciplines.[14] The humanistic disciplines, viewing this new opulence in the bench sciences, followed suit, with encouragement from administrators who wished to maintain rough equity in the arts and sciences.

Publication might be called academia's version of the arms race. As Smith tells it, "the faculty reward system reinforced the value of teaching less, teaching fewer students, teaching graduate rather than undergraduate students, upper-division rather than lower-division courses, seminars rather than lectures, of buying time out of teaching altogether."[15] These rewards are especially prominent at research universities, and graduate students see the faculty jockeying for them. By such displays we convey our values to the next generation.

This unbalancing act has an older history as well. As Len and others have pointed out, the British model of teaching college (which made the first higher educational footprint in colonial America) and the German model emphasizing research (arriving later, after the Civil War) were pushed together in the American version of higher education. It's always been as much a struggle as an alliance, as Vanessa L. Ryan neatly summarizes in a comparison of Germany's Wilhelm von Humboldt ("at the highest level, the teacher does not exist for the sake of the student: both teacher and student have their justification in the common pursuit of knowledge") to England's Cardinal Newman, who argues that the university is for "the diffusion and extension of knowledge rather than its advancement."[16]

The American system skews to the research side of the balance because research universities train all faculty, not just those who teach at research universities themselves. Yet Newman's separatist views notwithstanding, it would be difficult to argue against an ideal union of scholarly discovery and teaching. Without scholarship and research, after all, there would be nothing new to teach. But without the public act of teaching, no next discovery likely could be made. Academics, and especially those who serve as models for graduate students, need to stop short-selling pedagogy.

We owe it to ourselves to define our goals for doctoral students as neophyte teachers, even if those goals may be less obvious than not crashing the helicopter. Then we will find ourselves asking, What are the best and most economical means of training doctoral students as beginning teachers?

We view these challenges programmatically. Accordingly, our agenda for foundational improvement in developing graduate students (especially doctoral students) as capable teachers encompasses four basic challenges:

- *Sequencing.* What should be the order of teaching assignments over an approximately three-year period that would construct a staircase of experiences for graduate students, each building on those previous?
- *Range.* Since most doctoral graduates will not teach at research universities or selective colleges, how can the student-as-teacher gain experience in different kinds of higher educational institutions like public branch campuses, private colleges, community colleges, even K–12 schools, where curricular and classroom leadership by doctoral graduates could prove transformative?
- *Context.* Relatedly, how can graduate students gain a rudimentary understanding of the ecology of higher education, of the history of their discipline, and of the main challenges in the study of student learning, all without exacerbating the already excessive time to degree?
- *Vision.* Apart from classroom teaching and other necessities just mentioned, what goes into becoming a complete educator? Peering into the future of teaching, what do graduate students need to do? What kinds of teachers do they need to be?

Here's the good news: if the training of graduate students as teachers is the greatest embarrassment in PhD education, it is also an area where we're starting to wake up and catch up. Smith argues that the system that devalues teaching is being eclipsed because it "could not hold." Professors and administrators, Smith says, now "recognize that the escalating cost of an undergraduate education brought an obligation to provide students access to senior faculty" and more generally, an education "whose immediate and long-range value justifies its cost."[17] The challenge of preparing good graduate student teachers has produced more innovative responses than any other concern we identify in this book. Here is just one that is worth replicating: GradTeach Live, a competition at the University of Kentucky that parallels the well-known Three-Minute Thesis (TMT) contests that have proliferated around the country. In GradTeach Live, graduate student teachers have three minutes and one slide to showcase a component of their teaching philosophy and to demonstrate how they enact it in their classroom or lab. Prize levels are the same as for the university's version of the TMT.[18]

Here's the bad news: our values aren't changing with our practices. As long as we see teaching as sidecar attached to the research engine, and as long as we use research as the basis of measuring the value of an academic's work, our reforms will be endangered by our own priorities. Far from a building block, the institutional commitment to training graduate students as teachers crumples under the slightest pressure—because it's tissue thin. The implications of this tenuous commitment go far beyond the students' careers and reach to the heart of who we believe we are as professionals and what we think we're doing. Can we instead, in Emerson's good phrase, *realize* our rhetoric?

Blueprints and Building Blocks

Imagine we are cooking dinner and the book we consult for a recipe begins by saying, "Heat pan and stir in butter." For step two, "Heat pan and stir in butter." Then for step three, "Heat pan and stir in butter." Dinner would never happen until we found a better recipe. So it is with teacher training. We need a new recipe for developing great teachers rather than having graduate students teach the same courses over and over.

Our current failed recipe frequently begins by throwing graduate students into the undergraduate classroom, like butter into a pan, sometimes in their very first semester, without any real training at all. That deplorable practice mostly prevails at large public institutions. Usually there's a day or two of perfunctory orientation, and then into the machine march the new graduate student teachers. It's a sloppy approach that leads to some understandably poor teaching, and for the students affected on both sides of the lectern, there's little recourse.

After that, the graduate student teaches the same course or two again and again. The courses are necessary for undergraduates to take, but because the most experienced faculty don't want to teach them, they fall to apprentices. To be clear: we throw together our least experienced teachers with our least experienced undergraduate students. Because these courses effectively serve as potential gateways to liberal arts majors, we ill serve our disciplines and our students together in this way. (We'll discuss that problem further presently.)

At least for the undergrads, some good stuff comes later. For the doctoral students as teachers, it's Bill Murray in *Groundhog Day* with a negative difference.[19] Bill Murray's character repeats the same day over and over, but he learns. He improves his attitude and "graduates." But if the quality of the undergraduate experience may be redeemed by the enthusiasm of the neophyte teacher, that enthusiasm may well dim after multiple iterations of the same course.

Let's write a new recipe.

To do that, we need to avoid getting distracted by any but necessary details. Duke's graduate school sets a good example in requiring every doctoral program to submit a developmental plan for training grad students as teachers. The very requirement makes an important point. And by leaving the specific nature of the plan to each program, the requirement acknowledges disciplinary differences.

It is because of those differences, in the culture as well as the content of disciplines, that we will not ourselves become too detailed here. We will suggest some imperatives and offer some examples. The most obvious way to train beginning teachers is stepwise, through a series of thoughtfully sequenced teaching assignments. Start comfortable, and then raise the bar gradually.

The first teaching assignment given to doctoral students often involves grading for a faculty member's large class or grading while also leading a discussion section of a lecture course. (Scientists, if they teach, usually start out leading lab sections.) With luck, the student will receive some instruction on how to respond helpfully and constructively to student work. Sometimes a discussion leader will receive a visit or two to her section by the faculty member in charge of the course. (And, as we noted earlier, there is sometimes a one- or two-day compact orientation to teaching.)

Altogether, these bits and scraps fall short of a full meal. Consider instead a practicum run by the specific program that begins the spring semester before the student is to teach. Assign each beginner to a seasoned and successful graduate student teacher as a one-on-one mentor, and have the beginner observe classes by the mentor and others.

Then let the sequence wrap around to include the student's first fall term teaching. Assign readings to the new student-teachers, and bring them together weekly to discuss issues that arise from the reading and from the teaching that they observe and perform.[20]

We're aware that some programs require first-year graduate students to teach. We don't much like the practice, but we recognize that it's an economic necessity at some public universities. We hope that such institutions find a way to reduce their dependence on unskilled student labor, but during the time we have to live with that reality, we recommend an intensive one-week teaching bootcamp for rookies before they enter the classroom.

We hope that multiple program faculty will rotate the responsibility of teacher training among themselves. Sharing the labor of training helps to achieve a larger goal: to end the privacy of teaching that prevents such sharing among faculty themselves.[21]

How should graduate students be introduced to the classroom? Instead of throwing them into an introductory course (that might be better staffed by someone with more experience) and then forgetting about them, consider a one-to-one student-faculty partnership. By this we're suggesting that the student serve not as a teaching assistant but rather as an actual partner in the design and teaching of the course.

Teacher Training: A Requirement That Needs Some Teeth

In the humanities and some social sciences, just about every graduate student teaches. So, in departments with a training seminar, just about everyone in those fields completes it.

But what happens if a student flunks the teaching practicum? It's admittedly rare for a graduate student to prove an unfit teacher. But it does happen occasionally. And when it does . . . nothing consequential happens.

That's right, there are no prurient stories to tell about students who do poorly in their teacher training. No scandals break out. The students' failure at being taught to teach proves no deal breaker, and it never threatens their progress toward their degrees. Actually, that may be the scandal. One former dean at a large state university said that he "always suspected that there were a lot of bad TAs but had no real mechanism to deal with it." A current dean at a state university said, "I have seen faculty desire to expel students on account of lousy teaching, but it never gets anywhere."

We in the arts and sciences may say that we're training teacher-scholars (or scholar-teachers), but if someone fails to acquire the "teacher" part of that identity, we confer the degree just the same. PhDs aren't required to be teachers.

Viewed historically, that's not surprising. The United States borrowed the idea of the PhD from European universities, which train PhDs as scholars. But this isn't Europe. Utility has always mattered in American higher education. Today's roiling debates over the "use value" of a college degree didn't come out of nowhere. They've flared on and off for many generations.

The consistent push for utility helped create the expectation that in the United States, professors don't just do research. They teach. That's part of how society at large defines who they are, and it's also how professors view our own jobs. So if we confer a doctorate in the arts and sciences on a graduate student who can't teach, we invoke the European past and deny the American present.

At this point, you may ask: So what? All professors teach anyway, so what does it matter when they learn how? And if a student leaves academia, why should the ability to teach matter?

In fact, it matters a great deal. Most graduate students won't become professors, and the nonacademic workplace expects—and often demands—that graduate students know how to teach. "Only those graduate students with strong preparation as teachers will succeed" in today's workplace, say the authors of the Modern

Language Association's 2014 report on doctoral study in modern language and literature.[1] "The tendency to devalue teacher preparation in parts of doctoral education is at odds with the ever-growing national pursuit of effective teaching."

Put simply, if graduate students can't teach, they won't do well in any job market.

---

1. *Report of the MLA Task Force on Doctoral Study in Modern Language and Literature* (Modern Language Association, 2014), 10, https://www.mla.org /Resources/Research/Surveys-Reports-and-Other-Documents/Staffing-Salaries-and -Other-Professional-Issues/Report-of-the-Task-Force-on-Doctoral-Study-in-Modern -Language-and-Literature-2014.

We're imagining a moderately sized class that permits a mixture of lecture and discussion. In this scenario, the student and the professor collaborate to create a syllabus and then share the leading of the class (with the student receiving supervision from the faculty member) and share in grading written work. Stanford has experimented with such partnerships in an initiative originally funded by the Teagle Foundation.[22] The central idea is that the student learns through teaching and receives ongoing feedback from an experienced older colleague. (Note too that this is an inexpensive innovation. It simply entails the silent upgrade of a TA to a course partner.) A possible variation on this theme would have the student taking a graduate course on a certain topic while teaching a version of the same course to undergraduates, with regular check-ins between the two instructors.

One of the benefits afforded by this model is that students may get a chance to practice lecturing. A guest lecture, well-prepared and re-hearsed in front of the faculty instructor, prepares a student to com-municate with larger audiences in multiple possible settings later on.

Only after receiving carefully planned supervision of the sort we've described would the developing graduate student teacher lead an entry-level course such as composition, language, or calculus. Since solo flight would present new challenges, faculty should consider further orientation and sharing of experiences. Students also should engage faculty in dialogue about the learning goals of the course. These discussions benefit both parties, and may lead to new insights for faculty too.

Afterward, during the dissertating years, the student teacher should have an opportunity to develop and offer an elective course, again with faculty oversight, though by this point, such supervision would presumably be of the limited, just-in-case variety.

As graduate student teachers advance, programs might also consider a return to a faculty-student partnership but with a difference. This time, try flipping it. At the University of Virginia, graduate (and undergraduate) students trained by the Center for Teaching Excellence aid faculty members in designing courses and curricula as advisers. "Typically faculty teach to students," write the designers of UVA's PhD-Plus. "When students and faculty work together" and "each partner contributes equally, though not necessarily in the same ways, to curricular or pedagogical conceptualization, decision making, implementation, investigation, and analysis," new possibilities for learning emerge for all parties.[23]

Whatever the specifics, the underlying principle must be that graduate students progress not just as researchers but as teachers. Their research changes as they gain experience; so should their teaching. Alongside any such progression, doctoral students could be encouraged to consider the pedagogical implications of research assignments in graduate courses. Pedagogy could be part of the research—as Len's Fordham colleague John Bugg has tried with his graduate seminar Teaching the Nineteenth Century, in which students study literature with the specific aim of developing strategies to teach it.

Some programs now allow or even require students to include a pedagogical component in their dissertations.[24] What better means to assert the synergies between research and teaching? Similarly, teaching assignments could include a portfolio requirement, to be reviewed by a faculty advisor.

The quality of teacher training could be raised even further, but the obvious question of resources arises. Graduate students have been counted on to teach whatever is needed for reasons of economy rather than their own learning. It's cheaper by a ratio of about one dollar to five to pay a graduate student to teach rather than a faculty member. But with diminishing student cohorts (and rising numbers of adjuncts, and of adjunct unions), part-time teaching is getting more expensive, and more bureaucratic. To do the right thing costs less today than it once did.

What of the additional time required of faculty members to teach pedagogy more intensively? Certainly this will amount to additional work. Good teaching usually does. But professors need to do it. We see it simply as one of the responsibilities of teaching at the graduate level.

We should also acknowledge the elephant in the room. If graduate student teachers teach more upper-division courses, that will open up slots in the introductory courses that they usually get assigned to. If that means assigning a faculty member or two to a lower-division course once taught exclusively by TAs, well, it's about time. Teaching an intro course should hardly be considered low-caste labor or, worse, a punishment.

Let's consider a related, larger question: What if we saw our service courses more clearly as gateway courses? Because that's what they are. Well-intentioned educators wring their hands at declining enrollments in the liberal arts, with special attention given to dropping numbers in the humanities. Despite robust data showing that liberal arts majors fare very well in all kinds of job markets, anxious students nonetheless flock to courses in business and the professions.

The bottom line is simple: we can't save the liberal arts unless students sign up for liberal arts courses. So why not put our best and most experienced teachers in front of the classes most likely to yield undergraduate majors? Kurt Spelmeyer, a professor of English at Rutgers University who directs the expository writing program there, speaks often of how the required first-year expository writing course is the only experience that most Rutgers undergraduates will ever get of the English department. (Never mind that it's not a literature course; most students don't make that distinction.) Yet tenure-line faculty almost never teach the course. How does that help to persuade students to major in English? Instead of scorning "service courses," we might do better to see them as ambassadorial opportunities for ourselves. "Given the state of the liberal arts," says Melinda Zook, a designer of the new Cornerstone core curriculum at Purdue University, "it's time we got back into the classroom."[25]

We're aware that this proposal amounts to an overturning of our value system. But the old one isn't exactly serving us very well. Nor does it prevail elsewhere. The German model of graduate education prioritizes research, but it's also the practice at German universities for the most distinguished faculty in each discipline to be given the honor—*the honor*—of introducing new students to the nature of the discipline.* Given the obvious and widespread social pressures on our own universities, we need to privilege the importance of introductory courses apart from the quality of the doctoral experience. And as we consider what will best develop the doctoral student as educator, we need to take into account undergraduates and their educational needs. The two aims support each other.

But what of time to degree? Won't a greater emphasis on pedagogy make a bad situation worse? Not according to the Mellon Foundation, which found that while an excessive amount of teaching could slow progress to the degree, those who never taught were less likely to graduate than those who did. And the Mellon-funded researchers found that graduate students who teach gain "benefits that fellowship recipients do not necessarily enjoy—including the opportunities to confer with faculty members and other graduate students and relevant preparation for later teaching careers."[26]

Still, time is a real concern, especially given the additional elements we're recommending. As many programs now require a student to take as many as 15 semester courses in the discipline before proceeding to the exam and dissertation stages, might we reduce that number by a couple and allow for the greater focus on teaching to substitute? Imagine a doctoral program where a full half of the coursework and of the

---

* Some history departments also recognize the intro course as an honor to teach, though in these cases, it's usually a large lecture class.

dissertation involve pedagogy. It's unthinkable to us today, but that's because of how we ourselves have been socialized. Surely we can do much better to realize the symbiotic ideal of exchange between research and teaching.

Alternately or in addition, the full and final preparation of new teachers might allow for the possibility of a year-long postdoc. It could be made available as an incentive to the best student teachers to complete the degree with alacrity and to extend their teaching experiences, perhaps by interning in the teaching and learning center or by peer mentoring beginning graduate student teachers, while polishing the dissertation or staking out a nonacademic career application of one's research *and teaching* abilities.

But where might they teach? Not necessarily at the home campus alone. That's the subject of the next section.

Out of the Comfort Zone

"Only those graduate students with strong preparation as teachers will succeed" in today's workplace, say the authors of the Modern Language Association's 2014 report on doctoral study in modern language and literature.[27] That's just as true for those who don't join the professoriate. Any professional workplace expects—and often demands— that graduate students know how to teach. Employers value PhDs for their ability to work with complex information, to analyze it deeply, summarize it, redact it, synthesize it—and then to teach it to others. Sarah Iovan, who holds an English PhD, was hired by a large firm as a senior tax accountant in 2019. "They find my rather unusual background particularly exciting," she said, "because they are desperate for people to who can communicate technical concepts to clients with no technical background and who can teach junior staff and interns."[28]

But we need not venture beyond academia at all to see a gap in the preparation of students as teachers. Many doctoral students have little experience with the teaching-first environment of liberal arts colleges, public state branch campuses, and community colleges, even though those kinds of institutions constitute most of the professorial job market. Despite pneumatic rhetoric describing the interplay of research and teaching, research universities and a range of other types of institutions have unbundled the two functions by appointing full-time, non-tenure-track instructors along with the familiar legion of part-time adjuncts. (Part-time adjunct positions, which often exploit labor, are nothing we wish to promote and in fact hope, through career diversity, to restrict. But our point here is about where the jobs are and the obvious mismatch between training and career options.) "Students are not well-prepared to assume the faculty positions that are available," wrote Golde and Dore in 2001, "nor do they have a clear concept of their suitability . . . for work outside of research."[29] The situation has not improved nearly enough in the generation since those words were written.

This venerable concern has some history that informs some worthy current programs. It led in 1991 to the formation of Preparing Future Faculty, an initiative undertaken by the Association of American Colleges and Universities (AACU) and by the Council of Graduate Schools (CGS). Preparing Future Faculty, the workings of which we detailed in chapter 1, was designed to provide graduate students with experience at institutions other than the research universities where they receive their degrees: liberal arts colleges, community colleges, comprehensive universities such as branches of state universities. Through institutional partnerships, students were to observe and learn about faculty life and responsibilities in a variety of settings. "The key purpose of PFF," its leaders wrote, "is to promote expanded professional development for doctoral students."[30]

The plan was optimistic. The results proved less so. Presented with a range of possible activities on both sides of the partnership, host institutions tended to provide the minimum (an occasional workshop or job shadowing program, attendance at committee meetings). Further, the service component at the partner institution usually meant simply internal committee work without public engagement. Many PhD-granting institutions chose not to participate at all because the benefits did not seem to justify the amount of time required of the student. PFF soon lost momentum.

PFF nevertheless offered a superb conceptual design. It proposed to create vital liaisons between doctoral universities and a myriad of other kinds of higher education institutions where most graduate students could pursue a career. The program persists today in some graduate programs, usually in diluted form or with the PFF name tacked onto a program that no longer resembles the original.

Looking back, we might fault the program's architects for not having insisted on clear and sufficiently ambitious objectives. In particular, the failure to ask the graduate students to teach stands out. But that is not to say that the program offered no value. A 2002 survey of PFF alumni who secured academic positions showed a positive view of the program, with most believing that their PFF participation aided them in their job search, helped them make a smooth transition to their new jobs, and even allowed them to immediately contribute to the group mission of their new department colleagues.[31]

Perhaps PFF demanded so little because its leaders knew that they were doing something so new. By giving teaching and faculty career issues a space within the PhD degree, they were making an extraordinary assertion that these two matters deserved attention as something other than appendages to the research enterprise. Perhaps the most important effect of PFF is that it existed, and exists, as an important reminder that there is a world beyond the research university.

Some of its most ambitious institutional participants—interestingly, those with the most prestige—provided a helpful model for future collaborations between doctoral-granting universities and other kinds of institutions of higher education. At the University of Washington, nine students working intensively with mentors from their department or from a partner institution received scholarships for a quarter to design and teach a course or attempt an alternative instructional innovation. Stanford has lately forged a partnership with nearby San Jose State University, Preparing Future Professors, that brings Stanford doctoral students into the SJSU workplace. Adrienne Eastwood, an associate professor at SJSU said of the Stanford visiting students, "When they graduate, this is the kind of job that they can probably expect."[32] Similarly, the Mellon Foundation recently funded a four-year pilot program that will bring graduate students from CUNY into classrooms at LaGuardia Community College.[33] And earlier, Mellon had funded a program of exchange in which University of Michigan postdoctoral fellows in the humanities taught at Oberlin and Kalamazoo Colleges, while faculty members from these schools came to Ann Arbor to pursue their research work.[34]

At Indiana University, in a Future Faculty Teaching Fellowship Program, 20 advanced doctoral students at the main campus attend a three-day seminar to learn more about different academic environments and then relocate to branch campuses and other host institutions for one or two semesters of actual teaching. With guidance from a faculty mentor at the host institution, each student takes full responsibility for two courses—exactly what was lacking in PFF programs—while also participating in service activities. And at Duke, in a certificate in teaching program that we will discuss further in the next section, students are encouraged to make contact and teach at several nearby institutions, ranging from the Durham Technical Community College to the Osher Lifelong Learning Program.

At the University of Kentucky, PFF has evolved into a centralized program, housed in the Graduate School, and composed of a set of credit-bearing courses as well as workshops. One of its greatest strengths is that the courses are cross-disciplinary; students gain valuable insights from listening to and interacting with students from other disciplines in the contexts of teaching, service, and research. Preparing Future Professionals, for example, is a two-credit hour course for doctoral students across the disciplines who want to explore nonacademic careers and prepare for the broader job market. Through panel discussions and on-site visits, students interact with PhDs from Kentucky and elsewhere who work in fulfilling positions outside academia ranging from industry to nonprofits and start-ups. One of the students' key assignments is to conduct informational interviews with PhDs in the student's field who work outside of academia.[35]

More audaciously, the University of Wisconsin's NSF-funded K-through-Infinity program provides fellowships for doctoral students in the STEM disciplines to serve as resources in K–12 schools. Teams of student fellows, K–12 teachers, school administrators, and university researchers collaborate on curricular and pedagogical initiatives for one to three years. All fellows regularly work with students in classrooms, participate in meetings with school district liaisons, and take part in professional development seminars arranged by the district in tandem with the university. At the University of Virginia, graduate students may participate in a ReinventED Lab, cosponsored by the Charlottesville schools and various community groups, with an emphasis on innovation in public schools and in cocurricular aids for K–12 students.[36] Similarly, UC-Irvine's Humanities Out There program has had graduate students work with K–12 teachers to exchange disciplinary research and school classroom practices. Together, they develop new K–12 applications, learning at the same time to apply social science research methods.[37]

That Irvine program also supports 20-week internships for doctoral students in a range of cultural institutions ranging from PBS SoCal to repertory theaters and Orange County Parks. This public outreach represents a different kind of development from the PFF effort that has spread rapidly. At many universities, such public outreach adds to or replaces the sole career goal of "faculty" with "professional." Preparing Future Professionals programs are currently offered at the University of Kentucky, Marquette, Indiana, the University of New Hampshire, Old Dominion, Florida State University, and in a partnership between the University of North Carolina at Greensboro and North Carolina Agricultural and Technological State University. We will discuss their nature, their potential, and some dangers they may present in chapter 10, on public scholarship. (One caution we might mention here is illustrated by the otherwise laudable North Carolina effort, where the professionals program runs alongside the faculty program and students are asked to choose one or the other according to their goals. That seems sensible, but it misses an important point: that focusing on teaching adds to a student's capacities and credentials for a nonacademic career, just as workplace experiences can contribute powerfully to the success of a future professor. This example illustrates the peril of alternative PhD tracks. Learning of this sort is decidedly not a zero-sum game.)

Studying Teaching

We've discussed the value of more ambitious orientations for beginning teachers, but a number of graduate programs and entire graduate schools have gone well beyond that. They actually integrate the study of teaching and learning as subject matter into the doctoral experience.

The movement to focus more of the doctorate on teaching began with Ernest Boyer's *Scholarship Reconsidered* (1990), in which he proposed teaching as a form of active scholarship and urged that it be respected as a full partner to what he called "the scholarship of discovery," his term for research. Critics at the time considered Boyer's widened definition of scholarship a potential excuse for non-publishing faculty members and also argued that, in borrowing the status quo prestige inherent in research, he was undercutting his own argument. But Boyer's strategy demonstrated staying power. Along with Preparing Future Faculty and some subsequent reform initiatives such as the University of Washington's Re-envisioning the Ph.D. and the Woodrow Wilson National Fellowship Foundation's Responsive Ph.D., Boyer's work provoked conversation about the need to value teaching. Boyer's successor as director of the Carnegie Fund for the Advancement of Teaching, Lee Shulman, partnered with the AACU to establish the Carnegie Academy of Teaching and Learning in 1998 to support individual campuses interested in scholarly approaches to these matters. Carnegie's subsequent initiative in doctoral education (which we discussed in chapter 1 on reform efforts) furthered this emphasis.

Though Boyer and Shulman did not create a new normal, they did change the conversation. Very few graduate programs elide teaching as they once did, and a well-populated minority have sought to bring research into teaching and to treat teaching as a form of scholarship.

Examples of such efforts abound. Indiana's sociology department requires graduate students to take a three-course sequence on teaching and learning, with the third course consisting of a research project. Indiana also has extended the Scholarship in Teaching and Learning Program from faculty to graduate students, who partner with faculty in presentations, workshops, and group discussions. At Howard University, faculty-student pairs apply for small grants on teaching and learning and present their findings in a public roundtable. (For instance, nine programs considered how undergraduates acquire the language of their disciplines.) Another formal practice worth noting is the Scholar-Educator Option offered by the PhD program in the School of Biological Sciences at Illinois State University. This track combines research experience with formal training in teaching.[38] At the University of Michigan, an innovative program in chemistry employs training grants for students and faculty to design, implement, and assess an instructional project. The LEAD (leadership, excellence, achievement, diversity) Graduate Teacher Network at Colorado annually trains 45 advanced graduate students for an initial week, during which they develop a plan for departmental and group activities in consultation with their departmental chair and academic adviser. Each then contributes to the department's teacher training efforts throughout the academic year, while the students attend ongoing workshops and Friday Forums on issues of learning. Leaders of the program, which has enrolled more than 500 students in the past decade, believe it has shifted the campus culture to a learning-centered focus, while improving discipline-specific and general instructional skills—and even administrative abilities—for students. A similar program exists at the University of Washington.

Some universities have gone still further in providing formal recognition via a certificate in teaching. These credentials allow applicants to flag their specific skills in crowded markets. Howard University offers a certificate in college and university faculty preparation that entails "credit-bearing courses as well as practicum and field experiences that encompass teaching and learning as a scholarly activity, mentoring, assessment of learning outcomes, ways to achieve and maintain diversity, technology in higher education, and citizenship in the academic community."[39] At Colorado, students taking a number of workshops on teaching receive a similar certificate and lead teaching assistants are provided with small stipends to organize teaching activities in their departments. The University of Missouri offers a certificate of sorts as a graduate minor in college teaching for all doctoral students, consisting of a three-hour core course, a teaching practicum, and three to six elective hours.[40] Duke has taken a program pioneered by the biological sciences faculty and made it available to doctoral students in all fields. For the certificate in college teaching, students receive "sustained systemic training that promotes current best practices in teaching and learning, appropriate use of instructional technology, and systemic assessment of student learning outcomes."[41] Students take two courses in college teaching offered either by their department or by the graduate school. They lead a course and serve as a discussion, lab, or section leader with visits from at least two observers (who may be peers in the program or faculty). Further, they guest lecture on at least four occasions, and they document and reflect on these experiences in an online teaching portfolio designed to provide them with a competitive advantage in applying for academic positions emphasizing teaching.

Moving beyond individual institutions, the Mathematical Association of America runs Project NExT for graduate students and new faculty on all aspects of academic life, including teaching.[42] Such national programs can benefit individual programs that are strapped for time and resources. A more ambitious example on the national scale is the Center for the Integration of Research, Teaching and Learning (CIRTL), funded by the NSF and hosted by the Wisconsin Center of Educational Research. Focused on the sciences, the center today consists of a growing network of 23 research universities and serves more than 4,000 students each year. It has produced more than 100 publications and provides notes from hundreds of network presentations going back to 1997. CIRTL has a suggestive and intriguing online presence. In the fall of 2015, the center offered online courses on topics like teaching with technology, developing a teaching portfolio, diversity in the college classroom, teaching the STEM undergraduate, and bringing primary literature to the undergraduate classroom. The courses vary from year to year but always have the same four foci: learning through diversity, effective use of technology, teaching as research, and the academic career categories, which serve as well to organize the online learning communities.[43]

CIRTL offers a means for individual programs to supplement their teacher training. It can bring together graduate students and faculty, for the subjects matter to all who teach. Its greatest impact may be as a model, for we see no reason it could not be adapted by the humanities and social sciences as well.

We aim to showcase valuable ideas that deserve to spread. Even so, we would note two dangers. One is obvious: creating something of a separate track for students most interested in teaching may provide a free pass for others to ignore it and maintain an untenable status quo. That's the main problem with separate "teaching tracks" at the graduate level and of teaching specialists in specific disciplines.[44] The fact that these teaching-intensive graduate programs are almost always elective add-ons suggests that progressive graduate educators need to be more assertive. Or it may simply suggest the distance yet to be traveled.

The second danger is apparent only in its absence: a lack of background. No program that we know of includes a history of the discipline, a view of the overall higher education landscape, or a survey of the current debates and challenges in higher education (including the vanishing academic job market in some fields). We do not mean to turn all doctoral degrees into education degrees. Rather, we are suggesting hours, not semesters, and introductions, not full programs of study. (For several years Len taught a workshop for graduate students at Princeton that fits the bill, but it's cocurricular, not curricular.)

We need to know ourselves and the full variety of our academic world. Right now, such knowledge is confined to a few specialists and to those academics who pick it up along the way, as the authors of this book did. Professional self-consciousness should be part of the education of every faculty member, if only because it aids in the professional development of both our students and ourselves.

Beyond Teaching

In the end, graduate school should train educators, not just teachers. Educators know how to plan and teach in today's world, and they can adjust to the different kinds of audiences they may face, inside and outside the formal classroom.

To that end, we encourage you to take your graduate students backstage. In the coteaching with faculty members that we've suggested, students will learn more and faster if they see the workings of the whole, not just given a view from the audience. When students become junior partners and learn the challenges of organizing a course plan, they will be more self-aware when they do the same thing on her own. Similarly graduate students should witness and participate in discussion of curricular issues, even if that means they see a messy department debate.

Second, get your students off campus if you can. Organize a PFF-type link to teaching at a different kind of college or university or create opportunities for internships. In both cases, set up a sequence of learning, doing, and then teaching, to create a more capacious sense of what teaching may mean and where it can and should occur.

Third, get beyond the department. Higher education is increasingly recognizing that the disciplines may be useful, but they aren't sacrosanct, and that in any case, students can learn more about their own if they gain a perspective beyond it. A growing trend in undergraduate education is to organize college curriculum by major social challenges, not just disciplines. We discussed interdisciplinarity in more detail in chapter 6, but let us say here that another virtue of a complete educator is an awareness of how learning happens differently in different parts of the academy.

Fourth, spotlight teaching activities that aren't usually discussed, such as the best use of office time and now of digital communication. "The achievement of the MOOC [Massive Open Online Course] movement is, at this moment, very modest," says Sidonie Smith, but she rightly insists on the potential of technology to promote a community of learners.[45] Smith lists some positives of the online classroom, including its potential to make learning available to many who are too far away or can't afford it.[46] The COVID-19 pandemic has made many of these broadly familiar. We hope that the pandemic-necessitated shift to online teaching will eventually allow digitally based insight to generate new ideas for the traditional classroom. As Cathy Davidson points out, student learning is the important thing, and digital technology allows for new ways to think about that.[47] Put simply, the educators we train should know something of digital teaching and learning. These are conversations that we all need to have.

The ability of current faculty, especially senior faculty, to lead graduate students toward these new horizons is, at best, uneven. But just about every doctoral campus now has an office dedicated to digital instruction, and this is yet another place where we urge programs to make friends. We don't have to do everything by ourselves.

Which leads to our final injunction, to make teaching matters a continuing subject of public conversation in the workplace. We have public lectures in which scholars (both intra- and extramural) present their research. Why not hold public gatherings to showcase the scholarship of teaching? When we talk about teaching, we not only make it public but also show that it matters. When we don't talk about it, we imply that it's beneath notice.

Good teaching involves learning on both sides. Good teachers demonstrate to students that they're still learning. We aim for the same auspicious confusion between teaching and research. "We excite our students," Vanessa L. Ryan says, "because we are also creating and reinterpreting knowledge in our fields. Our research is strengthened by working with students at all levels who push us as scholars to reimagine our material." But Ryan also quotes critics who see "teaching and research as competing functions within a zero-sum game of resources"[48] Our teaching—and our teacher training—can and should push back against that view. Most of us know of examples of class discussion that leads to a scholarly project that extends beyond the classroom walls. We need to show that the synergy between teaching and research is an enabling reality, not a smokescreen.

Ryan ultimately finds in student-centered learning a valuable exchange between research and teaching: it "is inquiry-based and problem-based; it combines research-based learning and research-based teaching" and thus can "redefine teaching, and in consequence, also research."[49] This formulation follows Boyer in borrowing the prestige of scholarship to boost the impoverished status of teaching. That's a rhetorical concern, but we hope it signals that we're at an intermediate stage in a transformation of values. The path between research and teaching is a two-way street, as it should be, even with occasional collisions. One measure of the traffic flow up and down that street is how we educate our educators.

NINE

Degrees

What Should They Look Like? What Should They Do?

For most PhD students and their professors, the dissertation is the central and definitive part of the doctoral program. It's a conclusion and a beginning at the same time: a capstone scholarly experience in which the student brings her own voice to the conversation in her discipline in the final stage of an introduction to the next stage of professional life. But the dissertation may also become the most perplexing of mazes or an alienated and routine set of chores.

While the humanities disciplines are often dragged to center stage to illustrate the shortcomings of doctoral education, its problems are perhaps most fraught in the sciences. The current practice, as biologist Crispin Taylor describes it, entails lab leaders carving off projects from their own agendas and doling them out to students as thesis topics. This model of working within the adviser's grant-supported project discourages original thinking and makes the student, in the words of historian of science Yehuda Elkana, into "a minor technician in a huge machinery" whose education amounts to "the opposite of being trained for intellectual risk-taking."[1] That's bad enough, but worse still, this model is becoming economically less sustainable as competition for grants has intensified.

We have elsewhere pointed to the disciplinary difference between the overdetermined life of the laboratory for apprentice scientists and the laissez-faire advising that can go on in the humanities (see chapter 7, on advising). In the sciences, we observed, every major report over the past two decades has called for more training grants to provide a graduate experience that prioritizes the student's development. Instead, the research-grant-driven system persists—and in fact has increased its dominance. As a result of "being handed a thesis project on a plate," says Taylor, "students may lack intellectual engagement with their project, and it may take them longer to develop the facility for independent, strategic, and constructively critical thought that is a vital component of any doctoral program worth its salt." Elkana says that "defining a problem and locating the problem on the larger map of one's field" is "the single most significant and pivotal process in science training," but current practice doesn't teach students to do that.[2]

This is a damning critique—and it comes from scientists themselves. At minimum, science educators should consider Angelica Stacy's suggestion that part of the student's dissertation, at least, should focus on "something other than the student's portion of the adviser's research."[3]

At the other extreme, there can be too little thesis advising in the humanities and humanistic social sciences. If micro-vision characterizes the science dissertation and the research that leads up to it, a drifty laxness may beset the dissertation in the humanistic disciplines, ironically coupled with a dogmatism about format and scope. Professorial neglect in any field, writes Taylor, "can leave students feeling rudderless and frustrated," and this surely adds to time to degree—or to not completing the degree at all. Between this Scylla and Charybdis, Taylor sensibly calls for a middle way that will be "more valuable to the student."[4] In this chapter, we'll consider that middle way. We construe it as a wide road, with branches that lead to alternative dissertation possibilities, and with these, we include a proposal for a professional master of arts degree.

First Principles, Fundamental Questions

Let's start with the basics. What is a doctoral dissertation, and what is its purpose?

Here are a couple of things that a dissertation *is*. First, it's a substantial work of original scholarship that stands as the final credential for a graduate student to receive a PhD. Second, at the same time that the dissertation demonstrates mastery of learning, it's also the final and formal stage in a *process* of learning. That is, a dissertation doesn't just prove that a student has learned what graduate school has to teach; it's also part of that teaching and learning itself. You could say that it's the biggest single lesson in graduate school.

Here are a couple of things that a dissertation is *not*. First, it isn't a hazing ritual—or at least we can agree that it shouldn't be. (It can all too easily become one.)[5] Second, a dissertation isn't a book. It may become one later on, and that's fine when it happens. Or it might not become a book, which is not a bad thing. But as submitted, a dissertation isn't a book.

But how close to a book should a dissertation be?

Before we try to answer, let's expand the question. Some fields are "book fields," by which we mean disciplines or interdisciplinary programs (usually in the humanities and humanistic social sciences) in which PhDs might be one day be expected to turn their dissertations into books. When we talk about whether a dissertation can or should be turned into a book, we're using that possibility as an example of what the scope of a dissertation should be. Not all fields are book fields, of course. If you're not in a book field, please keep reading— because the conversation about whether a dissertation should become a book analogizes to the scope of the dissertation in other fields as well. The issues are the same.

We'll focus on the book fields for now because they illustrate the debate most clearly. Some tenure-track teaching jobs for PhDs in those fields will require that assistant professors turn their dissertations into books in order to get tenure. Most of the jobs where that requirement obtains are at research universities. (Teaching-intensive institutions do not typically require a book from their junior faculty.)

Because most professorships are not at research universities, we should recognize how relatively unusual the dissertation-to-book requirement is. (And professorships themselves are rarer these days, their ranks having been thinned and then supplemented by legions of full-time instructors who labor off the tenure track, with different job requirements. These faculty members generally face more modest research demands that don't include books.) Most fields have their own version of this problem. The dissertation-to-book requirement gets a lot of attention because it's a metonymy: within it the larger question of dissertation scope can play out.

When Stephen Greenblatt served as president of the Modern Language Association in 2002, he wrote a letter to the membership expressing concern over the fetishization of the "tenure book":

> Over the course of the last few decades, most departments of language
> and literature have come to demand that junior faculty members
> produce, as a condition for being seriously considered for promotion to
> tenure, a full-length scholarly book published by a reputable press. A
> small number of departments expect the publication of two such books.
> Whether these expectations are reasonable or necessary is a question that
> we should collectively ponder and debate.[6]

The MLA formed a task force in the wake of Greenblatt's letter, and it produced a report in 2006 containing some useful guidelines for how departments might evaluate scholarship more capaciously and thus free themselves from the tyranny of the book.[7]

The tenure-book fetish hasn't vanished in the generation since Greenblatt's letter, but it has receded from the front of professional consciousness of academics who work in the book fields. Perhaps the MLA task force report changed some minds. Since the report appeared, some departments have written tenure guidelines for assistant professors that mark out alternative paths to tenure: a collection of articles, for example. The rise of electronic repositories like JSTOR has helped boost the visibility of journal articles, advancing that cause. And digital scholarship now provides a new set of possible modes and venues for research and publication.

More likely, the continually narrowing economic straits of both academia and scholarly publishing changed something more than minds. Elite institutions may not have changed their tenure requirements—and their prestige continues to attract disproportionate publicity to everything they do—but like everyplace else, the elites hire fewer assistant professors these days. More PhDs go on to work at teaching-intensive colleges and universities or outside of academia entirely. The tenure-book hasn't exactly gone away, then, but it has become a marginalized phenomenon. The tenure-book problem seems less urgent these days because it affects fewer and fewer people.

But the dissertation hasn't adapted to this changed landscape. Graduate students write dissertations in different economic circumstances than their advisers did. That fact should matter more than it does. We began this book with a demographic example of a hypothetical incoming PhD cohort numbering eight people. Statistics tell us that of those eight, about four will finish the degree, and perhaps two will get full-time teaching jobs. Of those two, one at most will get a job at a research university or selective college—and those are pre-pandemic numbers. Yet the curriculum of most graduate programs remains aimed at that one person.

The dissertation requirement mirrors the needs of that one fortunate student particularly closely. The dissertation is obviously the central part of the curriculum of all doctoral programs in the arts and sciences. Broadly speaking, that curriculum needs to meet the needs of the students whose education brings it into being: it has to educate students in their field of study and help prepare them for the practical realities that they face as professionals-in-training. As we now conceive it, though, the dissertation best prepares the one (actually less than one) of those hypothetical eight entering students who will snag a job as an assistant professor at a research institution.

Should the dissertation requirement change? It's easy to say no. As we've observed, academia is small-*c* conservative, but graduate school is conservative even by academic standards. Graduate school has been around for centuries, but the doctoral dissertation is young by comparison. It was introduced in the late eighteenth and early nineteenth centuries in Europe and quickly worked its way to the center of the curriculum, first there and then here. Historian Roger L. Geiger credits Johns Hopkins University with "standardiz[ing]" the PhD in the United States. Hopkins awarded more PhDs than any other university during the formative decades of the 1870s and 1880s. Those PhDs in turn cultivated doctoral programs at public and private universities around the country. "By the turn of the century," says historian Laurence R. Veysey, "the PhD degree was usually mandatory" to get hired at "nearly every prominent institution."[8]

Graduate school practice has of course evolved since then. It introduced practices to accommodate increased numbers of students, such as bureaucratized admissions and comprehensive exams. But graduate study hasn't changed all that much since it was introduced in the United States in the decades leading up to the twentieth century. Graduate school today resembles graduate school in the 1890s much more closely than undergraduate school resembles its ancestors from that time.

Like many other features of graduate school, the dissertation has gone unexamined for a long time. As we will suggest, the question of whether to reform the dissertation is a matter for the faculty in each field—and each department or program within each field—to decide. We don't wish to prescribe the answer, but we do urge that faculty take up the question rather than ignoring it. In this chapter we'll outline the issues at stake.

The Case of History

History departments have staged the debate over the dissertation particularly vividly. Most historians agree that a history dissertation should be an extended work of scholarship. History is a book field, and many historians have argued that a history dissertation should be one revision away from a book.[9]

This conservative position contrasts with history's position at the forefront of the move toward career diversity for PhDs in the humanities.

The 2011 essay "No More Plan B," by American Historical Association executive director James Grossman and then-AHA president Anthony T. Grafton, remains a touchstone of that ongoing conversation, and it has been supplemented by many further projects by the association, including the Where Historians Work database, which we discussed in chapter 1.[10]

Some historians have been pushing back against the prevailing norm. The AHA's journal, *Perspectives on History*, published a forum, "History as Book Discipline," in 2015 in which a group of prominent historians argue that in these times of shrinking library budgets and burgeoning digital venues, the field has to rethink its priorities and become more flexible.[11] Lara Putnam, a participant in that forum, compares the emphasis on books to "living in a land of $100 bills. Maybe you'd like to be more flexible about what to buy. But the bottom line is you can't make change. . . . [I]f the irreducible unit of promotable scholarship is a seven-year research project leading to a 100,000-word monograph, it doesn't leave much room for flexibility." This practice hurts graduate students and junior faculty both. "The bottom line," says Putnam, "is that insisting historians' scholarly output arrive in book-size chunks in order to count for promotion radically reduces the flexibility of early and midcareer scholars to invest in anything else, be it peer-reviewed articles or public outreach or digital genres as yet uncreated." She asks, "Why should we so constrain the creativity of younger scholars when, truly, we don't have to?"[12] Indeed.

The idea that a history dissertation—or any dissertation, for that matter—should be an embryonic book has obvious implications for the amount of time it takes to finish a PhD. History dissertations typically entail extensive archival work: the graduate student, with the help of the adviser, identifies an archive and researches it deeply. The thesis emerges from that research. Graduate students in history usually learn the contours of their projects from their time in the archive. In the process, they may come to see the contours of a book their dissertation can become.

But should the dissertation be an early version of that entire book or instead some representative portion of it? It obviously takes much longer to write the whole thing. A representative portion would need to demonstrate that the candidate possesses the skills necessary to be a professional historian. It would imply, among other things, that the graduate is capable of finishing the publishable book later on.

The case of the history dissertation limns an ethical question: Where should graduate students finish their books? This question has multiple contexts:

- First, "where" is preceded by "if." Most graduate students in history won't turn their dissertations into books. Many of them won't work in academia at all.
- Second, if a graduate student does most (or even all) of the work to prepare a dissertation for eventual publication while in graduate school, the writer necessarily has done that work for apprentice wages: a graduate student stipend. If she revises and augments her dissertation into a book while employed as an assistant professor, she's doing the same work as a salaried, credentialed professional.

These questions surrounding history dissertations evoke the first principles we started with, the definition and purpose of a dissertation. But in recognition of the temporal dimension, we should now add a third: How long should it take to write a dissertation? All of these questions are interdependent and inseparable. Any reform of the dissertation process starts at their intersection—and with that in mind, we leave the specific precincts of history to return to the scene of the arts and sciences at large.

The Dissertation, Time to Degree, and Everything

The dissertation is a main ingredient in the stew of problems that plague graduate education in this country right now. The debate over how long it takes to earn a PhD has produced some entrenched positions. "The protracted character of doctoral study burns out one's scholarly interests," says one academic. Another argues that "the article-length dissertation is just common sense and is long overdue."

Yet another warns that "it would be a serious error to debase the Ph.D. in the interest of reducing its time." That back-and-forth ought to be familiar enough, but here's the rub: those quotations come from a book published in 1960.[13] We've been having the same arguments about time to degree for more than 60 years. While generations of us have fiddled, our graduate students remain in school for years on end.

The author of that 1960 study, Bernard Berelson, collected some of the first time to degree statistics, including the only numbers we've ever seen that measure the ABD period. Back then, the times-to-degree that people were complaining about were, ahem, rather lower than what we see today. The median number of years spent "directly working on dissertation" were 1.7 in the physical sciences, 1.6 in biological sciences, 1.1 in the social sciences, 1.3 in the humanities, 1.2 in engineering, and 0.9 in education.[14]

What has happened? We can make a few inferences:

- Because of the constricted academic job market, many graduate students stay in school longer to write the strongest possible dissertation. In book fields, that often entails writing a longer, more detailed, more book-like dissertation, with published articles as evidence at the job-market moment that the thesis is publishable. But the same logic applies to all fields.
- The requirements for a creditable dissertation went up at the same time, for similar reasons connected to the diminishing number of professorships. That is, as the academic job market tightened, the requirements for the PhD credential to compete for those jobs also tightened.
- Students stay longer in graduate school for other reasons too. They build up their teaching and service records, and most important, they publish as a way of distinguishing themselves. (Also, the dismal academic job market naturally affects the decision: Why leave sooner than necessary?)

The value of graduate student publication is hard to argue with— and it's intertwined with the market value of the student's dissertation. The logic is pretty clear: getting a part of your dissertation published suggests that the rest of it may be publishable too. And publication can allow a student to make the cut in a crowded field competing for academic jobs. Many professors on hiring committees behave just like Jason Brennan, a business professor at Georgetown, who says that "the scarcity of time" leaves him "no choice but to use some sort of heuristic rather than to give each candidate a thorough vetting." Faced with a stack of applications, Brennan will "cull anyone who doesn't already have a strong list of publications." In doing so, Brennan acknowledges that he may overlook an excellent candidate who hasn't published, but he considers the time saved worth the risk.[15]

We might disagree with Brennan's methods, but we must reckon with the fact that he's out there practicing them, and he's surely not alone. NYU philosophy professor J. David Velleman had those methods in mind in 2017 when he suggested banning graduate student publication. In "The Publication Emergency," a post on a popular philosophers' blog, *The Daily Nous*, Velleman makes a simple but radical two-part proposal: First, philosophy journals "should adopt a policy of refusing to publish work by graduate students." Second, to give teeth to the ban, Velleman suggests that philosophy departments "adopt a policy of discounting graduate-student work in tenure-and-promotion reviews" of junior professors.[16]

These policies, writes Velleman, would "halt the arms race in graduate-student publication." He caught a lot of flak for his suggestions, with hundreds of comments on his post. Some graduate students saw his proposal as an attack on their freedom. Such attacks don't recognize the extent to which Velleman is actually advocating *for* graduate students, who are caught in a system that's simply brutal. If they want to compete for the few tenure-track professorships that are out there, they have to publish while they're writing their dissertations. Doing so, however, not only puts extra stress on students in an already stressful period of their training but also can interfere with the maturation of those same dissertations.

First, some perspective: Velleman's suggestions can't become policy without widespread, virtually unanimous support; and even if that support were in evidence (which it most decidedly is not), his proposal would require unified cooperation among all philosophy journals and department personnel committees. Does anyone really think that's possible? To be clear: the authors of this book have no intention of legislating graduate student publication out of existence (we can't anyway) or of advocating for such a position.

Instead, we should take Velleman's post for what it is: a provocation. In this light, his thoughts inform a larger discussion of the gantlet that faces graduate students—not just in philosophy but also in other disciplines—and the role of the dissertation in it.

Even so, let's imagine the world Velleman is calling for, in which graduate student publication were forbidden. The culminating task for PhD students is to write a dissertation. Behind Velleman's hypothetical publication ban lies an assumption that the dissertation doesn't much matter in itself, or that it matters only if the student can publish chunks of it in high-profile journals before hitting what's left of the academic job market. That's a pretty dim assessment of the value of a dissertation, and it implies that a young scholar's application for an academic job gets a hearing only if he or she has published enough.

Velleman's position invokes a related and familiar academic complaint: that requiring a book for tenure outsources promotion decisions to university presses. The decision to publish (or reject) books written by assistant professors, in effect, decides most tenure cases ahead of time. If graduate student publication is what matters in hiring decisions, then the same argument applies at a lower level: hiring committees essentially outsource their scholarly judgment to journal editors. By accepting (or rejecting) graduate student submissions, the editors effectively pass judgment on the students' dissertations, verdicts that hiring committees then accept without looking at the dissertations themselves.

Does that happen? Sometimes, certainly. Numerous professors protested in response to Velleman's post that other attributes, such as demonstrated teaching ability, matter in hiring decisions. But very few of the hundreds of comments to the post had much to say about the dissertation.

It wasn't always that way. At one time, the dissertation mattered very much to hiring committees, and Velleman's imagined world without graduate student publication actually existed without any rules or bans. An emeritus professor in the humanities who worked for years at a high-ranking public university described hiring practices in his department during the 1980s and 1990s, a time when the academic job market had already tightened. "We read dissertation chapters," he said, "usually unpublished." His department usually requested two chapters. Every member of the committee would read them, the professor recalled. "We would ask: Is it fresh, interesting, consequential, learned, well written? We cared about possibilities of publication, but we didn't automatically dismiss someone who had only the germ of a book there. That sometimes guaranteed reach and intellectual ambition."

In the 1980s, most job candidates who were ABD hadn't yet published. "In rare cases," the professor said, an applicant "might have published an article, and of course we would read that as well. Certainly it was seen as a plus if published in a selective journal, but not if we didn't find it compelling." Ultimately, he said, "we gave more weight to the dissertation than to a published article."

In an eclipsed world where graduate students wrote their dissertations and mostly didn't publish while they were in school, the dissertation mattered more. That's the world that Velleman is encouraging us to imagine, and we've already been there. It's a return to futures past. Velleman calls the current situation a "publication emergency," but it's really more of a time-to-degree emergency. Publication takes time. Adding articles to a CV adds to the years that students spend in doctoral programs, where they earn apprentice wages and often take on debt.

"I was 26 when I was hired," said the emeritus professor. "The average age of the people we hired was probably 28–30." Today, with time to degree still hovering around the nine-year mark in humanities doctoral programs, new professors start earning a real salary only in their mid-30s. Often, they're older than that. When graduate students respond to the pressure to publish in graduate school, they postpone their professional launch and literally pay to do so with money they don't have. It doesn't take a philosopher to recognize that as unethical.

But as a number of Velleman's commenters pointed out, a ban on graduate student publication would boost the already-considerable influence of institutional prestige in faculty hiring. "Hiring committees use publication volume and venues as a way to judge the excellence of candidates," writes one commenter. "Take that away and committees are going to lean even more heavily on the prestige of the candidate's grad department." Right now, "the only way for low-prestige students to get an advantage over high-prestige students is to out-publish them."

Asks another poster, "As a graduate student not going to NYU [where Velleman teaches and the home of a well-regarded philosophy department], without a single publication, how do I distinguish myself?" Besides publications, "almost all other indications point purely at the reputation of the school you came from."

So the publication emergency that's also a time-to-degree emergency is also a prestige problem. We probably shouldn't be surprised by that, because problems that arise in graduate school tend to connect to each other. But what to do?

How much should the brand name on a degree matter? If we're so concerned with PhD program rankings that we don't take the time to look at a graduate student's actual work until late in the screening process, we might ask what sort of intellectual integrity our hiring decisions have. Like all of the problems that Velleman identifies, this one offers no easy solution. The debate over his ideas points not so much to a student publication ban as to the need for a collective look within. It's time that faculty members honored the work that we ask graduate students to do by actually scrutinizing it, as opposed to demanding that they produce more and more of it and then publish it under prestigious banners.

That imperative leads back to the dissertation. If we're going to require it, we need to make sure that its contours fit the needs of the faculty who read them, and especially the students who write them.

What Now?

Widening the Dissertation Possibilities

The higher the academic unemployment rate for PhDs, the less reasonable it is to demand that all graduate students write dissertations best suited for research-driven academic jobs. The book fetish—or its equivalent in nonbook fields—won't go away by itself, especially not when professors cling to the idea that a dissertation should be designed for the pursuit of those jobs. Faculty requirements, explicit and implicit, shape what a student's dissertation will look like, and that affects the student's graduate school career. Students need a chance to prepare themselves for the types of jobs that they are actually going to get, not just the one that traditional graduate school culture has deemed the ideal.

The faculty ought to be able to step in and do something. We're the ones who decide whether a dissertation is creditable, so we can decide what we're going to credit. But we're not filling our appointed space in this regard. Education scholar Jeannie Brown Leonard records a sense of student confusion about dissertation expectations, a sense that the adviser doesn't care very much or that the different members of a dissertation committee are offering contradictory advice.[17] We can't afford such inconsistency at any time, but especially not these days.

The requirements for the PhD have changed with the circumstances of the academic job market, and not just in recent years. When there were jobs for everyone, shorter theses abounded. When academic employment got scarcer, so did the quick finishers. Readiness for graduation, in other words, depended on the presence of jobs (in this case, professorships), not the length of the dissertation. We should keep in mind that *the requirements for a doctorate have always been under construction.*

Louis Menand suggested a few years ago that one peer-reviewed article serve for the dissertation. Menand's radically functional idea, like Velleman's hypothetical graduate student publishing ban, may be appreciated as provocation rather than policy proposal. As a provocation, it lays bare some of the sketchy ethics underlying the current prolonged time to degree. Menand argues that "if every graduate student were required to publish a single peer-reviewed article instead of writing a thesis, the net result would probably be a plus for scholarship," and of course they would finish much faster.[18]

In this spirit, we might consider a humanities dissertation comprising a small number of articles. (Science fields already credit dissertations with this format.) This suggestion would take the dissertation back to its nineteenth-century roots, when it was envisioned as a short publication (not a book) in the making. A dissertation made up of a small number of articles would acknowledge the reality that graduate students face and match their degree requirements to meet it. Such a change would meet our students where they are—which is a move we make far too rarely.

One version, advanced by the literature professor David Damrosch in 1995 and revived of late by current reformers, is to break the traditional monograph into a series of essays. The 2014 *Report of the MLA Task Force on Doctoral Study in Modern Language and Literature* offers this and other specific suggestions along those lines: an "expanded repertoire" of dissertation possibilities could include not only a suite of essays but also "Web-based projects," translations (with apparatus), "public humanities projects," and dissertations based in pedagogy.[19] Members of "The Future of the Dissertation," a 2016 workshop convened by the Council of Graduate Schools, called for a similar opening out of the social science dissertation. They proposed including community projects, ensemble dissertations, public scholarship, and visual mapping, among other ideas.

Faculty in the humanities and humanistic social sciences might also consider encouraging three-chapter dissertations. Most theses in these fields run four or five chapters, but the shorter alternative "has been with us for a long time," says John Bugg, the director of graduate studies in Fordham's English department. Bugg observes that graduate students don't usually consider the range of possible dissertations (which in the literature fields may include scholarly editions, translations, and the like as well as traditional formats of varying sizes); they just plan to slip (or wedge) themselves into the traditional mold. This

The Segmented Dissertation

The biostatistics department in the School of Public Health at Boston University asks students to complete a dissertation typically composed of three segments. Each segment is what department chair Josée Dupuis calls "a publishable unit"—that is, an article manuscript. The committee decides whether the units meet the "publishable" standard—meaning that the units don't have to be actually published or accepted when the dissertation is accepted—though at least one must be submitted for publication prior to the defense.[1]

The three segments don't have to form one tight whole. In practice they will often harmonize or connect, but they can be "loosely related," said Dupuis. If a student starts on a particular topic and then, after completing one unit, decides that she's not interested in it anymore, she can turn to a connected subfield, and she can still take that unit with her—that is, it can remain a part of her finished dissertation.

This modular quality of the segmented dissertation also gives the student more autonomy in her relations with her adviser. She may start working with her adviser and complete a segment or two, and then switch and complete the other segment(s) under the supervision of another committee member. In practice, this amounts to the ability to change advisers without having to alter or discard work already done. So the student loses no ground.

The segmented dissertation format is not a one-size-fits-all solution, but for some departments, it's an innovation to consider.[2]

---

1. Cassuto, conversation with Dupuis, October 2019. For a formal statement of dissertation requirements, see the Program Handbook, 17–19, https://www.bu.edu /sph/files/2019/11/MS-Handbook-2019-2020.pdf.
2. Carol Tenopir of the School of Information Sciences, College of Communication and Information, at the University of Tennessee describes a similar model, which she calls a "composite dissertation." "Technological Opportunities and Human Realities for Dissertations in The Future" (paper delivered at the CGS Future of the Dissertation Workshop, January 28–29, 2016), https://cgsnet.org /ckfinder/userfiles/files/1_4%20Tenopir2.pdf, 3-4.

sense of received expectations "isn't necessarily a bad thing," says Bugg, but there are cases, he says, when advisers should give students a three-chapter option.[20]

"The ecosystem of the dissertation is changing," says a valuable report on the CGS workshop.[21] In the sciences, where collaboration is already the norm in the laboratory, workshop members called for "acceptance of truly collaborative science dissertations in which students can avail themselves of the expertise of others."[22] Other salutary alternatives are starting to show themselves. The English department at Idaho State University, for example, "integrates research in literature with practical and theoretical training in the teaching of English." The degree integrates "research-oriented class work with courses in pedagogy," and it also includes "supervised teaching internships and a pedagogical component in every dissertation." In practice, students often include a chapter on the implications of their research for teaching. Department graduates who go into academia typically find positions at teaching-centered colleges.[23] (In the same spirit as their program, the department also sponsors a book prize on "the theory and practice of teaching literature.")[24]

And of course the digital environment presents a range of new possibilities. Amanda Visconti's 2015 dissertation at the University of Maryland took the form of a web-based, publicly generated annotated edition of Joyce's *Ulysses*. A. D. Carson became a minor academic celebrity after submitting his 2017 Clemson University dissertation in the form of a hip-hop album.[25] Nick Sousanis wrote his 2014 Columbia University dissertation in the form of a graphic novel. Anna Williams submitted a podcast dissertation at the University of Iowa.[26]

One argument against these new, boundary-pushing works is that they don't conform to existing categories in the academic job market. Writing a weird dissertation, this argument goes, will lead to a graduate becoming a pink elephant who won't fit in anywhere.[27] Perhaps that argument held at one time (though we wouldn't swear to it). But we certainly don't buy it now. The tightening of the academic job market has put enormous pressure on academic job market categories. When departments hire fewer people, they concern themselves more with intellectuals who bridge boundaries, not stay safely within them. Of course the dissertation has to be good, but hasn't that always been the case?

In the sciences, mindful of the insistence of both Taylor and Elkana that finding and developing a problem is at the center of any worthy doctoral education—requiring a creativity that present practice discourages—Angelica Stacy proposes that research funds go directly to students. The student then could decide in which faculty member's research she wished to invest her funding, which is to say her time and labor. That's a power flipper. Less radically, she notes that students could be offered dual advisers from the start and further notes that "some universities have had positive experiences offering students a year of rotating research positions in which students spend about three months at a time in three or four different labs before matching with a research advisor."[28]

Such innovations—including the ones not thought of yet—don't dilute the PhD so much as expand its horizons. One may object to specifics, but doctoral education needs a general spirit of experimentation because the reflexive conservatism of the past and present is not serving anyone very well. This conservatism also inhibits diversity. Many studies show that members of underrepresented groups want a PhD that is intelligible in their communities, where they often return. Greater flexibility promotes diversity, from recruitment to outcomes.

One important possible outcome is that a student may not finish the dissertation and will choose to leave the program with a master's degree. Or, now that "the master's is the new bachelor's," some students may choose the master's degree from the outset.[29] Some professional master's degrees, especially in the sciences, are thriving. In the humanities fields, not so much. In the next section we contextualize the problem and outline a proposal for a professional master of arts degree.

Reinventing the Master's Degree

The efficacy of the PhD dissertation for nonacademic careers seems obvious. The writing of a dissertation requires sustained reasoning, a range of research capacities, imagination, originality, and analytical abilities. Such skills are relevant to just about every career. Even so, some students deeply engaged by the subject matter of a discipline might wish to begin a career without spending years on a dissertation. That's one reason the professional science master's degree (PSM) has become highly popular, with hundreds of extant programs. Developed through consultation between industry and academia, the PSM is a two-year degree that was explicitly designed to get scientists hired at a higher level than if they entered with just a bachelor's degree.[30]

A similar terminal MA in the humanities or social sciences would prove equally valuable. To begin with, we are not suggesting a return to the kind of MA that many renowned research universities eliminated over the last several decades. That MA generally served as a torturous trial for students who almost universally desired the doctorate but had not been admitted directly into a PhD program. In cases where direct PhD admits and MA students with doctoral ambitions share courses, a nasty caste system may develop, with a large number of MA students competing for the few remaining spots in the doctoral class.

Not a down-market substitute for a PhD but a thoughtfully conceived degree in its own right, a new professional MA could offer a useful alternative to the choices of giving up on advanced study in a student's loved discipline or risking all for the doctorate. It also could serve students who depart a doctoral program when they discover it doesn't suit them. And to faculty members it would offer meaningful graduate-level teaching in a new context.

But far more important, where a sense of severely limited career options has discouraged undergraduates from majoring in various liberal arts disciplines, a professional MA (perhaps also offered as a combined BA/MA) could show students how they might apply their learning and skills to a range of professions. That kind of awareness may raise enrollments at the undergraduate as well as the graduate level.

Let's focus on that important matter of declining majors, primarily in humanities and humanistic social science disciplines. While our emphasis in this book has been on diversifying career outcomes for students, we're not ignoring the crucial issue of regaining professorial positions in those disciplines, chiefly the humanities, where mistaken assumptions of "uselessness" or dead-end job searches have contributed to sharply falling undergraduate enrollments—and thus to a reduction of tenure-track faculty positions.[31] A viable master's degree would encourage interested students to pursue a major in these fields. It would also establish relations between these fields and the professional programs at their universities and colleges that could lead to any number of interdisciplinary (and enrollment-building) opportunities.

Planned thoughtfully, a new professional master's degree in the humanities and humanistic social sciences would not cheapen the traditional fields of study. In fact, the result should be intellectually enriching. The means for growth, in other words, is to serve more fully the varied range of student goals.

The planning process for such a program might take the reverse-engineering process we described in chapter 2. With administrative approval, an accelerated planning process may be possible, as there will be fewer moving parts to consider than in a doctoral program. But master's programs aren't just "lite" versions of doctoral programs, and they need more than lite planning. The department and the institution have to clarify exactly why, and to what ends, the program is being instituted or reorganized. It's not enough just to want to add a graduate program. There needs to be a coherent curriculum and rationale.

Relatedly, this new kind of master's will require a strategy for publicizing its existence, which requires a clear sense of the potential audience. You can build it, but that doesn't mean they will come. Explaining the program to undergraduates at the home institution, to a regional and national set of students and undergraduate academic counselors at other institutions, and even to high school guidance counselors, will be vital to success. So too will a clear understanding of the program by faculty in other departments of the home institution.

Faculty leaders will be key to the effort, so they must truly want this, not just be willing to go along with it. Faculty leadership will likewise be key to securing and maintaining the interest and support of higher administration.

One encouragement for this planning process resides in the established success of the PSM, whose rationale and model can guide non-science disciplines. "We saw increasing numbers of science and engineering students getting MBA's," said Michael Teitelbaum, an adviser to the Sloan Foundation, which supported the advent of the new degree. Sloan saw a Goldilocks situation: a BA didn't provide the necessary level of science sophistication for employment, but the PhD took too long and didn't provide wider kinds of training appropriate to a nonacademic science endeavor. Teitelbaum described this as the difference between an "I-shaped" education (a narrow specialization) and a "T-shaped" one (which branches outward).[32]

PSM curricula supplement scientific coursework with instruction in areas relevant to careers in business and industry: management, communications, marketing, and finance. For instance, in pharmaceutical science, students might take a course on a regulatory agency like the FDA, or in computer science, courses on patent law and marketing.

The Council of Graduate Schools attempted a humanities version of the degree in the first decade of this century. The professional master of arts degree (PMA) received short-term funding from the Ford Foundation. The initiative had some early success on 18 campuses in fields like applied philosophy at the University of North Carolina, but the funding ran out before the degree could gain the necessary traction. Given the greater faculty resistance to business and related pursuits in these disciplines (compared to the prevailing attitudes in science faculties long accustomed to tech transfer) and to large numbers of students choosing careers in industry, sustained success for a PMA would have required more foundation buy-in than with the PSM, not less. The head of the program at CGS, Carol Lynch, nonetheless termed the project "a proof of concept success story" that led faculty members to recognize expanded possibilities. "Maybe the time will come," she said, "when somebody will start thinking about the students."[33]

Might that time be now? Here's a real-life recent case study of an English department at a public university. The department offers an

MA but no PhD, and it had lost much of its MA enrollment when public schools stopped funding their teachers to earn the degree part-time. Recently called upon to help propose a revised master's, we suggested a plan that differs in important ways from the PMS degree in its balance between disciplinary and beyond-academic training, but that is informed by the same commitment to applying advanced learning to workplace challenges. We suggested that this new MA, which could exist as an alternate branch of the existing one, could require features like an initial career packet, individual counseling, site visits to workplaces, and, in as many cases as possible, an internship. Developing such resources and opportunities will require greater communication between the department and both the career center and the alumni office. It also will require discussions of common interest with faculty in the several relevant professional schools on campus.

For this MA to succeed, the department will have to attend to every facet of the program. The master's thesis requirement should be flexible enough to allow for different possibilities, such as a thesis that might grow out of an internship experience. What is the student's initial career plan, and how will the internship experience meet or change that plan? Afterward, the department needs to ask, What part of the internship was most valuable? What would make it more valuable? How might its takeaway be of value to academia, to other students, to society? A master's thesis might simply take up an issue or interest that had arisen from this work experience.

We also proposed to this program a central new course called English at Work and two cognate courses in areas relevant to career interests. Adding these would require a corresponding reduction elsewhere—say, to eight traditional courses in the discipline rather than the existing 10. And in the disciplinary courses, faculty will need to develop a student-centered awareness that will make explicit to students how the techniques for interpretation and analysis that they are learning may apply in different occupational contexts. As we argued in chapter 3, it's important to show students the value of the skills they're acquiring so that they know they have them.

In this proposed master's program, and in doctoral programs emphasizing career options and public scholarship, we can conserve student time and faculty effort by simply rethinking assignments—something University of Michigan postdoctoral fellow Matthew Woodbury highlights in an essay on humanities careers. These might include op-eds, book reviews, digital exhibits, and team efforts with fellow students or with a community group or organization.[34]

These commitments, departmental and institutional, would be reasonably modest. The most laborious elements involve creating the course in English at Work, where the Michigan course model by Porter and Hartman that we outlined in chapter 3 or the emerging one at Emory (see chapter 10), could be readily adapted. The renovated MA might incorporate site visits or internships and work with other departments and schools to establish collaborative options. Faculty should also build in a way to assess the program and to make adjustments that will inevitably be necessary. At this writing, action on our proposal is pending.

Four important aspects of our report might form a road map for other institutions and programs. First is the matter of intramural collaboration. If several departments rather than one collaborated on a new PMA, the bevy of activities we've described elsewhere in this book at places like Duke, Louisville, and Irvine certainly could be adapted to the MA level. And while the PMA is a low-cost option even for an individual department, it gets even more affordable—and student outcomes are multiplied—if several departments share in the effort.

Second, we bring forward a point we've made elsewhere but that bears repeating here: success requires new relations among a program, the career office, and the alumni office. Departmental faculty need not suddenly be required to learn about off-campus careers. They need only learn how to become part of a team of experts that extends beyond the hallways of a given department. When professors learn to work with career service professionals, their efforts complement each other—and the students benefit. We want to make it easy for faculty to get to yes, and the best way to do that is to show them how a more public graduate education will ease their responsibilities, not make their jobs more difficult.

Third, nonacademic supporters of the discipline should be enlisted at the beginning of planning, not just when it's time to create internships and garner financial support. They will have important advice to offer, and the conversation will be far more interesting and edifying than if it took place in the faculty lunchroom. Collaborative planning will guard against unintentional academic insularity. It will also make the prospect of creating internships—daunting to professional humanists—less threatening.

Finally, the new PMA must be administered in such a way as to ensure its prestige. Len has documented elsewhere the mottled and frequently disreputable history of the master's degree in the history of American higher education. Faculty have done much to devalue the master's already, and that sustained effort accounts for perhaps the greatest obstacle to restoring its status. For instance, in 1959 Harvard graduate school dean J. P. Elder compared the master's degree to "a streetwalker—all things to all men (and at different prices)."[35] A new PMA will need to respond actively to such (not entirely unjustified) calumny. It may also need a new name, but we leave that to people who know more about branding than we do.

The program needs careful curation, especially at first. Admissions should be carefully selective, possible cognate courses for students should be well considered, and internships should be meaningful and challenging. (They should also be salaried when possible and supported by an institutional TA-ship when they're not.) The department should be explicit about the career orientation of a PMA. In the words of one of the higher education leaders we interviewed, "Be direct. Don't be ashamed to say the program emphasizes the career opportunities of its student graduates. Say in your public messaging about the new program, 'You love your discipline, but you are worried about a career. We can help.'"

We hope that a professional MA in the humanities or social sciences can prove self-supporting—and that student outcomes justify charging a reasonable tuition. But profitability is a bad reason for starting any new graduate program in the arts and sciences. The prime motive for a PMA should be the same one for opening out the PhD: to benefit society and the academic disciplines together by a more dynamic and continuous interchange between academia and the worlds beyond it. We should expect holders of any high degree to know things, but also something more than that. In the words of Robert Frost, "It's knowing what to do with things that counts."[36]

Coda

We suggested in chapter 2 that a graduate program plan its reforms backward from the outcome that the stakeholders want to see. Research and degrees would benefit from the same treatment. We started this chapter with big and fundamental questions about the dissertation: What is it, and what does it do? All of us who write and read dissertations need to reflect on those questions, and when we decide, we can use our answers to purpose-build dissertation requirements. We're calling for a reconsideration of graduate student scholarship. It should include a range of issues, including the scope of the discipline, the intended audience(s), the relation of teacher to student, the connections between coursework and capstone, and the distinction between skill building and publishable results.

We're not suggesting that the dissertation needs to change in any specific way—that's up to the professors in the disciplines. We are certainly not suggesting that its rigor be diluted or its legitimacy weakened as the qualifying credential for the highest degree that the university offers. Instead, we encourage adventurous student scholarship—what Taylor calls "independent, strategic, and constructively critical thought." Examining degree requirements (including the master's) is a practice we should get better used to. Environments change, and where appropriate, curricula ought to change with them.

TEN

Public Scholarship

What It Is, Where It Came From, and What It Requires

What Is Public Scholarship?

Public scholarship bridges the gap between traditionally hermetic graduate study and the socially versatile doctorate we have recommended. Its name suggests a social mission that appeals to graduate students and their teachers. While nonprofessorial career diversity may appeal to some doctoral students and not others, public scholarship has an integral role to play in the lives of all of them. And it has a special appeal to students from underrepresented groups who consistently express a desire to give back, to employ their learning for social betterment.

But the term "public scholarship" requires a clarity it has not yet achieved. Does it describe professorial types on PBS and the pages of the *New Yorker* and the *Atlantic*, figures like literary critic and historian Henry Louis Gates Jr., historian Jill Lepore, literary and cultural historian Louis Menand, physicist Brian Greene, and astronomer Neil deGrasse Tyson? Or would it apply to the engagement of advanced students and professors in civic projects, an upscale version of civic engagement and experiential learning now trending in undergraduate education? Or perhaps adult education, like the lecture series that York University professor emeritus Elaine Newton has given on modern and contemporary fiction for 40 years in Canada and throughout the

United States to packed houses? (Bob witnessed a recent Newton performance in Naples, Florida, on Philip Roth at which hundreds of people jockeyed for tickets at a large lecture hall.) Or might public scholarship include working in art museums and galleries, science museums, environmental law centers—unless such long-term endeavors belong to career diversity instead?

The answers to all of these questions is yes. The public figures we named do great work communicating sophisticated knowledge to mass audiences, but they are outliers. More common, but no less valuable, is the capacity of all doctoral graduates to practice, in historian Thomas Bender's phrase, "bilingualism," the ability to speak to both scholars and lay audiences. Current definitions of public scholarship tend to be too narrow. For example, the University of Michigan's Rackham Program in Public Scholarship defines its mission as supporting "collaborative and creative endeavors that engage communities and co-create public goods." The national organization Imagining America says that "Public Scholarship refers to diverse modes of creating and circulating knowledge for and with the public and communities."[1] The same organization elsewhere offers a better definition of public scholarship as "scholarly or creative activity integral to a faculty member's academic area . . . that contributes to the public good and yields artifacts of public and intellectual value," though that's still rather abstract.[2] The *Wikipedia* entry on public humanities defines the term as "the work of engaging diverse publics in reflecting on heritage, traditions, and history, and the relevance of the humanities to the current conditions of civic and cultural life."[3]

These definitions show that even supporters of public scholarship could use a lesson in talking with fewer marbles in their mouths, but we're quoting them for a different reason: together, they do help to characterize public scholarship. But can we perhaps define the concept more invitingly in plain language? To us, public scholarship encompasses all acts of communicating scholarly expertise to a nonexpert public to initiate interest and understanding.

By that definition, one might argue that college teaching, especially in introductory courses, is a form of public scholarship—and indeed it is. Not all faculty members are experts on nonprofessorial career opportunities, but just about every one of them has practiced that form of public scholarship. Just so, classicist Emily Watson, author of an acclaimed recent translation of the *Odyssey*, describes her highly popular Twitter account as "a virtual classroom." As in the live classroom, "you have to avoid patronizing your students just as you have to avoid losing them by assuming too much knowledge on their parts." Watson highlights the need for "clarity without dumbing down" as "the goal of any communication or conversation about scholarly work, "either inside the academy or beyond."[4] In the same spirit, the late historian Hayden White says, "I tell my students, 'Look, we're here to discuss the meaning of life.' The meaning of life is that I'm alive for the time being. I'm in a world which is making contradictory demands upon me. What do I do?"[5] Keeping in mind the everyday experience of teaching undergraduates as applicable to nonacademic settings, it's difficult to imagine any career, including a professorial one, where learning to communicate complexities to nonspecialists would be irrelevant.

To become more intentional about developing the capacity to explain and explore intricate concepts with the uninitiated is an evolutionary, not revolutionary, step in improving graduate education. Watson says that public scholarship is a key way for academics to gain understanding and popular support. She finds that it also improves her "ability to communicate in scholarly writing and in the classroom, too."

Students who engage with community groups and other public initiatives apply their learning, and they learn a great deal in the process. One could argue that such advanced students should be the most adept in this exchange between gown and town. Later in this chapter we will describe some undergraduate initiatives that could be readily adapted to doctoral education. Historically, doctoral education has helped to set the table for all educational levels, particularly for college. Now graduate education can benefit from the levels below it. It's a worthy and important game of catch-up.

Where Public Scholarship Came From

Linking deep research specialization with public scholarship is, like many of the topics we've raised in this book, less a brand-new idea than a restoration of the dual purpose of American higher education. David F. Labaree makes the point that colleges in the United States of the nineteenth century were deliberately located in "bucolic rural settings far from the centers of trade and finance." A significant corollary to the avoidance of cities was the notion of academia as a world elsewhere, where the slow time of chapel bells ringing, "marked off from its worldly surroundings by a wall," would replace the chaotic pace of a world of getting and spending.[6] But this notion of a pure, cloistered education was contradicted by the notion of learning as the basis for social improvement. The motive behind this practice was primarily moral (though also practical) in the case of the many colleges founded by religious denominations, and primarily practical (though also moral and ethical) in the case of state-supported universities.

The public application of knowledge informs the rhetoric of our major national visionaries, powered, perhaps in part, by the New England Puritan hope to meld the City of God with the City of Man. Emerson defined his American Scholar in 1837 as a public intellectual: "He" (and we should add, She) "is one who raises himself from private considerations and lives on public and illustrious thoughts."[7] Woodrow Wilson, president of Wesleyan before leading Princeton, the state of New Jersey, and then the nation, wrote in 1902 that "we are not put into this world to sit still and know; we are put in it to act."[8] Not long afterward, John Dewey, in *Democracy and Education* (1916), argued for continuing interaction between scholars and the public not only to meet social challenges but also to discover what those challenges are. For Dewey, this inquiry required an experiential pedagogy: methods that "give the pupils something to do, not something to learn." When "the doing is of such a nature as to demand thinking," says Dewey, "learning naturally results."[9] And from the civic side of the partnership between the academy and the nation, John F. Kennedy called in 1963 for an America "which will steadily enlarge cultural opportunities for all of our citizens."[10]

In citing these famous advocates of public scholarship, we neither hope nor wish to resolve the tension in US higher education between pure scholarship and the practical, for it has proved enormously fruitful. Too many demagogic reformers of doctoral education have viewed scholarship and research as a private, nefarious academic empire, and we need never apologize as scholars for pushing back the night. Scholarship and research center the PhD for long-demonstrated good reasons.

At the same time, we are aware of how crucial the application of learning is—to the good of the academic enterprise and to the good of the world. It was, after all, not a business magnate but John Milton who wrote, "I cannot praise a fugitive and cloistered virtue."[11] The growing enthusiasm for public scholarship in higher education, then, is less iconoclastic than restorative. The tension between the pursuit of knowledge and the education of students is coiled into the DNA of American higher education. Public scholarship means to repave the road between the academic grove and the city of social urgencies.

Where Public Scholarship Happens

We've given some definition to public scholarship and provided some historical context for it. But more particularly, where can public scholarship happen today? Before we answer our own question, it's worth noting how far public scholarship in PhD programs has come in less than two decades (in graduate school time, a mere moment).[12] It's certainly not everywhere or even an established norm right now, but public scholarship is perhaps the most rapidly growing practice in graduate education. There's even a handbook for aspiring public scholars, *Going Public*, recently published by the University of Chicago Press.[13] In its most ambitious form, it may lead students to create an entire career. A list of the two-year internships taken by ACLS Public Fellows, all recent PhDs, include an American studies graduate named digital engagement manager at the Science History Institute, a cultural studies graduate appointed as a cross-sector analyst at the Los Angeles County Arts Commission, a sociologist serving as a climate policy associate at the US Center of the Stockholm Environment Institute, a political scientist serving as program officer in the Media and Democracy Project of the Social Science Research Center, and a communications PhD appointed content strategist at the Innocence Project in New York.

Public scholarship need not be lifetime, all-consuming, or long term. It can occur in media settings ranging from TV channels like PBS, the History Channel, and Animal Planet to blogs and podcasts, to radio outlets like NPR and commercial talk radio, to all kinds of news outlets, newspapers, and magazines. All such media are likely candidates for creating internships, just as they can become career-diverse landing places. A range of institutions, such as museums of all kinds and libraries, serve as full-time centers for public scholarship that readily host discussions and lectures by scholars, and the hosts are often doctoral graduates in permanent positions. More formal adult education programs as well can take place on campus or in community centers.

Public scholarship can happen in K–12 schools where universities facilitate links between faculty members and graduate students to primary and secondary teachers and students. Such meetings can happen on campus, as universities may offer college facilities like laboratories or libraries or seminar rooms or the campus at large (as with summer programs designed for economically challenged potential college students). Or the groups can connect at primary or secondary schools, or in neighborhoods and in the streets, as in many community engagement projects. Public scholarship happens increasingly in prisons, where education programs have been proliferating for the past 15 years.[14] It's also enacted in lectures and seminars attended by retired people in any number of locales, including retirement communities adjacent to and affiliated with colleges. More than 10,000 students have benefited from the Clemente Program in the Humanities, begun by Earl Shorris in 1996, a nine-month course that meets for four hours each week to "equip motivated, low income adults to take charge of their lives." Students read great books and "build skills in critical thinking, written and oral communications, time management, teamwork, and self-advocacy" in seminar-sized discussions led by professors and housed in social service centers.[15]

Some senior faculty warn graduate students and junior faculty about where public scholarship should *not* be present: on their own CVs as they ready themselves for tenure. A 2019 column in the *Chronicle of Higher Education* warns junior faculty to avoid op-eds, blog posts, or other kinds of unrefereed public writing, and to be "calculating" about uses of time with the tenure decision looming. In a response, Sarah E. Bond and Kevin Gannon call that "the wrong advice." They point out that "lower-tier liberal arts colleges, teaching-oriented universities and community colleges—where the vast majority of academic jobs are found—have long championed the need for their faculty to pursue public outreach." Elite disdain for vulgar "popularizing" is simply out of step with the reality of today.[16]

We'd go further. Of course public scholarship should and can count as a professional credit if it is substantial and excellent. Beyond that, shaping and censoring yourself to external demands is a loser's game. The challenge for everyone, at all academic institutions and for intellectuals at other kinds of venues (including graduate students), is to do both—the choice between two kinds of valuable audiences is a false one. And we're reminded by this assertion that most doctoral graduates will work in endeavors that don't involve academic tenure decisions anyway. But more important, how does one want to live, as CEO of one's own career or as a fearful vassal?

The line between public and—what?—private or disciplinary or traditional scholarship is wavy, not straight and unyielding. Wherever it occurs, public scholarship will take two forms, separately or in combination. The first involves lingua franca. In 1999, Stanford University inaugurated the I-RITE program "to assist young scholars to communicate the significance of their research to a larger public, including undergraduate students, funders, policymakers, and laypersons." The program "requires connecting research to public concerns" and "asks

Three-Minute Films and Three-Minute Talks

When he served as dean of the graduate school at North Dakota State University, David Wittrock promoted the idea of three-minute dissertation videos. Making these short films, he suggested, would teach students valuable skills. They would learn to communicate in a different medium, to a nonspecialized audience.

Soon after Wittrock left the deanship. Graduate dean Claudia Tomany and associate dean Brandy Randall realized his plan. NDSU graduates about 100 PhDs each year. In 2014, faculty voted that each graduating PhD would have to produce a three-minute video about his or her dissertation. The deans saw that PhDs need to know how "to communicate information in a way that people can understand and use." But "we don't think enough about how to teach this to students," said Randall. "The dissertation video requirement does this."

The video requirement was not immediately embraced, but it soon gained its footing. Graduate students "are so good at talking the jargon of their fields that they don't even realize that they're doing it," said Randall. "After a couple of years, people started seeing the value of communicating with the lay person."

The same year that dissertation videos entered the picture, the NDSU graduate school adopted the Three-Minute Thesis competition. TMT, as it is known, is a public speaking contest in which graduate students give public presentations of their dissertation research to live audiences. The TMT idea first developed in the STEM fields (and was not invented at NDSU), but today it's spreading across campuses and disciplines.

Strictly limited to three minutes, TMT presentations are judged by a panel, which awards prizes. With these rewards come bragging rights and, in STEM, invitations to regional and national competitions.

TMT caught on at North Dakota State, and the friendly competition created a synergy with the emergent practice of dissertation video production. Perhaps that's not surprising, given that the videos are essentially three-minute thesis films.

The combination works in North Dakota. NDSU graduate students are positively eager to teach their research to audiences outside as well as inside their disciplines. It has spurred good-natured competition among departments, which further stokes the enterprise. And the program is growing and spreading. It's required of PhDs at NDSU, but the master's program in public health now plans to require it as well. "The culture is changing," said Randall. "It's valuable for students to be able to communicate to a general audience, and that awareness is catching on."

It's also valuable as outreach. "I'm very intentional about who I invite to judge the TMT competition," said Randall. "I always invite someone from outside the university," such as a potential employer, a newspaper editor, a K–12 teacher, or a member of the local Economic Development Corporation. "I want these external judges to see what happens at a research university," she said. "I want them to see what graduate education can do, and what our students are doing."

Higher education needs such exposure more than ever. "A lot of people don't understand graduate education," said Randall, "especially doctoral education." Some of those people work as legislators: between 2008 and 2016, 45 states reduced their per capita public funding of higher education.[1] Those legislators represent people like Randall's own family members. When she was in graduate school, Randall recalled, her family members would ask, "'What do you do all the time?' Research was such a mystery to them."

"We've been reluctant to share the story of what we do," said Randall. The space we don't claim is now occupied by a cynical narrative of "well-educated people wasting money," a prurient tale that "plays well in the media." We must, she said, "build a valuing of graduate education."

Friendly outreach helps to build that value. Randall named the head of the North Dakota Medical Foundation as the external judge of the first TMT competition at North Dakota State, and he was so compelled by the winner's presentation that he moved to fund her research on HPV prevention among Native populations. That example might inspire us all.

---

1. Michael Mitchell, Michael Leachman, and Kathleen Masterson, "A Lost Decade in Higher Education Funding: State Cuts Have Driven Up Tuition and Reduced Quality," Center on Budget and Policy Priorities, August 23, 2017, https://www.cbpp.org/research/state-budget-and-tax/a-lost-decade-in-higher-education-funding.

students beginning their dissertation work to write a brief description of their research that would be accessible to undergraduates in an introductory course in the field. A network of peer reviewers then provides feedback for revision."[17] Since its inception, the program has been adopted by more than 400 campuses in the United States and abroad.

As a new-media variant, North Dakota State University requires that all of its PhDs make three-minute videos describing their dissertations in order to graduate. The implied audience for these videos is the general public. And many programs now require students to develop compact "elevator speeches" describing their research or their dissertations.

When scholars take their work into the arena of public debate, they can influence the issues. They can also make a case for the value of what we do in colleges and universities. Sociologists Arlene Stein and Jessie Daniels remind us, "There's a big world out there that needs to hear from us." Our first job is to learn how to invite it to listen.[18]

A second kind of public scholarship puts learning into action. Public scholarship as experiential learning is not just about doing good. It also dramatically enriches the academic experience of a graduate student. Lee Shulman, president emeritus of the Carnegie Foundation for the Advancement of Teaching, says that applied learning addresses three common student complaints: "I knew it but forgot it" (you won't forget it if you apply it), "I thought I knew it but I didn't" (experience will be the test of that), and "I know it but I don't know what it is good for" (you will find out by experience).[19] And beyond that, as we have learned from the testimony of hundreds of doctoral students who have worked "out there," not all learning takes place in a classroom or lab.

How Public Scholarship Happens

It should not be the sole responsibility of faculty members to get themselves and their graduate students to the venues that we surveyed in the previous section. Though encouraging individual initiative should be an aspect of any public scholarship course or university-led initiative, many students and professors will need help in coming up with ideas, particularly in forging connections with local or national groups that might provide opportunities. Here, as with broadening career opportunities for doctoral graduates, the central administration must provide some encouragement and resources—for example, in the form of graduate versions of the offices of community engagement that now work solely for undergraduates.

More important, graduate programs should provide overall guidance. Professors need to teach students how to perform in the various settings we have described. This means encouraging intellectuals to change from "I-shaped" to "T-shaped": that is, to build a broad base of knowledge and communication skills across fields atop a column of specific expertise. Learning how to reach multiple audiences is not just a skill. It's a way of looking at the world that enables you to see complementary alternatives to specialization—and a need to forge ties outside the small world of specialists.[20]

Faculty aren't born knowing how to do this. At the University of Washington, they teach each other how to do it. In another initiative funded by the Mellon Foundation, Washington's Simpson Center for the Humanities has created Reimagining the Humanities PhD and Reaching New Publics: Catalyzing Collaboration, an exemplary program in which faculty work together "to create new graduate seminars with prominent public scholarship components." The work takes place in weekly workshops over a summer during which each professor develops a syllabus. The results have been compelling. For example, Leigh Mercer, an associate professor of Spanish and Portuguese, taught a course in which students organized and staged a film festival at Seattle's most diverse high school.[21] Richard Watts, a professor of French, challenged his students to take on "the public dimension of translation studies" and "design a collaborative network of translators and translation scholars within and beyond" the university.[22]

Because social challenges and issues do not come in labeled disciplinary packets, public scholarship necessarily encourages cross-disciplinary collaborations. Such interdisciplinary work widens both individual intellectual interests and the knowledge base of the university at the same time. Scholars are often surprised to find how welcome they are outside the campus walls—but only if they do not present themselves as gods bringing grace to needy sinners. Particularly in work with community organizations, listening and learning comes before speaking and participating.

Once oriented, we can identify concrete tasks. The first, says Gregory Jay, is "asset mapping of community and participants"—that is, figuring out what the job is and what there is to work with to get it done.[23] This move may include surveying a university community for potential advisers and partners. Here too, individual students and professors may require some institutional help. When academics work with nonacademic groups, all sides should agree on a realistic division of responsibilities. If the project is to be ongoing, it needs sufficiently deep roots on both the university side and in the partnering organizations, so that the work can continue even when some workers (like graduating students) move on.

Finally, we would underline the importance of creating an assessment method. As we suggested in chapter 2, assessment begins with a consensus on ultimate goals and the intermediate steps to get there, and it continues with midcourse adjustments. An assessment mechanism also provides a means for students and faculty to receive credit and criticism for their efforts, an especially important matter for faculty, as it is difficult to consider public scholarship as real (and tenure-evidential) work if its quality cannot be judged.

Jay's advice fits most closely with community engagement. On the lingua franca side of public scholarship, in *Going Public* Stein and Daniels advise scholars on how to vault themselves out of the ivory tower and into the public square. They show how to devise a pitch (the spiel for editors and other gatekeepers), a peg (something that connects your pitch to current events—and when to leap into the news cycle), and a hook (the bit that will really catch an editor's attention). And they include a useful primer on how to write in the "authoritative yet conversational voice" that general audiences appreciate.

"Why not try and write about your research in the same manner you would teach it to undergraduates?" asks classicist (and blogger) Sarah Bond. Like Stein and Daniels, she urges attention to "the world we are living in" from day to day. "Did you see a parallel with Cicero in the president's *State of the Union* rhetoric last night? Write about it." And she urges trumpeting the work of other academics doing socially consequential work.[24] Academic discoveries *are* news if we would only treat them as such. First, as Jay points out, university leaders must understand the long-term pragmatic benefits that public scholarship brings to a university: it helps colleges and universities to make friends, garner local and regional support that may become crucial at budget time or in the event of political controversies, and raise the quality of life in their own backyard. Furthermore, public scholarship has proven to be a very strong attraction to first-generation, underrepresented, and economically disadvantaged students. These groups made up a full 72 percent of participants in the University of Texas Intellectual Entrepreneurship program, which matches student learning and social challenges.[25] Opportunities to apply learning, or to bring expertise back home, attracts the diverse cohort that doctoral education needs but still lacks.

Administrators may be tempted to delegate public scholarship to individual faculty and departments to consider. Not so: a university administration has several key roles to play. In practical terms, bringing public scholarship into a graduate program means budgeting for it and especially linking it to curriculum. Cocurricular activities are good, but they inevitably (and properly) take second place to curricular obligations in the minds of students and faculty. If public scholarship (and other potential changes that programs may try) is to realize its potential, it needs to be linked to curriculum. In career terms, students and faculty both need professional credit for this work so that they don't see it as a spare-time hobby. Such credit, as the *Imagining America Tenure Team Initiative Report* makes plain, is essential because these efforts often consume time and energy beyond what might go into a traditional course or scholarly article.[26]

A Festival of Models of Public Scholarship

In this book we have often emphasized issues in doctoral education that cross disciplinary boundaries. Witness, for example, the striking similarity of the action issues identified in official communications like the 2018 National Academy of Sciences report *STEM Education for the 21st Century* compared to the 2014 *Report of the MLA Task Force on Doctoral Study in Modern Language and Literature* and the 2020 *Report of the MLA Task Force on Ethical Conduct in Graduate Education*. But when it comes to public scholarship, we should also differentiate among the humanities, social sciences, and bench sciences—even with the reminder that they can learn from each other's practices. (For instance, humanists have lately been experimenting with posters, a longstanding form of communication in the sciences.)

Public scholarship in the humanities often features a wise defensiveness, to show an increasingly skeptical public the practical value of study in these disciplines. Historian Ben Schmidt has crunched the numbers and shown that the humanities has been losing market share among majors for 20 years, with a still sharper decline after the economic downturn of 2008.[27] Mariet Westerman, then of the Mellon Foundation, describes it as "something close to a free fall," with English, history, and languages and literatures dropping fastest.[28]

The Humanities

Such findings suggest that the humanities have a healthy self-interest in demonstrating their practical usefulness to the civic well-being of a society. The obvious danger consists in succumbing to an impoverished notion of "use." Westerman cites Hannah Arendt's insistence that "the human work of creating a world structured by institutional and disciplinary formations only gains its full resonance and radiance in *action*."[29]

That is what the second form of public scholarship provides. Several institutions involve graduate students in community initiatives. In one such program, the Colorado Center for Public Humanities at the University of Colorado Denver seeks to "encourage interaction between the scholar and the wider public by matching scholars with particular communities, funding appropriate research activities, and supporting the production of books, film and web-based conversation that are aimed at extra-academic groups."[30]

Public humanities scholarship also can be taught directly as its own subject. Georgetown offers one such course, The Humanities at Work, to master's students over a month-long summer session. While it has some similarities to Porter and Hartman's Michigan course on career diversity (for example, in requiring students to analyze job advertisements), Georgetown's course emphasizes the public role of intellectual learning more than career options. Students read selections from the now-voluminous literature on public scholarship, practice describing research through story, interview public humanists, and finally design a project of their own.

Georgetown documents the participation of students by conferring a certificate in the engaged and public humanities. (The university will soon unveil a full-blown master's degree program in public humanities.)[31] Vanderbilt goes still further in offering a dual PhD in a traditional discipline (English, anthropology) and comparative media analysis and practice. Similarly, the African American Public Humanities Initiative at the University of Delaware provides stipend support for doctoral students in English, history, and art history over five years, with initial funding through an NEH Next Generation grant. Students in the joint program are trained in public scholarship, community outreach, and digital humanities as well as in archival research, the latter a provocative inclusion for an activity not usually thought of in terms of public scholarship.[32] Rice University, located in Houston, Texas, offers modular courses cotaught by faculty and expert curators and clinicians from the community linking the arts, culture, and medicine or other public endeavors. One recent module concerned the role of music in Houston and different ways to reflect on music in writing, while another took up the politics of cultural heritage in the Middle East, and a third provided "a brief history of madness."[33]

And finally, in one instance for which Bob was present, an entire department of history at Drew University reconceived itself in terms that included an emphasis on public scholarship and career diversity.

Case Study: Public Humanities at Emory

Humanists at Emory University have developed a seminar course in public humanities for spring 2020. Open to students across humanities disciplines, the course combines readings and discussion with a different internship for each student, selected from opportunities curated in advance through town-and-gown partnerships with cultural organizations. We consulted with the group of faculty members and students who together planned the course during a two-week summer workshop. Organized by Benjamin Reiss, chair of English, and Thomas Rogers, graduate director of history, the group of 18 listened to various presentations by leaders of civic organizations ranging from the water policy director of the Chattahoochee Riverkeeper to the editor of the *New Georgia Encyclopedia* to the director of the Decatur Books Festival. They also heard from campus leaders of such initiatives as Emory's African American Collections in its Rose Library, and the codirector of the university's Center for Digital Scholarship. The participating faculty and students split up into teams to read up on what other universities were attempting, to survey possible Atlanta-area partnering organizations and forward project ideas, and to consider on-campus opportunities and partnerships.

Many of the issues we discuss in this chapter were debated by the Emory group as the teams reported back. Some of the takeaways: "Start with the question, then draw together the disciplines." "How do we not only create knowledge but transfer and test it?" "Everything is a story and we should be able to tell it well." And our favorite: "If this is 'public humanities,' then what we have been doing until now is private humanities."

The group developed not only a master syllabus for the course but also an entire set of future goals, including an ongoing institute for public humanities. Though the seminar was shaken by the COVID-19 pandemic, it never lost its balance and successfully completed its launch in good style.

In a fifth-year assessment, Professor Jonathan Rose observed that a course on public history writing succeeded but that a seminar on public humanities was a disappointment: "You can't learn much of the world beyond the academy if you don't leave the classroom." As a result, the department substituted a term-long, credit-bearing internship for that course, leading to such projects as a study for the Irish Consulate in New York City on a firebrand who led the silk-workers strike of 1918 in Patterson, and another who created a food-justice kit distributed by the Global Justice Office of the United Methodist Church. The first graduate of the program to be hired serves as assistant director of the American Social History project at CUNY, designing teacher workshops and public history events.[34]

Arguably the national leader in humanities public scholarship has been the University of Washington, and more particularly its Institute for Public Humanities, a program led by Kathleen Woodward.[35] Washington's Connecting the Community program "addresses both the need for connection between the campus and the community" and career diversity. It encourages students to develop a portfolio on connecting with the community via public scholarship. This public humanities portfolio "will become part of a well-rounded career inside or outside academia." The organizers describe this portfolio as an addition to the traditional research/teaching/service triad used to describe academic work. (As such, we might view it as an attempt to expand service, the underemphasized third element of the tricolon, to mean something more extramural: service to society, not just committee work. As with so much of what we describe in this book, this innovation actually represents a move back to the future, for the idea of service in academia grew out of the early imperative, especially at state universities, to perform public service as part of their mission. This was the original basis of the "Wisconsin Idea" and other admirable motives from the early days of American research universities.)[36]

Washington's Simpson Center for the Humanities also offers a certificate in public scholarship for students who "are assigned a portfolio adviser and pursue a self-directed 15-credit course of study that includes a practicum project." A two-credit introductory course in scholarship as public practice meets three hours weekly on six occasions. The practicum, worth 5 credits, can consist of a community-engaged scholarly project, developing a community-based learning course, an internship, or the launch of a digital form of research designed for a wider public. The portfolio forms the 1-credit capstone and encourages reflection to link accomplishments to professional and personal goals. (The remaining credits consist of electives in the student's own program, and thus the 15-credit requirement is less daunting than it may at first appear, while remaining robust and real.) In addition, the Mellon Foundation has funded Summer Fellows for Public Projects in the Humanities at Washington, a program that links students' research to summer-long public projects—after the students complete a course originally titled Reimagining the PhD and Reaching New Publics and now reconceived as Catalyzing Collaboration.[37] New Public Projects in the Humanities, another Mellon-sponsored summer fellowship, supports two-person teams from English, history, and philosophy.[38]

Equally ambitious but less developed at this point, the City University of New York Graduate Center, funded by a five-year, $2.265 million Mellon grant, has created a PublicsLab. It will prepare students for careers "in the academy and beyond and share scholarship that contributes to the public good." The wording of the grant again suggests the strong connection between career diversity and public scholarship, for both involve applied and experiential learning. That this effort too is underwritten by an influential donor (the Mellon Foundation) shows how doctoral public scholarship is being mainstreamed.[39]

Public education is another likely venue, as several initiatives seek to bridge what one education scholar once termed the apartheid-like separation (especially in the humanities) between K–12 education and universities. Two programs at the University of California, Irvine, take the humanities into the schools. The Humanities Out There challenges doctoral students to create innovative K–12 curricula with a special focus on English language learners. Graduate students work closely with K–12 teachers and university faculty to understand both disciplinary research and K–12 classroom practice. They then retool their own

TH!NKing Outward

As devised by philosophy professor Marcello Fiocco, UC Irvine's TH!NK program has a simple design: A philosopher visits the same group of grade school students weekly for four weeks, for an hour or so each time. The philosopher reads a short piece aloud—usually a story—and then leads a philosophical discussion with the children based on it. A typical question, Fiocco says, might be "Can we have shape without color?" Or, following an excerpt from *The Little Prince*, the discussion leader might ask, "Could you own the moon?" The children respond eagerly to these challenges. "They all seem so excited to provide answers or get to the bottom of debates, and it is a joy to see," says Kourosh Alizadeh, a graduate student in philosophy who teaches in the program.

Fiocco designed TH!NK to fit California's primary-school curriculum—specifically to fulfill its California Common Core Standards for speaking and listening—and this attribute makes school principals more willing to participate. But the program also benefits the graduate students who teach in it. Funded by an intramural grant at Irvine, the program runs on a proverbial shoestring. Graduate students who take part receive stipends so modest as to be symbolic, and the children's classroom teacher gets a small payment to be an engaged observer ("so they don't sit in the corner grading papers," said Amanda Swain, executive director of Irvine's Humanities Commons and an administrator of the program).

Philosophy, Fiocco writes in a description of the program, is a "natural skill" of "the greatest practical importance"—and it's open to everybody. He wants to push back against the idea that the field "is only for geniuses and sages." Put simply, it's "critical thinking," which happens to be the phrase that defenders of the liberal arts invoke more often than any other. Says Fiocco, "I'm reaching kids who are going to be my fellow citizens."[1]

---

1. For more on Irvine's TH!NK program, see Leonard Cassuto, "It's Never Too Early to Learn to Think," *Chronicle of Higher Education* (November 28, 2017), https://www.chronicle.com/article/It-s-Never-Too-Early-to/241874.

disciplinary understandings for new public school applications, learning at the same time to apply social science research methods. The doctoral students design and test inventive, age-appropriate curricula by leading workshops in an actual classroom with the assistance of undergraduates who run break-out discussion groups. Once tested repeatedly in the classroom, the curricula are refined and published. Another Irvine initiative, TH!NK, brings philosophy to the K–12 population.

The Social Sciences

Public scholarship in the social sciences is more integrated into current academic study than it is in the humanities, as the name "social science" implies. The New School, for instance, offers regular programs on "critical and contested issues of our times with the intent of influencing public policy." And there are any number of links between government agencies and programs in these fields that are part and parcel of ordinary academic business.

A particularly active and successful example at the graduate level takes place at the City University of New York Graduate Center under the direction of social psychologist Michelle Fine. CUNY's public science program produces critical scholarship that focuses on educational equality and human rights, targeted for use in policy debates and in organizing movements. The program grew out of the Participatory Action Research collective, with its projects organized in schools or community organizations. It now brings together "activists, researchers, youth, elders, lawyers, prisoners, and educators" who collaborate not only in research but also its public application. Sample projects listed on the website for public science include one that studies the meaning of "'merit' in racially integrated public schools" and another that creates internships for public school students to "investigate finance inequity and college access."[40]

Fine's emphasis on participatory research characterizes much public scholarship in the social sciences. Her program privileges the different contributions by academics and nonacademics as part of an explicit move to democratize knowledge making and ground it in actual community needs and learning.

The progressive bent of this program raises an important question: How should community engagement state its social assumptions and aims? Is neutrality a virtue or a display of disingenuousness? Each program—and each public scholar—needs to address that question for themselves as we move forward.

You'd think that public projects in the social sciences would be common—and they are, on the undergraduate level. But doctoral education in these fields does not follow suit. It can and should do so. Several undergraduate examples feature models that doctoral education could adapt with ease. In fact, with more advanced students, such programs could have greater impact. The University of Texas program in Intellectual Entrepreneurship, which we mentioned in the previous section of this chapter and in chapter 1, began as an initiative for graduate students and then emigrated to the undergraduate level when a new graduate dean didn't get it. Before that happened, student engagement in community projects "where they discover and put knowledge to work, as well as requiring them to identify and adapt to audiences for whom their research matters," attracted more than double the percentage (20 percent) of students of color compared to the graduate school as a whole, according to its inventive and engaging leader, communications professor Rick Cherwitz.[41] In its later incarnation as an undergraduate program (which encourages students to seek a graduate education), 72 percent of participants were "first generation, underrepresented or economically disadvantaged students," and 28 percent were African American as of 2017, about seven times the percentage in the total University of Texas undergraduate population.

Intellectual Entrepreneurship originally offered a five-week, credit-bearing course each summer for graduate students across the disciplines. Designed as a catalyst for innovation, the course helped students envision creative ways to apply their intellectual training and expertise to scholarship, the community, the corporate world, or other arenas. Sometimes Cherwitz solicited challenges from local and regional organizations, and in many cases student teams developed their own ideas and strategies that the organizations adopted. Students also focused on developing their own visions into viable ventures using marketing research, teamwork, venture planning, and presentations. The program has worked wonders for undergraduates, and their scattered published accounts of their experience serve as strong testimonials. Why not return an idea like this to the doctoral level as well?

An equally likely undergraduate model is the late philanthropist Eugene Lang's Project Pericles. Now conducted at perhaps 20 undergraduate colleges and universities, Project Pericles encourages faculty to incorporate civic engagement and social responsibility into the curriculum. Students enroll in Debating for Democracy, a set of programs that teaches them how to sponsor projects that link campus and community, and advance their issues to elected officials, fellow students, community groups, and the media.

Many major campuses now house centers for public engagement, but they almost without exception skip over doctoral students to engage faculty and undergraduates (mostly in the social science disciplines). A wake-up call is overdue.

The Sciences

The bench sciences resemble the humanities in their active search for new footing in public scholarship. Scientists have the advantage of tech transfer, the robust interchange between academic sciences and for-profit technology. But the public-interest aspect of scientific work can be subordinated—not by hermetic traditions, as in the humanities, but by commercial interests. Everyone knows that scientific discoveries lead to economic benefits, but an emphasis on the "social profit" (to borrow David Grant's term) of the sciences is still at an early stage, though increasing rapidly.

That over half of all science PhDs work outside of academia does not translate automatically into momentum for public scholarship. Rather than prove their usefulness (a major motive for humanists to engage extramural publics), scientists tend to sponsor public scholarship to demonstrate their awareness of the social consequences, dangerous as well as salutary, of their work. Often their goal is to show that science can contribute to the common good and not just financial gain. In fact, because scientific and quantitative literacies lag badly behind expressive and historical literacies, the interest of scientists in going public encompasses a challenge to educate, from preschools to senior centers and everywhere in between.

The most established form of public science centers on "literacy," the work to inform nonscientific publics of what scientists do and why it matters. (Humanists and social scientists should pursue the same goal with equal energy.) Viewed in this light, science museums are brick-and-mortar embodiments of public scholarship in the sciences. Other traditional outlets for public science are new media and public and cable television.

Traditional outreach in the sciences also includes K–12 schools. The Graduate Molecular Biology Outreach Program at Princeton conducts activities for children such as science fairs and has students and faculty participate in an annual exposition on natural resources, NJ Wild. Adults are offered Science by the Cup (science-oriented tours of breweries and distilleries), and Science Quiz Night. The organization has also instituted a prison teaching initiative. MIT's biology department offers a week-long workshop on quantitative methods to undergraduates from many institutions, and Harvard's Life Sciences Outreach program helps high school teachers to develop new curricular materials. It also offers spring laboratory sessions for the students of 30 local high school teachers. We could provide many other examples without even leaving the Northeast.

Outreach by scientists to a larger public has steadily gained interest and attention since 1980, when *Time* magazine featured Carl Sagan on its cover. In the sciences, as in the humanities, many professionals understand the benefits of going public. In the *21st Century* report from the National Academies, more than half of the 11 desiderata listed for "an ideal graduate STEM education" include public scholarship. For example, students would "learn to consider ethical issues associated with their work as well as the broader implications of their work for society." In terms of lingua franca, they "would have opportunities to communicate the results of their work and to understand the broader impacts of their research," including "the ability to present their work and have exposure to audiences outside of their department, ranging from peers in other departments to the broader scientific community and nontechnical audiences," and so on.[42]

This powerful trend is further represented by the recently (1998) coined term, "open science," a controversial cognomen, which for our purposes may be characterized as the attempt to make scientific research available to "all levels of an inquiring society, amateur or professional."[43] While the term often refers simply to networking scientists who share information among themselves, one important strand is about explaining to nonexpert audiences the nature of research processes and their results.[44] Another recent coinage, "citizen science," bears some relation to the participatory efforts of the social sciences, in that it entails engaging nonscientists in research.

This is a global movement, but that's not to say that every science program is about to join it. As we've earlier pointed out, a half century of recommendations from the academies—for instance, to provide more money for training grants rather than to fund the faculty member's research alone—have been largely ignored. The proposal of "an ideal graduate STEM education," with "action steps for each stakeholder in the system to help achieve that goal" in the most recent report offers some reason for hope. And the report goes into real detail on strategies for making change appealing to reluctant stakeholders. Nonscientific disciplines require a similar goad.

In fact, science communication has become something of a movement. A national March for Science in 2018, intended to promote "a future where science is fully embraced in public life and policy" was held in part to combat the threat of a national undoing of the Enlightenment. "Lots of people out there are making reckless, wild claims about what is and isn't true, and about science itself," said Naomi Oreskes, a professor of the history of science at Harvard, and scientists have to step up and correct them.[45] Outside of the United States,

Cambridge has initiated Physics at Work for secondary students, and an educational outreach office for physics.

Women and nonwhite men are overrepresented in these science communication efforts, while white men are underrepresented. Oreskes sees this as both a result of reinforcing girls to care more about community and of the tough lot for women in academic science.[46] The data show that female graduate students in the sciences show more openness to nonprofessorial careers, which would help to account for their greater interest in alternatives enabled by better science communication skills.

Public scholarship in the sciences receives mandates and material rewards too. NASA requires all projects it funds to organize outreach efforts to the public and to universities, for instance. Humanists and social scientists may envy such widely scoped and well-funded efforts, as well as a wealth of award opportunities, such as the Award for Public Understanding of Science and Technology from the American Association for the Advancement of Science. Humanists and social scientists might gain inspiration from such models.

Not surprisingly, much public work takes place in virtual space. The University of Notre Dame received a five-year, $6.1 million grant to spread QuarkNet, a teacher development program established by the National Science Foundation and the Department of Energy.

We conclude this section with an especially interesting effort, The Science & Entertainment Exchange, which brings together all the disciplines. It was developed by the National Academy of Science to create "synergy between accurate science and engaging storylines in both film and TV programming."[47] Not only does it serve as a resource for writers and directors, who can literally call up for consultation, but the Los Angeles–based organization also offers regular well-attended forums, such as *The Most Unknown*, a documentary about scientists seeking answers to big questions who go on "dates" where they have conversations about topics like overpopulation or "cyber civics" (on secure voting).

Science Talk and the Importance of Public Communication

"It's tremendously important for scientists to get out there and explain what they do—to everyone, beginning with schoolchildren," says Naomi Oreskes, a professor of the history of science at Harvard University.

That message is spreading. Science communication courses have proliferated at colleges and universities in recent years. Janet Alder, an associate professor of neuroscience and cell biology and assistant dean of graduate studies at Rutgers University, teaches a good one in partnership with Nicholas M. Ponzio, a professor of pathology and laboratory medicine at the Rutgers New Jersey Medical School. "This course is about the importance of communication," they write in their joint syllabus. Their course teaches graduate students both to explain their research clearly and to "emphasize its significance."

Such outreach is multiplying outside the classroom too. Science Talk, a new science communication organization, holds an annual conference dedicated to that goal. Science Talk was founded in 2016 by Allison Coffin, a professor of integrative physiology and neuroscience at Washington State University Vancouver, and Janine Castro, a scientist at the US Fish and Wildlife Service. Both had taught science communication workshops and "wanted to create a forum for science communicators to come together, share ideas, and network," Coffin said.

To that end, the group's annual conference features discussions with people who work in science communication. They share their expertise on how to talk about controversial issues—like vaccine safety or gun control—in public settings. How do you control the room when things get loud? How do you defuse conflict? Just as important, participants practice their skills in workshops on subjects like using social media, creating an effective PowerPoint, or crafting a good elevator pitch.

Science Talk has grown swiftly, and its population skews young. Its biggest constituency is probably graduate students and postdocs. Panshak Dakup, a doctoral student in pharmaceutical science at Washington State University, said that "science communication is crucial in my life as a graduate student. In my interactions with professionals and laymen, there is almost always a forum where I need to explain what I do as a graduate student."

Jessica F. Hebert, a doctoral student in biology at Portland State University, is studying reproductive health, especially during pregnancy. "It is my goal to make science accessible," she said.

Accordingly, Hebert supplements her lab time by giving lectures and doing hands-on workshops at a science museum. She also extends her reach via cyberspace by contributing to podcasts like *This Week in Science* and *Geek in the City*. Hebert sees herself as a public educator: "I want to help fight misconceptions where I can."

The movement for public science matters for everyone today, not just scientists. As the astronomer Phil Plait put it in his Science Talk keynote address, "Science doesn't speak for itself. It needs an advocate—you."

Public Scholarship Going Forward

As public scholarship develops, its close relationship with career diversity emerges more and more clearly. Some graduate programs might see public scholarship as an end, while others might see it as a step toward greater career choice for graduates. For many, it could be both at once. By bringing social urgencies into the groves of academe, we can improve doctoral education without gutting what is already valuable in it and turn it into a beneficial, even critical, cultural lever. And it's very much worth noting that public scholarship pushes back against the harmful caricatures of higher education that have become so prevalent.

In the case of the humanities, Westerman recently voiced the counterargument that "translational activities" do not usually offer "shared and reciprocal interventions that use the *methods* of the humanities to solve problems defined by a community." Nor, she said, do they "generate new approaches within the academy to the grand challenges at whose table the humanities are trying to gain a seat"[48] In short, she's worried that public work may weaken the claim for intrinsic value and institutional support of the humanities.

We do not share this judgment or this anxiety. We do agree that public scholarship alone cannot cure what ails the humanities any more than arguments for the elevation of the soul can.[49] But the history of American higher education has always featured utility-based arguments, and we ignore them at our peril. (We are aware that this book engages with these positions.) We share Westerman's concern that the trivial not occlude the humanism of the humanities, but we contest the notion that institutional support adheres to an "either/or" logic. Institutions are influenced by public opinion, and every humanist (to say nothing of every social scientist) knows that there is a public relations problem to be fixed. Each of the forms of public scholarship we mentioned above is far more effective in forwarding the humanities than any number of testimonials or entreaties.

We end with the spotlight on the humanities because they are the canary in academia's coal mine. This is a time of public questioning of higher education generally. We are also engaged in an undeclared war against fact and disinterested reason amid a resource-draining viral pandemic and its inevitably straitened aftermath. In these times, public scholarship is integral to the future of the academy, not an amusing sideline. We need to put ourselves forward—and educate graduate students to do the same.

Conclusion

From Words to Actions

The One Thing Needful

American Historical Association executive director James Grossman is an optimist. His vision of a history department in the near future realizes the vision of this book, and it's so comprehensive that it applies equally well to many other fields.[1]

Grossman's future graduate director endorses career diversity. She foregoes discussing "placement rates" in introducing students to her department because that language carries the message of "the tenure track as the normative pathway." And curriculum, she explains, does not refer only to coursework but also to "internships, examinations, and the dissertation, with each element relating to the others in some intentional and articulated fashion." While the program emphasizes student versatility in expertise and career diversity, there are no separate tracks, she tells the cohort. She emphasizes the range of possible careers, even among professors, whose work "varies widely across higher education." And because many history occupations "will require additional skills and knowledge," she encourages students "to acquire that expertise via the whole university," including administrative offices and the like. Visit some other programs, as well, she adds, "not for the sake of interdisciplinarity itself, but for well-articulated intellectual and professional purposes."

Within the department and beyond it, the graduate director says, "you will become familiar with the institutional landscape of higher education, the scholarship on how people learn history, and the role of history in public culture." Have more than one adviser, she suggests, for "nobody is here to replicate themselves." But professors can't really provide good career advice for positions beyond academia, so she introduces the university's graduate student career director, who spotlights the leadership potential of PhD graduates. After that, the director of the university's center for learning and teaching talks to the students about the value of teaching—because even if a PhD decides to work outside of the professoriate, teaching will be a necessary skill.

Finally, the DGS concludes with a discussion of work, time, and money. Students' five-year support package, she explains, assumes a reduction in time to degree and a path to that goal. It will include stipends for teaching, for research, and for administration, with the latter referring to internships on campus in "community relations, international initiatives, communication/publications, admissions, development, student services," among others.

If Grossman's hypothetical introduction to doctoral study might seem too history centered for wider application, we would note that the *Graduate STEM Education for the 21st Century* report makes many of the same points—they're optimists also. Where it differs in field-related specifics, the STEM report retains a consistency in spirit and intention with Grossman's humanities-centered vision. Both call for a broadening of doctoral education, a diverse cohort, and the publication of transparent data on "costs incurred and viable career pathways and successes of previous students."[2] The authors of the STEM report recommend that students "encounter a variety of points of view about the nature, scope, and substance of the scientific enterprise" as well as "broad technical literacy coupled with deep specialization in an area of interest." Students would communicate the results of their work to varied audiences, including peers in other departments and also the general public, and they would "create their own project-based learning opportunities—ideally as a member of a team—as a means of developing transferable professional skills such as communication, collaboration, management, and entrepreneurship." They would "explore diverse career options, perhaps through courses, seminars, internships, and other kinds of real-life experiences." And faculty advisers "would encourage students to explore career options broadly and would not stigmatize those who favor nonacademic careers."

We're optimists too. When we began this book just two years ago, the move to a new PhD was still nascent, growing in national forums and reports like the ones we just quoted, but locally patchy and uneven. It's still far from assured or widely established, but my, how it has grown. We're encouraged by the local examples we've described in the previous pages, but the center does not yet hold. We second the plain statement of the STEM report that "unless faculty behavior can be changed . . . the system will not change."[3] We're aware that, even if faculty members become convinced of the necessity of changing doctoral education, the multivariable complexity of the task can be discouraging. Certainly the results we surveyed of past reform efforts inspire more caution than confidence.

So what to prioritize? Where to start?

"Okay," the reader may ask, "after all of this if you could change just one thing, what would it be?" Broader career opportunities? A doctoral cohort that looks more like America? Fewer years of schooling? More diligent advising and a student-centered dedication? Encouraging greater creativity in scholarship? Taking the teaching of teaching more seriously and integrating it into the content-based curriculum?

Each option is reasonable and even essential; but if we had to choose just one, we choose none of the above. To arrive at our alternative choice—which we believe might lead to all of the above—take a backward glance with us over the roads we've traveled in this book.

When we surveyed reform efforts of the recent past, in our first chapter, we saw a devastating disproportion. On one side lay the extraordinary number of reform efforts, their expense, and the talent involved, and on the other, the disappointing outcomes. Lots of smart people and lots of money led to few actual improvements. We've located the bright spots in these efforts to celebrate good ideas and more important, to show that this thing can be done—and to provide models that show how. But those bright spots remain the exception. The Carnegie initiative leaders observed that the "passionate zeal" of students is "unnecessarily eroded" and that doctoral study amounts to a "waste of human talent and energy in activities whose purpose is poorly understood." They call this waste "an urgent matter," but somewhere between thinking and acting, the urgency got misplaced.[4] The Carnegie leaders describe the results of their own strenuous efforts as modest, often simply accelerating reforms already underway, just as the abundantly funded Mellon Graduate Education Initiative found itself dependent upon the willing, who turned out to be few. Wistfulness is the dominant tone of the earlier reformers as they themselves look back.

For the students looking forward to their careers, the tone is frustration—which shouldn't be surprising. In the 2000 national survey of doctoral students, we recall, the organizers concluded, "Instead of brainstorming about what should happen, those involved in enriching graduate education should take well-considered suggestions that have already been made and turn those ideas into reality."[5] Twenty years later, those demands for change on the ground are even more insistent—and in light of the worsened academic job market, even more justified. Witness the outraged letter signed by English graduate students at Columbia to their faculty in May 2019, criticizing them for admitting 35 new students when not a single graduate had achieved a tenure-track position that year to that point. The students demanded preparation for career diversity and a wholesale reform of the department's advising system.[6] And that was before the COVID-19 pandemic.

This example illustrates a theme we have elaborated throughout this book, namely that most of the largely unexamined habits and traditions of doctoral study persist. It's worth repeating Derek Bok's plain and devastating observation that "graduate schools are among the most poorly administered and badly designed of all the advanced degree programs in the university." Doctoral programs, Bok continues, are "woefully out of alignment with the career opportunities available to graduates."[7] And given student frustration, the emphases of this book, Grossman's imagined future graduate orientation, and the twenty-first-century STEM report, among other warnings, career widening might well seem the one thing needful. But we want to focus on Bok's general statement about poor administration to get at a different idea.

We earlier quoted Grossman's mordant observation that each stake-holding group in doctoral education—faculty, students, administrators, employers—wants to change habitual practices, but cites recalcitrance on the part of the others as a reason nothing can be done. But why does such a confusion arise? Because no person or group appears to be in charge.

Grossman highlights an important point: lots of people want the system to change, but no one person or group believes that it is tasked with changing it. In other words, we see a lack of assigned and accepted responsibility. Meanwhile, Rome burns.

Now consider a key assertion by the public policy scholar Kenneth Prewitt, who surveyed the discipline-by-discipline essays on the Carnegie initiative in an essay in the very book where they were published. Those essays, wrote Prewitt, "are bold in the reforms recommended. But they are timid, in fact mostly silent, about who will have to align institutional habits, budgets, rules, and incentives if the reforms are to move from pages in this volume to practices in research universities."[8] Like Grossman, Prewitt observes that it's one thing to talk about what is to be done but quite another thing to identify who is to do it and how to encourage it in practical ways. The statement of responsibility from the STEM report includes a key clause we deleted when we referenced the statement a few pages ago. We now unveil it for dramatic effect: "Unless faculty behavior can be changed—*and changing the incentive system is critical in that regard*—the system will not change" (italics added).

Given the passion and intelligence that has been expended and the number of dollars spent to encourage innovations in doctoral education, we believe that the central barricade to action is *structural*. (One might be tempted to say instead that attitudes form the roadblock, but structure creates attitudes.)

And that leads to our designated priority, in two interrelated parts. The first is to *rethink the nature of the graduate school and empower the graduate deanship* to enable institutional change based on student-centered interests. The second is to *create incentives for change at every level*—from students to departments and their chairs, to provosts and presidents, and to foundation and disciplinary leaders, with an eye to government as well. If the graduate school and dean become the central conduit for all of these incentives, the two parts become one.

Prewitt says that "the genius of doctoral training in American higher education is that *no one is in charge*," but that's also the problem: when no one is in charge, that "cannot be taken to mean that no one above the faculty level has responsibilities." In other words, someone should lead. When we look from this angle, it's not difficult to understand why so much inertia impedes change in doctoral education in America. In higher education, says Prewitt, "reform co-evolves as a process that involves ideas from students and faculty with incentives designed by institutional and national leaders." But in the case of the PhD, "goals and incentives are misaligned," and this, he writes, constitutes "a leadership failure."[9]

Actually, it's more like a leadership vacuum. Consider that in calling upon presidents, provosts, and foundation leaders to step up, Prewitt does not even mention graduate deans. That's because graduate deans rarely have the power to change their own surroundings. The graduate deanship at some institutions is subordinated to the office of research, while at some others the job simply doesn't exist, and its responsibilities are subsumed within the larger duties of a vice president for research or sprinkled into the job descriptions of other deans. In most cases, the graduate dean is financially powerless and must seek alliances with the chairs and other deans to get anything done. "Follow the money," Bob wrote in 2005, "and it leads away from the graduate school to the faculty salary budgets of the other deans."[10]

This localized governance is not entirely a bad thing. Faculty ownership of graduate degrees can inspire extraordinary involvement. But the Carnegie leaders point out that "just as fish take water for granted, those inside the system find it hard to see . . . traditions and practices clearly."[11] Problems overlooked cannot be problems solved. As Damrosch puts it, "We academics are better placed to solve the world's problems than our own."[12] Faculty members are devoted to their disciplines and care about their students, but like everyone else, they're self-interested. Hence the defanged (or nonexistent) graduate deanship. Yet even when there is a graduate dean with her own headquarters, its very existence may be resented by the deans of schools whom the graduate dean must negotiate with for money. At too many universities, the graduate dean may serve tea more often than a clear purpose.

The dispersion of authority to the local program level harms the cohesion of the university and hinders the potential of its citizens— because in the end, the disciplines do not exist on separate planets but on a single campus, in an ultimately common enterprise. It's not only about successful management, then, but also intellectual quality: the graduate dean pilots a usefully wayward bus across the gridlines of the map of disciplines. En route, the deanship collects intellectual capital to create a graduate community and disperses best practices from one program to all the others.

The importance of a strong graduate deanship was elided by the Carnegie initiative a generation ago. Recent initiatives by disciplinary associations such as the Modern Language Association and American Historical Association elide it now. The Mellon GEI, on the contrary, depended on the graduate deans—and its disappointing results speak to the weakness of their oversight. The Woodrow Wilson Foundation's Responsive Ph.D. initiative sought deliberately to strengthen the graduate dean's position by working only through that office, but its success was limited because the authority of the graduate deans was likewise limited. It is worth repeating the recommendation from that initiative of nearly a generation ago: "The central notion of a graduate school requires strengthening so that it can become a vital force in breaking down barriers between programs and sponsoring a more cosmopolitan experience for doctoral students."[13] Today we would add that the most important barrier that graduate schools—led by their deans—should break down is the one between reform ideas that have gained a considerable consensus and the actual practices and policies of programs.

Dictatorial power is not at stake here. "Order me and I will fight you to the death," one faculty member noted at a Woodrow Wilson forum, but "invite my expertise and there is nothing I won't do for you." This sentiment argues for more carrots than sticks and for collaboration rather than fiat, but without resources the graduate dean cannot choose either. The dean of the graduate school requires an independent budget to encourage innovation, reward improvement, and, occasionally, withhold funds from programs. That is a key part of what deans do—except for graduate deans. University presidents and provosts, this is your alert.

An Example of an Empowered Dean

We saw the effect of an active and empowered graduate dean as we were finishing this book. *The New PhD* grew out of a report we completed for the Andrew W. Mellon Foundation on the recent history of doctoral program reforms. The graduate dean at Emory University, Lisa Tedesco, brought the report's recommendations, many of which have grown into our discussions in the book, to her faculty.

Reactions were predictable for a well-established university: they spanned a spectrum from enthusiasm to strong disagreement and included lack of interest too. That situation might have led nowhere without a persistent and creative and empowered dean. Tedesco formed committees to discuss possible change further, and the chair of English and the graduate chair of history subsequently encouraged other department chairs in the humanities to help them create a planning group to offer a graduate course next spring on public humanities.

We briefly consulted with the planning group of faculty members and humanities doctoral students, but the organizers had already invited a range of local nonprofit leaders and campus nonprofessorial intellectuals to discuss opportunities and possible partnerships with the group. The results include not only a most promising course but also a number of additional ways of promoting public scholarship, upon which the dean can now act.

The point of this story is that without a graduate dean's leadership, this exemplary process well might never have occurred. Clear leadership brings hope and action.

Assessment and the Student-Centered Graduate School

Even if the graduate dean gains authority, it will be meaningless without clearly stated standards and expectations for evaluating programs. Such assessment certainly should engage all faculty members, who then can bring back useful ideas to their own programs. "Assessment" has a bad reputation among faculty, mostly because many professors have, in the name of assessment, been mandated to measure the unmeasurable. Trying to figure out exactly what went into someone's success in the classroom is like trying to unbake a cake.

But really, haven't faculty members always been in the assessment business? We constantly assess our students, and we evaluate one another's research, writing, teaching, and service. We can rehabilitate the idea of assessment when we take the initiative to assess our own work and programs—and then act on our findings.

By what criteria might a graduate school evaluate its doctoral programs? Determining these criteria would require a discussion between graduate program directors and the graduate dean and school, but here's a list of potential candidates:

- A thoughtfully considered admissions policy that undergoes periodic faculty review
- Publication of attrition and time to degree statistics with a standard for each—perhaps five/six years and 75 percent retention and graduation in that time
- Clear goals and guidelines imparted to students at start of and throughout the program
- A diverse student cohort, assessed with an eye to national statistics in the particular discipline
- Pedagogical training as a developmental set of activities that create awareness of practices at a range of institutions
- Expanded career opportunities with curricular and cocurricular features to support them
- Explicit guidelines for faculty for advising at all stages of a program[14]

- Interdisciplinary opportunities and flexible dissertation alternatives
- Thorough data on outcomes for graduates that go back at least a decade

Any such list tends toward the quantitative. To ensure a thoughtful and qualitative evaluation, two further measures should be required: each departmental self-report ideally would be accompanied by a brief written discussion, and the graduate school would conduct periodic group discussions with a range of students in each program, perhaps once every three years.

While admissions criteria will differ from university to university, the primary incentive must be student support, which would help determine the size of the entering class. So as not to be draconian, one might imagine an assessment plan with a built-in delay of a year, whereby no support fund would be reduced without giving the program an opportunity to improve its student centeredness. In other words, the graduate school should encourage a discussion, but it is a discussion that requires student-first results and that may carry departmental consequences.

There are four other functions of the empowered graduate school. The first relates to one of the criteria listed above, the publication of data on student experience and outcomes in each program. Because some departments may lack the resources and the expertise to achieve such transparency (especially because there is little tradition of such data capture), the graduate school should be prepared to help at first. After that, each program reasonably could be asked to update the database continually.

A second function for the graduate school is to help programs link to the teaching and learning center, to help programs develop their students as teachers. A related move would be to connect programs with the alumni office and the career office to establish and regularize internships and nonprofessorial professional advice to students. As Grossman's imaginary graduate director proposed, this connection would invite the cooperation of administrative offices of the university in employing doctoral students to give them diverse academic work experiences.

A third function centers on the dean's global view: the graduate dean can and should inform programs of worthy innovations in other programs, at the home institution in particular but also elsewhere. Relatedly, the dean and the school can make multidisciplinary efforts more easily achievable and facilitate interdisciplinary initiatives by bringing representative faculty and students from the various programs together through dinners and presentations. (When Bob served as interim dean of the graduate school at the University of Michigan, for instance, he ran a monthly series of Monday dinner debates and presentations on matters of public interest. Less grand weekly dinners for graduate students, where each briefly discussed his or her work in sometimes distant fields, proved eye-opening as well.) How much more fruitful would doctoral education become if each part could become more aware of other parts—if the graduate school could become the intellectual center of a meaningful campus intellectual community?

And finally, the graduate dean can be the voice of the student in matters of concern. Even if a student never needs an ombudsman, it helps to know that one is available. In STEM fields, where intellectual ownership conflicts are frequent, this outlet matters especially.

Perhaps the empowered graduate dean and school we urge can seem too powerful. But when we speak of a graduate school, we are really speaking of a republic of faculty members and students, elected by their peers, who will work with the dean to establish policies. That's an institution that does not now exist at most universities. It really shouldn't be so hard to improve doctoral education, and this is one thing that can affect all the others.

The main reason we call for a strengthened graduate dean and school is because no other office is better positioned to institute major reforms whose scope extends beyond single programs. The graduate deanship can sponsor and drive transdisciplinary efforts. Collaborative and interdisciplinary preparation currently "is hostage to a reward system tailored to individual achievement within a discipline," said

Prewitt in 2006. Those hostages had been held for a long time when Prewitt wrote those words, and they remain captive today.

Consequently, the most important single action a president or a provost may take to address doctoral education is to appoint a strong graduate dean and to fund a dynamic graduate school.

We emphasize university leadership here because it may be the level that is most difficult to motivate. When it comes to approaching the administration, a complaint we hear frequently is, "My provost only cares how many students got tenure-track jobs at colleges and universities, preferably research universities." We suggest you begin with a simple response. Discuss student outcomes with the provost. Encourage her to read this book or some of the essays we cite here. Explain why you wish to have your program outcomes considered differently. Many provosts will welcome this discussion. Even today, many have not been invited to have it.

Next, the office of the president. As a former college president, Bob can vouch for the importance of the bottom line. If you see that a doctoral graduate who works outside the professoriate stands a good chance of making more money and having more to donate to the institution, your case will be heard. More idealistically, university presidents often have a breadth to their own professional biographies that makes diverse student outcomes not only understandable but emotionally and practically attractive to them.

Job one then: have the conversations, once, and then again, and again as program improvements take hold. In the initial conversations, explain your ambitions for your program and make the case for a strengthened dean of graduate studies. Tell the administration this: *change shouldn't have to be so hard.*

Six Departments, Six Possible Paths

Okay, the reader may say, we can try, but really, we can't do everything. We'll never reach consensus on everything, and we have our classes to teach and our research and scholarship to pursue, so will you slim it down for us?

To this reader, then, we respond by imagining the different paths chosen by six hypothetical departments after the kinds of student and alumni surveys and the consensus-seeking discussions that we described in chapter 2. And in outlining these six possible paths, we are also endorsing the idea that doctoral programs should differ significantly, so prospective students can have real choices beyond just comparing prestige. One size does not fit all at any stage of education, and the PhD is no exception.

Faster yet Broader

The faculty/student committee formed to improve the doctoral experience in a sociology department finds itself at odds, split between taking up career diversity and shortening time to degree. Sociology, some members of the committee say, is a natural fit with any number of social action careers in government, nonprofits, and community organizations, and the department is failing to train students for those careers. But others on the committee point out that, unlike in the humanities, many graduates already find their way into such careers, and that such an emphasis will make an already too-long program still longer. "And we still are given only six years of guaranteed student financial aid from the Grad School," they add. "This will make student debt even worse."

Two members speak to the dean. She can't decide the issues for them, but she is glad to see them earnestly seeking to improve the program. And she does have an idea to ease the tension. "If we're providing to students $25,000 for six years right now, as well as health coverage and a tuition waiver, you could take that $150,000-plus and instead provide $25,000 each year for five years of a faster program, and use the extra $5,000 for summer support each year. And that summer support might include nonacademic internships."

"Great," says a faculty member who wants to emphasize career diversity. "Currently our students teach during four of the six years to pay for a portion of that stipend. What if they graduated in four years, with two of those years teaching, and then spent a post-doc year teaching two courses in one semester and working part-time in the civic engagement center for the other, while receiving the stipend? You'd lose a course or two, but that should be paid for by the savings in health insurance and tuition waiver." The dean checks with the CEC director, who is enthusiastic. "Deal," she replies, "but only if your colleagues approve."

So the committee decides to urge the department to accommodate both goals—career diversity and a shorter time to degree, but they emphasize that the career diversity initiative will take place during summers and the postdoctoral year. A faculty member focused on time to degree reminds colleagues that if four years is the expectation for a BA, four years, plus summer semesters, is also reasonable for graduate students to gain a usable expertise that they will continue to develop after graduation. That is, one need not consider the doctorate the final stage of intellectual growth.

The committee chair adds, "We have a strong but not top-ranked department, and we need something distinct to attract students. Before this, we didn't look different enough from more prestigious programs. But if we adopt this faster yet broader track, we can set ourselves apart, maintain our academic standards, and give our students additional career opportunities. And those who want a professorial career can use their summers and postdoc year to strengthen their credentials."

The program faculty discuss how to set up summer internships and how to treat current students (to grandfather some of them into the new plan while allowing that some will proceed with the old). A follow-up committee develops a new plan: The renovated program begins with a written and verbally clarified timeline of expectations, so that expectations, and the funding that goes with them, are explicit. Advising—and monitoring—begins with the first weeks of the first year and remains active throughout.

Students will take courses and teach over a two-year period in four semester-long assignments that will develop pedagogical abilities. Summer stipends will be available, and courses will be offered during the first two years to speed their progress. In the postdoctoral year, an internship either in a campus administrative office like the civic engagement center or a nonprofit or for-profit corporation off campus will occupy one semester, with an option for the most academically career-oriented to teach at a community college or branch campus of a state university. This possibility will broaden the ranges both of academic and nonacademic career opportunities. As for the dissertation, this program replaces the book-length final project with two or three publishable major articles. Students will also have the option of writing a traditional dissertation, but faculty would keep a close eye on its shape so that it may be completed in 18 months. During this time, advisers agree to meet with their students on a biweekly basis.

In this instance, and in the others that follow, it's clear that discussions during the planning process with university administrators (deans, provosts, maybe even the president) are essential.

All-Purpose Pedagogy

A political science department is not fully persuaded by the career diversity movement, though it acknowledges the crisis in academic employment. "Not all of our students will become top scholars," says the director of graduate studies, "and some may not even aim for that. But just about all of them want teaching careers."

The faculty decides on a five-year program with a goal of graduating educators who can succeed across the full range of institutions of higher learning. A committee assigned the task of improving academic employment begins by broadening the definition of teaching venues to include high schools, independent schools, community colleges, branch campuses, and liberal arts colleges, as well as the usual research university preparations. The committee assigns teams to link with these different kinds of institutions in the region of the university. After the department votes to plan the new program, the committee reconvenes to establish internships based on the Preparing Future Faculty model, but with students actually teaching at these different institutions (following an apprenticeship period with a faculty member).

In this more traditional but still broadened program, students take 3 of their 12 courses outside the department to provide academic breadth beyond a single discipline, in part because most teaching-intensive colleges and schools require curricular breadth. They spend parts of two semesters in a teaching assignment at one or two of the venues. Because a few students might consider teaching or aiding in curricular design at a private or public high school, the department offers to swap some graduate student teachers with interested high school teachers who want an intellectual reboot at the university. (Who better to teach a first-year college student than a fine instructor who regularly teaches high school seniors just four months younger?) To minimize dropouts and meandering, the revamped program's qualifying exam includes the dissertation prospectus, and the committee works with the student to coordinate course choices to prepare for the exam. This bespoke preparation allows students to prepare on their own over an additional funded summer. The final project is a dissertation that combines traditional scholarship with a pedagogical component.

This hypothetical department also forges new connections with both the campus center for teaching and learning and the education school, while it also acknowledges that teaching challenges are sometimes discipline specific. The program develops and offers a new graduate course in the pedagogy and history of political science (also open to undergraduates who seek a teaching career on the secondary school level) and provides frequent opportunities for students and faculty to talk about teaching together.

This program complements its pedagogical aims with a pointed commitment to diversity. Fueled by awareness of the disparity at all levels between a mostly white faculty and a far more diverse student cohort, and of the voluminous research showing that students taught by a person who "looks like them" do better, the department invents new forms of local outreach and summer visitations, and also considers the effects of its policies on underrepresented groups. And finally, the program agrees to admit only that number of students who can be adequately supported, both financially and in their employment search.

Career Diversity

An English department goes all-in for career diversity. The faculty decide to open out to students the full range of professorial and nonprofessorial options, and to give equal standing to each. This program will establish local liaisons with a range of educational institutions similar to those forged by the pedagogically centered program and will also admit the possibility of academic careers in university administration that may come with some teaching opportunities. It will capitalize on the fact that every university is a small city, and so it will fund internships for graduate students in various offices like development, public relations, publications, admissions, and student affairs. (While some faculty worry that they are turning their program into a higher ed policy shop, the majority remind doubters that all options, very much including the professoriate, remain on the table and that the added possibilities hardly mark an end to intellectual inquiry.)

This program exerts its main effort to get outside the campus to propose different kinds of intellectual work in various social sectors. To get beyond the university walls, this program begins with links to two key partners within it: the career office, enlarged to include counselors who specialize in graduate students; and the alumni relations office, which connects students to alumni (including undergraduate alumni who also get pleasure from helping current students of every level) for internships and postgraduation employment.

Because lifelong academics aren't experts on nonacademic job searches, an expanded graduate role for career offices is a particular necessity. The program quickly learns the value of a suite of internship opportunities, and so it decides to fund a five-year, full-time position responsible for establishing a network of them, with cooperation not only from the career and alumni offices (and the graduate school) but also from faculty members themselves, who will learn to evaluate their personal connections for potential internships.

In this program also, advising begins in earnest the moment a student enters the program, with career advising that extends beyond graduation. Each student will maintain an independent career plan, revised each semester in consultation with a four-person committee chosen by the student, composed of two or three faculty members and one or two outside members employed outside the academy.

Accompanying this enhanced advising is a revision of admissions standards to prevent discrimination (intentional or inadvertent) against students with extramural career goals. (Imagine how most programs today would react to an applicant who expressed an interest in, say, technology applications of the discipline, or K–12 curricular design, or a job at the History Channel or another media outlet, rather than a college post.)

Upon graduation, in addition to the dissertation, students will be required to explain in lingua franca the importance of their projects, perhaps to a panel coming from different backgrounds. Such a requirement makes particular sense in a program such as this because as we have stressed in this book, career diversity and public scholarship dovetail.

Diversifying and Applying the American Intellect

With a chief goal of ethnic, racial, and gender equity, the faculty of a psychology program engages in a fruitful debate on the topic of career diversity, a term that some faculty members find problematic in itself. But this leads to an agreement to seek diversity in its more traditional sense, centering on race, ethnicity, class, and gender. The faculty agree that the program will intensify its efforts to recruit more students of color and more low-income students.

Some faculty argue that producing more college and university teachers of color must remain the focus, not preparing them for diverse careers. These colleagues argue further that the academic job shortage is less severe for able graduates of color because colleges and universities already recruit them actively. "Agreed," replies the department chair. "But why are these two goals inimical?" She cites research surveys showing that centering scholarship on urgent social issues especially attracts students with connections to minority communities. The program should privilege and appeal to this interest. A more diverse faculty, others argue, should also be a more socially aware and capable faculty, one that doesn't just talk progressive politics but actually addresses community needs. The program resolves the issue by emphasizing public scholarship and community internships at nonprofits and cultural institutions—but otherwise limiting its focus on career diversity.

Features of this diversity-centered program will include an opportunity to teach for at least one semester at a majority-minority institution and, following a series of workshops that survey community partnerships and prepare students to work helpfully with them, another semester of part-time internship at a nonprofit. Dissertation possibilities may include research tied to the interests of the organization where the student interns, and students must learn communication skills to explain their research effectively to various audiences, including those outside the discipline.

Students and faculty in this program meet together collegially to discuss the program's climate and to attempt to solve any difficulties together. Continuing in this spirit of collaboration, students contribute to the work of the department's various committees, including those on the undergraduate curriculum and admissions. Upon graduation, new PhDs will be offered the option to serve as mentors to beginning students and receive a stipend for this work (to be conducted in person, by telephone, by Zoom, and by email). In all, the program seeks to model the diverse community that is its larger social goal.

Scientific Creativity

Our fifth hypothetical program is in the sciences. This physics department, rather than seeking to replace faculty-directed research grants, takes several steps. We've talked in this book about how many problems confronting doctoral study cut across fields, but we've also pointed to some issues particular to the sciences, especially concerning outside research funding. Numerous national reports over the years have recommended that national funders replace the ever-increasing proportion of research grants awarded to faculty with grants that encourage students both to teach and to exercise greater freedom and creativity in formulating their own research projects. Yet the recommendations have been repeatedly ignored.*

Our hypothetical physics department chooses to meet this challenge. It decides to require a summer course on research methods, and its preliminary exam will center on inventing a research topic and a presenting a prolegomenon for developing it. For the dissertation, the department decides to establish guidelines to ensure that each student will have the freedom to develop a distinct and largely self-initiated project related to, but not wholly contained within, the adviser's grant project—with that faculty member's advice and consent, of course. Meanwhile, faculty will be encouraged to include in their research grants provisions for student experiences often associated only with training grants, and they will be assisted in doing so.

Funders should welcome such a move. To help make sure they do, representatives of the department along with the head of the university's research office, will visit with grant administrators at relevant federal agencies (NSF, NIH), and private funders such as the Howard Hughes Medical Institute and the Keck Foundation.

Many lab-oriented programs now ameliorate the scary autonomy of the faculty dissertation/lab research mentor by urging or requiring incoming students to rotate through three to five labs for a few weeks each, or at least interview with three different faculty members (six in the case of Stanford's chemistry doctorate) before ranking their choices as part of a process of matching student preferences to faculty research-funded needs. But that practice does not necessarily develop a student's scientific creativity. Nor do programs typically hold discussions among faculty members about issues of student advising and leading a lab group in a way that maximizes student growth. And students typically make their lab choice, or have it made for them, after just one or two semesters.

---

* Some individual programs in the sciences now provide greater independence to doctoral students. The chemistry department at the University of California, Berkeley, for instance, describes its program as "designed toward developing within each student the ability to do creative scientific research," though the program emphasizes the ability of students to design their own programs rather than a thorough rethinking of norms. https://chemistry.berkeley.edu/grad/chem/about.

Our hypothetical physics department understands that a shift to graduate student-centered science will require a concerted effort. Faculty will partner with alumni affairs and career services to seek opportunities for local industrial and technical internships for their students, and they will agree to accord a higher priority to teaching (which is now the stigmatized alternative, chosen only if a student is not supported by a faculty research grant). In conjunction with the graduate school, the department will increase stipends for teaching, and plan a thoughtful program to allow students experience teaching in both classrooms and labs. Perhaps most important, the department will institute a teaching requirement, and establish its own required course on pedagogy in physics.

Additional aspects of this renovated science program include a course on the social consequences of STEM research, a revamped admissions strategy that increases diversity, and regular reviews of program culture to ensure that the needs of a more diverse student cohort will be met. All of these suggestions are adapted from the *Graduate STEM Education in the 21st Century Report* and other recent calls for reform.

A New Kind of Master's

For several years, faculty in the art history department at a state university branch campus have struggled to maintain a doctoral program, but they face sharply decreasing student enrollments and inadequate financial resources for student aid. Or, alternately, we might imagine a history department at a master's level university that has lost much of its enrollment because federal and state supported programs that subsidized teachers to earn a graduate degree have been curtailed.

The faculty decides on a new master's of the kind we described in chapter 9. The history of art PhD program, after a particularly unpleasant discussion with the provost and graduate dean, proposes to replace the current failing program with a distinctive master's that will place graduates in museums, other cultural institutions, and galleries and auction houses, with a graphic and computer design track for the more studio oriented. If a few students wish to continue to the PhD, that could remain available via a tutorial system similar to those at British universities. But the emphasis will be on a one-of-a-kind master's with a strong and clear career orientation.

Our hypothetical history department determines to change its current master's program by adding career internships. To do this, it opens new channels of communication with alumni, regional and local businesses and nonprofits, and governmental agencies at all levels. The faculty comes to see that students may need additional foundational knowledge, so they sacrifice two departmental courses and require students to take two courses outside the department. As a result, department faculty for the first time engage with colleagues in other departments and schools—media, business, education, library studies, political science, public health, and environmental science, among others. The connections prove reciprocal: faculty in these other schools and departments decide to do what the history department is doing and send their students to receive cross-disciplinary instruction too—including graduate history courses.

Don't Stop There

We could go on to imagine a program that decides to prioritize diversity and rethinks its curriculum accordingly, or a program that emphasizes public scholarship rather than career diversity per se (because the faculty may be more amenable to it as a first step), and so on. Much of what we have written here about specific hypothetical programs could apply to any and all of them. The best advice we can leave our reader with is simple: empathize, imagine, plan, act.

National Organizations

We said that the new PhD should begin with the active encouragement of the president and provost. But why should they care? Here we move to the principle of providing motivation at every level.

Prestige—the "money" of higher education—motivates institutional leaders. Right now the prestige economy that surrounds graduate study is almost entirely research based. The problems with the current rating system need little elaboration. The National Research Council, for example, has a narrow ambit: it measures research output and ranks programs by the research productivity of their scholars. Because of the consequent emphasis on existing reputation, NRC findings can resemble the results of the hoaxes that routinely rank Princeton's (nonexistent) law school in the top 10.[15]

But the biggest problem with the research-based assessment is that it doesn't look at enough variables. Ranking graduate programs solely according to their research output (assuming that this were actually being done) would be like ranking cars solely by their engines. The engine is important, certainly, but anyone who drives knows that suspension matters, as do transmission, brakes, and so on.

Graduate schools need to be assessed by more student-centered measures. Prospective students need to know how well a program professionalizes its students, for example. How is the advising? The career counseling (for both professorial and nonprofessorial careers)? What kinds of support does the program offer students and for how long? What is the typical time to degree? These are just a few of the questions that prospective students increasingly want the answers to, and they're more important to students than how many citations the faculty earned for their publications.

What if students could get student-centered information by going to one place? A new assessment system wouldn't need to rank programs against each other according to some kind of absolute (and probably squishy) scale. Instead, it could gather information and present it in clearinghouse fashion. Think Yelp for graduate students.

Graduate students need their own Yelp. Right now they have no single place to go for information and can only investigate programs one by one. (And programs are not always forthcoming with information that students need.) Moreover, the shadow of research rankings looms all the larger because it has no competition. How best to move away from such a thorough reliance on this one pursuit?

We recommend a national website that rates (not ranks) programs and graduate schools. Funding and support for such a website could begin at any institution, with or without foundation support. (Think of the free advertising that would come from the association with such a project—and the goodwill it would generate among prospective applicants to graduate school.) A clearinghouse for student-centered information about graduate programs would be a public service. It wouldn't replace research rankings but would provide a counterweight to them. We can rate programs as they seek to achieve a limited number of goals such as those we listed, with the addition of publishing student support funding and activities.

Further, these categories or others provide an agenda for foundations to reward or incentivize graduate schools and their departments in particular areas:

- Self-assessments including student and alumni surveys
- Data keeping on student outcomes
- Innovative recruitment strategies to achieve a more diverse student cohort, by collaborations among academic institutions and through additional funding opportunities on both a need and racial/ethnic/gender basis
- Diverse career opportunities, professional development seminars, and viable links to the career and alumni offices
- Nonprofessorial internships, including those that might take place on campus in such areas as student services, development, publications, and university relations or in deans' offices
- Teaching opportunities for students, including the possibility of teaching at a diverse set of institutions
- Concrete proposals for improving rates of completion and time to degree

We all need to learn the accountability lesson together. National funding by foundations and agencies should focus on specific issues and set expectations. Proposals should also include a plan for sustainability beyond the funding horizon. Funders must insist on frequent periodic reports and continuing assessment (as we outlined in our second chapter). Further, and especially in terms of diversity efforts on a national scale, funders themselves should collaborate to create a unified effort.

Many of the items on our list surfaced in earlier reform efforts. It's fair to ask why they should work now—and spread to other institutions—if they didn't work then. They failed, we believe, for two reasons. First, suasion was not strong enough, even when early returns showed that programs were not performing according to expectations. Second, there may not have been enough time for faculty buy-in or sufficient means for replicating what worked at a larger number of schools.

We therefore suggest two waves of funding. A small number of pilot programs would lead off, followed by assessment of what works and does not, and a round of adjustments. Later funding for a larger group of programs would follow. In the case of national reform initiatives, we recommend dedicating a portion of the budget to getting the news out and helping the ideas spread. The American Historical Association is our model here. With financial support from the Mellon Foundation, the organization initially funded four history departments to integrate diverse career models into their doctoral programs and then later awarded smaller grants to a greater number of departments. The AHA has an information-rich website, and the organization has held various convenings to spread the word about what they're doing.[16]

The formula of choosing a few to influence the many requires thoughtful public relations. Spotlighting model programs likewise requires care. Funders need to consider the selection criteria for inclusion, to maximize the possibility that the few will become the many and the many will become the norm.

Many previous initiatives did not coordinate their efforts with each other. Even now, when technology makes it easy for institutions to work with and learn from each other, we often reinvent the same faulty wheels—and get the same flat tires. Foundations urge universities and colleges to collaborate, but the various foundations often fail to do just that with each other. This is most noticeable in efforts at representative diversity. One of the reasons we wrote this book was to call attention to old mistakes so that we don't expend precious resources and make them all over again.

Foundations, disciplinary associations, and other umbrella organizations have three other roles:

1. To seek to influence public policy. If every major report on the doctoral sciences has recommended awarding a greater percentage of training grants at the expense of research grants, major funders like NSF and NIH need to take their own advice. Not doing so results in Band-Aids rather than cures.
2. To provide economic advice. Reforms usually have a cost, sometimes modest but sometimes higher. A national group of strategic budget experts, working to serve the public good, may be able to suggest means to make the improvements less costly and thus more feasible.
3. To use their convening power. Faculty members, administrators, and doctoral students all need to know what the leadership considers good policy and practice. Public meetings get the word out.

We've already suggested that the power of the purse may be used to encourage individual departments and programs to reflect on their practices. How to begin? Enlightened graduate schools should solicit ideas from their own graduate students, so one possibility is the kind of survey of alumni (including non-completers) and current students that was conducted by Columbia's department of English and comparative literature under the auspices of the Carnegie initiative.[17] Another is to have funders and the university administration require responses to three simple questions—whether there is a will for reform, who can get it done, and by what means. And that might require a pre-beginning: to educate the faculty about the major issues facing graduate study, especially their surprisingly long history. Faculty idealism can help to create change, but not enough of it has been united and pointed toward doctoral education.

If prestige is comparable to money, so is money. What an institution spends money on shows that institution's values to its faculty. Students may require their own concrete incentives to develop their own self-aware and creative decision making as they consider their career prospects and whether a program fits their talents and temperaments. Workshops are good, but credited courses are better, and credentials (such as certificates) better still.

The initiatives of the past are themselves an education for the future. Too much sweat and treasure have been expended over the past generation to improve doctoral education for the results to be forgotten. Much that was done in the past generation can inform the work of this one. We have repeatedly held up the Carnegie initiative's three basic sets of questions for program self-assessment as exemplary. Preparing Future Faculty coalitions provide an excellent model for broadening students' teaching experiences. Similarly, Woodrow Wilson's summer fellowships for internship work beyond the academy and the matching of doctoral graduates with willing for-profits and nonprofits was intended to be taken over by individual campuses (which have their own regional businesses, cultural organizations, and interested alumni). Doctoral study is in trouble right now, and we can't afford to make the same mistakes when we try to fix it. Future reforms must begin with awareness of the strengths and weaknesses of past efforts. We must also assign and take responsibility. The American university has enshrined the idea of academic freedom, but it has proved less comfortable with its flip side of academic responsibility. But what freedom worth having doesn't come with responsibility?

Literary scholar David Damrosch rightly asks, "If everybody knows what needs to be done, why are so few programs doing it?"[18] He quotes Clark Kerr's observation that what is remarkable about higher education generally "is not how much has changed but how little." Kerr had a wide view of a large field, and he noticed that in "areas under faculty control," movements toward "academic reform" were "mostly overwhelmed by faculty conservatism."[19]

We've earlier invoked the conservatism of graduate school, but so little about it has changed that we might rightly describe it as rigid, not conservative. And even when we want to change, we frequently can't manage to do it. That isn't because we academics are uniquely poor change agents—sometimes the opposite is true. The failure begins with responsibility: we need to bring the responsibility to change together with the power to effect change. We must change *the process by which we change* if we are to effect the reforms we need. Right now the graduate school industrial complex has a leadership vacuum that disperses academic responsibility. But we have to take on that responsibility—to the university, to our fields of study, and especially to the professional lives and futures of our doctoral students.

The New PhD is a young movement, past its birth but still in early adolescence; and like an adolescent, it needs to embrace a variety of experiences and experiments. Neither of us has ever been accused of shying away from stating an opinion, but we have sought in this volume to balance advice and options. The only option we rule out is inaction.

Postscript

Graduate School after COVID-19

The coronavirus pandemic hit the United States just as this book went into production. The full effects of the economic catastrophe on higher education remain hazy at this point, but the main question is how bad they'll be. Hiring freezes began almost immediately, and even the most optimistic appraisals foresee painful budget reductions and downsizing at even the wealthiest colleges and universities.

We already had argued that any imminent increase in the number of professorships is unlikely. We should advocate for professorships, certainly, but we must also plan for the reality before us. Now that reality has been further battered. If the past—think 2008—is any guide, a further decrease in professorships now appears likely.

In these circumstances, we believe that career diversity matters all the more for graduate schools. The COVID-19 pandemic stands out as a destructive example of unexpected influences on the academic job market, but it also reminds us that others may well occur. At the same time, areas of concern not directly associated with career outcomes—admissions, say, or teacher training—remain worthy of bold innovation. They matter in themselves for the sake of the students' experience, but we need to rethink them in relation to a more widely purposed PhD.

Improvements in the range of outcomes should strengthen rather than compromise students' motives for pursuing the degree. "I love to read and interpret," "I'm a total lab rat," "I want to understand the world better"—these desires continue to motivate college graduates to enter doctoral programs. You don't have to become a professor to fulfill them. Now and more than ever, these life-affirming pursuits are undermined by a closed professorial economy—and they only benefit from a sense of multiple possibility.

We don't expect any silver lining to this pandemic. But we shouldn't let it deter us from making a new PhD. Changing PhD programs to meet current realities is not to let the tail wag the dog. It is to let the dog out of a shrinking cage.

It takes a village to raise any book, but this book needed a village more than most. A broadening consensus has emerged in recent years that graduate education has fundamental problems, but that doesn't mean the solutions are obvious. We've looked at many past and present reforms in this book, and we've drawn on the efforts of many people at different institutions to find those solutions. Without their work, we would not have been able to do ours.

This book germinated in a brief history of recent PhD reform that we were commissioned to write in 2015 by the Andrew W. Mellon Foundation. We studied the work of then and now, and when we finally looked to the future we wrote as hopeful advocates, for the largest disciplinary organizations had launched major reforms. Still, local examples of student-centered practices were rare. Now, as we bring this book to its readers, we find ourselves reporting as well as advocating, for innovation has begun to flourish on campus.

And so our first acknowledgment is to the hundreds of academics and their supporters who have braved the inherent, faculty-centered history of the doctoral degree to place students first. We've written about many of you in the pages of this book, but our coverage could not be encyclopedic. We honor all of you as the coauthors of our book.

Our second acknowledgment goes to Earl Lewis, former president of the Mellon Foundation, and his colleagues, particularly Eugene Tobin and Mariet Westermann, whose keen observations helped to shape our views. It's a mark of the foundation's rare integrity that we were not asked to change a word of our critique of Mellon's own efforts. However challenging the current moment is for the humanities and humanistic social sciences, it would be far more bleak without

Mellon, whose support of undergraduate as well as graduate education has been unique and literally vital.

The report that we wrote for Mellon required some special knowledge and expertise beyond our ken. Peter Bruns, professor of genetics emeritus at Cornell University and retired vice president for grants and special programs at the Howard Hughes Medical Institute, lent his capacious understanding of reform efforts in the sciences, and Johnnella Butler, professor of women's studies and former vice president and provost at Spelman College, contributed a similar mastery of the recent history of efforts to mirror the growing diversity of the US population and the collective national intellect in the PhD student cohort. Their insights inform not only the report but also this book.

Our book has benefited from the work of national organizations that have thoughtfully addressed issues in doctoral education. We're especially grateful to Pauline Yu and Joy Connolly and their colleagues at the American Council of Learned Societies; Judith Shapiro, Donna Heiland, and Andrew Delbanco at the Teagle Foundation; James Grossman, Emily Swafford, and Dylan Ruediger at the American Historical Association; and Paula Krebs and Stacy Hartman at the Modern Language Association. We've learned a lot from the writings of many colleagues, including Edward Balleisen, Chris Golde, Michelle Massé, Maresi Nerad, Julie Posselt, Maria LaMonaca Wisdom, and George Walker, who expertly led the Carnegie Foundation effort that we discuss in these pages. Special thanks to Katina Rogers for sharing the manuscript of her book while it was in production.

Teachers who write owe a lot to their students. Len taught a cocurricular workshop on American higher education at Princeton for three years beginning in 2017. Thanks to Anthony Grafton, Stan Katz, and especially Bill Gleason and Amy Pszczolkowski for their help to set it up and to Amy and James Van Wyck for their work to support it— and to the three cohorts of students who taught us all so much. Bob was gifted during his time at Woodrow Wilson with superb colleagues on graduate initiatives, in particular Elizabeth Duffy, Beverly Sanford, and Bettina Woodford. Similarly, the creative and dedicated work of Robert Ready, Richard Greenwald, and Jonathan Rose in rethinking graduate education at Drew University led to a number of important insights concerning public scholarship. And we are deeply grateful to our own graduate students at Fordham and Michigan for the trust they've placed in us and for the insight they've shared.

We've learned a great deal too from John Guillory, Morris Grubbs (who thoughtfully read the whole manuscript on short notice and provided enormously useful feedback), George Justice, John Kucich, Kerry Larson, Michael Schoenfeldt, James Van Wyck, Kathleen Woodward, and Rafia Zafar. Len's writing on higher education, especially his previous book, *The Graduate School Mess*, has led to many campus visits that enlarged our perspective. We thank his hosts: Rachel Adams, Nicholas Allen, Rebecca Alpert, Jonathan Arac, Herman Bennett, Russell Berman, Beth Boehm, Kathleen Canning, Jennifer Cason, Kinchel Doerner, David Downing, David Galef, Loren Glass, Josh Goode, Andrew Graybill, Morris Grubbs, Jaco Hamman, Phillip Brian Harper, Josh Hevert, Andrew Hoberek, Dorothy Hodgson, Sarah Hokanson, LeeAnn Horinko, Amy Hungerford, Coleman Hutchison, George Justice, Kate Hausbeck Korgan, Stephen Krason, Dan Kubis, Jerry Kukor, Michael Latham, Jenna Lay, Rodrigo Lazo, Julia Lupton, Michelle Massé, Keli Masten, Caroline Maun, Jeff Mayersohn, John McGreevy, Alene Moyer, Brian Norman, Dan Olson-Bang, Brandy Randall, Jordan Reed, Skip Rutherford, Vanessa Ryan, Susan Scheckel, Pamela Schirmeister, Jack Selzer, Lisa Sewell, David Shumway, John Stevenson, Amanda Swain, Jen Teitle, Kathryn Temple, Paul Thifault, Claudia Tomany, David Toomey, Johannes Voelz, Rob Watson, Eric Wertheimer, Glenn Wright, and Jessica Yood.

Some of the ideas in this book received their first airing in Len's regular column, The Graduate Adviser, in the *Chronicle of Higher Education*. Years' worth of thanks go to Denise Magner for her collaborative wisdom in shaping those essays for publication. Professors Benjamin Reiss and Thomas Rogers kindly allowed us to field-test some of the ideas contained in this book when they invited us to consult during the formation of their own public scholarship initiative at Emory University. And that initiative would not have been possible without the productive encouragement of Lisa Tedesco, Emory's vice provost for academic affairs and dean of the Laney Graduate School, and associate dean Rosemary Hynes. In thanking them, we also want to thank those administrators at many other universities who have goaded, encouraged, and funded efforts to create a new PhD.

We likewise extend thanks to those leaders in business, government, and finance who have cheered on the reform efforts. In naming a few of the former trustees at the Woodrow Wilson National Fellowship Foundation—the late Eleanor Elliott, Frederick Grauer, Nancy Malkiel, Louis Simpson, Marvin Suomi, and Steven Weiswasser—we mean to honor all those across social sectors who understand the value of PhDs in every imaginable pursuit and who act on that understanding. Len would like to single out Eva Badowska, John Bugg, and the late Stephen Freedman at Fordham University for their support. Thanks also to his graduate student research assistants Rhianna Marks-Watton and Joseph Daley.

Neither of us has ever cowritten a book before, and we can report that the clerical work increases exponentially as the number of authors multiplies. For his help in organizing the book—and more important, for his wise counsel in the process—we thank A. W. Strouse. Our most personal thanks go to our life partners, Debra Osofsky and Candy Cooper. They haven't read this book yet because they've been busy at their own work. Their dedication and expertise inspire us each day.

We thank our superb editor, Greg Britton, and his terrific colleagues at Johns Hopkins University Press, especially Kyle Gipson, for his careful attention to detail during production. We also thank Carrie Watterson for her thoughtful copyediting. We want finally to express gratitude to you, our reader, first for staying with us through many chapters. Second and more important, we are grateful in advance for what you will decide to undertake in your own life in higher education. Creating a more viable doctorate is a test of the professoriate, the students, and the national culture at large. The success of our work here will not be tallied by book sales or reviews, but only by whether we all choose to mark this important moment of change and participate in it.

Introduction

1. See Leonard Cassuto, "Ph.D. Attrition: How Much Is Too Much?," *Chronicle of Higher Education*, July 1, 2013, https://www.chronicle.com/article/PhD-Attrition -How-Much-Is/140045.

2. William Pannapacker, writing as Thomas H. Benton, "Graduate School in the Humanities: Just Don't Go," *Chronicle of Higher Education*, January 30, 2009, https://www.chronicle.com/article/Graduate-School-in-the/44846.

3. Derek Bok, *Higher Education in America* (Princeton, NJ: Princeton University Press, 2013), 240.

4. Katina L. Rogers, *Putting the Humanities PhD to Work: Thriving in and beyond the Classroom* (Durham, NC: Duke University Press, 2020). We are grateful to Rogers for sharing the manuscript with us in advance of its publication.

5. William James, "The PhD Octopus," in *Memories and Studies* (New York: Longmans, Green, 1917), 331.

6. Louis Menand, *The Marketplace of Ideas* (New York: W. W. Norton, 2010), 151–52.

7. William Rainey Harper, "First Annual Report" (1888), quoted in "From the History of the University," *University of Chicago Magazine* 8 (1915): 257.

8. This language occurs in title 7 of the United States Code. This is the context: "without excluding other scientific and classical studies and including military tactics, to teach such branches of learning as are related to agriculture and the mechanic arts, in such manner as the legislatures of the States may respectively prescribe, in order to promote the liberal and practical education of the industrial classes in the several pursuits and professions in life." US National Archives & Records Administration, "Transcript of the Morrill Act (1862)," November 25, 2019, http://www.ourdocuments.gov/doc.php?doc=33&page=transcript.

9. Nicholas Lemann, "The Soul of the Research University," *Chronicle of Higher Education*, April 28, 2014, https://www.chronicle.com/article/The-Soul-of-the -Research/146155.

10. Thomas Bender, "Expanding the Domain of History," in *Envisioning the Future of Doctoral Education: Preparing Stewards of the Disciplines*, ed. Chris M. Golde and George E. Walker (San Francisco: Jossey-Bass, 2006), 295.

11. See the National Science Foundation's *Survey of Earned Doctorates*, https://www.nsf.gov/statistics/srvydoctorates/. The survey is "an annual census conducted since 1957 of all individuals receiving a research doctorate from an

accredited U.S. institution in a given academic year." It is sponsored by the National Center for Science and Engineering Statistics within the National Science Foundation (with support from several other government agencies as well, including the National Endowment for the Humanities), but it includes numbers for doctoral graduates in all fields, including the humanities and social sciences as well as education and agriculture. It includes demographic characteristics of graduates as well as postgraduation plans.

12. William Bowen and Neil Rudenstine, *In Pursuit of the Ph.D.* (Princeton, NJ: Princeton University Press, 1992). The attrition rate has been high since the postwar era, as programs admitted scores of students with the social Darwinian expectation that most would drop out along the way, with only the fittest crossing the finish line.

13. The first graduate student union was organized in 1969 at Wisconsin; see R. G. Ehrenberg, Daniel B. Klaff, Adam T. Kezsbom, and Matthew P. Nagowski, "Collective Bargaining in American Higher Education," in *Governing Academia*, ed. Ronald G. Ehrenberg (Ithaca, NY: Cornell University Press, 2004), 222.

14. Of the sources that document the long-term withdrawal of public finding for higher education and its deleterious effects, see especially Christopher Newfield's *The Great Mistake: How We Wrecked Public Universities and How We Can Fix Them* (Baltimore: Johns Hopkins University Press, 2016).

15. Derek Bok and William G. Bowen, *The Shape of the River: Long-Term Consequences of Considering Race in College and University Admissions* (Princeton NJ: Princeton University Press, 1998).

16. Leonard Cassuto, "RIP William G. Bowen—and the Bowen Report, Too," *Chronicle of Higher Education*, November 22, 2016, https://www.chronicle.com /article/RIP-William-G-Bowen-and/238470.

17. See "Doctorate Recipients in the Humanities, 1970–2007," in *Humanities Indicators, 2008* (Cambridge, MA: American Academy of Arts and Sciences), http://www.humanitiesindicators.org.

18. Bowen is quoted in Jacqui Shine, "Blown Backward into the Future." *Chronicle of Higher Education*, September 23, 2014, https://chroniclevitae.com/news /717-blown-backward-into-the-future. Herb Childress's recent *The Adjunct Underclass: How America's Colleges Betrayed Their Faculty, Their Students, and Their Mission* (Chicago: University of Chicago Press, 2019) indicts these gradual changes in the workplace in scathing terms. Childress's book comes at what may be the tail end of an extended debate about the causes of adjunctification. One argument for intentionality holds that those at the top of the higher education pyramid engineered the situation by promoting the shift to a part-time labor force. An opposing argument holds that adjunctification occurred in part because the faculty wanted to teach less, especially at lower levels, with those same top administrators granting them lower teaching loads but without knowing where the money would come from to make up for lost courses. In this scenario, it's the tenure-track faculty who brought the problem on. There is much more to say on this subject, but it's ultimately tangential to the purpose of this book.

19. Chris M. Golde and Timothy M. Dore, *At Cross Purposes: What the Experiences of Today's Doctoral Students Reveal about Doctoral Education* (Pew, 2001), 5.

20. George E. Walker, Chris M. Golde, Laura Jones, Andrea Conklin Bueschel, and Pat Hutchings, *The Formation of Scholars: Rethinking Doctoral Education for the Twenty-First Century* (San Francisco: Jossey-Bass, 2008), 19.

21. We see a similar pattern in English though with a tailing-off: from 957 graduates in 1986 to 1,204 five years later to 1,493 in 1996 and the same number in 2001, still a 15-year increase of over 50 percent.

22. Marc Bousquet, "The 'Job Market' That Is Not One," *Chronicle of Higher Education*, December 15, 2014, https://www.chronicle.com/article/The-Job-Market -That-Is/150841; see also Vimal Patel, "How a Famous Academic Job-Market Study Got It All Wrong—and Why It Still Matters," *Chronicle of Higher Education*, September 9, 2018, https://www.chronicle.com/article/How-a-Famous-Academic/244458.

23. In 2003, 6 percent of PhD graduates in the arts and sciences were African American, rising to just 6.4 percent 10 years later. In 2003, 4.5 percent of PhD graduates in A&S were Hispanic Americans compared to 6.3 percent in 2013, but that trails the overall population increase of Hispanic Americans during that 10 years; See the NSF's *Survey of Earned Doctorates*.

24. Tony Chan, "A Time for Change? The Mathematics Doctorate," in Golde and Walker, *Envisioning*, 121.

25. Laurence Veysey brilliantly traces the usefulness idea in conjunction with research and "liberal culture" in the still-essential *The Emergence of the American University* (Chicago: University of Chicago Press, 1965).

26. John Dewey, *The Political Writings*, Debra Morris and Ian Shapiro, eds. (Indianapolis, IN: Hackett, 1993), 8. Dewey was speaking of philosophy, but his ideas apply generally.

27. David F. Labaree discusses the influence of the Morrill Act on institutions other than land-grant universities in *A Perfect Mess: The Unlikely Ascendancy of American Higher Education* (Chicago: University of Chicago Press, 2017), 38–42. The unity of the intellectual and the practical was also in evidence at sectarian private colleges, whose missions arose from the belief that higher education encourages an active life of moral generosity.

28. Douglas C. Bennett, "Innovation in the Liberal Arts and Sciences," in *Education and Democracy: Re-imaging Liberal Learning in America*, ed. Robert Orrill (New York: College Entrance Examination Board, 1997), 141–42; Andrew Delbanco, *College: What It Was, Is, and Should Be* (Princeton, NJ: Princeton University Press, 2012), 175–76.

29. Jacques Berlinerblau, "Survival Strategy for Humanists: Engage, Engage," *Chronicle of Higher Education*, August 2, 2012, https://www.chronicle.com/article /Survival-Strategy-for/133309.

30. Erin Bartram, "The Sublimated Grief of the Left Behind," February 11, 2018, http://erinbartram.com/uncategorized/the-sublimated-grief-of-the-left-behind/; Rebecca Schuman, "Thesis Hatement," *Slate*, April 5, 2013, http://www.slate.com /articles/life/culturebox/2013/04/there_are_no_academic_jobs_and_getting_a_ph_d _will_make_you_into_a_horrible.html.

31. Bartram's first follow-up essay in the *Chronicle*, "What It's Like to Search for Jobs Outside of Academe," *Chronicle of Higher Education*, August 24, 2018,

https://www.chronicle.com/article/What-It-s-Like-to-Search-for/243869, is written in a more even tone and offers practical advice. But when she says, "Academia didn't prepare me well for the nonacademic job market, but I can't blame it for that," she's being rather too generous to her former workplace.

32. John Paul Christy, who administers the valuable ACLS Public Fellows program (which facilitates government and other nonprofit opportunities for PhD graduates), says of graduate students in the humanities, "We keep learning, and our intellectual humility is highly valuable. A heuristic attitude makes for a good citizen and valued employee." Christy's point holds as true for the social and physical sciences as for the humanities. David Porter, chair of English at the University of Michigan, similarly urges teaching students to see that their own abilities have broad utility: "What does their experience of having commented upon and graded papers and exams given them? Their experience of leading a discussion? Their ability to bring a major research project to term?" All of these skills, argues Porter, are transferable. Christy and Porter, interviews with Weisbuch, 2019.

33. Joseph Cerny and Merisi Nerad's was one of the first of a now-growing number of such studies. Their "Ten Years After" survey documented the career paths of 6,000 doctoral graduates in six selected disciplines, and it showed that job satisfaction was actually slightly higher among those who left academia, compared to those who stayed in it. And those who left academia by choice or necessity remained glad that they earned the degree. Nerad notes that "another common assumption—that academic faculty enjoy the highest job satisfaction—also proved to be false . . . managers and executives in the BGN [i.e., business, government, and nonprofit] sectors" proved "most satisfied with their employment"—and not because of salary but "the intellectual challenges of work and autonomy at the workplace." See "Confronting Common Assumptions: Designing Future Oriented Doctoral Educa-tion," in *Doctoral Education and the Faculty of the Future*, ed. Ronald G. Ehrenberg and Charlotte V. Kuh (Ithaca, NY: Cornell University Press, 2009), 87. See also Merisi Nerad, Rebecca Aanerud, and Joseph Cerny, "So You Want to Become a Professor: Lessons from the PhDs—Ten Years Later Study," in *Paths to the Professoriate*, ed. Donald H. Wulff and Ann E. Austin (San Francisco: Jossey-Bass, 2004), 137–58.

34. Brian Croxall, "Graduate Humanities Education: What Should Be Done?," *Chronicle of Higher Education*, April 4, 2010, https://www.chronicle.com/article /Forum-The-Need-for-Reform-in/64887. Croxall recommends that graduate students not only teach but also seek an internship with a "business, nonprofit organization, government, or cultural-heritage organization."

When graduates of the six disciplines included in Nerad and Cerny's *Ten Years After* study were asked how their graduate programs could have been improved, they pointed to "the need for greater educational relevance to the changing world inside and outside academia and better labor market preparation." That report included science disciplines as well, and year after year, the National Science Foundation's survey of earned doctorates shows that just a bit less than half of all newly minted PhD graduates throughout the arts and sciences take their first jobs in academia. The six disciplines Nerad and Cerny surveyed were biochemistry (repre-senting the life sciences), computer science and chemical engineering (to represent engineering), English for the humanities, mathematics for the physical sciences, and political science for the social sciences. Sixty-one doctoral institutions were represented. For the rationale behind their selections, see Nerad, Aanerud, and Cerny, "So You Want to Become a Professor," esp. 158–59.

35. Sidonie Smith, *Manifesto for the Humanities: Transforming Doctoral Education in Good Enough Times* (Ann Arbor: University of Michigan Press, 2015), 139.

36. Julia Kent and Maureen Terese McCarthy, telephone interview with Weisbuch, summer 2018.

37. Cited by Marc Bousquet in "'Scientific American': Academic Labor Market 'Gone Seriously Awry,'" *Brainstorm* (blog), *Chronicle of Higher Education*, February 23, 2010, https://www.chronicle.com/blogs/brainstorm/scientific-american-academic-labor-market-gone-seriously-awry/21425. See also Alan Leshner and Layne Scherer, eds., *Graduate STEM Education for the 21st Century* (Washington, DC: National Academies Press, 2018).

38. Leshner and Scherer, *Graduate STEM Education for the 21st Century*, 113.

39. Six recent reports from the 2010s on graduate science education deserve special consideration. These begin with *The Path Forward* from the Council of Graduate Schools (2010; www.fgereport.org); and two from specific disciplines, the American Chemical Association's *Advancing Graduate Education in Chemical Science* (2012, https://www.acs.org/content/dam/acsorg/about/governance/acs-commission-on-graduate-education-summary-report.pdf); and NIH's *The Biomedical Research Working Group Report* (2012, https://acd.od.nih.gov/documents/reports/Biomedical_research_wgreport.pdf); a consideration of data on graduate science education from the National Science Board titled *Revisiting the STEM Workforce* (2014, https://www.nsf.gov/news/news_summ.jsp?cntn_id=134866); and a later Council of Graduate Schools report on Professional Development, *Shaping Effective Practices for STEM Graduate Education* (2017; https://cgsnet.org/professional-development-shaping-effective-programs-stem-graduate-students-0); concluding with a landmark 2018 study from the National Academies of Science and Engineering, *Graduate STEM Education for the 21st Century*.

40. Jacques Berlinerblau, "This Guy Got Tenure. You Probably Won't," *Chronicle of Higher Education*, June 29, 2016, https://www.chronicle.com/article/You-Probably-Wont-Get-Tenure/236957.

41. Michael Bérubé, "The Humanities, Unraveled," *Chronicle of Higher Education*, February 18, 2013, https://www.chronicle.com/article/Humanities-Unraveled/137291.

42. Julie R. Posselt, *Inside Graduate Admissions: Merit, Diversity, and Faculty Gatekeeping* (Cambridge, MA: Harvard University Press, 2016).

43. Derek Bok, *Higher Education in America* (Princeton, NJ: Princeton University Press, 2013), 232, 240.

44. Maria LaMonaca Wisdom, "Holding Open a Space for the Millennial Humanities Doctoral Student," *MLA Profession*, November 2019, https://profession.mla.org/holding-open-a-space-for-the-millennial-humanities-doctoral-student/.

1. National Institutes of Health, *Biomedical Research Workforce Working Group Report*, 2012, https://acd.od.nih.gov/documents/reports/Biomedical_research _wgreport.pdf.

2. Fellowships and teaching assistantships primarily accounted for the other forms of support in 2009. Fellowships increased moderately to 10,000 while support through teaching rose only slightly. See National Institutes of Health, *Biomedical Research Workforce Group: A Working Group of the Advisory Committee to the Director* (Bethesda, MD: NIH, 2012), http://acd.od.nih.gov/biomedical_research _wgreport.pdf, 7, 36. Angelica Stacy, "Training Future Leaders: Doctoral Education in Neuroscience," in *Envisioning the Future of Doctoral Education: Preparing Stewards of the Disciplines*, ed. Chris M. Golde and George E. Walker (San Francisco: Jossey-Bass, 2006), 201.

3. Harriet Zuckerman, Ronald Ehrenberg, Jeffrey Groen, and Sharon Brucker, *Educating Scholars: Doctoral Education in the Humanities* (Princeton, NJ: Princeton University Press, 2010), 248.

4. Kenneth Prewitt, "Who Should Do What? Implications for Institutional and National Leaders," in Golde and Walker, *Envisioning*, 23.

5. Zuckerman et al., *Educating Scholars*, 3.

6. See William G. Bowen and Neil L. Rudenstine, *In Pursuit of the Ph.D.* (Princeton, NJ: Princeton University Press, 1992).

7. Zuckerman et al., *Educating Scholars*, 5–7.

8. Zuckerman et al., *Educating Scholars*, 9.

9. Zuckerman et al., *Educating Scholars*, 258.

10. Zuckerman et al., *Educating Scholars*, 308, 101.

11. The median age of PhD recipients in the study was 31, and the mean 32.5. For those who attained tenure-track employment, the figures were 34 and 35.2. Those who graduated in five years or less, or in six years, got the highest percentage of tenure-track jobs, with the seven-year PhDs next, and the eight-year graduates after that. Publications helped these students secure such positions but so did finishing with alacrity. In all, "Having published increases a PhD's chance of getting a tenure-track position within three years of a degree. But taking as long as eight years to get the degree (or longer) has the opposite effect" (Zuckerman et al., *Educating Scholars*, 21). Here we must also consider that the programs in the study were among the best funded in the country, meaning that students who wanted to finish more quickly were often not required to teach to support themselves.

12. Zuckerman et al., *Educating Scholars*, 86.

13. "Of those employed after three years in a tenure-track position," write the authors, "50 to 60 percent of them are at doctoral institutions, about 15–25 percent at Masters-level institutions and another 15–22 percent at liberal arts colleges" (Zuckerman et al., *Educating Scholars*, 199). Here we note that this finding elides attrition, which was 43 percent of the sample surveyed—so the percentage of students placed at doctoral institutions by the 10 high-ranked universities in the study is really more like 12–15 percent of the entering class.

The success rate of graduates in attaining tenure-track positions at four-year institutions immediately upon graduation, and after up to three years, actually declined from the 1990–92 cohort (35 and 57 percent, respectively) to the 1998–2000 cohort (30 and 52). Those who left programs without graduating also had jobs, "a large majority of which are professional ones," which made clear "that the vast majority of them are not trapped in menial, low-level jobs and that they in fact received a payoff from their investment in doctoral education" (Zuckerman et al., *Educating Scholars*, 185).

14. Zuckerman et al. *Educating Scholars*, 86.

15. Zuckerman et al., *Educating Scholars*, 224.

16. Zuckerman et al., *Educating Scholars*, 248.

17. Jerry G. Gaff, Anne S. Pruitt-Logan, Leslie B. Sims, and Daniel D. Denecke, *Preparing Future Faculty in the Humanities and Social Sciences: A Guide for Change* (Washington, DC: Council of Graduate Schools, Association of American Colleges and Universities, 2003), 179.

18. Gaff et al., *Preparing*, 181.

19. Gaff et al., *Preparing*, 183.

20. Zuckerman et al., *Educating Scholars*, 154.

21. Gaff et al., *Preparing*, 189.

22. Jody D. Nyquist, Bettina J. Woodford, and Diane L. Rogers, "Re-envisioning the Ph.D: A Challenge for the Twenty-First Century," in *Paths to the Professoriate: Strategies for Enriching the Preparation of Future Faculty*, ed. Donald H. Wulff and Ann E. Austin (San Francisco: Jossey-Bass, 2004), 194.

23. Nyquist, Woodford, and Rogers, "Re-envisioning," 194.

24. Nyquist, Woodford, and Rogers, "Re-envisioning," 197.

25. Nyquist, Woodford, and Rogers, "Re-envisioning," 199–210.

26. Bob, who headed Woodrow Wilson at the time, confesses that he was at first skeptical of such a broad range of participants, with graduate deans and faculty much in the minority. Later, he would describe the Re-envisioning conference as the most dynamic and helpful meeting he ever experienced before or after, for precisely the varied extra-academic representation that had worried him at first.

27. Nyquist, Woodford, and Rogers, "Re-envisioning," 13.

28. Beverly Sanford and Hadass Sheffer, "Careers for Humanities Ph.D.'s in Museums," *Chronicle of Higher Education*, March 11, 2002, https://www.chronicle .com/article/Careers-for-Humanities-PhDs/45975.

29. The program attracted strong applicants, but Woodrow Wilson did not have a significant endowment, and no national funder was located. A few institutions continued the program on their own for another two years, but it gradually petered out.

30. Richard A. Cherwitz and Charlotte A. Sullivan, "Intellectual Entrepreneurship: A Vision for Graduate Education," *Change* 34, no. 6 (2002): 24.

31. Cherwitz and Sullivan, "Intellectual Entrepreneurship," 25–27.

32. In the original group, Yale, Howard, Penn, and Princeton represented the East; Indiana, Michigan, Wisconsin, and Washington University the Midwest; Duke, Texas, and Arizona State the South and Southwest; and Irvine, Colorado, and Washington the Far West. Later, both the University of Illinois at Urbana-Champaign and at Chicago joined, as did UCLA, Kentucky, Louisville, and Vanderbilt.

33. Robert Weisbuch, "Toward a Responsive Ph.D," in Austin and Wulff, *Paths to the Professoriate*, 217–35, 217–20.

34. Woodrow Wilson National Fellowship Foundation, *The Responsive Ph.D.: Innovations in U.S. Doctoral Education*, 2005, https://woodrow.org/news /publications/responsive-phd/, 3.

35. Woodrow Wilson National Fellowship Foundation, *Responsive*, 3.

36. Brown University Graduate School, "Graduate School to launch 'Open Graduate Programs' with $2M Mellon grant," press release, October 5, 2011, https://news.brown.edu/articles/2011/10/mellon just worked for me. See also Vimal Patel, "Brown U. Tests Approach to Interdisciplinary Graduate Work," *Chronicle of Higher Education*, March 24, 2014, https://www.chronicle.com/article/Brown-U -Tests-Approach-to/145487.

37. Woodrow Wilson National Fellowship Foundation, *Responsive*, 3.

38. George E. Walker, Chris M. Golde, Laura Jones, Andrea Conklin Bueschel, and Pat Hutchings, *The Formation of Scholars: Rethinking Doctoral Education for the Twenty-First Century* (San Francisco: Jossey-Bass, 2008), 32–33.

39. Prewitt, "Who Should Do What?," *Envisioning*, 23.

40. Pat Hutchings and Susan Clarke, "The Scholarship of Teaching and Learning: Contributing to Reform in Graduate Education," in Austin and Wulff, *Paths to the Professoriate*, 161.

41. Austin and Wulff, *Paths to the Professoriate*, 240.

42. Walker et al., *The Formation of Scholars*, 12.

43. Walker et al., *The Formation of Scholars*, 45.

44. David Damrosch, "Vectors of Change," in Golde and Walker, *Envisioning*, 41.

45. Walker et al., *The Formation of Scholars*, 46–47.

46. George E. Walker, "The Questions in the Back of the Book," Golde and Walker, *Envisioning*, 426–27 (emphasis in the original).

47. NSF Graduate Teaching Fellows in K–12 Education (GK–12) program solicitation online (2007).

48. Cited by J. A. Ufnar, Susan Kuner, and V. L. Shepherd in "Moving beyond GK–12," *CBE—Life Sciences Education* 11, no. 3 (October 13, 2017), https://www .lifescied.org/doi/full/10.1187/cbe.11-12-0119.

49. See Ufnar, Kuner, and Shepherd, "Moving Beyond."

50. For more information on the Ford awards, see http://sites.nationalacademies .org/pga/fordfellowships/.

51. For more information on the Gates Millennium Scholars Program, see https://gmsp.org/a-gates-millennium-scholars-program/.

52. For more on the Southern Education Regional Education Board Doctoral Scholars Program, see https://www.sreb.org/doctoral-scholars-program.

53. For more information on the Alfred P. Sloan Foundation Minority Ph.D. Program, see http://sloanphds.org/.

54. For more information on the Mellon Mays Undergraduate Fellows (MMUF) program, see https://www.mmuf.org. For the graduate initiatives program, see https://www.ssrc.org/programs/view/mellon-mays-graduate-initiatives -program/.

55. For more on the Ronald E. McNair Post-Baccalaureate Achievement Program, see https://www2.ed.gov/programs/triomcnair/index.html.

56. For more information on the National Science Foundation (NSF) ADVANCE Program, see https://www.nsf.gov/funding/aboutfunding.jsp.

57. For more information on the NSF Alliance, see https://www.nsf.gov/funding/pgm_summ.jsp?pims_id=5474.

58. For more information on the CGS Award for Innovation, see https://cgsnet.org/etscgs-award.

59. For more information on MOST, see https://www.asanet.org/sites/default/files/savvy/footnotes/julyaugust02/indexone.html.

60. For more information on IGERT, see http://www.igert.org/.

61. We should note that two totally distinct entities bear the Carnegie name. The Carnegie Foundation for the Advancement of Teaching, then led by Lee Shulman, organized the initiative we have described elsewhere in the book. The Carnegie Corporation of New York did not engage with doctoral education reform.

62. Steven C. Wheatley of ACLS, quoted in Leonard Cassuto, "Teaching in the Postdoc Space," *Chronicle of Higher Education*, April 17, 2011, http://chronicle.com/article/Teaching-in-the-Postdoc-Space/127150/.

63. For more information on the Public Fellows Program, see https://www.acls.org/programs/publicfellows/.

64. See https://www.acls.org/research/publicfellows/.

65. Weisbuch, interview with John Paul Christy, October 2015.

66. L. Maren Wood and Robert B. Townsend, *The Many Careers of History PhDs: A Study of Job Outcomes, Spring 2013*, a report to the American Historical Association, 2013, https://www.historians.org/Documents/Many_Careers_of_History_PhDs_Final.pdf.

67. See https://www.historians.org/jobs-and-professional-development/career-resources/five-skills.

68. Weisbuch, interview with James Grossman, executive director, American Historical Association, November 2015.

69. See "Mellon Foundation Grant Expands Impact and Scope of Career Diversity for Historians," *Perspectives on History*, December 19, 2016, https://www.historians.org/publications-and-directories/perspectives-on-history/december-2016/mellon-foundation-grant-expands-impact-and-scope-of-career-diversity-for-historians.

70. The AHA describes the responsibilities of fellows thus:

> The Fellow will work closely with a faculty team to coordinate programming and events with the department and to assist the faculty in the following activities:
>
> - Create links to career and alumni offices, centers for teaching and learning, and other appropriate units such as humanities centers
> - Create on-campus internships, following an assistantship model
> - Develop programming to expose students to different teaching environments

- Assist faculty in organizing/redesigning a departmental pedagogy course
- Assist faculty in organizing/redesigning a departmental professionalization course that shifts from the current emphasis on the transition from graduate student to "academic professional" (in the mode of research scholar) to the kinds of values and skills outlined in this proposal
- Administer AHA survey on graduate career aspirations, in collaboration with AHA staff

"About Career Diversity," American Historical Association, https://www.historians .org/jobs-and-professional-development/career-diversity-for-historians/about-career -diversity.

71. https://connect.mla.hcommons.org/.

72. Colleen Flaherty, "5-Year Plan," *Inside Higher Ed*, May 28, 2014, https:// www.insidehighered.com/news/2014/05/28/mla-report-calls-phd-program-reform -including-cutting-time-degree.

73. For a detailed discussion of the Porter-Hartman course, see Leonard Cassuto, "Can You Train Your Students for Diverse Careers When You Don't Have One?," *Chronicle of Higher Education*, August 22, 2018, https://www.chronicle.com/article /Can-You-Train-Your-PhDs-for/244323.

74. The CGS discussion of this ongoing project may be found here: https://cgsnet .org/ckfinder/userfiles/files/CGS_PhDCareerPath_report_finalHires.pdf. See also Leonard Cassuto, "Documenting What Ph.D.s Do for a Living," *Chronicle of Higher Education*, October 15, 2017, https://www.chronicle.com/article/Documenting-What -PhDs-Do-for/241449.

75. The website for myIDP is https://myidp.sciencecareers.org/.

76. National Science Foundation, *Science and Engineering Indicators*, 2012 and 2018. The 2018 report reads, "In recent decades, growth in the number of U.S.-trained doctoral scientists and engineers in the academic sector has been slower than the rate of growth in the business and government sectors, resulting in a decline in the academic sector's share of all U.S.-trained S&E doctorates, from 55% in the early 1970s to just under 50% in the mid-1990s to about 45% in 2015." https:// www.nsf.gov/statistics/2018/nsb20181/report/sections/academic-research-and -development/doctoral-scientists-and-engineers-in-academia#trends-in-academic -employment-of-s-e-doctorate-holders.

77. ImaginePhD is located at https://www.imaginephd.com/about.

78. https://www.nsf.gov/pubs/2018/nsf18507/nsf18507.pdf.

79. https://www.nsf.gov/funding/pgm_summ.jsp?pims_id=505015.

Chapter 2: Purpose, Then Path

1. Michael Fullan, *Change Leader: Learning to Do What Matters Most* (San Francisco: Jossey-Bass, 2013), 127.

2. Damrosch, "Vectors of Change," in *Envisioning the Future of Doctoral Education: Preparing Stewards of the Disciplines*, ed. Chris M. Golde and George E. Walker (San Francisco: Jossey-Bass, 2006), 35.

3. David Grant, *The Social Profit Handbook: The Essential Guide to Setting Goals, Assessing Outcomes, and Achieving Success for Mission-Driven Organizations* (White River Junction, VT: Chelsea Green, 2015).

4. Grant, *Social Profit Handbook*, 41.

5. A recent well-publicized example is the 2019 protest by graduate students in the Department of English and Comparative Literature at Columbia University. See Emma Pettit, "Columbia Had Little Success Placing English Ph.D.s on the Tenure Track: 'Alarm' Followed, and the University Responded," *Chronicle of Higher Education*, August 21, 2019, https://www.chronicle.com/article/Columbia-Had-Little-Success/246989.

6. Damrosch, "Vectors of Change," 41.

7. Damrosch, "Vectors of Change," 42–43.

8. Damrosch, "Vectors of Change," 43–44.

9. Steven Johnson, "How to Make a Big Decision," *New York Times*, September 1, 2018, https://www.nytimes.com/2018/09/01/opinion/sunday/how-make-big-decision.html.

10. Ronald S. Burt, *Neighbor Networks: Competitive Advantage Local and Personal* (Oxford: Oxford University Press, 2010), 257.

11. Damrosch, "Vectors of Change," 36.

12. Ronald S. Burt, "Structural Holes and Good Ideas," *American Journal of Sociology* 10 (2004): 355.

13. Leo Tolstoy, *The Kingdom of God Is within You*, trans. Constance Garnett (New York: Cassell, 1894), 46. The fake Twain quotation has an uncertain provenance. Both quotations—the misattributed Twain saying and the actual one from Tolstoy—relate to *The Big Short*: the Tolstoy quotation appears in Michael Lewis's 2010 book, while the quotation misattributed to Twain appears in the 2015 film adaptation. See Alex Shephard's explanation in the *New Republic*: https://newrepublic.com/minutes/126677/it-aint-dont-know-gets-trouble-must-big-short-opens-fake-mark-twain-quote.

14. Clark Kerr, *The Uses of the University*, 5th ed. (Cambridge, MA: Harvard University Press, 2001), 99. Kerr amended his great book several times on a decade-by-decade basis until his death.

15. Damrosch, "Vectors of Change," in Golde and Walker, *Envisioning*, 35–36.

16. Hence the nasty old joke told by frustrated university administrators: "How many faculty members does it take to change that light bulb?" Answer (grumpily): "That light bulb doesn't need changing."

17. David F. Labaree, *A Perfect Mess: The Unlikely Ascendency of American Education* (Chicago: University of Chicago Press, 2019).

18. Gary Klein, "Performing a Project Premortem," *Harvard Business Review*, September 2007, https://hbr.org/2007/09/performing-a-project-premortem. Johnson cites earlier psychologists on the importance of generating alternatives. In 1984, he reports, Paul Nutt studied 78 decisions made by high-level planners in corporations and nonprofits. Only 15 percent allowed for a stage for generating alternatives to a basic yes/no choice, and fewer than one in three contemplated more than one alternative—yet the rate of success in contemplating at least two alternatives was two-thirds while the yes/no had a success rate of less than half.

19. Grant's own formula for overcoming a resistance to sensible change is a modification of a formula known as the Beckhead model, after Richard Beckhead, a leading practitioner. It goes like this: Dissatisfaction times Vision times First steps overcomes Resistance to change. $D \times V \times F > R$.

In the case of the doctorate, an agreed-upon dissatisfaction results from our gaining a better sense of the actual experiences of our students in doctoral programs. V: The vision is our goal setting from which we plan backward to F: the first steps, which Grant defines as "concrete, manageable actions . . . knowing how to begin, and what to do next." Grant, *Social Profit Handbook*, 128–29.

20. Grant, *Social Profit Handbook*, 58.

21. Grant, *Social Profit Handbook*, 29–30.

22. Grant, *Social Profit Handbook*, 31.

23. To this model, Grant adds responsible leadership: "Only leadership can create and sanction mission time. It is up to leaders to create the spirit of ongoing learning that characterizes an assessment culture." And he cites the notion that dissatisfaction with the status quo coupled with a consensual vision and some successful first moves will overcome the fear of change (128–29). When that active leadership includes administrators (a university president, provost, and graduate dean, together with a department chair and director of graduate studies), we have an ideal situation. But even without the top administrative rungs, an energetic chair and the DGS will be sufficient—if the higher levels are at the least authentically interested and supportive.

24. No hyperbole here. That's the national average attrition rate for doctoral students in the arts and sciences.

25. A variation on Grant's process—or an addition to it—is suggested by Johnson. He urges all participants to write down the values most important to them—in our case, perhaps the list of PhD challenges—assigning to each a value from 0 to 1. (If you find, say, encouraging public scholarship a good idea but not a seminal one, you might give it a 0.4, while you view recruiting a more diverse student cohort more important and assign it a 0.8.) Then each participant considers how well each of the three or more alternative plans tackles each value on a scale of 1 to 100. Then you multiply the two figures (that is, goal priority and value of plan to meet each goal), add everyone's scores together for each item, and discover your best plan. We would use this math not to be definitive but to serve the conversation. In disciplines whose members distrust quantification, use it only in the case of a stalemate.

26. George E. Walker, Chris M. Golde, Laura Jones, Andrea Conklin Bueschel, and Pat Hutchings, *The Formation of Scholars: Rethinking Doctoral Education for the Twenty-First Century* (San Francisco: Jossey-Bass, 2008), 45.

Chapter 3: Career Diversity

1. Suzanne Ortega, remarks at the 2016 annual meeting of the Conference of Southern Graduate Schools, Charlotte, NC, February 2016.

2. Bob remembers using the "beyond academia" phrase in the 1990s in reaction against phrases like "alternative careers" that subtly denigrate PhD graduates who

don't become professors. The proliferation of listings under that heading, compared even to just five years ago, suggest it's an idea whose time has arrived.

3. Anthony T. Grafton and Jim Grossman, "'No More Plan B': A Very Modest Proposal for Graduate Programs in History," *Perspectives on History*, October 1, 2011. https://www.historians.org/publications-and-directories/perspectives-on -history/october-2011/no-more-plan-b.

4. Cathy Wendler, Brent Bridgeman, Fred Cline, Catherine Millett, JoAnn Rock, Nathan Bell, and Patricia McAllister, *The Path Forward: The Future of Graduate Education in the United States* (Princeton NJ: Council of Graduate Schools and ETS, 2010), http://fgereport.org/rsc/pdf/CFGE_report.pdf.

5. "Graduate Humanities Education: What Should Be Done?," *Chronicle of Higher Education*, April 4, 2010. https://www.chronicle.com/article/Forum-The -Need-for-Reform-in/64887.

6. Crispin Taylor, "Heeding the Voices of Graduate Students and Postdocs," in Golde and Walker, *Envisioning*, 48.

7. Homer L. Aanerud, Merisi Nerad, and C. Cerny, "Paths and Perceptions: Assessing Doctoral Education Using Career Path Analysis," in *The Assessment of Doctoral Education: Emerging Criteria and New Models for Improving Outcomes*, ed. P. L. Maki and N. Borowski (Sterling, VA: Stylus, 2006), 134.

8. C. M. Golde and T. M. Dore, *At Cross Purposes: What the Experiences of Doctoral Students Reveal about Doctoral Education (www.phd-survey.org)* (Philadelphia, PA: Pew Charitable Trusts, 2001).

9. Merisi Nerad, Rebecca Aanerud, and Joseph Cerny, "So You Want to Become a Professor: Lessons from the PhDs—Ten Years Later Study," in *Paths to the Professoriate*, ed. Donald H. Wulff and Ann E. Austin (San Francisco: Jossey-Bass, 2004), 146.

10. Maresi Nerad and Joseph Cerni, "From Rumors to Facts: Career Outcomes of English Ph.D.s—Results from the Ph.D.'s Ten Years Later Study," *CGS Communicator* 32, no. 7 (Fall 1999): 4, 2, 8, https://depts.washington.edu/envision/resources /TenYearsLater.pdf.

11. Katina L. Rogers, *Humanities Unbound: Supporting Careers and Scholarship Beyond the Tenure Track*, Scholarly Communication Institute, 2013, http:// katinarogers.com/wp-content/uploads/2013/08/Rogers_SCI_Survey_Report _09AUG13.pdf.

12. Barbara E. Lovitts, "Research on the Structure and Process of Graduate Education: Retaining Students," in Austin and Wulff, *Paths to the Professoriate*, 133.

13. Ehm is quoted in Leonard Cassuto, "What Do You Mean, 'Job'?," *Chronicle of Higher Education*, August 21, 2017, https://www.chronicle.com/article/What-Do -You-Mean-Job-/240951.

14. Interview with Weisbuch, summer 2018.

15. Susan Basalla and Maggie Debelius, *"So What Are You Going to Do with That?": Finding Careers Outside Academia*, 3rd ed. (Chicago: University of Chicago Press, 2015). Another promising new resource is Ashleigh H. Gallagher and M. Patrick Gallagher's *The Portable PhD: Taking Your Psychology Career Beyond*

Academia (New York: American Psychological Association, 2020). This book is less discipline specific than it appears. We also recommend Christopher L. Caterine's *Leaving Academia: A Practical Guide* (Princeton, NJ: Princeton University Press, 2020).

16. Michael Bérubé, "The Humanities, Unraveled," *Chronicle of Higher Education*, February 18, 2013, https://www.chronicle.com/article/Humanities -Unraveled/137291.

17. Though they are discipline specific, two guides may prove helpful as models for most other disciplines as well: "Career Diversity Faculty Resources from the American Historical Association (historians.org/jobs-and-professional-development /career-diversity-for-historians/career-diversity-faculty-resources) and "Doctoral Student Career Planning: A Guide for PhD Programs and Faculty Members in English and Other Modern Languages" (https://connect.mla.hcommons.org/doctoral -student-career-planning-faculty-toolkit/), published by the Modern Language Association.

Other examples in the humanities include the American Academy of Religion, Career Alternatives for Religion Scholars (https://www.aarweb.org/sites/default/files /pdfs/Career_Services/Articles/CareerAlternatives.pdf); "Beyond Academia: Profes-sional Opportunities for Philosophers," from the American Philosophical Association (https://cdn.ymaws.com/www.apaonline.org/resource/resmgr/docs/Beyond_Academia _2016.pdf); and "Careers for Classicists," from the Society for Classical Studies (https://classicalstudies.org/education/careers-for-classicists); along with "Careers for Classicists," from the Paideia Institute (https://www.paideiainstitute.org/careers_for _classicists).

18. Quoted in Leonard Cassuto, "Walking the Career Diversity Walk," *Chronicle of Higher Education*, July 23, 2017, https://www.chronicle.com/article/Walking-the -Career-Diversity/240693.

19. Kristina Markman, "Preparing Students for Career Diversity: What Role Can Departments Play?," *Perspectives*, June 26, 2017, https://www.historians.org /publications-and-directories/perspectives-on-history/summer-2017/preparing -students-for-career-diversity-what-role-should-history-departments-play.

20. Cassuto, "Walking the Career Diversity Walk."

21. Cassuto, "Walking the Career Diversity Walk."

22. Taylor, "Heeding the Voices," 49–50.

23. Taylor, Heeding the Voices," 49.

24. This argument is difficult but not impossible to make. During the Woodrow Wilson Humanities at Work effort, Elizabeth Duffy, then the vice president at Woodrow Wilson, succeeded in doing just that with 30 different corporations—and she did not have the advantage of appealing to alumni. This is where the attitudinal challenge links to the institutional one, for faculty cannot take the primary responsi-bility for educating employers.

25. Edward Balleisen and Maria LaMonaca Wisdom, the two main architects of Duke's Versatile Humanists program, have coauthored an exceptionally useful 2019 pamphlet, *Reimagining the Humanities PhD: A Guide for PhD Programs and Faculty*. Their work has benefited our own, and we're grateful.

26. Bérubé, "The Humanities, Unraveled."

27. The two-track model is actually a very old notion that goes back to the early days of research universities, especially public ones, in the United States, with different manifestations during the generation of postwar plenty (which featured the founding of a less onerous doctor of arts degree for those who would teach rather than research), and into the present day. See Leonard Cassuto, *The Graduate School Mess: What Caused It and How We Can Fix It* (Cambridge, MA: Harvard University Press, 2015), 142–50. The two-track idea also provides one of the rationales for the master's degree. We will consider the history and prospects of master's degrees in chapter 9.

28. "The Career Diversity Five Skills," https://www.historians.org/jobs-and -professional-development/career-resources/five-skills. We also discuss these in chapter 1.

29. For more on Arizona State's Preparing Future Faculty and Scholars Program, see https://graduate.asu.edu/current-students/enrich-your-experience/professional -development/preparing-future-faculty-and. For more on the UCLA "Many Professions of History" course, see https://www.historians.org/jobs-and-professional -development/career-diversity-for-historians/career-diversity-faculty-resources/the -many-professions-of-history-(ucla).

30. The syllabus for Professional Humanities Careers may be found at https:// sites.lsa.umich.edu/humanities-phd-proj/wp-content/uploads/sites/535/2018/02 /Professional-Humanities-Careers-Syllabus.pdf.

31. For more information on Indiana University–Purdue University Indianapolis's American Studies PhD program, see https://americanstudies.iupui.edu/new/ph-d -program/.

32. Katina L. Rogers, *Putting the Humanities PhD to Work: Thriving in and beyond the Classroom* (Durham, NC: Duke University Press, 2020).

33. For more on the Louisville PLAN program, see https://louisville.edu/graduate /plan. See also Leonard Cassuto, "The Problem of Professionalization," *Chronicle of Higher Education*, March 23, 2015, https://www.chronicle.com/article/The-Problem -of/228633.

34. Robin Wagner, "How a Career Fair Can Help You, and How It Can't," *Chronicle of Higher Education*, March 16, 2001, https://www.chronicle.com/article /How-a-Career-Fair-Can-Help/45369.

35. The Paideia Institute's Legion Project is located at https://www .paideiainstitute.org/legion.

Chapter 4: Admissions and Attrition

1. Leonard Cassuto, *The Graduate School Mess: What Caused It and How We Can Fix It* (Cambridge, MA: Harvard University Press, 2015), which came out the same year as Posselt's book, has an extensive historical discussion of graduate admissions. The MLA panel on graduate admissions that Len organized for the 2020 convention is possibly the first on the subject in the history of the convention.

2. Julie R. Posselt, *Inside Graduate Admissions: Merit, Diversity, and Faculty Gatekeeping* (Cambridge, MA: Harvard University Press, 2016).

3. Louis Menand, *The Marketplace of Ideas: Reform and Resistance in the American University* (New York: W. W. Norton, 2010), 105.

4. At wealthier universities, it *is* someone else's job. For example, Princeton has a separate office devoted to it: https://gradschool.princeton.edu/diversity.

5. Katina L. Rogers, *Putting the Humanities PhD to Work: Thriving in and beyond the Classroom* (Durham, NC: Duke University Press, 2020).

6. James Soto Antony and Edward Taylor, "Theories and Strategies of Academic Career Socialization: Improving Paths to the Professoriate for Black Graduate Students," in *Paths to the Professoriate: Strategies for Enriching the Preparation of Future Faculty*, ed. Donald H. Wulff and Ann E. Austin (San Francisco: Jossey-Bass, 2004), 111.

7. See for example, Tony Chan, "A Time for Change? The Mathematics Doctorate," in *Envisioning the Future of Doctoral Education: Preparing Stewards of the Disciplines*, ed. Chris M. Golde and George E. Walker (San Francisco: Jossey-Bass, 2006), 129; and Joyce Appleby, "Historians and the Doctorate in History," in Gold and Walker, *Envisioning*, 321. See also Robert Weisbuch, "Six Proposals to Revive the Humanities," *Chronicle of Higher Education*, March 26, 1999, https://www.chronicle.com/article/Six-Proposals-to-Revive-the/34597, in which Bob (wrongly, he now allows) argues for "doctoral birth control." He suggests that departments "should accept only 1.3 times the number of incoming students as the number of graduates in the previous year who found truly significant jobs—positions that they chose, not jobs that they accepted out of economic necessity. The extra 0.3 allows conservatively for attrition."

8. See Robin Wilson, "Cutbacks in Enrollment Redefine Graduate Education and Faculty Jobs," *Chronicle of Higher Education*, March 11, 2012, https://www.chronicle.com/article/Graduate-Programs-in/131123; and Scott Jaschik, "The Third Rail," *Inside Higher Education*, January 13, 2014, https://www.insidehighered.com/news/2014/01/13/speakers-mla-generally-are-skeptical-idea-shrinking-phd-programs.

9. Jeff Allum and Hironoa Okahana, *Graduate Enrollment and Degrees: 2004 to 2014* (Washington, DC: Council of Graduate Schools, 2015), 3.

10. The practical requirement that doctoral aspirants pursue a master's at their own considerable expense is common in the study of religion, for example.

11. Though Jon Marcus compiles compelling data from the US Department of Education.

12. See for example Mark Taylor, "Reform the PhD System or Close It Down," *Nature* 472, no. 261 (2011), doi:10.1038/472261a https://www.nature.com/articles/472261a.

13. Cassuto provides the first historical context for doctoral admissions in *The Graduate School Mess*. He notes that historically, professors have sought students who will fit the profile of the faculty, a practice Posselt calls "homophily" (17–56).

14. As a historian, Bender focused his study on history departments. Viewed across time, he says, "the range of professional careers in history has been much more various than contemporary graduate programs ordinarily recognize and grant. Let us start with demographics. Although it is often assumed that after World War II

all Ph.D.'s obtained academic jobs, the assumption holds, at best, for only one decade—1961 to 1971." Thomas Bender, "Expanding the Domain of History," in Golde and Walker. *Envisioning*, 299.

15. Posselt, *Faculty Gatekeeping*, 156.

16. Posselt, *Faculty Gatekeeping*, 36, 40.

17. Posselt, *Faculty Gatekeeping.* The Council of Graduate Schools has also promoted holistic review; see CGS, "Innovation in Graduate Admissions through Holistic Review," 2014, http://cgsnet.org/innovation-graduate-admissions-through -holistic-review. And even the Educational Testing Service (ETS), the owners of the GRE, has lately endorsed holistic admissions. See the ETS pamphlet, *Promising Practices*, https://www.holisticadmissions.org/curated-approaches/.

18. At the undergraduate level, after decades of questions about the predictive ability of the SATs and suspicions about the cultural biases of "the big test" (cf. Nicholas Lemann, *The Big Test: The Secret History of the American Meritocracy* [New York: Farrar, Straus and Giroux, 2000]), the College Board proposed an "adversity score" that purports to measure a student's overall disadvantage level. It included a neighborhood measure (including median family income, percentage of crime victims, percentage of adults with less than a high school or college diploma, vacant housing units, and so on), along with a high school measure (based on local area income, family structure, housing, and education). One need not be a political scientist to see the motivation. Anticipating possible future Supreme Court decisions against applying racial preferences in admissions, the board offered what was in effect a blind: instead of preferencing racial background, one could give extra weight to where people live. The idea is to avoid welcoming to home plate only students who start at third base. The same concerns apply to GRE scores. After a storm of criticism, the College Board withdrew the adversity score proposal in 2019.

19. *Advancing Graduate Education in the Chemical Sciences*, Presidential Commission, American Chemical Society Report, 2012.

20. In scientific fields where more students seek nonacademic careers, problems of overpopulation nonetheless have developed. Demand for PhDs is down both in academia and also in industry—yet programs lack an incentive to shrink because high numbers of students often guarantee research funding. Rightsizing as an issue, in other words, cannot be eliminated by expanding career opportunities, even if the right size may become larger.

21. Len tells a longer version of this story in *The Graduate School Mess* (50–51).

22. National Center for Science and Engineering Statistics Directorate for Social, Behavioral and Economic Sciences, *2016 Doctorate Recipients from U. S. Universities*, March 2018, https://www.nsf.gov/statistics/2018/nsf18304/static/report /nsf18304-report.pdf; also https://www.census.gov/quickfacts/fact/table/US /AGE775218.

23. We will add that graduate education underperforms in minority recruitment because structural racism, ethnocentrism, and sexism eliminate many potential candidates at every earlier degree level. You can't choose to get a PhD if you didn't graduate from college or high school.

24. For more on this initiative, see http://targethopechicago.net/college-support/.

25. Rafia Zafar, "Graduate Admissions and the other end of the diversity "pipeline," talk given at the MLA Convention, Seattle, WA, January 2020. We thank Professor Zafar for sharing her manuscript with us.

26. Though its partnership model deserves emulation, one concern is that Project Hope has been run for years by one person, Euclid Williamson, who has not identified any successor(s).

27. NBC News, "When Is Community College a Good Option for Latino Students?," June 15, 2015, https://www.nbcnews.com/news/latino/when-community -college-good-option-latino-students-n525116.

28. This kind of outreach in no way precludes the current efforts such as those associated with McNair and with National Science Foundation programs such as the Alliances for Minority Participation (AMP) and Alliances for Graduate Education and the Professoriate (AGEP). These valuable efforts help the undergraduates who have already made it to college by providing bachelor's students with early research opportunities and graduate students with the support that will encourage their success. For more on the AMP, see https://www.nsf.gov/funding/pgm_summ.jsp?pims _id=13646. For more on the AGEP, see https://www.nsf.gov/funding/pgm_summ.jsp ?pims_id=5474.

29. For this and other examples in this section, we are happy to acknowledge *The Responsive PhD*, a 2005 pamphlet published by the Woodrow Wilson National Fellowship Foundation. https://woodrow.org/news/publications/responsive-phd/.

30. See the program's website: https://www.fisk-vanderbilt-bridge.org/.

31. http://fisk-vanderbilt-bridge.org/program/description. The description in this paragraph is drawn from Vimal Patel, "Building a Better Bridge to the Ph.D.," *Chronicle of Higher Education*, May 19, 2016, https://www.chronicle.com/article /Building-a-Better-Bridge-/236529.

32. "Welcome SMART 2020," Colorado Diversity Initiative, University of Colorado, Boulder, https://www.colorado.edu/smart/undergraduates/smart-program -information/welcome-smart-2019.

33. At law schools, for example, retention rates are measured after the first year, and roughly correspond to the median LSAT score of the incoming class. The LSAT is scored on a scale between 120 and 180. At schools with the median LSAT score between 155 and 159, attrition after the first year hovers around 2%. At schools with a median score of 145 or lower, attrition jumps to around 25%, a rate that understand-ably alarms those in legal education but is still a lot lower than in doctoral programs in the arts and sciences. See https://lawschooli.com/law-school-dropout-rates/.

According to Derek Bok and William G. Bowen, "At leading schools of law, business, and medicine approximately 90 percent of black students complete their studies successfully." "The Arrival of the Bowen-Bok Study on Racial Preferences in College Admissions," *Journal of Blacks in Higher Education* 20 (1998): 120–22.

34. See Derek Bok, *Higher Education in America* (Princeton, NJ: Princeton University Press, 2013), 234; and Barbara E. Lovitts, "Being a Good Course-Taker Is Not Enough: A Theoretical Perspective on the Transition to Independent Research," *Studies in Higher Education* 30, no. 2 (2005): 144.

35. Harriet Zuckerman, Ronald Ehrenberg, Jeffrey Groen, and Sharon Brucker, *Educating Scholars: Doctoral Education in the Humanities* (Princeton, NJ: Princeton University Press, 2010), 7.

36. For further discussion of this human factor, see Leonard Cassuto, "Advising the Graduate Student Who Won't Finish," *Chronicle of Higher Education*, October 3, 2010, https://www.chronicle.com/article/Advising-the-Dissertation/124782.

37. Zuckerman et al., *Educating Scholars*, 99.

38. Council of Graduate Schools, *Ph.D. Completion and Attrition: Policies and Practices to Promote Student Success* (Washington DC, 2019), executive summary, 2. https://cgsnet.org/phd-completion-project

39. Zuckerman et al., *Educating Scholars*, 153. The Mellon researchers also found that 81 percent of those who did leave earned one or another higher degree—a sign that they were not intellectually incapable (265).

40. Barbara E. Lovitts, "Research on the Structure," in Wulff and Austin, *Paths to the Professoriate*, 116. Lovitts notes that non-completers had the same undergraduate GPA as those who completed the degree and had, if anything, more helpful background experiences such as publishing an article or working with a team. In fact, non-completers "had close collegial relationships with faculty and other students as undergraduates, went to graduate school expecting more of the same, and became disappointed and disillusioned when their experiences did not meet their expectations." Lovitts, "Research on the Structure," 120.

41. Lovitts, "Research on the Structure," 132–33.

42. Bok, *Higher Education*, 247.

43. Angelica M. Stacy, "Training Future Leaders," in Golde and Walker, *Envisioning*, 204.

44. Colleen Flaherty, "Bold Move in Graduate Education," *Inside Higher Ed*, October 9, 2019, https://www.insidehighered.com/news/2019/10/09/university -chicago-will-guarantee-full-funding-all-humanities-and-social-sciences. As part of this initiative, Chicago also announced a suite of new programs to be implemented in tandem with the funding un-cap/admissions cap, including UChicago Launch, a satellite of "the greater UChicagoGRAD program for placement and career diversity." The new program "will provide resources for students finishing their programs and recent graduates who want to work outside academe. Offerings will include one-on-one advising, funded internship placements and workshops on different sectors and the job hunt." See also Megan Zahneis, "Doctoral Education Is Flawed: What's One Solution from the U. of Chicago? Capping the Size of Ph.D. Programs," *Chronicle of Higher Education*, October 21, 2019, https://www.chronicle.com/article /Doctoral-Education-Is-Flawed/247384.

45. Lovitts, "Research on the Structure." See also, in Wulff and Austin *Paths to the Professoriate*, James Soto and Edward Taylor, "Theories and Strategies of Academic Career Socialization: Improving Paths to the Professoriate for Black Graduate Students," 92–114, especially their comment on "the traditional distance between service and research. Many faculty members model considerable separation between the two; the students in this study, however, operated in a value system that says research *must* be of service" (111). See also Andrea Abernathy Lunsford,

"Rethinking the Ph.D. in English" on expanding the canon to include popular modes, in Golde and Walker, *Envisioning*, esp. 363–64.

46. For more information on Michigan's Summer Institute for New Merit Fellows, see https://rackham.umich.edu/rackham-life/diversity-equity-and-inclusion/srop/.

47. See Leonard Cassuto, "Time to Degree Revisited: Back to the Future," *Chronicle of Higher Education*, April 21, 2014, https://www.chronicle.com/article /Time-to-Degree-Revisited-Back/146075.

48. All quotations from Bennett are drawn from an interview with Cassuto, November 2018.

49. Interviews with Robinson, Agbasoba, and other current and former Pipeline students are taken from interviews conducted by Cassuto, December 2018.

50. The Mellon Mays website is located at https://www.mmuf.org/.

Chapter 5: Student Support and Time to Degree

1. Quotations from John McGreevy are drawn from an interview with Cassuto in February 2017.

2. Alvin Kwiram, "Time for Reform?," in *Envisioning the Future of Doctoral Education: Preparing Stewards of the Disciplines*, ed. Chris M. Golde and George E. Walker (San Francisco: Jossey-Bass, 2006), 146; Chris M. Golde and George E. Walker, eds., *Envisioning the Future of Doctoral Education: Preparing Stewards of the Disciplines* (San Francisco: Jossey-Bass, 2006), 209.

3. See "The Age of New Humanities Ph.D.'s," American Academy of Arts and Sciences, Humanities Indicators, https://www.amacad.org/humanities-indicators /higher-education/age-new-humanities-phds. The report states that humanities PhDs "are almost three years older than the median doctorate recipient." Minor good news: the number is down from 35.7 in 1994.

4. Louis Menand, *The Marketplace of Ideas: Reform and Resistance in the American University* (New York: W. W. Norton, 2010), 153.

5. Roger L. Geiger, *Research and Relevant Knowledge: American Research Universities since World War II* (Oxford: Oxford University Press, 1993), 227–28.

6. Harriet Zuckerman, Ronald Ehrenberg, Jeffrey Groen, and Sharon Brucker, *Educating Scholars: Doctoral Education in the Humanities* (Princeton, NJ: Princeton University Press, 2010), 215.

7. John Adams, email correspondence with Cassuto, 2014.

8. See Stacey Patton, "Brandeis Tries a New Tactic to Speed Students to the Ph.D.," *Chronicle of Higher Education*, July 8, 2013, https://www.chronicle.com /article/Brandeis-Tries-a-New-Tactic-to/140139.

9. For more on Irvine's 5 + 2 program, see https://www.humanities.uci.edu /graduate/current/fiveplustwo.php. A below-the-radar precursor to these programs was introduced by chair John Adams in the geography department at the University of Minnesota in the early 2000s. Adams told students "that if they defended their dissertation in residence during the academic year, I would *guarantee* them employ-ment on a part-time basis for the following academic year teaching one or more courses on their own while they looked for a job elsewhere and prepared their

research for publication." Adams reported later that "it seems to have worked. These explicit rules motivated students to move through the program faster, and in their final year with us they developed teaching records (and student evaluations) and were able to present a completed dissertation during their job hunts." Adams, email correspondence with Cassuto, 2014.

10. George E. Walker, Chris M. Golde, Laura Jones, Andrea Conklin Bueschel, and Pat Hutchings, *The Formation of Scholars: Rethinking Doctoral Education for the Twenty-First Century* (San Francisco: Jossey-Bass, 2008), 60.

11. Kwiram, "Time for Reform?," 146.

12. Kwiram, "Time for Reform?," 146–47. The UK figure also excludes previous time pursuing a master's degree.

13. Zuckerman et al., *Educating Scholars*, 261.

14. Zuckerman et al., *Educating Scholars*, 263.

15. Zuckerman et al., *Educating Scholars,* 155.

16. For an extensive discussion of the denigration of the master's degree and where that has left us, see Leonard Cassuto, *The Graduate School Mess: What Caused It and How We Can Fix It* (Cambridge, MA: Harvard University Press, 2015), 150–55.

17. One problem is that the Ford Foundation has already funded an initiative to develop a professional master of arts degree. The funding ended in 2012 after nine years, before the degree could lift off, and it foundered as a result. Few concrete conclusions may be drawn from an abortive effort; we believe that the idea retains potential, especially if it's implemented in light of the knowledge we've gained since. We will discuss this possibility further in chapter 9, on degrees. See Cassuto, *The Graduate School Mess*, 159.

18. Quotations from Patrick Griffin are drawn from an interview with Cassuto in February 2017.

19. David Damrosch, "Vectors of Change," in Golde and Walker, *Envisioning*, 42.

20. Colleen Flaherty, "Fixing Humanities Grad Programs," *Inside Higher Education*, December 7, 2012, https://www.insidehighered.com/news/2012/12/07/mla -president-says-reforming-graduate-education-humanities-requires-hard-decisions.

21. See Vimal Patel, "Health Care Is a New Flash Point for Graduate Students," *Chronicle of Higher Education*, October 18, 2015, http://chronicle.com/article /Health-Care-Is-a-New-Flash/233797.

22. See the NSF's data set for "Doctorate Recipients from U.S. Universities: 2017," especially table 12; https://ncses.nsf.gov/pubs/nsf19301/data.

23. See Robert Weisbuch and Leonard Cassuto, *Reforming Doctoral Education, 1990–2015*, report for the Mellon Foundation, 2016, https://mellon.org/news -blog/articles/reforming-doctoral-education-1990-2015-recent-initiatives-and-future -prospects/, 37. Our commentary on the sciences here and throughout has benefitted greatly by a contributing author to our Mellon report, Dr. Peter Bruns, professor emeritus of genetics at Cornell University, who for many years served as vice president and led the Higher Education program at the Howard Hughes Medical Institute.

24. Kenneth Prewitt, "Who Should Do What? Implications for Institutional and National Leaders," in Golde and Walker, *Envisioning*, 30.

25. Zuckerman et al., *Educating Scholars*, 267.

Chapter 6: Curing the Curriculum and Examining the Exam

1. Here's one version of the story: https://www.beliefnet.com/love-family /parenting/2000/10/teaching-tales-the-way-you-like-it.aspx.

2. Alan Leshner and Layne Scherer, eds., *Graduate STEM Education for the 21st Century* (Washington, DC: National Academies Press, 2018), 95–97.

3. For examples, see HistoryLabs: Collaborative Research Seminar at the University of Michigan, https://lsa.umich.edu/history/history-at-work/programs/u-m -historylabs.html; the Price Lab for Digital Humanities at the University of Pennsylvania, https://pricelab.sas.upen.edu, Matrix: The Center for Digital Humanities and Social Sciences at Michigan State University, https://msustatewide.msu.edu /Programs/Details/1219; and Humanities Lab at Arizona State University, https:// humanities.lab.asu.edu. In some of these cases, faculty, graduate students, and undergraduates work together, thus affording graduate students additional growth opportunities in professional development and in becoming a broadly based educator.

4. Eric Wertheimer and George Justice, "Connecting the Curriculum: A Collaborative Reinvention for Humanities PhDs." *MLA Profession* (May 2017), https://profession .mla.org/connecting-the-curriculum-a-collaborative-reinvention-for-humanities-phds/. Wertheimer and Justice argue for individual, digitally based curricula for graduate students, an experiment they have pioneered at Arizona State University, where they both work.

5. Leonard Cassuto, interview with Russell Berman, June 2012, quoted in Cassuto, *The Graduate School Mess: What Caused It and How We Can Fix It* (Cambridge, MA: Harvard University Press, 2015), 65.

6. Judith Shapiro, *Community of Scholars, Community of Teachers* (Chicago: Prickly Paradigm Press, 2016).

7. The application of cognitive science to the disciplines is in a beginning stage, but it holds some promise as a way to approach these problems. See Carnegie Mellon University, Eberly Center, The Simon Initiative, http://www.cmu.edu/teaching /simon/index.html; and http://www.cmu.edu/teaching/.

8. President's Council of Advisors on Science and Technology, *Report to the President—Transformation and Opportunity: The Future of the U.S. Research Enterprise*, 2012, https://obamawhitehouse.archives.gov/sites/default/files/microsites /ostp/pcast_future_research_enterprise_20121130.pdf.

9. Douglas C. Bennett, "Innovation in the Liberal Arts and Sciences," in *Education and Democracy: Re-imagining Liberal Learning in America*, ed. Robert Orrill (New York: College Entrance Examination Board, 1997), 141–42.

10. Chris M. Golde and Timothy M. Dore, *At Cross Purposes: What the Experiences of Today's Doctoral Students Reveal about Doctoral Education* (Pew, 2001), 13.

11. A department might consider an interdisciplinarity requirement of students during the coursework stage. The resulting intellectual cosmopolitanism would serve students well both inside and outside the academy.

12. See information for the Summer Dissertation Retreat at https://writingcenter .wustl.edu/2019/04/23/summer-dissertation-retreat-call-for-applications/.

13. See Brown University Graduate School, "Graduate School to Launch 'Open Graduate Programs' with $2M Mellon Grant," press release, October 5, 2011, http://www.news.brown.edu/pressreleases/2011/10/mellon; and Vimal Patel, "Brown U. Tests Approach to Interdisciplinary Graduate Work," *Chronicle of Higher Education*, March 24, 2014, https://www.chronicle.com/article/Brown-U-Tests -Approach-to/145487.

14. Woodrow Wilson National Fellowship Foundation, *The Responsive Ph.D.*, https://woodrow.org/news/publications/responsive-phd/, 17.

15. See Cassuto, *The Graduate School Mess*, 83.

16. Computer science, which does turn away business, is a notable exception to this austerity.

17. William James, "The PhD Octopus" (1903), in *Memories and Studies* (New York: Longmans, Green, 1917), 331.

18. George E. Walker, Chris M. Golde, Laura Jones, Andrea Conklin Bueschel, and Pat Hutchings, *The Formation of Scholars: Rethinking Doctoral Education for the Twenty-First Century* (San Francisco: Jossey-Bass, 2008), 41.

19. David Jaffee, "Stop Telling Students to Study for Exams," *Chronicle of Higher Education*, April 22, 2012, https://www.chronicle.com/article/Stop-Telling -Students-to-Study/131622.

20. For these and other examples, see Cassuto, *The Graduate School Mess*, 89–90; and the *Report of the MLA Task Force on Doctoral Study in Language and Literature*, 2014, https://apps.mla.org/pdf/taskforcedocstudy2014.pdf.

21. Walker et al., *The Formation of Scholars*, 54, 55.

22. Walker et al., *The Formation of Scholars*, 55.

23. See Balleisen and Wisdom, "Reimagining the Humanities PhD: A Guide for PhD Programs and Faculty" (2019), http://site.duke.edu/interdisciplinary/files/2020 /01/options-for-reimagining-humanities-phd-external.pdf.

Chapter 7: Advising

1. Zoe Greenberg, "What Happens to #MeToo When a Feminist Is the Accused?," *New York Times*, August 13, 2018, https://www.nytimes.com/2018/08/13 /nyregion/sexual-harassment-nyu-female-professor.html.

2. William Clark, *Academic Charisma and the Origins of the Research University* (Chicago: University of Chicago Press, 2006).

3. Laurence Veysey, *The Emergence of the American University* (Chicago: University of Chicago Press, 1965), 157, 158.

4. James Grossman, "Hierarchy and Needs: How to Dislodge Outdated Notions of Advising," *Perspectives*, September 1, 2018, https://www.historians.org /publications-and-directories/perspectives-on-history/september-2018/hierarchy-and -needs-how-to-dislodge-outdated-notions-of-advising.

5. David Damrosch, "Vectors of Change," in *Envisioning the Future of Doctoral Education: Preparing Stewards of the Disciplines*, ed. Chris M. Golde and George E. Walker (San Francisco: Jossey-Bass, 2006), 38.

6. Thomas Bender, "Expanding the Domain of History," in Golde and Walker, *Envisioning*, 305.

7. See the Duke University Graduate School's website: https://gradschool.duke.edu/professional-development/cultivating-culture-mentoring.

8. Angelica M. Stacy, "Training Future Leaders," in Golde and Walker, *Envisioning*, 200.

9. See the NIH website: https://loop.nigms.nih.gov/2014/10/new-requirement-to-describe-idp-use-in-progress-reports/. For specific examples, see Iowa State's requirement at https://www.grad-college.iastate.edu; the University of Nebraska at https://www.unl.edu/gradstudies/professional-development; and for Brown, https://www.brown.edu/academics/biomed/graduate-postdoctoral-studies/resources-and-programs.

10. George E. Walker, Chris M. Golde, Laura Jones, Andrea Conklin Bueschel, and Pat Hutchings, *The Formation of Scholars: Rethinking Doctoral Education for the Twenty-First Century* (San Francisco: Jossey-Bass, 2008), chapter 6.

11. See Leonard Cassuto, "Changing the Way We Socialize Graduate Students," *Chronicle of Higher Education*, January 10, 2011, https://www.chronicle.com/article/Changing-the-Way-We-Socialize/125892.

12. David Porter and Stacy Hartman, Professional Humanities Careers, syllabus, https://sites.lsa.umich.edu/humanities-phd-proj/wp-content/uploads/sites/535/2018/02/Professional-Humanities-Careers-Syllabus.pdf.

13. On the master's level, the program in English at Villanova University offers students a Professional Research Option, an independent study in which they study "the history and future prospects" of one or two fields of interest and, in addition to a research paper, write a sample cover letter in which they detail how their graduate study helps to prepare them for entry into that field. https://www1.villanova.edu/villanova/artsci/english/gradenglish/academics/mainenglish/PRO.html

14. Bender, "Expanding the Domain of History," 305

15. This multiheaded advising practice was recommended by the 2020 MLA Task Force on Ethical Conduct, and Columbia's English department already practices it with its advising committees. However, this is one idea that would not work particularly well in the sciences, because of the economically based division of labor: the student works in the adviser's lab, on the adviser's nickel. Committee members usually do little more than "advise and consent."

16. John Adams, email correspondence with Cassuto, 2014.

17. Russell Berman et al., "The Future of the Humanities Ph.D. at Stanford" (unpublished manuscript). See Leonard Cassuto, "The Multi-track Ph.D.," *Chronicle of Higher Education*, September 30, 2012, https://www.chronicle.com/article/The-Multi-Track-PhD/134738.

18. Jim Grossman, "Imagining Ph.D. Orientation in 2022," *Chronicle of Higher Education*, August 28, 2017, https://www.chronicle.com/article/Imagining-PhD-Orientation-in/240995.

19. Professor David Porter developed and taught Professional Humanities Careers, the professional development course at the University of Michigan in collaboration with Stacy Hartman, project manager of the Modern Language Association's Connected Academics Program, which explores ways to prepare doctoral students in the

humanities for a variety of careers. See Leonard Cassuto, "Can You Prepare Your Ph.D.s for Diverse Careers When You Don't Have One?," *Chronicle of Higher Education*, August 22, 2018, https://www.chronicle.com/article/Can-You-Train-Your -PhDs-for/244323.

20. See Graduate School, University of Tennessee, https://gradschool.utk.edu /training-and-mentorship/.

21. For a more detailed discussion of Louisville's PLAN, see Leonard Cassuto, "The Problem of Professionalization," *Chronicle of Higher Education*, March 23, 2015, https://www.chronicle.com/article/The-Problem-of/228633.

Chapter 8: Students as Teachers

1. Chris M. Golde and Timothy M. Dore, "The Survey of Doctoral Education and Career Preparation" in *Paths to the Professoriate: Strategies for Enriching the Preparation of Future Faculty*, ed. Donald H. Wulff and Ann E. Austin (San Francisco: Jossey-Bass, 2004), 25.

2. Austin and Wulff, *Paths to the Professoriate*, 89.

3. *Report of the MLA Task Force on Doctoral Study in Language and Literature*, 2014, https://apps.mla.org/pdf/taskforcedocstudy2014.pdf, 10.

4. See William H. Brackney, *Congregation and Campus: Baptists in Higher Education* (Macon, GA: Mercer University Press, 2008), 221.

5. See, for example, *Academically Adrift: Limited Learning on College Campuses*, the widely noticed study by Richard Arum and Josipa Roksa (Chicago: University of Chicago Press, 2010).

6. Gerald Graff, personal conversation with Cassuto, 2014.

7. One urban college dean at a Woodrow Wilson National Fellowship Foundation panel several years ago commented, "Our new faculty members do not understand students for whom school comes after family and job. Sometimes I don't think they even like this type of student, but they represent the future." Robert Weisbuch, "Toward a Responsive Ph.D.," in Wulff and Austin, *Paths to the Professoriate*, 222. Nobel Prize–winning physicist Carl Wieman declared on NPR that too many programs fail to take teaching seriously: "Hey Higher Ed, Why Not Focus on Teaching?," June 7, 2017, https://www.npr.org/sections/ed/2017/06/07/530909736 /hey-higher-ed-why-not-focus-on-teaching.

8. Smith, *Manifesto for the Humanities* (Ann Arbor: University of Michigan Press, 2016), 88. Smith's data comes from *The Condition of Education* (2010), published by the US Department of Education, Institute of Education Sciences, National Center for Education Statistics.

9. Smith, *Manifesto*, 89.

10. Woodrow Wilson National Fellowship Foundation, *The Responsive Ph.D.: Innovations in U.S. Doctoral Education*, 2005, https://woodrow.org/news /publications/responsive-phd/.

11. Golde and Dore, "Survey," 25–26. Their data derives from a 20-page survey sent to enrolled doctoral students at 27 universities in 11 arts and sciences disciplines, garnering 4,114 completed surveys—though Golde and Dore's essay focuses "only on

those students who said that, at some point in their careers, they desired a faculty position." We would guess that the discrepancy between the widespread student interest in teaching (and teaching beyond the campus) and the low level of training available would appear still greater if students planning a nonprofessorial future were included.

12. See Leonard Cassuto, "Teach While You're at It," *Chronicle of Higher Education*, January 5, 2015, https://www.chronicle.com/article/Teach-While-Youre -at-It/150963.

13. Bob received full funding for a doctorate in literature in the late 1960s via the National Science Defense Act. Indeed, Bob's doctoral education—during those halcyon days when time to degree was more reasonable—was financed fully by a National Defense Education Act Fellowship, even though no one ever told him how Emily Dickinson was contributing to military preparedness. Perhaps there was more to national defense than the inscribers of the act understood.

14. R. C. Lewontin, "The Cold War and the Transformation of the Academy," in *The Cold War and the University: Toward an Intellectual History of the Postwar Years*, ed. Richard Simpson (New York: The New Press, 1998).

15. Smith, *Manifesto*, 86.

16. Quoted in Vanessa L. Ryan, "Redefining the Teaching-Research Nexus Today," *MLA Profession*, November 2016, https://profession.mla.org/redefining-the -teaching-research-nexus-today/.

17. Smith, *Manifesto*, 86–87.

18. More info and video examples of Kentucky's GradTeach Live can be found here: https://gradschool.uky.edu/gradteachlive.

19. *Groundhog Day*, dir. Harold Ramis (Columbia Pictures, 1993).

20. The contours of this suggested practicum are based on current practice in Fordham University's English department. Design credit to Professors Moshe Gold and Anne Fernald.

21. The Carnegie Fund for the Advancement of Teaching in 2004 skewered the privacy that paradoxically surrounds the quintessentially public act of teaching, noting that "habits and conversations that would allow faculty to share what they know and do as teachers, and to build on the work of other teachers, are almost nonexistent. In this respect, the contrast with research is striking." See Weisbuch and Cassuto, "Reforming Doctoral Education, 1990–2015," 73, https://mellon.org/news -blog/articles/reforming-doctoral-education-1990-2015-recent-initiatives-and-future -prospects/. See also Gerald Graff, "MLA 2008 Presidential Address," http://www .mla.org/pres_address_2008; Pat Hutchings and Susan E. Clarke, "The Scholarship of Teaching and Learning," in Wulff and Austin, *Paths to the Professoriate*, 163.

22. For more on this coteaching initiative, see "The Advantages of Coteaching for Graduate Students," Teagle Foundation, http://www.teaglefoundation.org/news-insights /news/articles/teagle-in-the-news/the-advantages-of-coteaching-for-graduate-students.

23. See University of Virginia's PhDPlus website, https://phdplus.virginia.edu/.

24. The English department at Idaho State University teaches literature and teaching together. We discuss their example in chapter 9, on degrees.

25. Zook is quoted in Leonard Cassuto, "A Modern Great Books Solution to the Humanities' Enrollment Woes," *Chronicle of Higher Education*, November 10,

2019, https://www.chronicle.com/article/A-Modern-Great-Books-Solution/247481. Purdue's Cornerstone program is a modern great-books core curriculum staffed by full-time instructors in an effort to revitalize enrollments in the way we're describing. Initial results are highly auspicious.

26. Harriet Zuckerman, Ronald Ehrenberg, Jeffrey Groen, and Sharon Brucker, *Educating Scholars: Doctoral Education in the Humanities* (Princeton, NJ: Princeton University Press, 2010), 260.

27. *Report of the MLA Task Force on Doctoral Study in Language and Literature*, 2014, https://apps.mla.org/pdf/taskforcedocstudy2014.pdf, 10.

28. Sarah Iovan, interview with Cassuto, October 2019.

29. Chris M. Golde and Timothy M. Dore, *At Cross Purposes: What the Experiences of Today's Doctoral Students Reveal about Doctoral Education* (Pew, 2001), 5.

30. Jerry G. Gaff, Anne S. Pruitt-Logan, Leslie B. Sims, and Daniel D. Denecke, *Preparing Future Faculty in the Humanities and Social Sciences: A Guide for Change* (Washington, DC: Council of Graduate Schools, Association of American Colleges and Universities, 2003), 179, 181.

31. Gaff, Pruitt-Logan, Sims, and Denecke, *Preparing Future Faculty in the Humanities and Social Sciences*, 189.

32. Audrey Williams June, "Navigating Culture Shock," *Chronicle of Higher Education*, May 5, 2014, https://www.chronicle.com/article/Navigating-Culture -Shock/146365.

33. CUNY's account of this grant initiative may be found at https://www.gc.cuny .edu/News/All-News/Detail?id=53784.

34. Mellon's record of this grant may be found at https://mellon.org/grants /grants-database/grants/university-of-michigan/20100636/

35. Kentucky's PFF and PFP info is here: https://gradschool.uky.edu/sites /gradschool.uky.edu/files/PFF%20Brochure_SCREEN%20VIEW.pdf.

36. See "UVa Student Launches Education Nonprofit," *Charlottesville Tomorrow*, September 5, 2015, https://www.cvilletomorrow.org/articles/uva-student -launches-education-nonprofit.

37. Humanities Out There curricula may be found at https://historyproject.uci .edu/hot/.

38. For more on Illinois State's scholar-educator option, see https://illinoisstate .edu/academics/biological-sciences-doctorate/.

39. For more information on Howard's program, see https://gs.howard.edu /graduate-programs/college-and-university-faculty-preparation.

40. For Missouri's teaching minor, see http://catalog.missouri.edu /undergraduategraduate/interdisciplinaryacademicprograms /additionalminorsandcertificates/collegeteaching/. The University of Illinois at Chicago offers a teaching practicum open to students from all departments and programs: https://grad.uic.edu/programs/foundations-college-instruction/gc-594/.

41. For more on Duke's certificate in college teaching, see https://gradschool.duke .edu/professional-development/programs/certificate-college-teaching.

42. For more information on Project NeXt, see https://www.maa.org/programs -and-communities/professional-development/project-next.

43. See https://www.cirtl.net/, especially the pages on "About," "Courses," and "Resources."

44. For a discussion of the pitfalls of special teaching tracks (or worse, special teaching degrees, which have their own history), see Leonard Cassuto, *The Graduate School Mess: What Caused It and How We Can Fix It* (Cambridge, MA: Harvard University Press, 2015), chapter 5.

45. Smith, *Manifesto*, 95, 97.

46. Smith, *Manifesto*, 96, 97.

47. Cathy Davidson, *The New Education: How to Revolutionize the University to Prepare Students for a World in Flux* (New York: Perseus, 2017).

48. Ryan, "Redefining the Teaching-Research Nexus Today."

49. Ryan, "Redefining the Teaching-Research Nexus Today."

Chapter 9: Degrees

1. Yehuda Elkana, "Unmasking Uncertainties and Embracing Contradictions: Graduate Education in the Sciences," in *Envisioning the Future of Doctoral Education: Preparing Stewards of the Disciplines*, ed. Chris M. Golde and George E. Walker (San Francisco: Jossey-Bass, 2006), 90. He excoriates the practice of "simply distributing research topics among the incoming batch of new doctoral students" as "one of the most anti-intellectual, and even morally least acceptable, aspects of otherwise very efficiently organized departments" (89–90).

2. Crispin Taylor, "Heeding the Voices of Graduate Students and Postdocs," in Golde and Walker, *Envisioning*, 53; Elkana, "Unmasking," 66, 90.

3. Angelica Stacy, "Training Future Leaders," in Golde and Walker, *Envisioning*, 197.

4. Taylor, "Heeding," 53.

5. Dian Squire, a graduate student, wrote in 2014, "A dissertation is a singular, extended Medieval hazing ritual whereby graduate students spend countless hours engrossed in a singular topic that itself 'encourages "hasty specialization" and a loss of "a period of exploration, risk-taking, and learning from mistakes."'" "A Response to 'An Open Letter to Journal Editors,'" *Chronicle of Higher Education*, October 15, 2014, https://www.chronicle.com/article/A-Response-to-An-Open-Letter /149365.

6. "A Special Letter from Stephen Greenblatt," May 28, 2002, https://www.mla .org/Resources/Research/Surveys-Reports-and-Other-Documents/Publishing-and -Scholarship/Call-for-Action-on-Problems-in-Scholarly-Book-Publishing/A-Special -Letter-from-Stephen-Greenblatt.

7. *Report of the MLA Task Force on Evaluating Scholarship for Tenure and Promotion*, December 2006, https://www.mla.org/content/download/3362/81802 /taskforcereport0608.pdf.

8. Roger L. Geiger, *To Advance Knowledge: The Growth of American Research Universities, 1900–1940* (Oxford: Oxford University Press, 1986), 8; Veysey, *The Emergence of the American University* (Chicago: University of Chicago Press, 1965), 175–76.

9. A 1989 study found that about 35 percent of history dissertations eventually became books. It's true that 1989 is a while ago, but the high number makes the point well. Cited in Timothy Gilfoyle, "The Changing Forms of History," *Perspectives on History*, April 1, 2015, https://www.historians.org/publications-and -directories/perspectives-on-history/april-2015/the-changing-forms-of-history.

10. Anthony T. Grafton and James Grossman, "No More Plan B," *Perspectives on History*, October 1, 2011, https://www.historians.org/publications-and-directories /perspectives-on-history/october-2011/no-more-plan-b. Where Historians Work: An Interactive Database of History PhD Career Outcomes, https://www.historians.org /wherehistorianswork.

11. "History as a Book Discipline," *Perspectives on History*, April 1, 2015, https://www.historians.org/publications-and-directories/perspectives-on-history/april -2015/history-as-a-book-discipline-an-introduction.

12. Lara Putnam, "The Opportunity Costs of Remaining a Book Discipline," *Perspectives on History*, April 1, 2015, https://www.historians.org/publications-and -directories/perspectives-on-history/april-2015/the-opportunity-costs-of-remaining-a -book-discipline.

13. See Leonard Cassuto, *The Graduate School Mess: What Caused It and How We Can Fix It* (Cambridge, MA: Harvard University Press, 2015), 11; and Bernard Berelson, *Graduate Education in the United States* (New York: McGraw-Hill, 1960), 181.

14. Berelson, *Graduate Education in the United States*. In the late 1960s, Bob's dissertating period lasted 1.6 years, not only typical but almost uniform in his department. A generation later, Len took almost twice as long to get through that stage: about 3 years. In his entering cohort of 14 students, only 3 finished faster.

15. Jason Brennan, "Meritocracy Is All We Have Time For," *Chronicle of Higher Education*, September 20, 2019, https://www.chronicle.com/interactives/20190911 -meritocracy-forum, B14.

16. J. David Velleman, "The Publication Emergency," *Daily Nous*, July 31, 2017, http://dailynous.com/2017/07/31/publication-emergency-guest-post-j-david-velleman/.

17. Jeannie Brown Leonard, "Doctoral Students' Perspectives on the Dissertation," in *The Assessment of Doctoral Education: Emerging Criteria and New Models for Improving Outcomes*, ed. P. Maki and N. Borkowski (Sterling, VA: Stylus, 2006), n.p.

18. Louis Menand, *Marketplace of Ideas: Reform and Reaction in the American University* (New York: W. W. Norton, 2010), 152.

19. *Report of the MLA Task Force on Doctoral Study in Language and Literature*, 2014, https://apps.mla.org/pdf/taskforcedocstudy2014.pdf, 14.

20. John Bugg, email to Cassuto, September 2019.

21. The CGS report is "Imagining the Dissertation's Many Futures," *GradEdge* 5, no. 3 (March 2016): 3, https://cgsnet.org/sites/default/files/March%20FINAL2.pdf. The Canadian Association of Graduate Schools has also produced a valuable resource, the *Report of the CAGS Task Force on the Dissertation—Purpose, Content, Structure, Assessment* (September 2018), https://secureservercdn.net/45.40 .148.221/bba.0c2.myftpupload.com/wp-content/uploads/2018/09/Dissertation-task -force-report-FINAL-Sept-EN-1.pdf.

22. "Imagining the Dissertation's Many Futures," 2, 3.

23. "The PhD in English and the Teaching of English," Idaho State University, https://www.isu.edu/english/graduate-programs/phd-in-english-and-the-teaching-of-english/.

24. "Teaching Literature Book Award," https://www.isu.edu/english/scholarships—awards/teaching-literature-book-award/teaching-literature-book-award-information-/.

25. Ashley Young and Michel Martin, "After Rapping His Dissertation, A. D. Carson is UVa's New Hip-Hop Professor," NPR, July 15, 2017, https://www.npr.org/2017/07/15/537274235/after-rapping-his-dissertation-a-d-carson-is-uvas-new-hip-hop-professor.

26. MLA Executive Director Paula Krebs interviews Williams about her dissertation in Anna Williams, "Dissertation Innovations: A Podcast Dissertation," *MLA Profession* (2019), https://profession.mla.org/dissertation-innovations-a-podcast-dissertation/.

27. Vimal Patel, "Ph.D.s Embrace Alternative Dissertations: The Job Market May Not," *Chronicle of Higher Education*, February 28, 2016, https://www.chronicle.com/article/PhDs-Embrace-Alternative/235511/.

28. Stacy, "Training Future Leaders," 201.

29. Laura Pappano, "The Master's as the New Bachelor's," *New York Times*, July 22, 2011, https://www.nytimes.com/2011/07/24/education/edlife/edl-24masters-t.html.

30. In planning for the PSM, the Sloan Foundation, its main backer, insisted on collaboration between academic scientists and industry from the outset, along with an ongoing board of industry advisers once the program got going. Begun in the mid-1990s with a three-year grant to just three universities—Michigan State, Georgia Tech, and the University of Southern California—PSM programs at dozens of universities have now graduated well over 5,000 students.

For a brief history of the master's degree, including the PSM, and the subsequent failed attempt to create a humanities and social science version of a professional degree initiated by the Council of Graduate Studies, see Cassuto, *The Graduate School Mess*, 151–61.

31. See Matt Reed, "The Decline of Humanities Enrollments and the Decline of Pre-Law," *Inside Higher Ed*, September 16, 2018, https://www.insidehighered.com/blogs/confessions-community-college-dean/decline-humanities-enrollments-and-decline-pre-law.

32. Cassuto, interview with Michael Teitelbaum, April 2015. See "A Degree of Uncommon Success," *Chronicle of Higher Education*, June 29, 2015, https://www.chronicle.com/article/A-Degree-of-Uncommon-Success/231199.

33. Cassuto, interview with Lynch, April 2015. See "The Sad Story of the P.M.A.," *Chronicle of Higher Education*, August 4, 2015, https://www.chronicle.com/article/The-Sad-Story-of-the-PMA/232113.

34. Matthew Woodbury, "Preparing for Humanities Careers: Suggestions for Doctoral Students and Departments," The Humanities PhD Project, April 28, 2016, https://sites.lsa.umich.edu/humanities-phd-proj/2018/04/16/preparing-for-humanities-careers-suggestions-for-doctoral-students-and-departments/.

35. J. P. Elder, "The Master's Degree for the Prospective College Teacher," *Journal of Higher Education* 30, no. 3 (1959): 133.

36. Robert Frost, "At Woodward's Gardens" (1936).

Chapter 10: Public Scholarship

1. For more on Michigan's Rackham Program in Public Scholarship, see https://rackham.umich.edu/professional-development/program-in-public-scholarship/. The quotation from Imagining America is taken from the Rackham Program site.

2. Julie Ellison and Timothy K. Eatman, *Scholarship in Public: Knowledge Creation and Tenure Policy in the Engaged University* (Syracuse, NY: Imagining America, 2008), https://surface.syr.edu/ia/16, 16.

3. https://en.wikipedia.org/wiki/Public_humanities, accessed February 20, 2020.

4. Paula M. Krebs, "From the Executive Director: Translating Scholarship," *MLA Summer Newsletter*, 2019, https://execdirector.mla.hcommons.org/2019/06/18/translating-scholarship/.

5. Hayden White and Robert Pogue Harrison, "'We're Here to Discuss the Meaning of Life,'" *Chronicle of Higher Education*, April 3, 2019, https://www.chronicle.com/article/We-re-Here-to-Discuss-the/246047.

6. David F. Labaree, *A Perfect Mess: The Unlikely Ascendancy of American Higher Education* (Chicago: University of Chicago Press, 2017), 31.

7. Ralph Waldo Emerson, "The American Scholar," in *Selected Writings*, edited by Stephen E. Whicher (Boston: Houghton Mifflin, 1957), 73.

8. Woodrow Wilson, "Princeton for the Nation's Service" (1902), http://infoshare1.princeton.edu/libraries/firestone/rbsc/mudd/online_ex/wilsonline/4dn8nsvc.html.

9. John Dewey, *Democracy and Education: Introduction to the Philosophy of Education* (New York: Macmillan, 1916), 181. For a more detailed account of Dewey's influence, see Amy L. Chapman and Christine Greenhow, "Citizen-Scholars: Social Media and the Changing Nature of Scholarship," *Publications* 7, no. 1 (2019): 11; and Robert Weisbuch, "Imagining Community Engagement in American Higher Education," *Diversity and Democracy: Civic Learning for Shared Futures* 18, no. 1 (Winter 2015), 8–11.

10. John F. Kennedy, "Remarks at Amherst College, 26 October 1963" (transcript), https://www.arts.gov/about/kennedy-transcript.

11. John Milton, "Areopagitica" (1644).

12. A graduate student at the Re-envisioning conference at the University of Washington in 2000 noted, "The academic environment is still very insular. And our society is not insular, and people who are well prepared should have a multitude of experiences and interactions with people in different sectors. And that's still not happening, it's still not there. And it's desperately needed." Quoted in Woodrow Wilson National Fellowship Foundation, *The Responsive Ph.D.: Innovations in U.S. Doctoral Education*, 2005, https://woodrow.org/news/publications/responsive-phd/.

13. Arlene Stein and Jessie Daniels, *Going Public: A Guide for Social Scientists* (Chicago: University of Chicago Press, 2017).

14. See for example Gregory Jay, "The Engaged Humanities: Principles and Practices for Public Scholarship and Teaching," *Journal of Community Engagement and Humanities*, June 19, 2012, http://jces.ua.edu/the-engaged-humanities-principles -and-practices-for-public-scholarship-and-teaching/. Jay reviews recent critiques of biases of race, class, gender, and nationality in the study of humanities disciplines, and he urges "expanding what we mean when we say 'the public' and to whom our work is accountable."

15. See https://clementecourse.org/; Earl Shorris, *Riches for the Poor: The Clemente Course in the Humanities* (New York: W. W. Norton, 2000); and a subsequent book by Shorris, *The Art of Freedom* (New York: W. W. Norton, 2013).

16. Sarah E. Bond and Kevin Gannon, "Public Writing and the Junior Scholar," *Chronicle of Higher Education*, October 16, 2019, https://www.chronicle.com/article /Public-Writingthe-Junior/247342. In response to Manya Whitaker, "Which Publications Matter at Which Stages of Your Career?," *Chronicle of Higher Education*, September 23, 2019, https://www.chronicle.com/article/Which -Publications-Matter-at/247192. It should also be said that Whitaker doesn't speak for everyone. Julie Ellison and Timothy K. Eatman question tenure standards— including at the most prestigious research universities—that don't encompass public scholarship. *Scholarship in Public: Knowledge Creation and Tenure Policy in the Engaged University* (2008), http://imaginingamerica.org/wp-content/uploads/2015 /07/ScholarshipinPublicKnowledge.pdf.

17. George E. Walker, Chris M. Golde, Laura Jones, Andrea Conklin Bueschel, and Pat Hutchings, *The Formation of Scholars: Rethinking Doctoral Education for the Twenty-First Century* (San Francisco: Jossey-Bass, 2008), 79.

18. Stein and Daniels, *Going Public*, 5.

19. Lee S. Schulman, "Taking Learning Seriously," *Change* 31, no. 4 (1999): 10–17.

20. Leonard Cassuto, *The Graduate School Mess: What Caused It and How We Can Fix It* (Cambridge, MA: Harvard University Press, 2015), 234.

21. See Nancy Joseph, "A Spanish Language Film Festival, Curated for Teens," *Perspectives Newsletter*, April 2018, https://artsci.washington.edu/news/2018-04 /spanish-language-film-festival-curated-teens.

22. Richard Watts, syllabus for French 590 (spring 2019).

23. Gregory Jay, "The Engaged Humanities: Principles and Practices for Public Scholarship and Teaching," *Journal of Community Engagement and Scholarship* 3, no. 1, June 19, 2012, http://jces.ua.edu/the-engaged-humanities-principles-and -practices-for-public-scholarship-and-teaching/.

24. Sarah Bond, "Vox Populi: Tips for Academics Transitioning to Public Scholarship," *Forbes*, January 31, 2018, https://www.forbes.com/sites/drsarahbond /2018/01/31/vox-populi-tips-for-academics-transitioning-to-public-scholarship /#45fc44d31a60.

25. See our previous discussion; and Richard A. Cherwitz and Charlotte A. Sullivan, "Intellectual Entrepreneurship: A Vision for Graduate Education," *Change* 34, no. 6 (2002): 22–27, esp. 24.

26. See the Imagining America website, https://imaginingamerica.org/initiatives /tenure-promotion/.

27. Benjamin Schmidt, "The Humanities are in Crisis," *Atlantic Monthly*, August 23, 2018, https://www.theatlantic.com/ideas/archive/2018/08/the-humanities-face-a-crisisof-confidence/567565/.

28. Mariet Westerman, "Promise and Perils of the Public Humanities Pivot" (talk at Mahindra Center for the Humanities, Harvard University, February 2019). We are grateful to Dr. Westerman for sharing her manuscript with us.

29. Westerman, "Promise and Perils of the Public Humanities Pivot," 9.

30. Jay, "The Engaged Humanities."

31. For more details on the Georgetown program, see https://publichumanities.georgetown.edu/. Its start, originally scheduled for fall 2020, has been delayed by the COVID-19 pandemic.

32. For more information on Delaware's program, see http://www.afampublichumanities.udel.edu/.

33. Rice's offerings are described here: hrc.rice.edu/publichumanities/modular-courses.

34. Jonathan Rose, "Rethinking Graduate Education in History," *Perspectives on History* (February 1, 2009), https://www.historians.org/publications-and-directories/perspectives-on-history/february-2009/rethinking-graduate-education-in-history; and Rose, "Rethinking Graduate Education in History: A Five-Year Assessment," *Perspectives in History* (December 1, 2014), https://www.historians.org/publications-and-directories/perspectives-on-history/december-2014/rethinking-graduate-education-in-history.

35. For more details on Washington's public humanities program, see https://simpsoncenter.org/programs/initiatives/public-scholarship/archive/institute.

36. For a fuller historical explication of academic service, see Leonard Cassuto, "University Service: The History of an Idea," *MLA Profession*, November 2016, https://profession.mla.org/university-service-the-history-of-an-idea/.

37. For more information on this summer program, see https://simpsoncenter.org/programs/mellon-summer-fellows-public-projects-humanities.

38. For a description of this program, and of the projects that the fellows devised, see https://simpsoncenter.org/programs/mellon-summer-fellows-public-projects-humanities.

39. Mellon also funded a substantial public humanities initiative at NYU in 2019. It is in development at the time of this writing.

40. For more on the Public Science Project, see http://publicscienceproject.org/about/.

41. Richard Cherwitz, "Increasing Diversity through Intellectual Entrepreneurship, *Huffington Post*, April 29, 2012, https://www.huffpost.com/entry/increasing-diversity-thro_b_1305588.

42. Alan Leshner and Layne Scherer, eds., *Graduate STEM Education for the 21st Century* (Washington, DC: National Academies Press, 2018), 3, 5. Students also "would be encouraged to create their own project-based learning opportunities—ideally as a member of a team—as a means of developing transferable professional skills such as communication, collaboration, management, and entrepreneurship." The other desiderata include two on giving students "time, resources, and space to

explore diverse career options," while two others concern improving faculty mentoring and another requires recruiting a more diverse population of scientists in terms of race and gender.

43. M. Woelfle, P. Olliaro, and M. H. Todd, "Open Science Is a Research Accelerator," *Nature Chemistry* 3, no. 10 (2011): 745–48, https://www.nature.com/articles/nchem.1149.

Some of the controversy arises from anxieties among some scientists over losing academic and financial recompense for their discoveries. For others, open science offers the promise of accelerating knowledge and encouraging interdisciplinary collaborations.

44. Benedikt Fecher and Sascha Friesike list five distinct forms of open science, but only two (public and democratic) have to do with outreach and nonexpert participation, while the other three (infrastructure, measurement, and collaboration among scientists) do not. See Fecher and Friesike, "Open Science: One Term, Five Schools of Thought," in *Opening Science*, ed. Bartling and Friesike (New York: Springer, 2014), 17–47, https://www.hiig.de/publication/open-science-one-term-five-schools-of-thought/. For an emphasis on accelerating knowledge and encouraging interdisciplinary collaboration, see Chapman and Greenhow, "Citizen-Scholars."

45. Quoted statements on science communication from Cassuto, "As Scientists Speak Out about Science, Women and Young Scholars Lead the Way," *Chronicle of Higher Education*, April 19, 2018, https://www.chronicle.com/article/As-Scientists-Speak-Out-About/243155.

46. See Leonard Cassuto, "As Scientists Speak Out about Science, Women and Younger Scholars Lead the Way," *Chronicle of Higher Education*, April 29, 2018, https://www.chronicle.com/article/As-Scientists-Speak-Out-About/243155.

47. For more on the Science and Entertainment Exchange, see http://scienceandentertainmentexchange.org/.

48. Westerman, "Promise and Perils of the Public Humanities Pivot."

49. Another counterargument, Stanley Fish's odd "Stop Selling the Humanities," based on a faulty logic that a single weakness in an argument invalidates it entirely, simply suggests giving up. *Chronicle of Higher Education*, June 17, 2018, https://www.chronicle.com/article/Stop-Trying-to-Sell-the/243643.

Conclusion

1. Jim Grossman, "Imagining Ph.D. Orientation in 2022," *Chronicle of Higher Education*, August 28, 2017, https://www.chronicle.com/article/Imagining-PhD-Orientation-in/240995.

2. Alan Leshner and Layne Scherer, eds., *Graduate STEM Education for the 21st Century* (Washington, DC: National Academies Press, 2018), 114ff.

3. Leshner and Scherer, *Graduate STEM Education for the 21st Century*, 114.

4. George E. Walker, Chris M. Golde, Laura Jones, Andrea Conklin Bueschel, and Pat Hutchings, *The Formation of Scholars: Rethinking Doctoral Education for the Twenty-First Century* (San Francisco: Jossey-Bass, 2008), 5.

5. Adam P. Fagen and Kimberly M. Suedkamp Wells, "The 2000 National Doctoral Program Survey: An On-line Study of Students' Voices," in *Paths to the*

Professoriate, ed. Donald H. Wulff and Ann E. Austin (San Francisco: Jossey-Bass, 2004), 88.

6. Of the 35 students admitted, 19 eventually enrolled. One student got a tenure-track professorship in the months following the students' letter. See Leonard Cassuto, "Anatomy of a Polite Revolt in Columbia's English Department," *Chronicle of Higher Education*, October 3, 2019, https://www.chronicle.com/article/Anatomy -of-a-Polite-Revolt-in/247247. See also Emma Pettit, "Columbia Had Little Success Placing English Ph.D.s on the Tenure Track: 'Alarm' Followed, and the University Responded," *Chronicle of Higher Education*, August 21, 2019, https://www .chronicle.com/article/Columbia-Had-Little-Success/246989.

7. Derek Bok, *Higher Education in America* (Princeton, NJ: Princeton University Press, 2013), 232, 240.

8. Kenneth Prewitt, "Who Should Do What? Implications for Institutional and National Leaders," in *Envisioning the Future of Doctoral Education: Preparing Stewards of the Disciplines*, ed. Chris M. Golde and George E. Walker (San Francisco: Jossey-Bass, 2006), 23.

9. Prewitt, "Who Should Do What?," 23–24.

10. Robert Weisbuch, "Toward a Responsive Ph.D.," in Wulff and Austin, *Paths to the Professoriate*, 218.

11. Walker et al., *Formation*, 3.

12. Damrosch, "Vectors of Change," in Golde and Walker, *Envisioning*, 35.

13. Woodrow Wilson National Fellowship Foundation, *The Responsive Ph.D.: Innovations in U.S. Doctoral Education*, 2005, https://woodrow.org/news /publications/responsive-phd/, 233.

14. The MLA's *Task Force Report on Ethical Conduct* had not been released in its final version as this book went to press, but it was approved by the MLA delegate assembly in January 2020 and covered by the press at that time. The version approved by the delegate assembly may be found at https://www.mla.org/content /download/115847/2439024/J20-Item-8e-Report-from-the-Task-Force-on-Ethical -Conduct-in-Graduate-Education.pdf.

15. See "Mistaken and Fictional References," in https://en.wikipedia.org/wiki /Princeton_Law_School. See also Jan Hoffman, "Judge Not, Law Schools Demand of a Magazine That Ranks Them," *New York Times*, February 19, 1998, https://www .nytimes.com/1998/02/19/nyregion/judge-not-law-schools-demand-of-a-magazine -that-ranks-them.html.

16. See the AHA's website, https://www.historians.org/jobs-and-professional -development/career-diversity-for-historians/about-career-diversity.

17. David Damrosch, "Vectors of Change," in Golde and Walker, *Envisioning*, 34–45, 41.

18. Damrosch, "Vectors of Change," 34.

19. Quoted in Damrosch, "Vectors of Change," 37–38.

assessment, of doctoral programs, 19, 29, 92, 327–28, 340–42; ongoing, 92, 93–94, 111; three questions for, 108–9, 345

Association of American Colleges and Universities, Preparing Future Faculty, 43–47, 91, 255–56, 257, 258, 259, 263, 333, 345

Atlantic Philanthropies, 43, 56, 69

attrition, of faculty, 146

attrition and retention, of graduate students, 1, 2, 26, 38, 118, 166–67, 172–76, 327, 342; funding and, 40–41, 42; solutions, 168, 169–71; timing, 168

Balleisen, Edward, 220

Bartram, Erin, 14–15

Basalla, Susan, 16, 120

Bender, Thomas, 6, 225, 292

Bennett, Douglas C., 14

Bennett, Herman L., 172–74

Berelson, Bernard, 274

Bergholz, Peter, 207, 208

Berlinerblau, Jacques, 14, 21, 25

Berman, Russell, 79, 204

Bérubé, Michael, 22, 25, 29, 120, 126

Boehm, Beth A., 235–36

Boge, Andrew, 136–37

Bok, Derek, 3, 9, 29, 167, 169, 322–23

Bond, Sarah E., 297, 302–3

boot camps, 78–79, 80, 82, 83, 248

Boston University, School of Public Health, 281

bottom-up approach, 138, 140, 152–53

Bousquet, Marc, 120

Bowen Report, 9–12

Bowen, William G., 7, 9–12, 39, 40, 41

Boyer, Ernest, 259, 265

Brennan, Jason, 275

Bugg, John, 251, 280, 282

Burt, Ronald S., 99

Busch, Nancy, 140

Butler, Johnnella, 64

career counseling. *See* career services office

career diversity, 26, 32, 113–43, 319, 335–36; admissions and, 152,
157–61; advising for, 124–25, 139, 229–30, 233–35, 321, 335–36; challenges of multitasking the degree; 122–27; connection to public scholarship, 114, 115, 116, 129–30, 291–93, 295–97, 300, 308, 317, 336; COVID-19 pandemic and, 347–48; definition, 119; Humanities at Work program, 50–53, 55, 72, 305; increased acceptance, 114–16; internships for, 128, 129, 130–31, 132–39, 197, 335; multitasking PhDs for, 122–27; nonacademic, 19; practicing of, 128–32; Preparing Future Faculty program, 43–47, 91, 255–56, 257, 259, 263, 333, 345; principles, 137–43; of revised master's degree, 287–88; student support component, 197; teaching ability and, 249–50, 254–59; time to degree issue, 119, 127, 129, 132, 137, 331–32; versatility of graduate students, 121–22

Career Diversity for Historians (AHA), 52, 72–74, 76

career offices, 125, 288, 335, 342

career outcomes, 19–20, 146, 328; as admissions issue, 153; curriculum and, 1–3, 8, 199–203, 206, 207–12; tracking, 84, 122, 342; transparency in reporting, 19, 328

career paths, 3, 7; academic *vs.* nonacademic, 3, 8, 12, 14–17; job satisfaction relationship, 117–18; PhD-to-professor, 152

career services office, 139–40, 234; graduate career specialist, 320

Carnegie Academy of Teaching and Learning, 259

Carnegie Corporation, 70

Carnegie Foundation for the Advancement of Teaching, 35, 36, 53, 70, 259, 300. *See also* Carnegie Initiative on the Doctorate (CID)

Carnegie Initiative on the Doctorate (CID), 12, 13, 59–62, 123, 182, 259, 322, 324–25, 344; three questions for PhD reform assessment, 108–9, 345

Cassuto, Leonard, 9, 142, 161, 218, 251

Castro, Janine, 316

Center for the Integration of Research, Teaching and Learning (CIRTL), 261–62

Cerny, Joseph, 117–18

Cherwitz, Richard, 53

Christy, John Paul, 72

City University of New York Graduate Center: Pipeline Fellows Program, 172–76; public scholarship program, 310–11

Clemente Program in the Humanities, 296–97

Coffin, Allison, 316

collaboration, 155, 189, 205, 214, 288, 289, 329–30, 337, 343; as skill, 129, 130, 138, 201

Columbia University, 61, 97–98, 192

communication skills, 19, 129, 130, 201, 202, 302–3, 316–17. *See also* public scholarship

community colleges, 160–61, 164, 254, 256–57

community engagement, 57, 311. *See also* public scholarship

community engagement offices, 300–301

community service, 117, 119

Compact for Faculty Diversity, 65

comprehensive examinations, 28, 187–88, 203, 207, 217–19, 226, 271; substitutes, 219–21

Connected Academics: Preparing Doctoral Students of Language and Literature for a Variety of Careers (MLA), 78–80, 81, 82, 115

conservatism, institutional, 101, 102–3, 225, 283, 345–46

Council for Basic Education, 69

Council of Graduate Schools (CGS), 17, 35, 114, 148, 168; "The Future of the Dissertation," 280; Award for Innovation in Promoting an Inclusive Graduate Community, 68; Degree Completion initiative, 170; Next Generation Humanities Ph.D., 82–84; nonacademic career pathways report, 115; Ph.D. Career Pathways, 84; Preparing Future Faculty, 43–47, 91, 255–56, 257, 259, 263, 333, 345; professional master's degree program, 286

COVID-19 pandemic, 4, 10, 21, 69, 160, 213, 347–48

credentialing, 6, 345

Croxall, Brian, 16

curriculum, 12, 16, 19, 27–28, 123, 270, 319; for career diversity, 127, 129–32; core, 200–202, 206, 253; courses *vs.*, 203–14; faculty research interests and, 98; interdisciplinary approach, 27, 213, 214–16, 263; outcomes-based, 199–203, 207–12; of professional master's degree, 286; public scholarship, 303; reform process, 206–12; research emphasis, 2, 147; seminars, 149, 150, 204; student outcomes relationship, 1–3, 8; students' dissatisfaction, 98

Damrosch, David, 61, 92, 97–98, 99, 101–2, 225, 280, 324, 345

Daniels, Jessie, 302

Davidson, Cathy, 264

deans, graduate, 55, 56, 58, 95, 138, 140; empowerment, 31, 56, 324–26, 328–30

Debelius, Maggie, 16, 120

Dewey, John, 14, 294

digital analysis, 128

digital format dissertations, 282

digital learning, 242

dissertation committees, 231–33

dissertations, 19, 20, 203, 266–90; as admissions issue, 158; advising for, 28, 188–89; article-length, 269–74, 332; collaborative, 282; comprehensive exams and, 218–20; definitions and purpose, 268; digital format, 282; format change recommendations, 279–83, 328; historical perspective, 270–71, 280; interdisciplinary, 216; in literature fields, 280, 282; noncompletion, 118; pedagogical component, 251; public scholarship component, 297–300; published as books, 268–75, 279; in the sciences, 266–67; segmented, 281; substitutes/alternatives, 182–83, 184; three-minute, 246, 298–99, 300; time to degree and, 188–89, 190, 274

mission time, 93–95, 103, 110
Modern Language Association (MLA), 35, 81, 96, 120, 142, 150, 238, 249–50, 269, 280, 325; Connected Academics: Preparing Doctoral Students of Language and Literature for a Variety of Careers, 78–80, 81, 82, 115; Graduate Student Caucus, 120; *MLA Task Force on Doctoral Study in Modern Language and Literature,* 249–50, 254, 303–4; *Report of the MLA Task Force on Ethical Conduct in Graduate Education,* 303–4
Morrill Act, 5–6, 13–14
MOST (Minority Opportunities through School Transformation), 68
myIDP (Individual Development Plan) (AAAS), 20–21, 84–85, 86, 116, 227

National Academies of Science, Engineering, and Medicine, 65
National Academy of Sciences (NAS), 35; *Graduate STEM Education for the 21st Century,* 21, 200–202, 203, 213, 303–4, 313–14, 320, 321, 323, 339; Science & Entertainment Exchange, 315
National Conference on Graduate Student Leadership, 242
national disciplinary associations, 96, 205, 344
National Endowment for the Humanities (NEH) Humanities Next Generation Grant, 82, 83, 125, 305
National Institutes of Health, 34, 35, 227, 343
national organizations, role in doctoral education reform, 340–46
National Research Council (NRC), 341
National Science Foundation (NSF), 35, 43, 96, 216, 344; ADVANCE-Organizational Change for Gender Equity in STEM Academic Professions, 67; Alliance for Graduate Education and the Professoriate (AGEP), 67, 165–66; career path survey, 117; Center for the Integration of Research, Teaching and Learning

(CIRTL), 261–62; Graduate Teaching Fellows in K–12 Education (GK–12), 62–64; Integrative Graduate Education, Research, and Teaching (IGERT) program, 56–57, 68; K-through-Infinity program, 257–58; Ph.D. Career Pathways, 84; QuarkNet funding, 315; Research Traineeship Program, 87–89
Nelson, Cary, 22
Nerad, Marisi, 117–18
networking, 151
New, Jennifer, 134, 135–36
Newton, Elaine, 291–92
New York University, 150
Next Generation Humanities Ph.D. (CGS; NEH), 82–84
nonacademic career paths: bias toward, 122–24; faculty support, 124–25; job satisfaction with, 117–18. *See also* career diversity
nonprofit organizations, fellowships with, 70–72
North Dakota State University, 206, 207–9, 217; three-minute dissertation videos, 297–99, 300
Notre Dame University, 177; 5 + 1 program, 181, 184, 186–90, 194
Nyquist, Jody, 47–50

office of career services. *See* career services office
O'Neill, Tip, 153, 155
online learning, 213, 261–62, 263–64
Oreskes, Naomi, 314, 316
Ortega, Suzanne, 114

Paideia Project, 142
Pannapacker, William, 120
part-time faculty, 147, 255
part-time graduate students, 154
Participatory Action Research collective, 310
Pedicone, Jason, 141
Pew Trusts, 43, 56, 59
Ph.D. Career Pathways (CGS), 84
PhD degree: assessment of, 19, 29, 92, 93–94, 108–9, 111, 327–28, 340–42, 345; costs, 148, 177, 182; history of,

Rose, Jonathan, 307
Rudenstine, Neil R., 7, 40
Ruediger, Dylan, 75–76
Rutgers University, 252, 316
Ryan, Vanessa L., 264–65

Sagan, Carl, 313
Schlumberger Foundation Faculty for the Future Awards, 68
Schmidt, Ben, 304
scholarship, as PhD focus, 295
Schuman, Rebecca, 15
Science & Entertainment Exchange, 315
science education, funded research and, 8–9, 338
science PhD. *See* STEM disciplines
scientific creativity, 337–39
service courses, 239, 241, 252, 253
sexual harassment, 222–23, 225
Sharma, Ghanashyam (Shyam), 235–36
Shorris, Earl, 296–97
Showalter, Elaine, 120
Shulman, Lee, 259, 300
site visits, 133, 137, 288
Sloan Foundation, 286; Minority Ph.D. Program, 65, 67
Smith, Sidonie, 16–17, 242, 244, 245–46, 263–64
Snow, C. P., 18, 20
social profit, 93, 101
social sciences: projected faculty shortage, 9–10; public scholarship initiatives, 310–12; time to degree, 7–8
Society for Classical Studies, 141, 142
sociology departments, 331–32
Sosa, Julie Ann, 9–12
Southern Regional Education Board Doctoral Scholars Program, 65
Spelman College, 64
Spelmeyer, Kurt, 252
Stacy, Angelica, 34, 283
Stanford University, 80, 82, 204, 256
Stein, Arlene, 302
STEM disciplines: academic career paths, 7; academic job market, 7, 149; advising, 224–25, 226, 227; attrition rate, 168; career diversity,

57, 62–64, 84–85, 86, 87–89, 116, 159–60, 257–58; career outcomes, 159–60; curriculum, 200–202; dissertations, 266–67; financial support, 193–94; gender equity, 67; government funding, 243–44; intellectual ownership conflicts, 224–25, 329; nonacademic career paths, 17, 26; as percentage of all PhDs awarded, 193; program size, 149; public scholarship, 312–17, 320–21; relationship with humanities, 18; research orientation, 159–60; shared challenges with nonscience programs, 18–25; social profit value, 312; student diversity, 65, 67, 68; suggested reforms, 337–39; time to degree, 7
Stroud, Dina M., 165
student debt, 148, 190–91, 192, 331
student diversity, 12–13, 26–27, 29, 64–68, 327; in admissions, 25–26, 144, 172–76, 339; advising for, 165, 166, 173; attrition/retention issue, 167, 170–71, 172–76; funding for, 342–43; recruitment initiatives, 55, 57, 58, 144–45, 162–66, 172–76, 342. *See also* diversity, social
student-centered graduate education, 202–3, 206, 328–30
surveys, 97–99, 117, 236, 342, 344
Swafford, Emily, 73–74, 75–76

Target Hope, 163–64
Taylor, Crispin, 117, 123, 124, 266, 267, 283
Taylor, Edward, 146
teaching, 12, 19, 327, 328–29, 333–34, 342; for career diversity, 128–32, 249–50, 254–59; as career path, 160–61, 339; as career skill, 254–255, 320; certificates in, 260–61; devaluation, 236–42, 250; communal approach, 204; digital 261–62, 263–64; faculty-student partnership, 248, 250–51, 263, 264; faculty's role, 252, 263–64; historical perspective, 243–44, 249; inadequacy, 238,

Wilson, Woodrow, 294
Wisdom, Maria LaMonica, 29, 134–35, 220
Wittroch, David, 298
Woodford, Bettina, 47–50
Woodrow Wilson National Fellowship Foundation, 35, 120–21, 128, 130–31, 345; "Diversity and the PhD" pamphlet, 55; Humanities at Work, 50–53, 55, 72, 305;

Responsive Ph.D. initiative, 36, 52–53, 55–58, 59, 91, 216, 259, 325
Woodward, Kathleen, 307

Yale University, 41, 57

Zafar, Rafia, 162–63
Zimm, Michael, 141
Zook, Melinda, 253